W9-AEV-780

Vern L. Bullough, RN, PhD
Editor

Before Stonewall
Activists for Gay and Lesbian Rights in Historical Context

*Pre-publication
REVIEWS,
COMMENTARIES,
EVALUATIONS . . .*

"**B**efore Stonewall is a collection of short biographies of early gay and lesbian activists. The book serves as both primary and secondary source material. While its editor, Vern Bullough, skillfully places these life stories in context, with his usual wide historical grasp, and some biographers (e.g., Tripp) provide full discussion of their subjects (in this case, Kinsey) with fascinating detail, much of the volume contains intimate accounts by friends and lovers of these early pioneers.

Most striking to the twenty-first century reader is the vivid picture of American gay life forty and fifty years ago. We learn about a bartender's arrest on a restaurant's opening night for a 'two-month unpaid parking ticket' (Charlotte Coleman), an almost-fatal beating administered at the whim of an arrest-ing officer because his victim was dressed 'butch' (Billye Tallmadge), and the immense importance of a lesbian publication such as *The Ladder* in a world where there were no gay images (Barbara Grier). Tidbits such as the account of Betty Friedan deliber-ately discontinuing lesbian couple memberships in NOW (Del Martin), or conscious imitation of Stokely Car-michael's 'Black is Beautiful' in coin-ing the slogan 'Gay is Good' (Kam-eny) are not found in other studies of gay history, and set this volume apart from the rest."

Helen Rodnite Lemay, PhD
Professor of History
and Distinguished Teaching Professor,
Stony Brook University

More pre-publication
REVIEWS, COMMENTARIES, EVALUATIONS . . .

"*Before Stonewall: Activists for Gay and Lesbian Rights in Historical Context* is a book for everyone. Here the story of an all-but-forgotten era and people is presented beautifully through four dozen mini-biographies without sacrificing the message of group organization and larger themes. General readers and younger queers will discover, in accessible terms, the contributions of such fascinating individuals as Jim Kepner, Barbara Grier, José Sarria, and the still-anonymous "Lisa Ben" (anagram for lesbian) to the twentieth-century struggle for gay and lesbian rights.

This is a celebration of the movement's successes that made Stonewall possible, with the focus simultaneously on individual courage and organized action, especially through homophile organizations ONE, Inc., Mattachine Society, and the Daughters of Bilitis. The book is by no means confined to those groups or to the 1950s, though; as editor Bullough says of Salt Lake City resident Berry Berryman, 'her life emphasizes how rich and varied were the lives of gays and lesbians before it became possible to be publicly recognized as such.' *Before Stonewall* also reminds all of us that change depends upon human action, and the stories within can inspire us to that action in our time."

Vicki L. Eaklor, PhD
Hagar Professor of Humanities
and Professor of History,
Alfred University

"*Before Stonewall* provides a welcome and much-needed introduction to the lives and contributions of many of the key figures in the history of the American lesbian and gay movement. Full of intriguing information and insights about forgotten gay pioneers and straight allies as well as some of the movement's most famous leaders, this volume should become a standard reference work for those interested in the queer past."

George Chauncey, PhD
Professor of History
and Director, Lesbian
and Gay Studies Project,
The University of Chicago

"This is a marvelous book, with multiple insights into the strategies and techniques that were used by pioneering activists to challenge heterosexism and begin the struggle for gay and lesbian equality. Included here are the individual stories of the most effective early leaders in one of the great social movements of the twentieth century. They are presented with all of their accomplishments, defeats, dedication, and eccentricities. Many of these activists gave up the chance for material wealth, while focusing their energies on making the world a less prejudiced place. Both heterosexual and homosexual, these pioneers were united in the conviction that change can occur with direct action and individual perseverance. This book is a collection of fascinating stories, brought together by one of the most respected scholars in the field of sexology."

Walter L. Williams, PhD
Professor of Anthropology
and Gender Studies,
University of Southern California,
Los Angeles

More pre-publication
REVIEWS, COMMENTARIES, EVALUATIONS . . .

"*Before Stonewall*" is a poignant verbal photo album for those of us who are Family. When lesbigays stand tall today, we do so on the shoulders of those who went before, with far tougher challenges. Our foremothers, forefathers, and foreaunties demonstrated again and again the courage possible in ordinary people. Vern Bullough has painstakingly collected the details, written as tributes by many LBGT scholars. The text is uncluttered and easy to devour. This is food for the heart."

Louie Crew,
Author of
The Gay Academic

HPP

Harrington Park Press®
An Imprint of The Haworth Press, Inc.
New York • London • Oxford

NOTES FOR PROFESSIONAL LIBRARIANS
AND LIBRARY USERS

This is an original book title published by Harrington Park Press®, an imprint of The Haworth Press, Inc. Unless otherwise noted in specific chapters with attribution, materials in this book have not been previously published elsewhere in any format or language.

CONSERVATION AND PRESERVATION NOTES

All books published by The Haworth Press, Inc. and its imprints are printed on certified pH neutral, acid free book grade paper. This paper meets the minimum requirements of American National Standard for Information Sciences-Permanence of Paper for Printed Material, ANSI Z39.48-1984.

Before Stonewall
Activists for Gay and Lesbian Rights in Historical Context

HAWORTH Gay & Lesbian Studies
John P. De Cecco, PhD
Editor in Chief

Before Stonewall
Activists for Gay and Lesbian Rights in Historical Context

Vern L. Bullough, RN, PhD
Editor

Judith M. Saunders, RN, PhD
Sharon Valente, RN, PhD
Associate Editors

C. Todd White, PhD (cand.)
Assistant Editor

VCTC Library
Hartness Library
Vermont Technical College
Randolph Center, VT 05061

HPP

Harrington Park Press®
An Imprint of The Haworth Press, Inc.
New York • London • Oxford

Published by

Harrington Park Press, an imprint of The Haworth Press, Inc., 10 Alice Street, Binghamton, NY 13904-1580.

© 2002 by The Haworth Press, Inc. All rights reserved. No part of this work may be reproduced or utilized in any form or by any means, electronic or mechanical, including photocopying, microfilm, and recording, or by any information storage and retrieval system, without permission in writing from the publisher. Printed in the United States of America.

Cover design by Jennifer M. Gaska.

Library of Congress Cataloging-in-Publication Data

Before Stonewall : activists for gay and lesbian rights in historical context / Vern L. Bullough, editor.
    Includes bibliographical references and index.
        p. cm.
    ISBN 1-56023-192-0 (alk. paper)—ISBN 1-56023-193-9 (alk. paper)
    1. Gay activists—Biography. 2. Gay liberation movement—History. I. Bullough, Vern L.
HQ76.5 .R56 2002
305.9'0664'0922—dc21

                                                                                    2001051858

CONTENTS

ABOUT THE EDITOR

Vern L. Bullough, RN, PhD, is a Distinguished Professor Emeritus from SUNY. Currently, he is serving as Adjunct Professor of Nursing at the University of Southern California. For ten years, he served as Dean of Natural and Social Sciences at SUNY Buffalo, and prior to that, he was a professor at California State University, Northridge, for twenty years. He is the author, co-author, or editor of fifty books, including *Sexual Variance in Society and History, Women and Prostitution, A Short History of Homosexuality, Science in the Bedroom,* and *Encyclopedia of Birth Control.* He was one of the founders of the Center for Sex Research at California State University, Northridge, and of the gay caucuses in the American Historical Association and the American Sociological Association.

Professor Bullough wrote the ACLU policy on gay and lesbian rights in the 1960s for the ACLU of Southern California, which was the first affiliate to hear court cases for gay and lesbian rights and served as a model for the national ACLU. He contributed to various groundbreaking gay journals such as *One, Tangents,* and *Ladder.* He served as Vice President of the Institute for the Study of Human Resources for One, Inc. and for a time ran a gay hotline out of his house that was eventually taken over by the ACLU of Southern California. He was a charter member of the original Parents and Friends of Lesbians and Gays, which had been founded in Los Angeles and later went national. Two of his children, a daughter and a son, both adopted, are gay. His late wife, Bonnie Bullough, was co-author or first author on many of his books. Her mother, who was a lesbian, was the motivating factor in the Bulloughs' studies of homosexuality and lesbianism, and a biography of her mother's longtime companion is included in the book. Professor Bullough has received numerous awards for his activism and scholarship from the gay, lesbian, and transgender communities as well as from his colleagues. He is past President of the Society for the Scientific Study of Sex and is the recipient of its award for distinguished research.

CONTRIBUTORS

Lee Arnold is Director of the Library of the Historical Society of Pennsylvania in Philadelphia. He is also a writer and researcher. Previous works include biographical essays, travel writing, and book reviews.

Roberta Bobba is in her seventies and has lived in San Francisco and the Bay Area for over sixty-six years. Her close friendship with Charlotte Coleman has covered a forty-year period in which both women have been active in the gay movement.

Gwen Brewer, PhD, is Professor Emeritus of English at California State University, Northridge.

Victoria A. Brownworth has authored and edited numerous books including the award-winning collections *Too Queer: Essays from a Radical Life* and *Coming Out of Cancer: Writings from the Lesbian Cancer Epidemic*. She is a columnist for several publications, including *Curve, Bay Area Reporter, Lambda Book Report,* and the *Baltimore Sun*. She lives in Philadelphia where she teaches writing and film at the University of the Arts.

Susan Bullough drives an eighteen-wheel truck, plays rugby, is a semiprofessional drummer, and is the daughter of the editor of this book.

John P. De Cecco, PhD, is Professor of Psychology and Human Sexuality Studies at San Francisco State University. He is the long-time editor of the *Journal of Homosexuality* and is editor of the Harrington Park Press program in which this book appears.

Holly Devor, PhD, is Professor of Sociology at the University of Victoria, in Victoria, British Columbia, Canada.

Wayne R. Dynes, PhD, is Professor of Art at Hunter College, City University of New York. He is perhaps best known as the editor of the *Encyclopedia of Homosexuality*.

Virginia Elwood-Akers is a librarian at California State University, Northridge. She presently is preparing an index to materials in the Bonnie and Vern Bullough collection at that university.

William Fennie is a writer and translator, as well as author of *Some Kind of Courage: Scenes from the Life of Billye Talmadge*.

Florine (Flo) Fleischman was a licensed minister in the Metropolitan Community Church. In 1984 she left the MCC to found the New Hope Christian Church of Van Nuys. In 1995 she retired from the ministry and became a board member and eventually president of ONE Institute/Gay and Lesbian Archives. She was a close friend of the late Jim Kepner.

Lewis Gannett is a professional writer who has published two novels, *The Living One* and *Magazine Beach*.

Joseph Hansen is one of the most widely read gay authors of the latter part of the twentieth century. Among his almost forty books are the twelve Dave Brandstetter detective novels. His autobiographical novel *Living Upstairs* won the 1994 Lambda Award.

Jim Kepner, now deceased, has his biography included in this book.

David K. Johnson, PhD, is Adjunct Lecturer in the History Department at Northwestern University. His writings on gay and lesbian history have appeared in the *Washington Blade, Washington History,* and the anthology *Creating a Place for Ourselves: Lesbian, Gay, and Bisexual Community Histories.* His book *The Lavender Scare: Homosexuality and the National Security State, 1950-1975,* is forthcoming from the University of Chicago Press.

Kay Tobin Lahusen, the first openly gay photojournalist, joined Daughters of Bilitis in 1961. In 1964 she began photographing lesbians for covers of *The Ladder,* a breakthrough in gay publishing for the first national lesbian magazine. She marched in the 1960s' gay picket lines and took pictures also. In the early 1970s she helped found Gay Activists Alliance; wrote and photographed for *Gay,* a New York newsweekly; and co-authored *The Gay Crusaders,* the pioneer book of gay biographical sketches. Her current photo exhibit is "Opening the Closet Door: Photos of the Early Gay Rights Movement." She lives with veteran activist Barbara Gittings.

John Lauritsen is an independent scholar and author of, among other books, *The Early Homosexual Rights Movement (1864-1935)* and *A Freethinker's Primer of Male Love.*

Phyllis Lyon is an author, sexologist, lesbian feminist, and civil rights activist. Her biography is included in this book.

Donald Mader, MDiv, PhD candidate, is an assistant at Pauluskerk in Rotterdam, The Netherlands.

Del Martin is a lesbian feminist who, despite claims to the contrary, knows the homophile movement still lives. Her biography is included in this book.

Jesse G. Monteagudo is a freelance writer who lives in South Florida with his domestic partner of over fifteen years. His biweekly columns, "The Book Nook" and "Jesse's Journal," appear in over a dozen print and online publications. He is in the process of writing his first book.

Stephen O. Murray earned a PhD in Sociology from the University of Toronto and is one of the major researchers into all aspects of homosexuality. He is the author or co-author of a dozen books, including *American Gay* and *Homosexualities.*

Jack Nichols is senior editor, <www.gaytoday.badpuppy.com>, and author of *The Gay Agenda: Talking Back to the Fundamentalists.* His biography is included in this book.

William A. Percy III is Professor Emeritus of History at the University of Massachusetts, Boston. He served as associate editor of *The Encyclopedia of Homosexuality.* He is the author of *Outing: Shattering the Conspiracy of Silence* (with Warren Johansson) and *Pederasty and Pedagogy in Ancient Greece.*

Felice Picano is the author of some twenty volumes of fiction, poetry, memoirs, etc., and is considered a founder of modern gay literature. Among other accomplishments, he founded two publishing companies: the SeaHorse Press and Gay Presses of New York. His most recent novel, *Onyx,* was published in 2001 by Alyson Publications.

Stella Rush, a longtime activist, has her biography included in this book.

Judith M. Saunders, RN, PhD, is an associate editor of this book.

James T. Sears, PhD, is the award-winning author or editor of twelve books, among them *Growing Up Gay in the South* (The Haworth Press, 1991). His book *Rebels, Rubyfruit, and Rhinestones,* the second volume of a projected multivolume work on queer southern life, was published in 2001 by Rutgers University Press.

Karen C. Sendziak holds an AB degree from the University of Chicago and is employed as a legal assistant. She has been affiliated with Gerber/Hart Library in Chicago for over fourteen years, and is currently the Curator of the Archives and the organizational historian.

Charles Shively, PhD, is Professor in American Studies at the University of Massachusetts, Boston.

C. A. Tripp, PhD, a research psychologist, was an associate of Kinsey at Indiana University and is probably best known as the author of *The Homosexual Matrix* (1975).

Sharon Valente, RN, PhD, is Assistant Professor of Nursing at the University of Southern California where she teaches a course on human sexuality.

C. Todd White is completing his PhD at the University of Southern California in the Department of Anthropology.

Leslie Warren is an advocate for women and a lifelong friend of Pat Walker.

Preface

This book has had a long gestation period and in the process lost its original parent. The book was originally conceived by Wayne Dynes nearly a decade ago and some of the articles that appear in it now were commissioned then. One of them, by the late Jim Kepner, has been revised and finished by William A. Percy III. Due to other commitments and some difficulties with potential contributors, Dynes decided to withdraw from the project. A couple of other possible editors were approached by John De Cecco, the editor at The Haworth Press who originally commissioned the work, but finally, at the urging of Percy, he requested that I take over. The book has changed considerably from what Dynes envisioned, and for this I take responsibility. I have included many more individuals than he would have, but in spite of this it is by no means all-inclusive. Many people, such as Martin Block, made important contributions but are not included here. In Block's case, it is because this book is intended to be more than Mattachine, Los Angeles, or ONE, Inc., and although he was significant, there is still a disproportionate number of Angelenos, as residents of Los Angeles call themselves, included in this collection.

The purpose of the book is to cast as wide a net as possible, and suggestions and nominees were made by many people who played significant roles in the organization or emergence of the gay and lesbian community. It also includes a number of individuals who have not self-identified as gay or lesbian but who made significant contributions and were active on the firing line, which, in the long run, is what counted. There is also some disparity in length of biography because, although all of those in the book were out there "fighting" the battle, some had more important roles or were better known than others. The hardest decision was to cut out those who were more or less quietly in the struggle before 1969 but only later emerged as prominent in the cause. C. A. Tripp, for example, one of the contributors, played a significant role, particularly in his influence on Kinsey, but it was only after 1969 that he made his most significant and public contributions. Although Allen Ginsberg is included, in part because he was so outspoken about his homosexuality, Gore Vidal is not. Vidal, although he wrote a significant gay novel, was not so much in the public arena for the gay cause. Still, some feel he should have been included; the decision was not to do so. Other more closeted gays of the pre-Stonewall period were not even considered.

It is difficult for those who were not active in the 1950s or 1960s to realize the stigma that the activists suffered, and the actual fear and hostility their presence aroused. The reader will find, however, that these early barrier breakers were a varied lot, and about the only thing they had in common was a commitment to change public perceptions of gays and lesbians. They often disagreed on methods and on specific action, and much internecine warfare existed. Some, such as Lisa Ben, worked anonymously and are still reluctant to come out publicly. The ultimate key, however, was to stand up and be counted, even if under a pseudonym, and this book is essentially about those who did.

I wish to acknowledge the help and encouragement of John De Cecco, William A. Percy III, and William Palmer, Publications Director of The Haworth Press. All of my contributors are owed a special thanks because of their willingness to suggest others to be included and for their willingness to meet my deadlines. Two women, Sharon Valente and Judith M. Saunders, were particularly helpful; I have listed them as associate editors. C. Todd White, a doctoral student, rounded up photos and found missing documents, therefore he is listed as an assistant editor. I would also like to thank the staff at The Haworth Press for their assistance, particularly Karen Fisher and Peg Marr.

Introduction

Same-sex relations are not new. They have existed in every culture and every time period. Occasionally, as in the Greek world, they were open and tolerated and even institutionalized, but until recently most modern historians refused to talk about such subjects. The English translations of Plato, for example, used all sorts of subterfuges to avoid mentioning the subject, and it was only in the last part of the twentieth century that this defect was remedied. It is perhaps no wonder that at least some of the founders of modern Greek studies, such as Johann Joachim Winckelmann (1717-1768), were gays who probably achieved pleasure in realizing the contribution of same-sex people to history, although they themselves did not come out openly. This was because Western culture, since Christianity had become the official religion at the end of the classical period, forced such discussions underground, stigmatizing and officially condemning same-sex activities. In spite of this, we know that in many of the royal courts there were homosexual coteries and in the large urban centers there was an underground gay and lesbian culture which was often harassed by the police and authorities but which continued to grow and expand. There were even covert organizations of gay men (although so far no record of lesbian organizations has been found) since at least the eighteenth century, and others have argued that they existed before then. Informal alliances were formed through male brothels, bars, and clubs. Often, however, individuals and occasionally whole groups were publicly exposed, ostracized, and even imprisoned. This happened frequently enough that few men or women were willing to publicly proclaim their same-sex preferences. Some who had great power or influence did not hide their same-sex interests, but even in this case they usually acted with caution. Most homosexuals attempted to exist invisibly in society at large without making too many waves.

The first modern challenges to this sub-rosa existence came in Germany, a consequence of the result to unite the disparate German-speaking states into what came to be called the German Empire under the leadership of the Prussian royal house, the Hohenzollerns. This unification was accompanied by an attempt to unify the German legal code. Generally, until the end of the eighteenth century, Europeans outside of England had been governed under a civil law tradition that had been heavily based on Roman law and that since the medieval period had condemned homosexuality. Matters changed during the French Revolution, and one of the lasting accomplishments of the revolution was the legal revision that came to be called the Napoleonic Code. At the beginning of the nineteenth century it was adopted in most of the areas of Europe under French occupation, including parts of Germany. In terms of sex, the code adopted two standards to determine whether a sex act was legal or illegal: age and consent. Children were a protected class, but otherwise sex activity taking place between those who had reached the age of consent (usually fourteen) was not against the law. When Germany was being unified, the question was whether the Prussian law (traditional civil law which made sodomy a crime) would become the basis for the legal code of the new empire or the provisions about homosexuality and other sexual issues that the Napoleonic Code had adopted would be followed. The threat of abandoning the Napoleonic Code emboldened a few daring spokespersons to make the debate public, notably Karl Heinrich Ulrichs (1825-1895), a homosexual himself, who set out to publicly challenge attitudes on same-sex relationships and to urge the adoption of the Napoleonic code. He argued in a series of longish pamphlets and short books that the instincts which led men and women to same-sex relationships were inborn and therefore natural to a significant percentage of human beings. Sex between such individuals was not any more dangerous to society than was procreative sex between married persons, and there was no basic reason to outlaw such relationships. Ulrichs developed a complex schematic for the development of homosexuality, which those who are interested in the subject should read; it was finally translated into English in the 1990s. Ulrichs sent his publications to important people everywhere, from the kaiser to members of the medical community. Others contributed to the campaign to recognize same-sex relations. Karoly Maria Benkert (or Kertbeny) (1824-1882) coined the term *homosexuality* to describe such relationships. Although it was homosexuals themselves who raised the issue and started the discussion, the questions also aroused interest among many in the legal and medical communities. Most notable among these was forensic physician Richard von Krafft-Ebing (1840-1902), who adopted, in part, Ulrichs' biological explanations. Krafft-Ebing, however, also held that certain behavior patterns such as masturbation, which he condemned, were also crucial in "perverting" heterosexuality. Still, the major contribution of Krafft-Ebing's work, in spite of many of its negative qualities, was to bring homosexuality out of the closet, making it a subject fit for scientific discussion, and ultimately to political action.

The leader in such action was Magnus Hirschfeld (1868-1935) who began the first public movements for what might be called the emancipation of homosexuals. A researcher into homosexuality as well as a homosexual himself, Hirschfeld organized the Scientific Humanitarian Committee in 1897 in Germany designed not only to carry out research but to remove from the German legal system (which had ultimately rejected the Napoleonic solution) the negative laws on homosexuality. Although he was unsuccessful in attaining such a revision, his organizing efforts led to the establishment of committees in Germany and elsewhere in Europe to campaign for the rights of gays. The existence of such organizations was often precarious not only because of the stigma its members might suffer but also because the trauma of World War I, the Great Depression, and the rise of the Nazis and communism undermined their financing, their right to proclaim their identity, and in many cases led to the imprisonment of their members. Americans were not unacquainted with these groups, and some such as Henry Gerber wrote for continental publications and tried unsuccessfully to initiate a similar organization in the United States. Although initially many individual communists had urged a change in the law toward gays, including Emma Goldman (1869-1940), the Russian Communist Party, by the time Stalin came to power, had come to regard homosexuals as a product of capitalist degeneracy, and the USSR did little to improve their lot. The Nazis were more openly hostile; shortly after they came to power they destroyed the research materials that Hirschfeld had collected, and by the end of World War II they had embarked on a program of putting homosexuals into concentration camps where thousands died. Some of the organized groups in Europe still managed to survive despite the Nazi and communist policy, and the oldest continuous group is that associated with the publication of *Der Kreis,* which started in Zurich in 1932. In the Netherlands, still another group originally affiliated with Hirschfeld's group in Berlin continued to exist after the destruction of his institute by the Nazis, but it disappeared with the Nazi occupation of that country. Immediately after the end of World War II, surviving members began publishing *Vriendschap,* and this was soon followed by the emergence of a new reinvigorated organization. The Dutch group also began publishing *Lesbos,* a lesbian-oriented publication, one of the earliest to deal with topics of special interest to women. Other postwar groups were established or revived in Germany, France, England, and elsewhere, although not in the Eastern bloc countries.

Progress was not easy, however, since even the most innocent effort to organize groups could be made to sound sinister to those willing to exploit the existing homophobic tendencies in large segments of the population, particularly in the United States. For example, an early attempt to bring various gay and lesbian groups together in the International Committee for Sexual Equality in 1951 led to a sensationalist denunciation of the committee by an American, R. E. L. Masters. He portrayed the mostly letterhead group as the the most powerful body in the history of homosexual organizations, and a major threat to the world through its attempt to put forth policies favoring same-sex toleration.

In the United States, informal groups centered around bars, taverns, and bathhouses in most urban areas served as a haven for various gays in the last part of the nineteenth century and first part of the twentieth. Prohibition destroyed the bar culture, but bathhouses continued to be a meeting place for male gays, and so eventually did some speakeasies. We know that some gays and lesbians found refuge in other kinds of groups. In Salt Lake City, for example, not a city noted for its bars or taverns, the Bohemian Club attracted a mixed group of nonconformists, many of whom were gay or lesbian. Certain neighborhoods such as the Tenderloin in San Francisco, Greenwich Village in New York City, the Near North Side in Chicago, and other similar neighborhoods were islands of toleration in a hostile world. Few gays or lesbians, however, dared to come out openly to their nongay friends because exposure could mean disaster if not imprisonment. Some even adopted public attitudes of hostility toward the lesbian and gay community; some would claim J. Edgar Hoover as a sad example of this.

This fear of exposure continued almost until the end of the twentieth century. The pianist and performer Liberace serves as a good example, since he continued publicly to deny he was homosexual (even in a court case) until his death, although significant numbers of people knew otherwise. He was such an exaggeration of the gay queen that although many of his fans probably suspected, they wanted to accept his denial—and he was afraid of exposure. Rock Hudson, who had publicly denied his same-sex preference, revealed himself only as he was dying, but his deathbed admission struck a major blow for the gay and lesbian community.

Although police and law enforcement agencies frequently kept records on suspected homosexuals, they often adopted a policy of ignoring these files except when it was convenient to do otherwise. As a police reporter in the mid-1940s, I had access not only to the official reports and complaints about alleged sexual indiscretions but to the informal notes and cards compiled by the police on the sexual activities of a large number of individuals in the city in which I lived. Although only a handful of these people were arrested during my tenure in that job, their activities were observed (perhaps unknown to them) and their files were periodically updated. Such a practice could pose threats to any gay person whenever the police wanted to interfere, and could act as a paralyzing force in any attempt to elicit change.

There was also a kind of unofficial censorship on the topic. The Bell Telephone Company, for example, refused to list any group with the word *homosexual* in its title until the late 1960s, and it was not until after this situation that the words *gay, lesbian,* and *homosexual* could be listed in any public directory or "family" newspapers. Instead, circumlocutions were used to avoid open discussion of the subject and large numbers of people remained totally ignorant about the extent of homosexuality in their community.

Several factors worked to bring about a change in attitudes, although ultimately it was the action of the people in the gay and lesbian community themselves. Undergirding the potential for such action, however, was a growing body of research about sexuality itself and same-sex relations in particular. Much of the research was done in the United States. One of the first studies of same-sex relations was conducted by Katharine Bement Davis in her study of the *Factors in the Sex Life of Twenty-Two-Hundred Women,* carried out in the 1920s. She found that about half of her college-educated sample of women had experienced "intense emotional relations with women" (Davis, 1929, p. 248). The number giving these feelings of overt sexual expression, and whom she classified as lesbian, however, was about 200, slightly under 10 percent. The study was one of many underwritten by the Rockefeller-supported foundations and bureaus.

Interestingly, for a brief time in the United States during the first few decades of the twentieth century considerable research on homosexuality was undertaken, but little of it was published. The sociology department at the University of Chicago, as part of its efforts to understand the changes in social and sexual mores resulting from the growing urbanization of the United States, had begun researching homosexuality in 1910, and a number of student papers and dissertations appeared which included some discussion of the phenomenon. Chicago researchers also found large homosexual networks in Illinois penitentiaries and reform schools, and also reported that some of the individuals involved in same-sex activities seemed to engage in such practices only while confined to prisons. What is known sometimes as the "pansy craze" in the 1920s attracted sightseeing tourists to gay and lesbian haunts and led to novels with gay or lesbian themes such as Radclyffe Hall's *Well of Loneliness* (1929), Blair Niles' *Strange Brother* (1931), and Robert Scully's *A Scarlet Pansy* (1933). Realistic novels by such writers as James T. Farrell also included discussions about same-sex relationships.

This brief outpouring of research and publication declined in the 1930s as American psychoanalytic explanations of homosexuality increasingly gained popularity and convinced both local authorities and the general public that homosexuality could best be explained and dealt with in terms of individual psychopathology. Homosexual and lesbian staff and professors, as well as those who were not but who had participated in the early research projects, more or less ceased such research and went underground. The University of Chicago, the early example of tolerance, for example, admitted in the year 2001 that as late as the early 1950s Paul Goodman, a not-so-closeted gay man, was dismissed from the university because of his same-sex activities. The U.S. government itself in the 1950s and 1960s moved against known homosexuals in government; among those dismissed was Franklin Kameny, whose biography is included in this book.

Most psychoanalytic studies of the time are now more or less rejected because of sampling errors and false assumptions, but one or two of the better ones can still be mined for information. The first large-scale American study was by psychiatrist George Henry who subscribed at least in part to a biological origin of homosexuality. The data in his *Sex Variants* published in 1941 were better than his conclusions, which were influenced by his own prejudices and reflected the general attitudes of the time. Henry had the support of large segments of the underground New York gay and lesbian community who recruited subjects for his study, and it is the information that they provided which makes the study important. Both the earlier Chicago studies and the Henry study indicate the existence of widespread gay and lesbian communities even though much of the public knew little about them.

Although such scholars as Howard S. Becker (1965) and Erving Goffman (1959) questioned the assumed pathology of homosexuality, arguing that it received its "deviant status" because of rules and sanctions imposed by society, it was Alfred Kinsey's work that raised the whole issue of homosexuality to national attention, especially in his book, *Sexual Behavior in the Human Male* (1948). Homosexuals found in reading the report that they were more numerous than the general public (or perhaps they themselves) realized and that many "heterosexuals" had also had same-sex experiences. Popular reports of the percentage of gays in the population ranged from one person in twenty to one person in ten, to even higher, depending on which Kinsey statistic was used. Still, at the heart of the report was that 4 percent of Kinsey's male subjects could be labeled as exclusively homosexual. Although low, this was still a number the public could not ignore, and it caused an impassioned public debate.

The gay community was deeply involved in this debate, and its power and influence was growing, even though it was still not fully out in the open. World War II had helped many rural and small-town Americans find others similar to themselves in the military service. Although the various services occasionally dishonorably discharged a person for being homosexual, vast numbers of gays and lesbians went through the World War II experience either undetected or ignored and were able to make lifelong friendships. It was this factor that stood them in good stead when they went back to civilian life and began to seek other gays and lesbians.

There had already been some glimmering of gay organizations in the 1920s, such as Henry Gerber's Society for Human Rights in Chicago which was quickly abandoned after the "leaders" were put in jail. Lisa Ben had produced some nine issues of *Vice Versa* in Los Angeles in 1947-1948; she quit after a year, yet her efforts proved symbolic of what was to come. In 1948, a group of mostly gay men in Los Angeles campaigned for Henry A. Wallace under the euphemism "Bachelors for Wallace." Some of the same people in this group emerged to organize or join the Mattachine Society, a group founded by Harry Hay and four others. The Mattachine Society itself was initially secret, but many of its leaders became publicly known and eventually the group went public. The formation of the Mattachine Society marked the beginning of what might be called gay activism; without this period there could have been no Stonewall. Dale Jennings, one of the Mattachine Society's founders, is called "the Rosa Parks of the gay movement" in this book because of his willingness to confront the authorities.

The groundwork for the gay movement was also helped by studies and reports such as the Wolfenden Committee in London which had advocated legalization of homosexuality, as had the model penal code of the American Law Institute and the ninth International Congress on Criminal Law, the American Civil Liberties Union, the Quakers, and other religious groups, all of whom argued for equal rights for gays and lesbians. Unofficially, even the U.S. government had begun to change its attitude under the leadership of the National Institute of Mental Health (NIMH) which had established a commission to study the issue. The commission, headed by Evelyn Gentry Hooker, whose research into homosexuality was an important factor in changing scientific opinions, urged that homosexuality be decriminalized and that discrimination in employment against those labeled as gay or deviant be eliminated. There was an attempt by some to bury the report, but it was published by the gay community itself.

Also aiding the gay movement was the demand of other groups for equal civil rights and the elimination of discrimination. These movements followed the leadership of those involved in gaining civil rights for blacks, a movement that helped pave the way for demands for changes by other groups, including homosexuals. Although no single leader in the gay and lesbian communities achieved the fame and reputation of the Reverend Martin Luther King Jr., a large number of activists put their careers and reputations on the line, many of whom are commemorated in this book. In retrospect the radical drop-off in public hostility toward homosexuality came about in a remarkably short period of time. One reason it is so remarkable is that the gay and lesbian movement, unlike the civil rights movement, had more or less to build their legal case from scratch because there was not the centuries-long foundation of struggle and legal advances which had been won over several generations by the National Association for the Advancement of Colored People (NAACP), Congress on Racial Equality (CORE), and the American Civil Liberties Union, which had built up a caseload of law and precedents—all of which had been lacking in the fight for gay rights.

Also building on the civil rights movement was a well-orchestrated campaign to give women equal rights with men, a struggle that had begun in the United States in the middle of the nineteenth century, again a much longer history of activism than existed in the gay movement. Here, as in the gay movement, the leadership was more dispersed than in the civil rights movement, although the National Organization for Women (NOW) seemed at times to have a dominant position. The passage of civil rights and anti-discrimination legislation again served as a model for the gay community. Other groups also struggled to be heard and to have the laws changed including Latin Americans, Americans of Asian descent, the physically disabled, and others. Although they all had difficult struggles, none of them had been so long officially ostracized as the gay and lesbian community. Thus although all of these factors were important in the growing success of the gay movement, it was the activism of the homosexual community itself that carried the brunt of the battle in changing medical, scientific, social, and political opinions about homosexuality and lesbianism. It was a motley crew of radicals and reformers, drawn together by the cause despite personality and philosophical differences, who helped lay the foundation for a successful battle that brought gays into the twenty-first century as a stronger community than ever before.

It is their story that is told in the following pages.

BIBLIOGRAPHY

There is a vast literature out there on every point mentioned in this introduction. Some of the basic sources or translations of them, as well as the references, include:

Becker, Howard. "Deviants and Deviates," *Nation,* 201 (September 20, 1965), 20-21.

Bullough, Vern L. *Homosexuality in History.* New York: Meridian Books, 1979.

Bullough, Vern L. *Science in the Bedroom: A History of Sex Research.* New York: Basic Books, 1994.

Bullough, Vern L. *Sexual Variation in Society and History.* Chicago: University of Chicago Press, 1976.

Bullough, Vern L., W. Dorr Legg, Barrett W. Elcano, and James Kepner, *An Annotated Bibliography of Homosexuality,* 2 volumes. New York: Garland Publishing, 1976.

Cory, Donald Webster. *The Homosexual in America.* New York: Greenberg, 1951.

Cutler, Marvin (Ed.). *Homosexuals Today: A Handbook of Organizations and Publications.* Los Angeles: One, Inc., 1956.

Davis, Katharine Bement. *Factors in the Sex Life of Twenty-Two Hundred Women.* New York: Harper, 1929.

Goffman, Erving. *The Presentation of Self in Everyday Life.* New York: Anchor Books, 1959.

Hall, Radclyffe. *The Well of Loneliness.* New York: Covici Friede, 1929.

Henry, George. *Sex Variants: A Study of Homosexual Patterns,* 2 volumes. New York: Hoeber, 1941.

Hirschfeld, Magnus. *Homosexualities.* Translated by Michael Lombardi-Nash. Introduction by Vern L. Bullough. Buffalo: Prometheus Books, 2000.

Hooker, Evelyn. "The Adjustment of the Male Overt Homosexual," *Journal of Projective Techniques,* 6(1-4) (1957), 18-31.

Kertbeny, Karoly Maria. His two pamphlets were reprinted in *Jahrbuch für sexuelle Zwischenstufen,* 6 (1905), i-iv, 3-66.

Kinsey, Alfred, Wardell B. Pomeroy, and Clyde E. Martin. *Sexual Behavior in the Human Male.* Philadelphia: W. B. Saunders, 1948.

Krafft-Ebing, Richard von. *Psychopathia Sexualis,* Twelfth Edition. Translated by F. J. Rebman in 1906. Reprinted Brooklyn, NY: Physicians and Surgeons, 1933.

Lauritsen, John, and David Thorstad. *The Early Homosexual Rights Movement (1869-1935).* Albion, CA: Times-Change Press, 1974.

Livingood, John M. (Ed.). *National Instiute of Mental Health Task Force on Homosexuality: Final Report and Background Papers.* Rockville, MD: National Institute of Mental Health, 1972.

Masters, R.E. L. *The Homosexual Revolution.* New York: Julian Press, 1962.

Niles, Blair. *Strange Brother.* New York: Harris Pub., 1931.

Scully, Robert. *Scarlet Pansy.* New York: Faro, 1933.

Towards a Quaker View of Sex. London: Friends Home Service Committee, 1964.

Ulrichs, Karl Heinrich. *The Riddle of Man-Manly Love.* Translated by Michael Lombardi-Nash. Introduction by Vern L. Bullough. Buffalo: Prometheus Books, 1994. This is the English translation of the twelve titles published by Ulrichs in German in the nineteenth century.

Wolfenden, Sir John (Chairman). *Report of the Committee on Homosexual Offences and Prostitution.* London: Her Majesty's Stationery Office, 1957.

PART I:
PRE-1950

Probably the most influential force in changing attitudes toward homosexuality was the Kinsey report issued in 1948. As C. A. Tripp writes in his biography of Kinsey, homosexuality became front-page news, and much of the hostile criticism toward the report was due to its data on the same-sex experiences of American males. Although the report on women did not come out until five years later and faced even more hostile criticism, the revelation of same-sex activity among women did not raise the stir that the report on men did. Because, as Tripp indicates, Kinsey was determined to force Americans to face up to the existence of homosexuality, he must be regarded as a pioneer in the gay movement. This point should perhaps be emphasized, because changing public attitudes toward homosexuality was crucial and Kinsey played a large part in this. He made not only the public but also those who were gay and lesbian realize that a lot of people were homosexual.

Yet no matter how much research is done, the political battles necessary for gay men and women to be recognized have to come from the gay community. This section includes a discussion of a number of individuals from the then mostly secretive gay community. Henry Gerber, whom authors Jim Kepner and Stephen Murray call the grandfather of the American gay movement, emphasizes that the American gay movement did not appear from nowhere but was influenced by developments in Europe.

One who attempted to communicate some of these developments was Edward Irenaeus Prime-Stevenson, who wrote under the name Xavier Mayne. He was the first American to write extensively about homosexuality, first in a novel and then in a long scholarly monograph, both of which were published in Europe and eventually smuggled into the United States. He has rightly been called the father of American homophile literature. Somewhat more open about his homosexuality was the Boston Brahmin, Prescott Townsend, who traced his ancestry back to the Mayflower. He was a fixture in Boston who publicly advocated for homosexuals. During World War II, while working in a shipbuilding yard, he was arrested and served time in jail for the "abominable and detestable crime against nature," an event which he reported on in his Harvard class report for that year. He later went on to organize Mattachine Society in Boston. Somehow he managed to retain his leadership in the arts community of Boston. Few gays, however, had the savoir faire of Townsend, or the money and family connections that allowed him to be somewhat different.

Jeannette Howard Foster, a librarian, troubled by a lack of knowledge about what she called "female homosexuality" began investigating it and in the process compiled and published a comprehensive bibliography of sex variant women under her own name, which made it possible for a new generation of scholars, of which I was one, to build upon her research. If Harry Hay was the grandfather of the gay movement in the United States, then Jeannette Howard Foster is the grandmother of lesbian scholarship.

Not quite so open about her own lesbianism but very willing to fight for the cause of homosexuality was Pearl M. Hart. She had as one of her missions in life the representation of the underserved in court, and she defended literally thousands of male homosexuals as part of her practice. She was an early closeted member of the Daughters of Bilitis, lived openly with another woman, and was a major force in the Chicago gay community even though she was not public about her own sexual preference.

Lisa Ben is an interesting paradox. She published and distributed an early gay newsletter in the 1940s under her pseudonym. As of this writing, she is still alive and was very reluctant to use her real name in this book. Since, however, she is identified online as Edyth Eyde, it seems permissible to so identify her here. Her biography emphasizes that it takes a variety of people and attitudes to make a revolution, and sometimes a very small step can, in retrospect, seem to have been quite influential and daring.

Berry Berryman was more of a fighter than Lisa Ben but her pioneering study was not published until after she died. Scholarly journals simply did not accept studies such as hers and there was no gay press to publish it. She also lived in Utah, a state that might seem unlikely to have spawned a gay activist, but her case again emphasizes that a lot of gays and lesbians were doing their best to improve the conditions for their compatriots and whose contributions have not yet come to public attention.

Alfred C. Kinsey (1894-1956)

C. A. Tripp

Photo by C. A. Tripp

For many, "pre-Stonewall" versus "post-Stonewall" defines the decisive turning point in the fight for gay liberation. At the time of the 1969 Greenwich Village riots, however, few anticipated that Stonewall would go down in history as the dividing line between radically different eras; in fact, the riots barely penetrated the consciousness of the public, gay and straight alike. This stands in sharp contrast to another major turning point that had seized widespread attention some twenty years earlier, in 1948. Almost overnight it created a divide between radically different eras of sexual understanding: pre-Kinsey versus post-Kinsey. It brought homosexuality out in the open, and Kinsey's willingness to do so marks a major step in gay liberation.

The publication of *Sexual Behavior in the Human Male,* popularly known as the Kinsey Report, ignited a firestorm among scientists, psychiatrists, clergy, moralists of every stripe, and, not least, the general public. Indeed, the report raised a furor the likes of which had not been seen since the debut of Darwin's theory of evolution. Dr. Alfred C. Kinsey, the senior author (and writer of the report's every word), rocketed from obscurity to international prominence, the nature of which ranged, depending on point of view, from sublime distinction to what struck some as shameful notoriety. The report's 804 pages of dense prose, replete with 335 graphs and tables charting the activities of 5,300 male subjects, put under the microscope a world of sexual experience that never before had received rigorous scientific scrutiny. In the process it demolished many myths about sexuality in general, and homosexuality in particular.

Such a text demanded a great deal of the casual reader, of course. But then, many readers had no need to crack Kinsey's tome for themselves. The popular press, which knew a hot story when it saw one, trumpeted the central findings throughout the world.

The findings included astonishing statistics: 37 percent of adult males at least once had experienced sex with another male to the point of orgasm; fully 50 percent of adult males had acknowledged occasional sexual attraction to other males; and although "only" 4 percent were exclusively homosexual, 10 percent of married males in their twenties had made overt homosexual contacts *after* getting married. Kinsey expected this to be his biggest bombshell, and was much surprised when no reviewer or commentator even noticed it. Instead, all eyes focused on his next comment: "This [37 percent] is more than one male in three of the persons that one may meet as he passes along a city street" (p. 623). Later in the report, in a discussion of demands from some quarters that homosexuals be "institutionalized and isolated," Kinsey noted that "there are about six and a third million males in the country who would need such isolation" (p. 665).

The figures rocked the boat of conventional wisdom, to put it mildly, for it had been widely assumed that homosexuality arises from rare diseases, or from impaired maleness, or from immaturities that thwart heterosexual development. But the report made it plain that male-male attractions were woven into the fabric of ordinary, everyday life. In that light, notions of rarity, illness, impaired maleness, and immaturity suddenly were subject to challenges which, pre-Kinsey, had lacked scientific substantiation. (A terminological note: "Gay" will be used sparingly because few of Kinsey's homosexual subjects thought of themselves as gay in the identity-group sense of the term.)

The report presented several lines of evidence that showed that homosexual males, far from exhibiting "impaired maleness," fully measure up to or even exceed the maleness of ordinary straights. One such indication emerged from some remarkable discoveries about the timing of puberty in boys. Although it is perhaps obvious that, regardless of sexual leanings, early puberty signals a certain hot-to-trot virility—a rush into sexual maturity—Kinsey's examination of that reality uncovered a major difference between homosexual and heterosexual males.

Kinsey found that boys who reach puberty early (by age eleven) are much more sexually active than boys who reach puberty late (after age fifteen), not only during adolescence but, in fact, for the rest of their lives. This link between early puberty and high lifetime sexual activity was a discovery with far-reaching implications. It took on even more significance when coupled with another Kinsey finding: Boys who mature early are *much* more likely to engage in homosexual behavior than boys who mature late. By age sixteen, for example, 31.9 percent of the early-pubescent boys in his sample had had sex with another male, whereas only 12.3 percent of the late-pubescent boys had experienced homosexual contact. One could suppose that this disparity might flow from the early-maturing boys having had more opportunities to experiment, simply by virtue of their head start. But the trend persists: By age twenty-seven, 42.2 percent of the early-pubescent males had had homosexual contact, versus 22.2 percent of the late maturers— a ratio of almost two to one.

In other words, homosexuality looms very large indeed among males whose sex drives kick in early and continues to stay strong. Early puberty, of course, by definition, is a fairly rare occurrence in the male population as a whole. But Kinsey's data made it clear that for homosexual males, early puberty very nearly approaches the norm. To put it plainly: Gays tend to want and get sex sooner and have more of it than straights, *from adolescence all the way through to old age.*

Furthermore, the data revealed that boys strongly inclined to homosexual activity tend to attain puberty at an especially early age. Indeed, to his amazement, Kinsey found that the greater the homosexual inclination, the earlier the puberty, and the greater the lifetime sexual experience—by a very large margin! A converse finding is equally striking: Boys who arrive at puberty late not only tend to be less sexually active throughout their lives, but also are highly prone to an exclusively heterosexual orientation.

Initially, the findings seemed compatible with conventional psychological or sociological explanations. The day these findings first poured from the Kinsey lab's IBM computer-card sorters, someone hypothesized that a boy who matured at ten or eleven was ready for sex long before he had sufficient heterosexual opportunities, and thus may get into pattern-setting homosexual experiences. It was tempting, that is, to dismiss the association between early puberty and homosexual behavior as an almost accidental by-product of timing combined with having all-male playmates. But another researcher present that day, Dr. Frank Beach, a distinguished experimental psychologist who chaired the psychology department at Yale, was more cautious and wanted to check it with experimental data in his animal lab. Months later, Beach established that the same basic trends prevail in rats: The first to mature are "champion mounters" strongly inclined to homosexual behavior. This confirmed that Kinsey had uncovered a deep, previously unsuspected connection in the biology of sex.

But that wasn't quite all. Previously, laypeople and sex researchers alike had assumed that homosexual males suffer from a deficiency of sex hormones. The report shattered that theory by pointing out that although injections of male sex hormones do amplify sex drive, they do not change the direction of sexual interest; they simply intensify preexisting attractions. Many researchers also assumed that "inversion," the capacity to switch back and forth between male and female sexual roles, stems from impaired virility. Building on Frank Beach's research, the report found quite the reverse: A propensity for inversion implies not a "weak" sexuality but an especially robust hormonal situation. The report quotes Beach's findings on lower mammals: "[M]ales who most often assume the female type of behavior are the ones who 'invariably prove to be the most vigorous copulators,' when they assume the more usual masculine role in coitus" (p. 615). Translation: Males who readily switch from being a top to a bottom are kings of the hormonal hill—and deliver performances to prove it!

Among the other myths the report exploded was the old chestnut propagated by Boy Scout manuals and the like that masturbation robs the young of their future ability to perform sexually. Kinsey's data indicated exactly the opposite: Sexually precocious boys, the ones most prone to "self-abuse," are destined to enjoy the lustiest adulthoods. Moreover, the folklore that masturbation brings on such calamities as blindness and hairy palms did not square with the report's finding; irksome in the extreme to guardians of purity, the report found that at least 95 percent of males engage in the practice.

Beyond showing that long-standing stereotypes of gays were ludicrously wrong, the report also presented surprisingly high figures on premarital and extramarital sex among heterosexuals in a context that suggested that the prohibition of such activities does far more harm than good. Many found this all the more alarming because of the prestige of Kinsey's backers: Indiana University, the National Research Council, the Rockefeller Foundation, and a roster of consultants that read like a cross-section of mainstream science.

Yet the substance and value of the Kinsey research lay elsewhere than in what seemed sensational. Then, as now, its great value flowed from the establishment, for the first time, of reliable baseline data on sexuality. Since the Kinsey data now are more than fifty years old, a question arises: Have the figures significantly changed in the intervening years as a result of the sexual revolution and other social forces?

Some certainly have changed. The average age at first intercourse is clearly down from age seventeen, where it once was, just as the amount of premarital intercourse is decidedly higher than it was in Kinsey's time. The proportion of homosexual individuals in the population, which Kinsey found to be stable for five generations, has probably remained so. At least, judging from several subsequent studies, nothing indicates it has either increased or decreased significantly.

*   *   *

The marked originality of Kinsey's work frequently raises the double question of how he came to sex research, and how he was able to make such a fresh start. The standard answer (true as far as it goes) is that when Indiana University instituted its first marriage course in 1938, Kinsey was elected to teach it. As his students began asking far-ranging questions about sex, he would try to answer them or look them up in the existing literature. What he found in the literature appalled him: a general lack of evidence and rigor.

Kinsey quietly decided to collect his own data. He began to interview people, to ask basic questions about their sex lives, and to polish and greatly expand his questions. Out of both generosity and a desire to learn more about "the reality," as he liked to call it, he provided a good deal of private counseling to students in his course, most of whom were either married or planning to marry. During the spring semester of 1939 alone he conducted some 280 of these personal conferences.

One could not have predicted from Kinsey's rigidly religious upbringing that he would follow this path. His straitlaced father, a devout Sunday school teacher who insisted that the family walk rather than ride to church, enforced a triple Sabbath: Sunday school, church, and evening prayer meeting. Part of this moralism stayed with young Kinsey until at least his first year in college, during which, he later recalled with amusement, a classmate once sought him out to confess to "excessive" masturbation. Kinsey took his friend back to their dormitory and knelt down beside him to pray for God's help to make the youth stop.

Although Kinsey soon rejected religion, in other respects he continued to lead a conventional life. After receiving a PhD in zoology from Harvard, he secured an assistant professorship at Indiana University, got married, fathered four children, and pursued a career of teaching, writing, and fieldwork in entomology (the study of insects). The fieldwork presented physical and social challenges that Kinsey greatly enjoyed. In fact, a theme never to reverse itself was his lifelong fascination with nature and its effect on his interpersonal relations.

As a boy he was entranced by the outdoors. He loved to go alone on long hikes across the countryside, everywhere noticing the characteristics of plants and animals, particularly the differences and similarities between individuals of the same species. He was fascinated, too, by the sorts of people he found—farmers and country folk from generally less-educated backgrounds than his own, whose permission he often needed to cross land or camp out. He learned to meet strangers very different from himself, to tune into their views and attitudes, and to quickly establish rapport and gain cooperation.

For twenty years Kinsey put these abilities to extensive use while conducting field research on his first great academic passion, the gall wasp. "Bug hunting," as he called his pursuit of the tiny insect, took him on treks for thousands of miles across the then forty-eight states, and into Guatemala and Mexico, during which he met an even more diverse array of strangers. In Mexico, for example, he would hike for days into mountainous back regions that the government warned were inhabited by hostile Indians. At one point, officials required him to sign a document absolving them of any responsibility should he come into harm's way. Kinsey took the alleged perils in stride. His colleague, friend, and biographer Wardell Pomeroy gave this account of how he dealt with them:

> On the first night [out in the wilderness] he set up his tent and went to sleep quickly, exhausted by a long day of collecting specimens. Next morning he emerged to find himself virtually surrounded by a circle of impassive Indians, who sat on the ground and studied him solemnly, with what purpose he did not know. Casually he set up his camp stove, then drew a chocolate bar from his pocket. He bit off a piece and ate it, to show that it was not poisoned, and offered a piece to the man nearest him. Then he divided the bar, giving a small piece to each man. When they had eaten it, he invited one of the Indians to examine his galls. The offer was accepted. After a few minutes of peering at them, the Indian called on the others to join him, and they took turns looking, equally interested. A few hours later, the hills were covered with natives searching for galls to bring to the American professor. (Pomeroy, 1972, p. 39)

From such experiences Kinsey developed "a system for discharging danger in strangers," the cardinal principles of which proved extremely useful in his sex research: "Try never to move forward or back, especially in dangerous situations, be they dealing with the Mafia, interviewing prostitutes, or getting around the nervousness of ordinary people" (Pomeroy, 1977, p. 39). ("Moving forward" can seem intrusive, "moving back" can look defensive or rejecting.) "Be considerate and thoughtful, never selfish in your pursuit." "Let people know what you want, then allow them to bring it to you" (Pomeroy, 1972, pp. 39-40). These are but a few examples; there were many others.

The boyhood hiking, the bug-hunting expeditions, and the sexual counseling thus laid the groundwork for Kinsey's development of one of his most consummate skills: making interview subjects comfortable. His kindly, nonjudgmental manner and simple language almost instantly put strangers at ease. He always reminded his college-bred interviewers to use the vocabulary of their subjects: "The lower-level individual is never ill or injured, though he may be sick or hurt. He does not wish to do something, though he wants to do it. He does not perceive, though he sees. He is not acquainted with a person, though he may know him" (Kinsey, 1948, p. 52). Everywhere in Kinsey's approach it seemed that even plainness and politeness were powerful stuff, part of his respect for each person's makeup and the right to be himself or herself regardless of current position or predicament. Kinsey insisted that anyone generous enough to give a sexual history deserved to be treated as a friend or guest: "The tottering old man who is a victim of his first penal conviction appreciates an interviewer's solicitation about his health, appreciates being provided with tobacco, candy, and other things the institution allows. The inmate in a women's penal institution particularly appreciates the courtesies that a male would extend to a woman of his own social rank, in his own home" (Kinsey, 1948, p. 48).

*   *   *

Kinsey early on recognized a need for broader knowledge of what sex is like in special and diverse contexts; he wanted to see behind the curtains of privacy that people use to disguise or to entirely hide what they do from others, and sometimes from themselves. By July, 1939, he had collected some 350 sex histories. The material persuaded him that he needed more information on homosexual behavior. A student whose history he had taken told him of someone in Chicago who could introduce him to homosexuals and show him how they live. Acting on this tip, he arranged for a trial visit to meet the contact and soon was making weekly trips. "He would leave Bloomington after his last class on Friday, drive the more than 200 miles to Chicago, work through the weekend, then drive back on Monday morning in time for his 8:30 a.m. class" (Christenson, 1971, p. 107).

Within two months he had collected scores of homosexual histories and was astounded by the variations among them. Although the subjects he met in Chicago did indeed constitute valuable urban samples, he later was amused by how naive he had been about "the homosexual." The kinds of histories he'd traveled great distances to gather could have been found in abundance, had he but known it, within walking distance of his Bloomington office.

On other occasions he traveled far and wide to study particular groups: prisoners, prostitutes, paragons of virtue in religious sects. Nothing he ever saw diverted or defeated him for, as a colleague put it, "He was always able to look through any ugliness to something lovely beyond" (Earle M. Marsh quoted in Pomeroy, 1972, p. 166). Whenever he ran into something unique, he immediately tried to investigate it. Once, when a sixty-three-year-old man claimed that he could come to orgasm in ten seconds from a flaccid start, Kinsey reacted with a skeptical glance, whereupon the man demonstrated this particular feat on the spot. Deep in rural Kansas, Kinsey searched out a community where, remarkably, all the women were easily able to reach orgasm in ordinary intercourse—unusual the world over, both then and now. It turned out that the community's prevailing style of pacifying babies involved a particular patting and stroking technique that soon induced sleep. Unbeknownst to the caregivers, the technique accidentally brought their baby girls to orgasm, thereby leaving traces in their sexual substrates that made them "easy responders" for life. Other special cases (tabulated separately to keep them from biasing the averages) involved such things as the sexual responses of people who had had brain surgery, others who for religious reasons had struggled all their lives against any sexual expression, members of nudist colonies, and paraplegics.

In addition to investigations of people plain and special, Kinsey and his co-workers made an extensive study of the differences between the sexes that so affect their psychology and compatibility. (A central finding revealed that males tend to be genitally focused, and females are more "peripheral," i.e., tend to place more value on the moods and ambiance *around* sex than on genital stimulation.) Kinsey also pursued literally dozens of subprojects, including studies of fourteen mammalian species, and of human neurology and physiology. He launched cross-cultural surveys of ancient and modern societies, including a detailed investigation of sex practices in pre-Columbian civilizations and a study that traced shifts in Japanese sexual mores over 400 years. Legal experts were brought in to gauge the relationship between a man's education and how well he fared in the legal system. A bevy of scholars worked to accurately translate into English important classical literature, previous translations of which distorted or outright omitted sexual passages, particularly ones dealing with homosexual themes. For example, Kinsey asked Dr. Hazel Toliver, an authority on ancient Latin and Greek, to check the prestigious Oxford-published Benjamin Jowett translation of Plato's *Symposium*. She found, among many others, the following instances of censorship:

JOWETT: He who under the influence of true love rising upward begins to see that beauty is not far from the end.

WHAT PLATO REALLY WROTE: Through the nightly loving of boys a man, on arising, begins to see the true nature of beauty.

JOWETT: As Pausanias says, The good are to be accepted, and the bad are not to be accepted.

PLATO: As Pausanias says, It is honorable for a man to grant sexual favors to the good among men and shameful for him to grant them to the unbridled.

JOWETT: Now I thought he was seriously enamoured of my beauty and this appeared to be a grand opportunity of hearing him tell what he knew.

PLATO: Now I thought he was eager for my bloom of youth and I believed that it was a windfall and my marvelous piece of good luck that it should fall to me to sexually gratify Socrates in order to hear everything he knew.

*   *   *

As noted at the outset of this chapter, the report generated enormous commotion. Its most controversial elements, by far, were those that explored homosexual issues. For although homosexuality was only one of the six basic forms of sex examined (the others were nocturnal emissions, masturbation, heterosexual petting, heterosexual intercourse, and sex with animals), and although it represented only a fraction of the research effort, nothing disturbed critics more or brought them to such a fever pitch of hate and rage than did the findings on homosexual behavior. A. H. Hobbs, an associate professor of sociology at the University of Pennsylvania, issued a typical denunciation: "There must be something wrong with Kinsey's statistics, which [coupled with] the prestige of the Rockefeller Foundation, give unwarranted weight to implications that homosexuality is normal, and that premarital relations might be a good thing" (Jones, 1997, p. 734). Others insisted that homosexuality just can't be that prevalent—and, anyway, by talking about it you encourage it. The president of Princeton University, Dr. Harold Dodds, actually likened the report to "toilet-wall inscriptions" (Pomeroy, 1972, p. 287). Clare Boothe Luce, author of the racy play *The Women,* felt obliged to proclaim at a lecture for the National Council of Catholic Women in 1984 that, "The Kinsey Report, like all cheap thrillers, would fall into obscurity if so much attention was not paid to it."

Similar sentiments came from congressmen, from a handful of anthropologists and psychoanalysts, and more stridently from Union Theological Seminary's Henry Van Dusen (who, dangerously, sat on the board of the Rockefeller Foundation). A respected scientist had poked a stick in the eye of American prudery, and the leading prudes, aghast at the sudden airing of heretofore forbidden topics, ferociously lashed back. The hue and cry raised such doubts about Kinsey's data that the National Research Council asked the American Statistical Association (ASA) to examine the work in detail. Kinsey was well prepared for this challenge, but not for the delay it entailed, during which his financial backing began to evaporate. Originally he had envisioned publishing nine further volumes on human sexuality; of these, only *Sexual Behavior in the Human Female* (1953) saw print.

When the ASA finally weighed in, it rated Kinsey's research as the best ever done in the field. The last three words of its summation characterized the report as "a monumental endeavor." (Strangely enough, even here, homosexual behavior was the central issue; it was the only one of the six kinds of sex that Kinsey studied to appear in the index of the ASA's 338-page report.) But by then, the battle with reaction had been lost.

Heartsick at losing support for his "right to do sex research," as he always put it, and exhausted by efforts to seek new backing, Kinsey's health began to fail. He died on August 25, 1956. Shortly before, he memorably commented: "There isn't a day that I do not regret that we do not have a raft more of our material in print for people to use" (Christenson, 1971, p. 169).

In fact, one of the more haunting aspects of Kinsey's legacy is that perhaps as much as 90 percent of the data that he and his staff gathered has yet to be published or even prepared for publication. Furthermore, changing political winds, budgetary constraints, and mismanagement have severely restricted scholars' access to the treasure trove of information still held by the Kinsey Institute for Sex Research at Indiana University. It is both shocking and sad that many decades after Kinsey started gathering the information, those who control it still consider it too hot to handle.

*   *   *

A few comments are in order about a pair of recent Kinsey biographies, *Alfred C. Kinsey: A Public/Private Life* by James Jones (1997), and *Sex the Measure of All Things: A Life of Alfred C. Kinsey* by Jonathan Gathorne-Hardy (1998). The Jones book, although a tour de force of meticulous detail distributed over nearly 1,000 pages, makes serious misjudgments throughout that cumulatively destroy the uninitiated reader's ability to grasp Kinsey's character, either his size as a man or his stature as a scientist of great merit. With regard to the nature of Kinsey's homosexuality, his alleged lifelong masochism, and, above all, his "sense of shame," Jones' mistakes are simply too coarse and careless to warrant rebuttal. More serious by far are other misperceptions, such as Jones' notion of "Kinsey the reformer," of a "compulsive" obsessed with revolutionizing sexual mores. This is absolute nonsense. For although the report made a landmark contribution to the intellectual underpinnings of the sexual revolution, Kinsey always maintained that the whole matrix of our mores is stubborn, ancient in origin, glacial in pace, and quite often indifferent to scientific facts. His vision, focused on the individual's striving to understand his or her particular sexuality, was almost exactly the opposite of what Jones portrays. To sum up the vision: If you as a person, whoever you are and wherever you live, can "get ahold of the facts" (a favorite phrase of his), *you can work out your own solutions*. This was not the credo of a man who would impose a new sexual order.

Fortunately, no such complaints can be leveled against the Gathorne-Hardy biography. Every time it comes to hand, I'm amazed anew at how good it is—rich, important, lively, greatly detailed in its own way, and occasionally hilarious in a fashion that only a polished writer can manage to bring off. For instance, while evaluating how studies subsequent to Kinsey have tried to measure some of the same variables he explored, Gathorne-Hardy takes us behind the scenes to meet the "Blue Rinse Brigade," a group of elderly ladies hired by a Chicago research organization to gather sexual histories. The "extensive training" that these women were said to have received turned out to consist of only a single page of guidelines and three days of actual practice—a woefully inadequate level of preparation that has plagued many other post-Kinsey studies as well. Kinsey, who wrote extensively on interviewing techniques, in contrast demanded that his history takers receive training for a *full year* and set extremely rigorous standards to maximize their "people skills." He would have laughed out loud at the very notion of the Blue Rinse Brigade. For as one of its potential subjects asked with plaintive bewilderment, "Do they think I'm going to tell some old woman who reminds me of my mother that I'm a cocksucker?" (Gathorne-Hardy, 1998, p. 286).

*   *   *

Numerous researchers have stepped in since Kinsey's death to continue his work, with some achieving success in a few areas. But no one has matched his cutting edge or has come close to the quality and detail of the *Male* and *Female* volumes (both of which have recently been republished). They endure as the standard reference works on what people did and mostly still do in sex. They also endure as the first, and to this day the most comprehensive, refutation of myths associated with homophobia.

REFERENCES

Christenson, Cornelia V. *Kinsey, A Biography.* Bloomington: Indiana University Press, 1971.

Gathorne-Hardy, Jonathan. *Sex the Measure of All Things: A Life of Alfred C. Kinsey.* London: Chatham and Windus, 1998.

Jones, James H. *Alfred C. Kinsey: A Public/Private Life.* New York: Norton, 1997.

Kinsey, A. C., Pomeroy, W., and Martin, C. *Sexual Behavior in the Human Male.* Philadelphia: W.B. Saunders, 1948.

Kinsey, A. C., Pomeroy, W., Martin, C., and Gebhard, P. *Sexual Behavior in the Human Female.* Philadelphia: W.B. Saunders, 1953.

Pomeroy, Wardell B. *Dr. Kinsey and the Institute for Sex Research.* New York: Harper and Row, 1972.

Henry Gerber (1895-1972): Grandfather of the American Gay Movement

Jim Kepner
Stephen O. Murray

If everyone keeps aloof, nothing will be done. As Goethe said: "Against human stupidity even the gods fight in vain."

Henry Gerber, October 23, 1945, letter to Manuel Boyfrank

Henry Gerber (1895-1972), the crotchety Bavarian-born forefather of a gay movement in the United States, arrived in the United States in 1913. In 1917 he was briefly institutionalized in a mental institution for being homosexual. After the United States declared war on Germany, Gerber was given a choice between joining the U.S. Army or being interned for the duration of the war as an enemy alien. He chose to join the army, working as a printer and proofreader in Coblenz (in the Rhineland) as part of the American Army of occupation during the early 1920s. Gerber contacted the then-thriving Bund für Menschenrecht (Society for Human Rights, founded in 1919 by Hans Kahnert) and worked either on *Blätter für Menschenrechten* (*Journal for human rights,* a gay periodical published in

Chicago Historical Society

Shortly before his death, Kepner drafted a two-and-a-half-page biographical sketch for a precursor of this book. Murray edited this sketch and added material from Gerber's letters—letters that Kepner had collected and that are now in the ONE/IGLA collection at the University of Southern California—and from the material Kepner supplied Katz (1978). Dates following quotations are those of letters to Manuel Boyfrank. Page numbers that are not part of a fuller reference are from Katz (1978). Kepner did not supply citations for the direct quotations in his sketch.

Berlin for which Gerber wrote two bylined articles from the United States that appeared in 1928 and 1929) or, more likely, on an army post newspaper. His 1962 article in *ONE Magazine* recalled subscribing to a German homophile magazine and traveling several times to Berlin.

After the war, his citizenship status still uncertain because of the psychiatric hospitalization, he worked for the U.S. Postal Service in Chicago. With some help from his supervisor there, he founded a Society for Human Rights (SHR) in Chicago. The SHR's December 1924 charter from the state of Illinois as a nonprofit corporation had the stated objective

> to promote and protect the interests of people who by reasons of mental and physical abnormalities are abused and hindered in the legal pursuit of happiness which is guaranteed them by the Declaration of Independence and to combat the public prejudices against them by dissemination of factors according to modern science among intellectuals of mature age. The Society stands only for law and order; it is in harmony with any and all general laws insofar as they protect the rights of others, and does in no manner recommend any acts in violation of present laws nor advocate any matter inimical to the public welfare. (Katz, 1978, pp. 386-387)

Gerber signed the application as secretary. The Reverend John T. Graves, an African-American preacher, who was the only clergyman Gerber seems to have found congenial, signed it as president, and the document lists seven directors, including Gerber and Graves.

Gerber was deeply disappointed by his inability to gain support for SHR from any physicians or advocates of sex education and sexual freedom: "The most difficult task was to get men of good reputation to back up the Society." He tried to get medical authorities to endorse the new organization, but as he said "they usually refused to endanger their reputations." He was dismayed that "the only support I got was from poor people"; the only men willing to join were "illiterate and penniless." Gerber did all the work and bore all the costs. He recalled that he had been "willing to slave and suffer and risk losing my job and savings and even my liberty for the ideal" (Katz, 1978, pp. 388-393). Years after SHR collapsed, Gerber reported that he had come to realize that "most people only join clubs which already have members" (June 22, 1946).

Very few individuals were even willing to receive the Society's publication, *Friendship and Freedom* (of which there were two issues), by mail, regarding it as akin to thieves publicly subscribing to a thieves' journal, making it easy to find criminals (as those engaging in any same-sex sexual contact were then considered). Postal censors eagerly cooperated with local law enforcement agencies to identify "sex deviants." A picture of *Friendship and Freedom* appeared in a German magazine (it is reproduced in Katz 1978, p. 587), and a brief review of the first issue appeared in the French journal *L'Amitée* in April of 1925 (originally titled *Inversions*).

In his 1962 retrospect, Gerber wrote that upon his return to the United States,

> I realized that homosexuals themselves needed nearly as much attention as the laws pertaining to their acts. . . . The first difficulty was in rounding up enough members and contributors so the work could go forward. The average homosexual, I found, was ignorant concerning himself. Others were fearful. Still others were frantic or depraved. Some were blasé.
>
> Many homosexuals told me that their search for forbidden fruit was the real spice of life. With this argument they rejected our aims. We wondered how we could accomplish anything with such resistance from our own people. (Katz, 1978, p. 388)

Gerber never said where he tried to recruit, other than through pen pals. There were speakeasies where homosexual men gathered, but Gerber neither drank nor smoked and did not like to associate with queeny or with older homosexual men. Surreptitious homosexual activity in parks, restrooms, and theaters limited, if not precluded, conversation, at least any discussion about joining a legal reform organization. The few pen pals who admitted they were homosexual were interested in direct sex contacts, in trading erotic photos, or in ethereal romanticism.

Nevertheless, Gerber and his original group had a plan for gradual expansion with two cautious principles, both of which prefigured 1950s' homophile organizations:

> (1) We would engage in a series of lectures pointing out the attitude of society in relation to their own behavior and especially urging against the seduction of adolescents.

> (2) Through a publication named *Friendship and Freedom* we would keep the homophile world in touch with the progress of our efforts. The publication was to refrain from advocating sexual acts and would serve merely as a forum of discussion.

The final part of the plan aimed to convince authorities of the need for change:

(3) Through self-discipline, homophiles would win the confidence and assistance of legal authorities and legislators in understanding the problem: that these authorities should be educated on the futility and folly of long prison terms for those committing homosexual acts, etc. (Katz, 1978, pp. 386-387)

Gerber and Graves had decided to exclude bisexuals from SHR. Unbeknownst to them, SHR's vice president, Al Weininger, called by Gerber an "indigent laundry queen," had a wife and two young children. The members of SHR were jailed when Weininger's wife told a social worker about an organization of "degenerates," and the social worker passed on the information to the police. The police brought along a newspaper reporter when they came calling on Gerber. As Gerber recalled:

> One Sunday morning about 2 a.m., I returned from a visit downtown. After I had gone to my room, someone knocked at the door. Thinking it might be the landlady, I opened up. Two men entered the room. They identified themselves as a city detective and a newspaper reporter from [the Hearst newspaper] the *Examiner*. The detective asked me where the boy was. What boy? He told me he had orders from his precinct captain to bring me to the police station. He took my typewriter, my notary public diploma, and all the literature of the Society and also personal diaries as well as my bookkeeping accounts. At no time did he show a warrant for my arrest. At the police station I was locked up in a cell but no charges were made against me. (Katz, 1978, p. 390)

The next morning he was taken to the Chicago Avenue Police Court, where he found John, Al, and George, a young man who had been in Al's room at the time of arrest. The *Examiner* reported the story under the headline, "Strange Sex Cult Exposed." The reporter claimed that Al had "brought his male friends home and had, in full view of his wife and children, practiced 'strange sex acts' with them." He also wrote that a pamphlet of this "cult" was found that "urged men to leave their wives and children," a statement totally antithetical to the SHR policy of including only exclusive homosexuals.

On Monday the detective produced a powder puff in court that he claimed to have found in Gerber's room. This was understood by everyone as evidence of effeminacy, although Gerber heartily denied that it was his or that he ever used powder or owned a powder puff. The judge wondered aloud about whether *Friendship and Freedom* violated federal laws about sending obscene materials through the U.S. mail—the obscenity being discussion of homosexuality or the persecution of homosexuals, rather than anything particularly prurient.

The case was dismissed and the prosecution reprimanded (by a different judge), but his legal defense cost Gerber his life savings of $600 and resulted in dismissal from his job for "conduct unbecoming a postal worker." Al pled guilty to disorderly conduct and was fined $10. Most undistributed copies of *Friendship and Freedom* were confiscated by the police, along with Gerber's private papers and typewriter. Despite a judge's order, they were never returned to him. No action on obscenity was taken although two postal inspectors were present in the court. The case left Gerber very bitter that none of the more affluent Chicago homosexuals helped him in a fight which he regarded as one for the collective good. Gerber was left without a job or savings, and his dream of a Society for Human Rights was ended.

It is not clear what Gerber did to earn a living during the next few years. On a 1927 visit to New York City, a friend from his newspaper days in Coblenz introduced him to a colonel (who had been a brevet major general during World War I) who told Gerber he would be glad to have him in his unit if he reenlisted. Gerber did so; in 1945, he received an honorable discharge and a $100 a month military pension. Making New York City his home, Gerber made some further efforts to organize homosexuals, although he increasingly believed that "most bitches are only interested in sex contacts," not challenging legal and social stigmas of homosexuality. "I have absolutely no confidence in the dorian crowd, mostly a bunch of selfish, uncultured, ignorant egoists who have nothing for the ideal side of life," Gerber wrote Boyfrank (April 9, 1944). "Since it gets me nothing and prevents me from enjoying my liberty in private, why bother to help others?" was the bitter view of the one-time idealist reformer. "Why waste your time and run risks of jail over a few stupid homos who are bound to get in dutch and spill everything? I have gone through all this and swore to do it no more" (January 4, 1945).

Gerber also ran the pen-pal club *Contacts* from 1930 until 1939. It had about 150 to 200 members when he began. Although most members were heterosexual, it was possible for Gerber and a few other homosexuals to blend in, thereby avoiding attention and interference from the postal authorities. Members were not informed who was running the club. He produced a monthly newsletter, generally a single mimeographed sheet for "Contacters." He also worked on a 1934 freethinking publication, *Chanticleer,* writing many articles in defense of homosexuality, including an early report on the persecution of homosexuals in Germany. He missed the fact that a similar witch-hunt against homosexuals had begun in the Soviet Union months earlier: Russia was still thought to be the only Western country that had been freed from legal oppression. So convinced was Gerber that religion was the source of antihomosexual bias that he hardly saw atheism and what we might now label gay pride as separable.

In the final (1939) issue of *Contacts,* #10, Gerber provided a lengthy self-description of a vaguely (pop-)Nietzschean misanthrope whose misogyny is dwarfed by his anticlericalism:

> NYC Male, 44, proofreader, single. Favored by nature with immunity to female "charms," but do[es] not "hate" women; consider[s] them necessary in the scheme of nature. Amused by screwey antics of Homo Sapiens. Introvert, enjoying a quiet evening with classical music or non-fiction book. Looking at life, I understand why monkeys protested Darwin's thesis.
>
> Of Bavarian descent. Brought up Catholic, now an avowed atheist. (God loves atheists because they do not molest him with silly prayers.) Believe[s] in brotherhood of man, but sees no hope for mankind to free itself from exploitation of the entrenched money changers. Religions is a racket and one who believes in supernatural powers is ready to swallow anything, including Jonas' whale.
>
> Believe[s] in French sex morality: that it's not the state's business to interfere in the sexual enjoyment of adults so long as rights of others are not violated. If I had designed this world, I would have designed a less messy and filthy modus operandi of procreation than "sex" and birth. . . . Nature is plain, although there is no meaning beyond multiplication of existing forms. Like cats, men and women create children, which in the case of cats are drowned every time a litter appears. It is still against the law to drown unwanted children. Nature will always favor procreation and is distinctly on the side of women in trapping man and drafting him for his natural duties. Birth control makes slow headway, but is considered legal, although natural forms of birth control which do not depend on artificial goods sold in drugstores [homosexual contacts] are still considered grave moral misdemeanors. . . . Religious racketeers realize that man's emotions, if freely expressed by sex activity, would leave nothing for religion. But sex represt [repressed] and inhibited leads to religious hysteria, and priests get rich thereby. Thus sex must be suprest [suppressed]. No intelligent man will find certain anatomical parts of man's body more moral than others and would naturally reject the word "obscene." But it is part and parcel of a scheme to deprive man of sex pleasure for the ultimate profit of others. Man must not enjoy himself too much or God will weep and punish him! Absurd theology, accepted by millions of Christians and Jews.

Life itself is not a great gift, but those who have a good income without having to work too hard manage to find life tolerably interesting and enjoy the pleasures of mind and body. . . . A genuine introvert, consider[s] solitude the greatest blessing of man. Can get along without friends and prefer[s] to be alone rather than waste my time with morons who have only learned phrases such as You said it, You are damn[e]d right, Search me. It is impossible for a person conducting his business in a big city to be alone most of the time, and contacts in the line of business prevent a solitary introvert from becoming lopsided. Books, the radio, the newspaper bring the world into his home, without forcing him to endure painful contact with nitwits. Brainless people fear being alone with their empty selves and run from party to party and from the many amusements offered such unthinking people. I am fond of reading non-fiction books and have quite a library of selected volumes. Very fond of classical music. Have about 1000 gramophone records (all classical) and a radio-combination, also play the piano. Fond of outdoors in summer. Like foreign, especially French, films, and the few worthwhile Hollywood pictures, but am disgusted with the hypocrisy and "goody-goody" filmware which shows all men honest and all women "pure." Firmly for realism even if it shakes a few pious spinsters out of their "Alice-in-Wonderland" revery. Rather particular about correspondents. Not interested in smut or "obscenity," not because it is a "sin" but believe my private affairs personal and sacred, not to be divulged to gossip. Not interested in the gossip-mongering of the average Contacts female nor inclined to waste time on brainless male "old wives" who are too lazy or cowardly to solve their own problems. Consider myself civilized and self-sufficient, but always welcome people of like minds who can discuss life intelligently, and can share the simple pleasures of discussion, music, and travel.

This diatribe drew at least one response, the beginning of correspondence with Manuel Boyfrank. In a January 27, 1940, letter Gerber wrote Boyfrank, "I was surprised to find you a homosexual, too, but let me tell you from experience [that] it does not pay to do anything for them. I once lost a good job trying to bring them together. Most men of that type are too scared to join any association trying to help them; the other half are only interested in physical contacts and have no interest in helping their cause, as I found to my sorrow." Gerber continued, immediately, with specification of his own sexual conduct, circa 1940:

Personally I am only interested in young boys around 20 who are willing to do all the "dirty" work for say a dollar. . . . Fortunately there are
many of that type who deliver the goods for a price, and I am more or
less consorting to this business. How should I worry how others get
theirs? As they say in the South, I get mine; why worry how he gets
hisn?

In a letter to Boyfrank (March 23, 1944), however, he said that mutual
masturbation in movie theaters was the extent of his "love affairs."

He might have been not quite honest, since in another letter to Boyfrank
(July 5, 1945), he wrote, "I prefer prostitutes who have their price and do a
good job. . . . Thousands are willing to make a couple dollars and get pleasure on top of it." In addition to their abundant supply, he stated that another
advantage in this choice of sexual partners was that "prostitutes would no
more call the police than a bootlegger would ask a revenuer for protection of
his illegal business."

Generally unsociable, Gerber longed for that "ideal friend," but by his
midforties he had settled for quick anonymous sex, primarily masturbating
military men in theaters. Intellectual companionship for him was at a geographic distance, maintained cautiously (given his experiences with the
U.S. Postal Service) by mail. From 1939 to 1957 he engaged in extensive
correspondence with Manuel Boyfrank, Frank McCourt, and several others
about how to organize homosexuals, and how to answer the prejudice and
misinformation in the press.

Gerber and his friends suffered periodic beatings, theft, and blackmail by
the "dirt trade." They were further harassed by postal snoops who opened
"suspicious or obscene" mail and reported homosexuals to the police. In
February 1942 Gerber's quarters were searched by G-2, the U.S. Army investigative unit. Although they found no damaging evidence, Gerber spent
weeks in the guardhouse. Gerber recalled that "they put me before a Section
VIII (undesirable) board and tried to get me out of the army on that. When I
told the president of the board I only practiced mutual masturbation with
men over 21, the psychiatrist told me 'You are not a homosexual.' I nearly
fell out of my chair! Imagine me fighting all my life for our cause and then
be told I was not a homosexual!"

Although he recurrently discussed the need for a homosexual advocacy
group, Gerber felt that it was virtually impossible to find enough reliable
people to start one. On Governor's Island in 1948, Fred Frisbie, a nineteen-
year-old soldier who had gone home with a friend of Gerber's, enthusiastically joined such a discussion over breakfast, but Gerber argued that most
homosexuals would never support any organization designed to improve the

general social position of homosexuals. Frisbie was later a participant in Mattachine and ONE, Inc.

Some of Gerber's long-winded letters in defense of homosexuality (also attacking corrupt politicians, conservative moralists, and religion) appeared in *The Modern Thinker, The Freethinker, American Mercury,* and District of Columbia newspapers, signed by "Doctor Gerber," since only a doctor was presumed to know anything about such abnormality.

Gerber, Boyfrank, and McCourt were masculine in appearance and demeanor and felt they had little in common with effeminate queens or lesbians. In particular, Gerber regarded women as nest builders, allies of priests, and as natural enemies of homosexuals. "Women are good psychologists and [it] did not take long to find out that homosexuals are their deadly enemies in the capture of the male" (January 4, 1945) was a leitmotif of Gerber's letters to Boyfrank. Although knowing little of the gay bar scene, they knew the park and movie theater cruising scenes well. Each had been rolled a few times. They argued among themselves about what homosexuality was and what to do about the problems homosexuals faced. Gerber initially viewed homosexuality as innate, then as a preference, and, after a Freudian conversion, as potential in all men ("There are no homosexuals. There is only sex pleasure and various forms of acquiring it"—July 5, 1945, letter to Boyfrank; reiterated October 23, 1945). However, he continued to vacillate about the existence of a homosexual kind of person as indicated by his rhetorical question, "What homosexual in his right mind wants to marry or to be 'cured'?" (August 9, 1947).

After a few relatively early partnerships with young queens, Gerber rarely had sex with friends or with anyone much over twenty-five years of age. Although publicly opposing racism, he often expressed his own. He viewed psychoanalysis as liberating and angrily cut off any friends, such as Jan Kingma (who was involved in or founded Philadelphia's Foundation for Social Development in 1948) simply because he espoused mysticism or religion or sought to work with sympathetic clergy. Except for the Reverend Graves, Gerber regarded any seemingly supportive clergy as a hypocrite, ignoring Christianity's implacable and essential opposition to homosexuality.

He worked some, though at a distance with Mattachine–New York and *ONE Magazine* during the 1950s. He wrote an account of the Society for Human Rights that appeared in the September 1962 issue of *ONE Magazine,* and translated part of Magnus Hirschfeld's (1914) *Die Homosexualitait des Mannes und des Weibes* for the *ONE Institute Quarterly.* Although Gerber pressed Boyfrank to join ONE, he continued to doubt that these organizations could win support from most gays or substantially change public prejudices. In a June 18, 1957, letter to Boyfrank he commented that "ONE and Mattachine have lots of financial trouble because the average homosexual is mainly interested in contacts with other homosexuals. When neither of these publications help in this matter but beg for contributions all the time . . . people are discouraged. . . . So the average homosexual, unless he is unselfish, can see nothing in it for him and he returns to the solitary hunt for trade."

During the 1950s he began to explore the gay bar scene and was astonished to discover that more men than he had previously supposed did engage in anal intercourse. Except for brief trips to Mexico and Europe during 1951 and 1952, he spent his final years at the U.S. Soldiers' Home in Washington, DC. He worked on an autobiography "admitting my homosexuality but not going into details," a critique of religion, a book on ethics, and a book on sex laws. The last he titled *Moral Delusions* (January 4, 1945). He also worked on rewriting translations he had done years earlier of two German gay novels he collectively titled *Angels in Sodom* (December 7, 1946). He mailed some manuscripts to Boyfrank. Either they all were lost—perhaps seized by postal inspectors—or they disappeared into Boyfrank's never-finished cut-and-paste manuscript. Boyfrank told Kepner he did not recall receiving them, although they are discussed in their correspondence around that time (e.g., in an October 23, 1945, letter). Gerber also produced a recreational bulletin at the soldiers' home and wrote letters and prepared tax forms for other veterans, most of whom he despised as idiots.

Although his fledgling organization was crushed by a cabal of social control agents, Gerber sowed the seed of gay pride and the idea of fighting for gay rights in scores of correspondents, directly and indirectly influencing Harry Hay, Jim Kepner, Tony Segura, Donna Smith, Fred Frisbie, Manuel Boyfrank, and others who worked to establish the homophile movement of the 1950s. Gerber is also a clear link between the German movement to remove Paragraph 175 of the German penal code and the 1950s' law reform movement that still remained extremely high-risk activism for people who were not just stigmatized but whose relations—even nonsexual associations—were criminalized. He was keenly aware of the centrality of postal inspectors interfering with association at a distance by those seeking to organize around homosexuality and its repression, an obstacle to nonlocal mobilization that ONE finally succeeded in removing in 1958.

BIBLIOGRAPHY

Gerber, Henry. 1929. "Die Strafbstimmungen in den 48 Staaten Amerikas und den amerikanischen Territorien für gewisse Geschlechtsakte." *Blätter für Menschenrechte* 7(8):5-11.

Gerber, Henry. 1962. "The Society for Human Rights—Chicago." *ONE Magazine* 10(9):5-10. Abridged version in Katz, 1978:584-592.

Hirschfeld, Magnus. 1914. *Die Homosexualitait des Mannes und des Weibes.* Berlin: Louis Marcus.

Katz, Jonathan Ned. 1978. *Gay American History.* New York: Avon. (Many of the documents are in Katz, 1978.)

Kepner collection. Jim Kepner collected material on Gerber including many of his letters which are now in the ONE/IGLA collection at the University of Southern California. He also supplied material to Katz. Unfortunately, Kepner, who started this biography, did not supply citations for the direct quotation in this sketch. There is often some conflict in dates in Gerber's recollections.

Edward Irenaeus Prime-Stevenson
(Xavier Mayne) (1868-1942)

John Lauritsen

Novelist, journalist, independent scholar, and music critic, Stevenson was the first American to deal openly with homosexuality, both in a fictional setting and as a transmitter of the ideas about homosexuality as put forth by Karl Heinrich Ulrichs, Magnus Hirschfeld, and Richard von Krafft-Ebing.

Edward Stevenson was born on July 23, 1868, in Madison, New Jersey, the youngest son of Paul E. Stevenson, a Presbyterian minister who became principal of a classical school in Bridgewater, New Jersey, and then in Madison. Stevenson's mother, Cornelia Prime, came from a family of distinguished literary and academic figures; she was fifty-two at the time of Edward's birth.

Although admitted to the New Jersey Bar, Edward Stevenson never practiced law but instead pursued a career as a writer, which he had begun while still in school. His first novel, *White Cockades* (1887), is a boy's book about Bonnie Prince Charlie. Twenty years later Stevenson, writing under the pseudonym of Xavier Mayne, commented on this work: ". . . passionate devotion from a rustic youth towards the Prince and its recognition are half hinted as homosexual in essence" (1908, p. 367). Many novels and short stories followed, of which several were based on the theme of passionate male friendships.

Stevenson developed an international reputation as a man of letters, specializing in musical, dramatic, and literary criticism. He was at various times on the staff of the *Independent, Harper's Weekly,* and other publications. In the 1890s, he began dividing his time between Europe and the United States, and his life and outlook became increasingly cosmopolitan. Eventually he claimed mastery of nine languages, Asian as well as European. After the turn of the century he became an expatriate, residing mostly in Italy. His reasons are clearly expressed in his writings: the United States (as well as England) had an atmosphere that was oppressive and laws that were dangerous to a man such as himself, who was a lover of other males.

Stevenson's place in homophile literature is assured through two works: *Imre: A Memorandum,* the first American novel to deal openly and sympathetically with male homosexuality, and *The Intersexes,* the first book in the English language to discuss all aspects of homosexuality.

Imre: A Memorandum was self-published in Naples in 1906. It is best appreciated as a didactic work, an apologia for "The Friendship which is Love—the Love which is Friendship" (these words appear on the book's title page). We may presume it is also an expression of Stevenson's own tastes and opinions.

The novel's plot is meager enough. In a small Hungarian town, Oswald, an Englishman who is "past thirty" meets and falls in love with Imre, a twenty-five-year-old Hungarian officer who is from an old and proud but impoverished Transylvanian family. Imre "was of no ordinary beauty of physique and elegance of bearing, even in a land where such matters are normal details of personality." He possessed "a pair of peculiarly brilliant but not shadowless hazel eyes." Though his features were delicate, they were "without womanishness," for "Imre was not a pretty man; but a beautiful man." His body is described thus: "Of middle height, he possessed a slender figure, faultless in proportions, a wonder of muscular development, of strength, lightness and elegance." Imre was a star athlete in sports ranging from gymnastics to swimming, fencing, target shooting, and horse riding:

> Yet all this force, this muscular address, was concealed by the symmetry of his graceful, elastic frame. Not till he was nude, and one could trace the ripple of muscle and sinew under the fine, hairless skin, did one realize the machinery of such strength. (Mayne, 1908, p. 367)

Oswald and Imre spend much time together, mostly in conversation. About halfway through the book, following an intense discussion of friendship, Oswald begins a confession, which goes on for almost fifty pages. He tells the story of his life; reviews the work of Krafft-Ebing and others on uranianism; discusses the love-friendship of Ancient Greece; cites many famous men who were lovers of their own kind; and finally, using the familiar form of address, declares his love for Imre.

Imre appears to rebuff Oswald. In an anguished speech he pledges undying friendship, but implores Oswald never again to speak of what he had told him—"Never, unless I break the silence." Circumstances separate the two friends for awhile. Imre's communications become increasingly affectionate, and at last they are reunited. In a hotel room, Oswald is sexually aroused when Imre puts his arm around Oswald's shoulder, and struggles "in shame and despair to keep down the hateful physical passion which was making nothing of all my psychic loyalty" (Mayne, 1908, pp. 367-368). Apparently with a visible erection as a sign of his "sensual weakness," Oswald falls away from Imre, certain that his friendship would be lost forever.

However, Imre, voluntarily breaking the agreed-upon silence, delivers a confession of his own. Declaring his love for Oswald, he recounts his own experiences and love inclinations, which parallel those of Oswald. The dramatic high point of the novel is reached in Imre's resounding declaration: "Look into thyself, Oswald! It is all *there*. I am a Uranian, as thou art. From my birth I have been one. Wholly, wholly homosexual, Oswald!"

After more talk, they take a walk in the moonlight. Finally, back in the hotel room, Imre puts his arm around Oswald and delivers the final speech, which concludes: "Come then, O friend! O brother, to our rest! Thy heart on mine, thy soul with mine! For us two it is surely is . . . Rest!" (Mayne, 1908, pp. 368-369). It is by no means described, but we may dare to imagine that they then take off their clothes and get in bed.

Stevenson's magnum opus, *The Intersexes: A History of Similisexualism As a Problem in Social Life,* was also privately printed, apparently in Rome in 1908, in a limited edition of 125 copies. It is dedicated to the memory of Richard von Krafft-Ebing (1840-1902), the author of the best-seller *Psychopathia Sexualis* (1886).

An astonishing range of topics is covered in the 646 pages of Stevenson's book, including animal studies, similisexual love in the ancient world and among primitive peoples, gay geniuses, literature with homoerotic themes, ancient and modern legislation, male prostitution, blackmail, and violence.

Stevenson begins by addressing the book to the "individual layman," paying tribute to "medical psychologists," and explaining the basic concepts and terminology that he uses. Throughout *The Intersexes* Stevenson employs the terminology of Karl Heinrich Ulrichs (1825-1895), as popularized by Magnus Hirschfeld (1868-1935) and Krafft-Ebing. The term "intersexes" is a translation of the German *sexuelle zwischenstufen* (intermediate sexual types or sexual intergrades), the notion being that homosexuals are psychologically, and sometimes also physically, in between real (i.e., heterosexual) men and women.

In Ulrichs' sexual taxonomy, males are divided into three main categories: (1) the *Dioning* or normal male (called *Urianaster* when he acquires Urning tendencies!); (2) the *Urning* or homosexual male; and (3) the *Urano-dioning,* a male who is *born* with a capacity for love in both directions. Stevenson uses the English form, uranian, with its female counterpart uraniad for lesbians. (In Plato's *Symposium,* Pausanias postulates *two* gods of love: the Uranian [Heavenly] Eros governs principled male love, whereas

the Pandemian [Vulgar] Eros governs heterosexual or purely licentious relations.)

The reliance upon Ulrichs, Hirschfeld, and Krafft-Ebing is unfortunate,
as it dates the book and creates a conceptual muddle. Elsewhere in *The
Intersexes,* Stevenson shows that gay men can be every bit as masculine as
straight men and sometimes more so. One of the longest chapters in the
book covers the uranian and uraniad in the military and athletics. We are assured that "In the army and the marine we find the Uranian in enormous proportion," and that these uranians are characterized by "bodily vigour" and
"virile courage." A dozen pages are enthusiastically devoted to the phenomenon of soldiers who sell their bodies to other males.

Ulrichs and Hirschfeld notwithstanding, Stevenson is fascinated by the
concept that man-to-man love is "a supremely virile love": "Is there really
now, as ages ago, a sexual aristocracy of the male? a mystic and hellenic
brotherhood, a sort of super-virile male?" (Quotation in *Imre,* p. 1, attributed to "Magyarbol", another of Stevenson's pseudonyms).

Stevenson places great emphasis on the aesthetic dimension of male love,
especially for the more masculine type of uranian who possesses a "super-
seding sense of the beauty of the male physique and male character." He
praises the Ancient Greeks for having: "a temperament at once rugged and
yet aesthetically sensitive as in no other race."

Stevenson eloquently describes the high esteem with which male love
was held in the ancient world, especially Greece. He puts forward the "startling but irresistible conclusion" that the condemnation of similisexual love
is entirely a product of Christian morality which, going against our classical
heritage, is "simply a relic of ancient Jewish semi-civilized dispensations."
Throughout the book he characterizes the source of oppression in such
terms as the "narrow Jewish-Christian ethics of today."

Stevenson drew upon almost everything that had been written on similisexualism in the early homosexual rights movement and in psychiatric literature. In addition, he recorded his own extensive observations of the Uranian scene in the cities of Europe and the United States. There are hundreds
of case studies, newspaper accounts, and stories from the grapevine.

In his final chapter, "Is the Uranian a Higher or a Lower Sex and Type in
the Scale of Humanity?," Stevenson grapples with a paradox that tormented
him. On one hand, uranian types included vigorous and masculine men of
the highest character. On the other, there could also be "countless ignoble,
trivial, loathesome, feeble-souled and feeble-bodied creatures." He was horrified that the ranks of man-loving men included:

Those patently depraved, noxious, flaccid, gross, womanish beings! Perverted and imperfect in moral nature and even their bodily tissues! Those homosexual legions that are the straw-chaff of society; good for nothing except the fire that purges the world of garbage and rubbish! (a passage from *Imre,* p. 116, cited in *The Intersexes,* p. 588)

Nevertheless, Stevenson is convinced that the "uranian passion . . . is largely salutary," and he holds up the ideal:

Happiest of all, surely, are those Uranians, ever numerous, who have no wish nor need to fly society—or themselves. Knowing what they are, understanding the natural, the moral strength of their position as homosexuals; sure of right on their side, even if it be never accorded to them in the lands where they must live; fortunate in either due self-control or private freedom—day by day, they go on through their lives, self-respecting and respected, in relative peace. (Mayne, 1908, p. 515)

Considering their scarcity, it is difficult to gauge the influence of Stevenson's books on the homophile movement. *The Intersexes* is cited in Magnus Hirschfeld's 1914 magnum opus, *Die Homosexualität des Mannes und des Weibes*. Some members of the homophile intelligentsia read them. Both *Imre* and *The Intersexes* were reprinted in 1975 as part of the Arno Press series on homosexuality. Unfortunately, they were so poorly reproduced that many pages are almost illegible.

At any rate, both books are precious repositories of information, and should be studied by every aspiring gay scholar.

BIBLIOGRAPHY

Austen, Roger. *Playing the Game: The Homosexual Novel in America*. Indianapolis: Bobbs-Merrill, 1977.

Garde, Noel I. (Edgar Leone). "The Mysterious Father of American Homophile Literature: A Historical Study," *ONE Institute Quarterly,* 1:3 (Fall 1958), pp. 94-98.

Johansson, Warren. Entry on Stevenson in the *Encyclopedia of Homosexuality,* edited by Wayne R. Dynes, New York: Garland, 1990, volume 2, p. 1250.

Katz, Jonathan. *Gay American History: Lesbians and Gay Men in the U.S.A.* New York: Crowell, 1976.

Katz, Jonathan. *Gay/Lesbian Almanac: A New Documentary*. New York: Harper and Row Books, 1983.

Lauritsen, John, and David Thorstad. *The Early Homosexual Rights Movement (1864-1935)*. New York: Times Change Press, 1974; Second Revised Edition, 1995.

Levin, James. *The Gay Novel*. New York: Irvington, 1983.

Mayne, Xavier. *Imre: A Memorandum*. Naples: npl, 1906.

Mayne, Xavier. *The Intersexes: A History of Simisexualism As a Problem in Social Life*. Privately printed (apparently in Rome, Italy), 1908.

Prescott Townsend (1894-1973): Bohemian Blueblood— A Different Kind of Pioneer

Charles Shively

Courtesy Boston Atheneum

Born in the Mauve Decade of Oscar Wilde's ascendancy, Prescott Townsend came of age in the roaring 1920s and lived to embrace hippies in the 1960s and Boston's Gay Liberation Front with its newspaper *Fag Rag* in the 1970s. During his nearly eighty years, Townsend participated in a multitude of progressive movements in the United States. He fostered an early counterculture in Boston and Provincetown, worked with the Kinsey Institute, produced his own "snowflake" theory of sexuality, established a Mattachine chapter, and later his own "demophile" group in Boston. After World War I and until his death, he called for the repeal of the Massachusetts antisodomy laws enacted by seventeenth-century Puritans. As of this writing, Chapter 272, Section 34 of the General Laws of Massachusetts still prohibits "the abominable and detestable crime against nature, either with mankind or with a beast" and provides as punishment "imprisonment in the state prison for not more than twenty years."

Prescott maintained a deep self-regard for his biological bloodline. His family claimed direct descent from twenty-three passengers on the Mayflower. One of his revolutionary heroes was an ancestor, Roger Sherman, the only person to sign three significant American documents, the Declaration of Independence, the Articles of Confederation, and the Constitution. Sherman, similar to Townsend, may not be much remembered today, but the grouchy second U.S. President John Adams described Sherman as "an old Puritan, as honest as an angel and as firm in the cause of American Independence as Mount Atlas" (Cathcart manuscript). Like Townsend, Sherman also demonstrated a "personal awkwardness and rusticity of manner." Townsend himself claimed that Sherman was the only Founding Father "to be so inconsistent" as to sign all three foundation documents. Sherman, however, probably did not share his descendant's later sexual interest in his fellow males.

Born in Roxbury, Massachusetts, June 24, 1894, into a comfortable and conventional Yankee family, Prescott Townsend was the third son and fourth child of Kate (Wendell) and Edward Britton Townsend. He prepared at the Volkman School, entered Harvard College (as did his brothers), graduated with the class of 1918, and attended the Harvard Law School for one year. His third class report listed his membership in the Harvard Club of Boston and New York as well as the Masonic Order. Prescott regularly attended his class reunions and marched in Harvard's annual procession for graduating students and alumni; at his fiftieth reunion he carried the class stanchion. His family attended the very high Anglican Church of the Advent, at the foot of Boston's Beacon Hill, where Ralph Adams Cram, the fashionable Yankee architect, designed much of the interior, including a retablo for Prescott's mother. His own funeral, however, took place in the Unitarian Arlington Street Church, which hosted gay youth groups, antiwar rallies, and other causes dear to Prescott's heart.

Townsend early embraced "paths untrodden." He came through Harvard when manliness was the norm and when Bull Moose Theodore Roosevelt was a hero. If TR's Rough Riders inspired him, Prescott certainly deviated from TR's ideal of what that might constitute. Like Roosevelt he went west for adventure, and in the summer of 1914 worked in the logging and mining camps of Idaho and Montana. Here he came in contact with the freewheeling Industrial Workers of the World (IWW, also popularly known as "Wobblies"), who were organizing unskilled and itinerant workers. Their anarchist politics left a strong imprint on the impressionable youth; he probably witnessed camp dances, where the men got along without women and lived outside the norms of traditional society. At the very least, the lumber camps and the IWW gave Townsend a view of the world far beyond Harvard in Yankee Boston. He himself reported in his papers that he always loved street boys and drifters and said that wherever he went he took them in and provided them with "love."

Another quite different summer trip into Mexico's backwaters opened him to other unconventional experiences. In the Rio Blanco Canyon, he was codiscoverer of some Toltec stone heads and a had a new species of salamander named after him: *Salamandra oedipustownsendentis*. Townsend himself early on developed an interest in Freud and his theories; the naming of the salamander reflects this, and is not an incidental reference to his father who had built a fortune in the coal business. Although his father died relatively young, he left the family in comfortable circumstances. Townsend's relationship with his father at best was "distant," but it was surely less tragic than that of Oedipus. He always remained on good terms with his mother. Her only advice to him when he announced his homosexuality was that he should be careful because not everyone would be as generous as she was in accepting his life choices.

The United States' entry into World War I in 1917 offered another interruption from the traditional Ivy League life, and Prescott's stint in the U.S. Navy helped wean him further from his Puritan past. In April 1917 he enrolled as chief boatswain's mate U.S. Naval Reserve Force, was appointed ensign September 18, and was assigned to the U.S.S. *Illinois* in the Atlantic fleet. After a short time at sea, he transferred to New Orleans and then attended the Texas A & M Naval Unit to learn the secret military codes. He was released from active duty January 25, 1919, shortly after the end of the war.

After desultorily pursuing law school for a year, he dropped out and later left for an eight-month stay in Paris. Although he may not have known Gertrude Stein, F. Scott Fitzgerald, Robert McAlmon, André Gide, T. E. Lawrence, H. D. (Hilda Doolittle), or Ernest Hemingway as well as he later implied, he did absorb the postwar culture and values of Bohemian Paris and he carried these ideals back to Boston.

As a member of the Harvard Travelers Club, Prescott made several memorable trips, one into North Africa and another into Communist Russia. The free life of the Bedouins attracted him as it has so many gay men. One of Prescott's prized possession was a *djellabah* which he claimed Lawrence of Arabia had given to André Gide, who in turn gave it to him. Since the garment, along with many other prized manuscripts and mementos, was lost in one of his several disastrous fires, DNA tests can never be run to see whether either Gide or Lawrence once wore it. Nonetheless, the existence of the garment and Townsend's attachment to it (similar to that of Christians to their relics) demonstrates how highly he regarded the homosexuality of the Bedouins, his connection with Gide, and fantasies of Lawrence in the Arabian sands.

Prescott himself was unconventional, but far from revolutionary in sentiments. His travels in Algeria seem to have left him with little understanding of the problems of colonialism. He did undertake to have *The Perfumed Garden* retranslated into English, but that gesture would hardly shield him from today's antiorientalism critics. Likewise, his trip to Russia in 1962 with a "people to people" program "working for world peace" had its conventional touches. He proudly reported: "I traveled on the farms and in the cities, giving out my forty pounds of *Life, Look,* and Sears Catalogs"

(Harvard University *Class Reports,* 1962). Unlike many gay pioneers of his day, he never flirted with communism. Rather like W. Dorr Legg, whom he had met in 1953, Prescott almost always voted Republican. His personal friendship with Adlai Stevenson, who had a purported lavender streak, may have led him to break ranks and vote Democrat in 1952, but if so he returned in 1956 to Eisenhower and Nixon.

Although a political conservative on most issues, he was an intellectual and cultural radical. Townsend was a moving force in the bohemian underground both on Beacon Hill and in Cape Cod's Provincetown. He backed theater productions, experimented with new architecture, encouraged authors, and played an active part in the city's gay life. He had met expatriate novelist Eliot Paul in Paris, and they brought together an intellectual, artistic, and often sexual avant garde caliber of women and men in Boston. The back of Beacon Hill, where Prescott lived most of his adult life, approximated New York's Greenwich Village and in some ways even the Left Bank in Paris. Before, during, and after Prohibition, the bars on the back of the Hill catered to a miscellaneous crowd of sailors, transvestites, poets, prostitutes, and gay men. For a time during the 1920s, Townsend participated in a speakeasy, eatery, and theatrical establishment on Joy Street in what was formerly a stable, one of several buildings he owned on Beacon Hill. In November 1922, with his backing and collaboration, the Barn Theater opened, offering experimental theater with links to Paris, Provincetown, and Greenwich Village.

Lucius Beebe, in his book, *Boston and the Boston Legend* (1935), described Townsend in this period as wearing "a raccoon skin overcoat that was the envy of Cedar Street"; and that the "rangy" youth could easily "talk informatively on any given subject for the space it required his auditor to consume precisely a quart of gin." A great talker, Prescott spoke to classes at Harvard, gave talks on the radio, and expounded his theories at length in the local restaurants, meetings, bars, his own special soirees, and underground films. Other than interviews, however, he left little extended work, and the publications or organizations he founded did not outlast his life.

Townsend's "snowflake theory" of homosexuality provided an interesting mix of Freud, Kinsey, and other sexologists. He intended it to be simple and illuminating for those confused or uncertain about their sexuality; in his words, it was "Freud pared to the bone . . . designed to provide enlightenment and save thousands of dollars" in psychotherapy. He held that certain conditions of early life are nonreversible: "left-handedness, homophile libido, sexuality, fetishes, inherited super-ego, and main vocational drives." The individuals who had these conditions were each different as were snowflakes and the question was what to do about it. His answer, somewhat oversimplified, was, "Hit, Miss, Submit," and "Work, Love, Play." In short, be yourself; and although he recognized that his work had some basis in academic research, he wanted others to follow through on such research and left money to the Harvard psychology department to be "used in connection with research and study of the homophile and also the study of sexual variants."

Townsend's greatest work (beyond his extraordinary personality and public agitation for gay causes) was in his architectural experiments, both on Beacon Hill and in Provincetown. He built five A-frame houses in Provincetown; had he patented his A-frame, he might have become better known. He also built his own absolutely unique house, the "Gangway" assembled from driftwood, plastic castoffs, and other detritus. Because of his open welcome to the homeless (and young gays) some believe that his house was torched deliberately. This was because shortly before the fire three of the selectmen of Provincetown had issued "An Appeal to All Decent People," complaining that "We are not getting the support we should in our effort to rid our town of these degenerates." The appeal concluded with a call: "Let us not permit our town to become a Sodom or Gomorrah" (Cathcart manuscript). Undaunted by the fire, Townsend soon rebuilt on the site with a more conventional and very expensive guest house.

He was ever conscious of being gay even in the 1920s; he had examined ways of repealing the state's "crime against nature" law. During World War II, he worked two years at the Fall River shipbuilding yard and while there had charges brought against him for an "abominable and detestable crime against nature." He did not hide his arrest and wrote in his Harvard class report: "I was thrown into jail for refusing to pay $15.00 graft for an act that is not against the law in England nor in Illinois." According to legend, when the judge asked what he had to say for himself, he replied, "So what's wrong with a little cocksucking on the Hill?" Consequently, he served over a year's sentence in the Deer Island House of Correction before being released on the day that Germany surrendered in 1945.

Because of the dangers of arrest, blackmail, and imprisonment, detailed accounts of Prescott's sexual life are relatively sparse. During his time in the U.S. Navy he recalled never having had any sexual relations, although later he made up for lost time by inviting many sailors into his Beacon Hill quarters. Street boys and runaways likewise always received a warm welcome from him, both in Boston and in Provincetown. Fellatio seems to have been one of his favorite activities, and he was always generous to a degree with those who needed food, shelter, and money.

During the 1950s, he convened meetings every Sunday at his house at 75 Philips Street (also then operating as the Paul Revere Bookstore), which he called "the first social discussion of homosexuality in Boston." The circle soon moved into a meeting room of the Parker House Hotel, more fashionably located next to King's Chapel and the old City Hall. One more formal member of the group (called "The Professor") did not like the informal atmosphere. "The purpose of the groups was for public education," he complained, "not for assignations, which is what they were trying to make it. Prescott was defending his creamy-meamy, bubble-headed, faggy types" (Mitzel, 1973).

The division between what in Boston has often been called the "Good Gays" and the "Bad Faggots" carried over into the Mattachine Society in 1957. Prescott organized the first chapter in Boston and he also attended meetings of ECHO, the East Coast Homophile Organization. As the Boston group grew with larger meetings, newsletters, and prominent speakers, the "Good Gays" soon voted Prescott out of leadership. Pushed aside, he then left to organize his own Boston Demophile Society. Although the Boston Mattachine Society soon collapsed, the Demophile Society managed to publish several newsletters, hold meetings, invite speakers, and organize outings for demonstrations and trips. The society continued more or less until Prescott's death, but one of his secretaries unfortunately used copies of the Boston Mattachine and the later Demophile newsletters for firewood. Later, Townsend's house caught fire, engulfing a vast treasure trove of early gay liberation records.

From the beginning, Townsend had always been something of a hippy and he went on to become a flower child in the 1960s. When groups of young teenagers began camping out in the Boston Common, Prescott himself joined them, gearing up his mimeograph machine to turn out flyers announcing "The Boston Common Be-In" for the Summer of 1967. This set the example for the Boston Gay Liberation Front "Be-In" in 1970 in which Townsend was involved. Townsend also became a star in underground filmmaker Andrew Meyer's 1966 *An Early Clue to the New Direction*. In it, Townsend propounds his snowflake theory of sexuality to "Joy Bang," a young star described as "a half Lolita-half Jane Fonda type." In the films Townsend explains that everyone is unique, like a snowflake, but that all sexual relations fit into hit, miss, or submit patterns. John Waters also captured some of Townsend's ideas in his works. His work inspired a number of young people to come out and be themselves. One of them, John Murray, after being in a Boston gay male liberation consciousness-raising group, went to live with Prescott at his final residence on Beacon's Hill's Garden Street until the elderly Yankee stopped eating and then stopped breathing on May 18, 1973. A large group showed up for his memorial to honor him and watched a screening of Meyer's *An Early Clue to the New Direction*.

BIBLIOGRAPHY

The Boston Atheneum contains letters from Prescott Townsend in Montana and Idaho to his mother and also letters from his World War I service. Each year he provided details of his life for his class reports at Harvard.

Beebe, Lucius. *Boston and the Boston Legend.* New York: Appleton-Century, 1935.

Boston History Project. *Improper Bostonians: Lesbian and Gay History from the Puritans to Playland.* Boston: Beacon Press, 1998.

Cathcart, Adrian. Queer for Justice: An Autobiographical Memoir. Manuscript by Townsend deposited in the Boston Atheneum with accompanying letters and documents.

Harvard University. "Prescott Townsend." *Class Reports for the Class of 1918.* Cambridge, MA: Harvard University Press, 1921-1968, 3rd to 50th Year Class Reports.

Mitzel, John. "Beans, Cod and Libido: The Life of Prescott Townsend, 1894-1973." *Manifest Destiny* 3 (Summer 1973): 1-8.

Shand-Tucci, Douglass. *Boston Bohemia 1881-1900.* Volume one of Ralph Adams Cram's, *Life and Architecture* (Amherst: University of Massachusetts Press, 1995).

Jeannette Howard Foster (1895-1981)

Virginia Elwood-Akers

Photo by Tee A. Corinne

In the early years of the twentieth century, a young and very innocent college junior named Jeannette Foster was on the student council at Rockford University in Illinois, when a meeting was called to discuss two young women who were to be judged in a "morals case." No details of the offense were given, beyond the fact that the two young women had locked themselves in their dormitory room together at every opportunity. Bewildered, Foster realized that the other students all seemed to know the nature of this serious offense and she was mortified by her ignorance. As soon as the meeting ended, Foster went to the library to search for answers. Having reached the conclusion that the embarrassment of her fellow council members, and the use of the term "morals case," seemed to indicate that the offense had been sexual, she looked in Henry Havelock Ellis's *Studies in the Psychology of Sex,* which she later said she had passed many times "without once having the impulse to look inside." There, in a chapter titled "Sexual Inversion in Women," in which Ellis discussed sexual relationships between women, Foster found her answer.

Perhaps Foster recognized herself in Ellis's study. She would later say that she had been attracted to women since she was a child. Perhaps, as a serious scholar, she was merely troubled by what was later described as "her lack of knowledge regarding female homosexuality." Whatever her reason, she began to compile a bibliography on the subject of what she called "sex variant" women. Foster selected the term "sex variant" because, as she said in her book, *Sex Variant Women in Literature,* it was neither rigid nor emotionally charged, and because its meaning was "no more than differing from a chosen standard" (Foster, 1985, "Introduction"). She defined the term to mean an *emotional* attraction between women, which is passionate and sex-

48

ual in nature, even if the sexual component is not conscious. At first concentrating on scientific and factual studies, she gradually added literary titles to the bibliography. Ultimately, she decided to limit the scope of her bibliography to literature, or what she called "imaginative writing." The bibliography grew into a narrative and was published more than forty years after it was begun. Foster's pioneering effort has been influential on virtually every subsequent scholar in the field of lesbian literature, and has led Karla Jay to acknowledge her as the "unchallenged foremother in this field" (1976, p. 34).

Jeannette Howard Foster was born November 3, 1895, in Oak Park, Illinois. Little is known of her youth or of her family. She was bookish and precocious, entering the University of Chicago when she was only seventeen, and going from there to Rockford College in Rockford, Illinois, from which she received an AB in chemistry and engineering in 1918. She returned to the University of Chicago and changed her studies completely, receiving an MA in English and American literature in 1922. For nearly ten years she taught literature and creative writing at Hamline University in Saint Paul, Minnesota, before deciding upon a career as a librarian. Graduating with a degree in library science in 1932, she found a position as science librarian at Antioch College in Ohio. Although she had continued to work on her bibliography, it was taking a position as a professor of library science at Drexel Institute in Philadelphia in 1937 that gave her access to library collections in the eastern United States and allowed her to begin her work.

Blessed with the ability to see herself and her scholarly efforts with a sense of humor, Foster told interviewer Karla Jay that "lots of funny things happened" to her during her years of research (1976, pp. 34-35). As an example, she told the story of her search for a book called *Mephistophela* by Catulle Mendes, published in France in 1890. Mendes' book was wildly popular at the time of its publication, when it had half a dozen printings in both French and English. By the time Foster was looking for it in Philadelphia, however, there were only four known copies in the United States. One was in Philadelphia but was in the library of the exclusive Rittenhouse Club, which allowed no women to enter its doors. Foster pleaded that she wanted only to use the library, which was in the front of the building, and none of the members of the club would even have to see her. She was archly told that women would not be admitted for *any* reason. Fortunately, Foster was acquainted with a member of the club, then an assistant librarian at the University of Pennsylvania. Amused, he agreed to check the book out for her to read, if she would read it in his office. Foster readily agreed, and read the more than 350 pages of *Mephistophela,* in French, sitting in a corner of the librarian's office. Foster found the ridiculous situation to be funny. She also saw the humor in an occasion when she dropped out of a library school field trip—reasoning that the graduate students were adults and didn't really need her for a chaperone—in order to visit the Yale University Library, which held a rare copy of *Mary, a Fiction* by Mary Wollstonecroft. She had one day to read the entire book in order to include it into the bibliography; an important inclusion, since she described Wollstonecroft's book as "the first novel on female variance to be written by a woman" (Foster, 1956/1985, p. 55).

In 1948 Foster accepted a position as librarian at the Kinsey Institute for Sex Research in Bloomington, Indiana, which gave her access to a large collection on the subject of sexuality and allowed her to complete her research. It would be another ten years, however, before her own book would be published. Foster decided that it would be a good idea to start the title of her book off with the word *sex,* as "I had learned from searching bibliographies," she said, "a title beginning with the word *sex* couldn't be ignored." Still, Foster realized that it would not be easy to find a publisher for her book in the United States in the 1950s. Trade publishers were out of the question, and a dozen university presses also turned the book down. Rutgers University Press held the manuscript for over seven months before finally deciding they were unwilling to take a chance with publication. Finally Foster self-published the book with Vantage Press, investing $2,000 of her own money. The experience with Vantage was an unhappy one. Editors changed Foster's prose, which infuriated the former professor of creative writing. She sent the manuscript back with edited parts reinstated, declaring, "That *stands,* or else." The editors capitulated, but charged her extra for "author's alterations" in order to return the manuscript to its original wording. Vantage published *Sex Variant Women in Literature* in 1956, but when the publishers asked for more money and Foster refused, she was told her that her royalties would be kept against what she owed them. Vantage then sold the rights to the British publisher Frederick Muller, Ltd., which published the book in 1958. Foster, who learned of the sale by reading an article in the periodical *Publishers Weekly,* did not receive any money from the sale or publication. The only monetary reward she received from her forty years of work was a check for $240 when a secondhand dealer bought the 2,400 remaining copies of the book, from an original printing of 3,500, at ten cents a copy.

By the time the book was published, Foster was working as a reference librarian at the University of Kansas in Kansas City, Missouri. *Sex Variant Women in Literature* received only one review, and that a negative one, in a psychology publication. It was also briefly mentioned in a newspaper article. Foster's book seemed to be destined for oblivion. But fate, in the form of a young lesbian working in the catalog department of the Kansas City Public Library, intervened. Barbara Grier had seen the title mentioned in a library publication. The twenty-three-year-old Grier had been working on a bibliography of lesbian literature for seven years and had collected nearly one hundred titles. Since she had been planning to write a book on what she thought was an original subject, she was both delighted and chagrined to learn that Foster had already done so. When she discovered that the author of *Sex Variant Women in Literature* was living in the same city, Grier immediately called her, and began a lifelong friendship with Foster.

Grier also became Foster's successor as bibliographer of lesbian literature. In 1956 the Daughters of Bilitis, a recently founded lesbian organization, began publication of a periodical called *The Ladder* which "soon instituted a careful recording of lesbian literature" (Grier, 1985, p. 355). Foster taught Grier review checking techniques and the younger woman began compiling records of new titles and also of old titles that may have been missed in prior years. Often Grier had to rely on intuition to recognize a title that might contain lesbians or lesbian literature, since mainstream reviewers rarely mentioned the subject. Many of the titles Grier selected were reviewed in *The Ladder,* which in 1967 published a bibliography of 2,000 titles, *The Lesbian in Literature,* co-authored by Gene Damon and Lee Stuart. Gene Damon is the pseudonym of Barbara Grier. Not surprisingly, *The Lesbian in Literature* was reviewed in *The Ladder* by Jeannette Foster, who had begun to contribute occasionally to the periodical.

"Writing a favorable review of a work in which one has been overgenerously cited might be taken as reciprocal back-scratching," Foster wrote (Foster, 1967, p. 17). But she went on to say that she considered Damon and Stuart's work "an excellent bibliography." Foster defended the inclusion in Damon and Stuart's book of the semipornographic original paperbacks that had proliferated at the time and that the bibliography identifies with a "T" for "trash." She pointed out that the paperbacks, although probably written by men as pornography, did include lesbians as subjects, and that inclusion was therefore justified.

During the late 1960s Jeannette Foster contributed both fiction and nonfiction articles to *The Ladder.* Besides reviewing *The Lesbian in Literature,* she wrote reviews of books such as Maurice Collis's *Somerville and Ross: A Biography,* which recounts the lives of writers Edith Somerville and Violet Martin, Frederick Brown's *An Impersonation of Angels: A Biography of Jean Cocteau,* and C. P. Snow's *The Sleep of Reason.* She also contributed fiction, using the pseudonyms Hilary Farr, Jan Addison, and Abigail Sanford. "Temple of Athene" by Hilary Farr, for instance, appeared in three parts in late 1967. It is the somewhat melodramatic story of poor Theodora's crush on the improbably named Lenox VanTuyl, and of lesbian tensions in a campus setting. Foster's contributions to *The Ladder* were not the first time she had contributed fiction to a periodical. In October 1927 her short story "Lucky Star" had appeared in the mainstream publication *Harper's Maga-*

zine. "Lucky Star" is also about an unrequited crush, but in this story the erstwhile lover is male, a visitor to a small town who has completely misinterpreted the lighthearted flirting of a married woman. Since the married woman does not seem to particularly care for her husband, it is possible that this story might also have been about two women if the circumstances of publication had been different.

Between the years 1914 and 1938 Jeannette Foster wrote passionate love poetry. In 1976 Foster's poems were published, along with poetry by Valerie Taylor, by Womanpress in a volume called *Two Women*. In the same year Naiad Press published *A Woman Appeared to Me*, Foster's translation of *Une Femme M'Apparut* by Renée Vivien. Since Diana Press had reprinted *Sex Variant Women in Literature* in 1975, Foster was delighted to have three of her creative endeavors in print at the same time, all of them published by lesbian-oriented presses. She was especially pleased with *A Woman Appeared to Me*, which was the first translation of the work based on the poet Vivien's affair with Violet Shilleto and her relationship with Natalie Barney; with the exception of a few poems, this was the first major Vivien work to be published. Vivien was one of the writers discussed in *Sex Variant Women in Literature* who was essentially "discovered" by Foster, although her work was known to a select few. Foster called Vivien a poet whose poetry "has been pronounced most perfect in form of any French verse written in the first quarter of the [20th] century" (Foster, 1985, p. 158). Foster is also credited with the "discovery" of Natalie Barney, a woman known as much for her salon in Paris, and for her open and daring lesbianism, as she was for her writing.

Little is known of Foster's private life. In interviews given at various times in her life she disclosed few details. She was quoted as saying that her circumspection was due to a wish to respect the privacy of her friends. It is known that she knew writer Janet Flanner when the two writers were both at the University of Chicago, and that she formed a friendship with poet May Sarton when Sarton was poet in residence at Lindenwood College, now Lindenwood University, in St. Charles, Missouri, where Foster had begun work as the assistant librarian in 1963. She was close to Barbara Grier and to writer Valerie Taylor. The poems in *Two Women* are clearly written to more than one woman, but the women are not named. In a recent article in Zimmerman's (2000) *Lesbian Histories and Cultures: An Encyclopedia*, Andrea Peterson disclosed that Foster had a long relationship with Hazel Toliver, a professor she had met at Lindenwood College. Foster was a member of the Daughters of Bilitis and did not disguise her identity as a lesbian, although she said that she was a member of a generation that, as she put it, "concealed our gayness as if it were syphilis" (Hogan and Hudson, 1998, p. 218).

Foster was not a political person, but she did weigh in on the issue of whether lesbians should have a strong national organization. In 1968 she wrote a letter to the editor of *The Ladder* on that subject. The editor decided that Foster's comments on dominance within lesbian relationships were of sufficient interest to print the letter as a short article, and invited further comments from readers. In the article, "Dominance," Foster described herself as a member of the Daughters of Bilitis who had listened over the years to debates, discussions, and arguments among the members and who had found herself curious as to why a group of people "as closely homogeneous as any except a racial group" (Foster, 1968, p. 17) would have such dissentions. Foster's conclusion was that some members of "the sisterhood" had a strong need to dominate the others. Oddly, she identified these women as those who refused to marry men, insisted on taking a job whether or not they needed money, dressed as they pleased rather than in fashion, and openly proclaimed themselves as lesbians. Even in 1968 Foster's conclusions must have seemed strange to some readers of *The Ladder.* Foster went on to make the point, however, that even within homogeneous groups dissension will occur, and that forming a national organization such as the National Association for the Advancement of Colored People (NAACP), American Association of University Women (AAUW), or American Association of University Professors (AAUP) would be advantageous for the Daughters of Bilitis, because there is "quite literally safety in numbers."

Foster's comments indicate that she must have been circumspect in her personal life, and she never reported that her life had been difficult because of her lesbianism. The library environment in which she spent her life is not a hostile one for homosexuals, and it is unlikely that Foster would have encountered a great deal of open discrimination, especially because she was discreet in her personal life. In fact, librarians acclaimed her accomplishment in writing *Sex Variant Women in Literature;* in 1974, she was honored by the American Library Association with its third annual Gay Book Award. She was delighted. "My long respected ALA is willing to admit the existence . . . and even honor it . . . of Gaiety!" she is quoted as saying in Steven Hogan and Lee Hudson's (1998) *Completely Queer.* The publication of three of her works, and being honored by her peers, made the mid-1970s a happy time for Foster. Upon her retirement, she moved to Pocahontas, Arkansas, where she shared a home with Toliver and with a third friend, Dorothy Ross, who had been head of the physical education department at

Lindenwood College. But Foster was growing old and ill, and by the end of the decade she was partially paralyzed and living in a nursing home.

Lesbian scholars and others who admired her work made pilgrimages to Pocahantas, Arkansas, to meet Foster, now more than eighty years old. When it became apparent that Foster's financial resources were depleted, Valerie Taylor and photographer Tee Corinne placed an appeal in gay and lesbian publications for funds to assist her. Benefits and fundraisers were held to raise money for Foster's expenses. On July 26, 1981, Foster died at the age of eighty-six.

Jeannette Foster would be an important figure in the field of literature even if she had never written a word other than her massive literary study. At the time of its publication, little had been written on the subject of lesbian literature and in fact it was a subject rarely discussed in "polite" company. Foster boldly stated in her book that "feminine variance has persisted in human experience since the beginning of literary records." She went on to say that such variance had "repeatedly aroused sufficient interest to be the subject of literature, some of it good enough to have survived through many centuries against all odds." She carefully explained that she selected the term *sex variant* because it was neither rigid nor emotionally charged and reminded her readers that the word *variant* simply means different. She reserved the word *lesbian* for instances of overt sexual expression, and used the word *homosexual* as a synonym for *sex variant*. "It will be employed here," she wrote in her book, "only when needed to relieve verbal monotony" (Foster, 1985, p. 13).

Foster began her study with Sappho, the Greek poet from the sixth century B.C., and made her way briskly through the centuries to 1951, ending with a discussion of (Patricia Highsmith) Claire Morgan's *The Price of Salt*. In the book's nearly 400 pages Foster discussed both the literary efforts and the personal lives of well-known figures such as George Eliot, George Sand, Emily Dickinson, and Emily Brontë. More important, she wrote also of little-known writers such as sixteenth-century poet Louise Labé, twentieth-century novelist Gale Wilhelm, and the French poets and literary figures Renée Vivien and Natalie Barney. *Sex Variant Women in Literature* also devotes many pages to lesbian and variant characters in literature, many of them created by male authors. *Sex Variant Women in Literature* is often cited as one of the most important works in the field of lesbian literature. According to the online service Literature Resource Center, Foster's courageous early work, "contributed significantly to the development of a lesbian culture in the twentieth century."

BIBLIOGRAPHY

Many of the quotes appear from Foster's *Sex Variant Women.*

Books, Articles, Poems, and Reviews by Jeannette Foster

"Dominance," *The Ladder,* XIII (I-II: October-November 1968), 17-18.

"The Lesbian in Literature: A Bibliography" (Review), *The Ladder* XI (X: September 1967), 17-18.

"Lucky Star," *Harper's Magazine,* 155 (October 1927), 624-635.

Sex Variant Women in Literature. Reno, NV: Naiad Press, 1985. Reprint of the 1956 Vantage Press edition with material added.

"Somerville and Ross, A Biography" (Review), *The Ladder,* XI (V-VI: February-March 1969), 26-27.

"Temple of Athene," *The Ladder,* XII (I: December 1967), 20-28; XII (II: January 1968, 4+; XII (III: February/March 1968)7+; and XII (V:April 1968), 22-27.

Two Women Revisited: The Poetry of Jeannette Foster and Valerie Taylor. Chicago: Womanpress, 1976. Revised from 1976 edition. Austin, TX: Banned Books, Edward Williams Publishing Company, 1991.

"Whipped Cream," *The Ladder,* 14 (1/8 April/May 1971), 31-32.

Translated by Jeannette Foster

A Woman Appeared to Me. Translation of *Une Femme m'Apparut* by Renee Viven. Reno, NV: Naiad Press, 1976.

About Jeannette Foster

Grier, Barbara. "Afterword" in *Sex Variant Women in Literature* by Jeannette Foster, 1985 edition (pp. 355-357). Reno, NV: Naiad Press.

Hogan, Steven, and Lee Hudson, *Completely Queer: The Gay and Lesbian Encyclopedia* (pp. 218-220). New York: Henry Holt and Company, 1998.

Jay, Karla. "Jeannette Foster, X-Rated Bibliographer," *Lesbian Tide,* 5 (May-June 1976), 34-35.

Jay, Karla, and Allen Young (Eds.), *Lavender Culture* (pp. 257-261). New York: New York University Press, 1994.

Literature Resource Center (online database), <http://www.galenet.com>.

Malinowski, Sharon (Ed.), *Gay and Lesbian Literature,* Volume 1 (pp. 140-141). Detroit, MI: St. James Press, 1994.

Zimmerman, Bonnie (Ed.), *Lesbian Histories and Cultures: An Encyclopedia* (pp. 308-309). New York: Garland, 2000.

Pearl M. Hart (1890-1975)

Karen C. Sendziak

Gerber/Hart Library

Pearl M. Hart practiced law in Chicago from 1914 to 1975 as an advocate for children, women, immigrants, and gay men and lesbians. One of the first female attorneys in the city to specialize in criminal law, she was remarkable for her commanding physical and intellectual presence. The size of her five-feet, eleven-and-a-half-inch and 200-pound frame was surpassed only by her generosity of spirit. Journalist I. F. Stone describe her affectionately as a "big benevolent Brunnhilde of a woman, six feet tall with gray hair, grandmotherly expression, and one of those round unmistakable Russian Jewish faces" who was "famous throughout the Midwest for a lifetime of devotion to the least lucrative and most oppressed kind of clients" (Stone, 1953, p. 31). Hart's direct involvement with one of these groups, gay and lesbians, did not emerge until the final two decades of her life, although she early on had defended gay men.

Pearl Hart was born in Traverse City, Michigan, on April 7, 1890, as Pearly Minne Harchovsky, but she was known as Hart for most of her life. Both her father, David, an Orthodox rabbi, and her mother, Rebecca, had emigrated from Russia. She was the youngest of the couple's five daughters, and the only one born in the United States. By her own account, her childhood was happy: " . . . I was particularly fortunate in that everyone loved me a lot, and spoiled me" (Weiner, 1975).

The family moved from Traverse City to Chicago when Hart was a preschooler and settled in the bustling neighborhoods of the near west side among fellow Jewish emigrés from Eastern Europe. She was educated in the Chicago public school system, and according to the poet and author Valerie Taylor, labored in a garment factory as a teenager. Evidence of her leadership qualities emerged early when she was elected president of her predominately male local union.

Hart entered the night-school program at Chicago's John Marshall Law School in 1911, earning her tuition by working during the day as a law clerk and stenographer. Graduating in 1914, she was admitted to the Illinois Bar on October 7 of that same year and began to build her criminal law practice. From 1915 to 1917 she held a position as one of the first female adult probation officers in Chicago. Her early legal career focused on the needs of children, and in the mid-1920s, she began working with prominent social reformers such as Sophonisba Breckenridge of the University of Chicago to rehabilitate the juvenile court system. Regarded as an expert on juvenile justice, she drafted legislation, served on committees, and spoke before a variety of civic groups, all in an effort to protect Chicago's most vulnerable citizens. Hart remained dedicated to this cause throughout her life and her expertise in the field was recognized nationally.

Another of her major concerns was the welfare of women passing through the legal system. In 1933, she volunteered to serve as the first public defender in morals court to stem the tide of women being arrested for alleged prostitution. Women walking alone were particularly vulnerable to this charge. After four years serving in morals court, she had reversed the 90 percent conviction rate for these women to 10 percent.

In the 1950s, Hart devoted increased time to defending individuals accused of subversions against the U.S. government. The three major laws under which her clients were prosecuted were the Alien Registration Act of 1940 (popularly known as the Smith Act), the Internal Security Act of 1950, otherwise known as the McCarran Act, and the Immigration and Nationality Act of 1952, also known as the McCarran-Walter Act.

The government brought charges against many of Hart's clients based on organizations they well might have joined decades earlier but had severed ties with or drifted away from long ago. Sadly, a good portion were elderly, already retired, and declining in health. Hart's most prominent case from this era was *U.S. v. Witkovich*. George Witkovich received an order of deportation on June 15, 1953. In a subsequent hearing before the Immigration and Naturalization Service, he was asked twenty-two questions about his activities and affiliations. On Hart's advice, he refused to answer the questions because they were not relevant to whether or not he should be deported. The United States filed a lawsuit compelling his answers, and Hart countered with an appeal that eventually made its way to the U.S. Supreme Court. She won the case in 1957 when the high court agreed with her contention that the attorney general's power to question aliens subject to deportation was limited by constitutional safeguards. Hart's victory was extraordinary, particu-

larly for a solo practitioner. Her creative legal analysis and compelling oral
arguments are a testament to her commitment and skill.

Pearl Hart also carried a heavy caseload defending individuals subpoe-
naed to testify before the House of Representatives Un-American Activities
Committee. From the late 1940s to the mid-1960s, the committee held hearings in Chicago during which Hart was present with her clients.

Her activism is manifest in the large number of organizations in which
she participated and/or helped found in her sixty-one–year career. The most
prominent of these was the National Lawyers Guild, a bar association of liberal attorneys. She was a founding member of the group in late 1936 and
early 1937. She also helped establish the American Committee for the Protection of the Foreign Born in 1933. In 1947 she was a founder of the Midwest version of that committee. In 1960 she helped the Chicago Committee
to Defend the Bill of Rights come into existence. She was a force in the
Women's Bar Association of Illinois, of which she was president in 1925. In
her presidental address to that group she stated that "years ago we were still
regarded as a useless novelty" (Hart papers, March 16, 1925). In 1943 she
joined with other women to found what eventually became the George and
Anna Portes Cancer Prevention Center in Chicago.

Two other activities to which Hart devoted considerable interest throughout her life were politics and teaching. She ran for judgeships four times:
1928, 1932, 1947, and 1948. She also ran for a seat as Chicago alderman in
1947 and again in 1951. She lost all six elections; her campaigns as an
Independent or Progressive Party candidate were completely overwhelmed
by the Chicago Democratic machine. Her lack of success in electoral politics was balanced by her commitment to education. She taught criminal law
at her alma mater, John Marshall Law School, for a quarter-century, from
1946 until 1971. She also taught at the Northwestern University School of
Social Work. In addition, she was affiliated with the Abraham Lincoln
School, an adult-education enterprise founded in 1943. The school was
added to the Justice Department's list of subversive organizations in 1953.

By all accounts, Hart was an engaging public speaker. In the 1940s she
addressed groups as diverse as a neighborhood Kiwanis Club, the Catholic
Women's League, and the American Society for Russian Relief. After out-
lining the social and political ills of the days to attendees of the 1962 annual
dinner of the Jewish Cultural Schools in Chicago, Hart urged those who
grapple with the major problems of society not to be fearful of being called
radical but rather to revel in the knowledge that they did not walk away from
problems but rather were willing to stand up and fight for that which they
knew was right.

It was only in the final two decades of her life that she became directly involved with the gay and lesbian community, although she had represented

many gays in court before that. She cofounded the Mattachine Midwest, which had its first public meeting on July 27, 1965, and served on its legal counsel until her death. In addressing one of the early meetings of the group, she urged the members to stop viewing themselves as members of a minority and assert the equal rights which are guaranteed to them by the Constitution. According to former president Jim Bradford, 75 percent of the Mattachines' job was "making the police behave." The pace of bar raids was unrelenting, and a defendant arrested in such a sweep could expect a difficult journey through a legal system infested with corruption. Pearl fought two major fronts in the battle to check police abuses in this area. First, she defended clients arrested for alleged criminal activity. Second, she communicated directly with the Mattachine membership through the articles in the organization's monthly newsletter. Covertly, notes Bradford, she passed along information gained from her clients about the names of officers that were causing trouble, which part of the parks were currently hot; she would pass along information, without revealing sources, that her clients would tell her—in her terms, where the "pinch bugs infest the bushes" (Bradford interview, p. 21).

Hart defended scores of gay men arrested for soliciting sex in a public place, those entrapped to do so, and those caught in the crossfire of a bar raid. In representing her clients, she defended each case on its own merit. She refused to be involved in the bribery so often involved in such cases, and usually demanded jury trials since juries were less likely to convict than judges. Her reputation was so immaculate that she was affectionately referred to as the "Guardian Angel of Chicago's Gay Community."

An occasional contributor to the *Mattachine Midwest Newsletter,* she usually focused on civil rights and police procedures. She and Bradford cowrote an article that first appeared in the September 1968 issue on "Your Rights If Arrested," which was reprinted as a pamphlet, and distributed by the thousands.

In a May 1969 address to the Mattachine membership, she urged those in attendance and the Mattachine Society as well to be "more aggressive" in their public stance. Although her involvement in Chicago was, for the most part, with gay men, lesbian activists around the country knew her as well. Del Martin, editor of *The Ladder,* solicited her opinion on the 1961 repeal of Illinois' sodomy laws. In a March 1962 article in that magazine, Hart noted that new legislation would not guarantee social approval of same-sex activities. Instead, she emphasized that only through a protracted educational campaign could lesbians and gays achieve far-reaching results. Shirley Willer, the newsletter editor of the New York chapter of the Daughters of Bilitis, sent Hart a letter in 1966 thanking her for the financial contributions to the chapter and expressing hope that she would become more directly involved in the organization.

Hart never openly identified herself as a lesbian. According to Valerie Taylor, any inquiry into her sexual orientation would be rebuffed with a cold stare and a reply, "That's none of your business. Why do you want to know that?" She did have two long-term relationships in her life. The first was with the actress and singer J. Blossom Churan. From 1918 until 1924, Hart had shared a law office with Churan's father, and sometime during this period she met Blossom, some six years her junior. Probably no relationship developed fully until the death of Hart's father in mid-1923. By 1926 when her mother died, Hart felt freer to express her own sexuality. In the early 1940s, however, Churan seemed to be bored with Hart and began an affair with a physician, Bertha Isaacs. Instead of relinquishing Churan to her new lover, Hart proposed that all three live together, which they did until Churan died in October 1973.

Hart's second major relationship was with the poet and author Valerie Taylor whom she had met in 1961 but did not become close with until 1963 when Taylor returned from living overseas. So secretive was their affair that many people known to both women did not realize their bond, and some old-time acquaintances even as of this writing claim that nothing happened between the two. Taylor, however, spoke fondly and affectionately of Hart as a profound influence on her life. She moved into an apartment around the corner from Hart's home, and for eleven years their intimacy was sustained by Hart's weekly Sunday visits. Taylor wrote at least a half-dozen poems for Hart, and dedicated her 1982 book, *Prism,* to P. M. H. Taylor's short story "Generation Gap," published in the anthology *Intricate Passion,* is based on her relationship with Hart. Taylor considered Hart the love of her life, but the feeling was not necessarily mutual; Hart's primary attachment was to Blossom Churan until Churan died.

Hart remained close to her family throughout her life. She was the favorite aunt of all her nieces and nephews, indulging them with outings and an occasional five-dollar bill. She formed a particularly strong relationship with the daughter of her sister Bessie, Tess Hart Weiner. Although separated by half a continent, the two remained in weekly contact for thirty-five years, and it was Weiner who cared for her beloved aunt during her final illness. For the most part, Hart's relationships with women were hidden from her family.

The highest honor that Hart received during her life was an honorary doctor of law degree from her alma mater, John Marshall Law School. The recognition came in 1964 as part of the ceremony marking the fiftieth anniversary of her graduation. The City of Chicago has since honored Hart twice, posthumously. In 1992 she was chosen to be inducted into the Chicago Gay and Lesbian Hall of Fame. In 2001 Hart was the recipient of a Chicago Tribute Marker of Distinction. Under this program, the city recognizes outstanding deceased individuals by placing a large plaque on the sidewalk in front of their former homes or other pertinent location.

Hart died on March 22, 1975, of pancreatic cancer complicated by heart disease. In reflecting on her inevitable death in earlier healthier times, Hart bemoaned the fact that she had no sons or grandsons to say kaddish for her. The president of the Matttachine Midwest Society consoled her by saying that members of the organization were her sons and grandsons, and would gladly say kaddish if she felt the need.

She loved practicing law, and did so illuminated by her belief that the downtrodden—be they wayward juveniles, marginalized women, demoralized homosexuals, or browbeaten immigrants—deserved equal representation under the law. The Bill of Rights provided her moral compass, and she was fond of saying that the Constitution was a wonderful document that should protect everyone, if everyone would really obey it. Beloved by her clients and esteemed by her colleagues, Hart practiced law with compassion, integrity, and an unwavering passion for social justice. She devoted her life to protecting civil liberties and, in the words of the citation upon her honorary degree, was "a source of radiant confidence in the ultimate supremacy of the law and the goodness of man."

BIBLIOGRAPHY

Pearl Hart papers and Gregory Sprague papers, Chicago Historical Society.
Special collections, Gerber/Hart Library.
Pearl Hart clipping file.
Mattachine Midwest Newsletters, 1965-1975.
"New Illinois Penal Code –What Does It Mean?" *The Ladder,* March 1962.
Del Martin, "Pearl Hart is Remembered on the Anniversary of Her Passing." *Chicago Gay Life,* March 15, 1976.
Valerie Taylor; A Resource Book, revised 1999, compiled by Tee A. Corinne, and accompanying volumes of poetry.
Jack Rinella papers. Letter from Shirley Willer to Pearl M. Hart, February 13, 1966.
Ron Pajak video interview with Valerie Taylor, 1997.
Jim Bradford, "Interview by Gregory Sprague." Jack Rinella papers.

Books and Articles

Buhle, Mari Jo, *Encyclopedia of the American Left.* Paul Buhle and Dan Georgakas (Eds.). New York: Oxford University Press, 1988.
Corinne, Tee (Ed.). *Intricate Passions.* Banned Books, 1989.

Gatland, Laura. "Guardian of Justice," *John Marshall Comment,* Winter 1998.

Ginger, Ann Fagan. *Caroll Weiss King: Human Rights Lawyer, 1895-1952.* Niwot: University Press of Colorado, 1993.

Ginger, Ann Fagan. *The National Lawyers Guild: From Roosevelt Through Reagan.* Philadelphia: Temple University Press, 1987.

Hemmes, Michael. "Pearls of Justice," *Gay Chicago Magazine,* March 8, 2001.

Kuda, Marie J. Biography of Pearl Hart, in "Chicago's Gay and Lesbian History: From Prairie Settlement to World War II," *Chicago Outlines,* February 24, 1999.

Stone, I.F. "Bleak Landscape of the Resistance," *I.F. Stone's Weekly,* December 21, 1953; republished in Stone, *The Haunted Fifties.* New York: Random House, 1953.

Sullivan's Law Directory. Chicago: Law Book Publishing Company, early editions from 1914-1975.

Schultz, Rima Lunin, and Adele Hast (Eds.). *Women Building Chicago, 1790-1990: A Biographical Dictionary,* Bloomington: Indiana University Press, 2001.

Other Sources

"Pearl Hart and Valerie Taylor: A Chicago Love Story?" Marie J. Kuda slide show.

Personal interview with Tess Hart Weiner, April 6, 1998.

Weiner, Tess Hart. "How I Remember My Aunt Pearl," Gerbert/Hart Library publication, September 1998.

Weiner, Tess Hart. Audiotape recording of her remarks at memorial service for Pearl Hart, April 13, 1975.

Lisa Ben (1921-   )

Florine Fleischman
with Susan Bullough

Charles Faber Feature

The pseudonymous Lisa Ben broke the barrier of silence within the American gay community by publishing what some regard as the first lesbian newsletter/magazine, *Vice Versa,* beginning in June 1947. Ben said she started the newsletter to keep herself company; she called it *Vice Versa* because when she began publishing it, her kind of life was considered a vice. She distributed it free of charge.

Ben was an unlikely pioneer: although she had enough courage to publish a newsletter (for some twelve issues) and distribute it to friends and bar patrons, she did so anonymously. Later when she began writing for *The Ladder,* she adopted the name Lisa Ben (an anagram of lesbian). As of this writing she still refuses permission to include her real name for fear of discovery by people who would "not understand," even though her close family has long been deceased, as are most of her former employers and workmates. Since, however, Lisa Ben's real name, Edythe Eyde, has been publicized online, it seems permissible to note it in this biography.

Lisa, an only child, was born in 1921 in San Francisco. Her father was an insurance agent, her mother a housewife; she was raised for the most part in Los Altos on a thirty-three–acre apricot ranch where she spent a lot of her time playing with animals as there were few children her age in the area. She went to college for two years, then her father insisted she quit and go to secretarial school even though she did not want to. She wanted to be a violinist in a symphony orchestra, but the obedient daughter, discouraged by her parents, did what they wanted as she was never allowed to argue with them. When she began working, she continued to live at home and her parents required her to pay a third of her salary to them as rent. Finally, shortly before the outbreak of World War II, she got up enough courage to move to Palo Alto where she was then working. Ever mindful of finances, she paid for her rent by watching three children at night. Gathering up her courage, she moved to Los Angeles where she had a friend and she has lived there ever since.

Lisa was not interested in boys and did not date in high school. She knew nothing about homosexuality, although she had a crush on a girl in the high school band which included some hugging and kissing. When the girl broke off the relationship, a devastated Lisa confided to her mother about losing her girlfriend, and when her mother questioned her so intently about the matter, Lisa began to wonder if she had done something wrong. Lisa never brought up the subject again with her parents.

In Los Angeles she fell in with a group of women who did not talk about men all the time, as most of her other friends did. When one of the women asked her if she was gay, Lisa thought she was being asked if she was happy. Her affirmative reply led them to invite her to a club where Lisa noticed that the men and women were in separate areas. That evening it gradually dawned on her what gay meant and that she was not the only woman who found other women attractive. She gradually extended her lesbian contacts.

In 1947, she was working as a secretary in a Hollywood movie studio. She had been told by her boss that there were long periods when she might not have much to do in the office. He said he did not want her to knit or read a book during these periods, but she could do anything else she wanted providing she looked busy. She felt that since there were magazines and newsletters for every type of interest, it would be logical to have a magazine for gay women. She began typing a newsletter and decided to distribute ten copies. This meant she typed each letter twice, producing four carbon copies. Most of what was included in the magazine she wrote herself and distributed to other "gay girls" (her term). Originally she had intended to mail them, but a friend warned her that she could be prosecuted for using the mail to distribute obscene material and so she then depended upon personal contacts to pass them on. She could have cut a stencil and used a mimeograph to make more copies, but this would have exposed her activities to others. She quietly sought a printer to make more copies, but her initial experiences convinced her that this was not a viable alternative. She wrote movie and book reviews, poems, and news. She requested contributions from others, but never received any, although the magazine aroused much interest in the gay community. The publication ceased after nine months and twelve issues because her studio job ended. She went on to other things, among them writing gay parodies of popular songs and singing them at the Flamingo, a club that allowed gay shows and acts on Sunday afternoon.

She dated and went out with a number of other women and finally, at age thirty-six, entered into a special relationship with a woman she is unwilling to identify. The two lived together for three years, but their affair was ended by Ben after her partner went to Las Vegas and lost everything gambling, including the rent money. Although she continued to have casual relationships after that, Ben never again was interested in any long-term relationship. She keeps up correspondence with her friends and writes poetry in her spare time. In 1997 she was recognized as a founder of the Los Angeles gay community. She remains proud of what she has accomplished but reluctant to seek publicity. Still, her willingness to come out as she did in the 1940s makes her almost unique among the lesbians of the time.

Berry Berryman (1901-1972)

Vern L. Bullough

Homosexual and lesbian friendships and social groups were long part of the American social scene, although most of these groups avoided public exposure. As historians try to trace down the histories of these groups, some serendipitously come to light and we find they left studies or autobiographies that are important to helping us to understand same-sex life in the past. One such "find" was a study by Berry Berryman who began interviewing her lesbian and gay friends perhaps as early as the 1920s and began writing them up in the early 1940s only to abandon the project, which was eventually completed by Bonnie and Vern Bullough in the 1970s. Her study was significant even though flawed because it is one of the few studies we have of a rather loosely knit lesbian (and gay) community in an unlikely place, such as Salt Lake City was. She was a pioneer in her study and in her public lifestyle.

Born Mildred J. Berryman in Salt Lake City, Utah, she grew up there. Like many other young women conscious of her same-sex attraction, she had difficulty coming to terms with herself. She married twice, first an elopement at sixteen, which was annulled, and later in her early twenties in a more formal ceremony, which resulted in a quick divorce. After these efforts at conformity, she began to come to terms with her lesbianism and over the years lived with several different women for shorter or longer periods. It is not clear what caused her to begin her studies of the gay and lesbian community in Salt Lake City, but she was undoubtedly influenced by the writing of Krafft-Ebing and Havelock Ellis, whose books were in her library.

A short and somewhat overweight woman, she eventually settled down with Ruth Uckerman in 1942 and the two lived together running a small business making jewelry from semiprecious stones, small carvings, various tourist items, and ribbons for state and county fairs. They later expanded their business to include various injectable plastic items. Similar to Lisa Ben, Berryman began typing up her notes while working in an office—not for a film studio office, but for the American Red Cross in early 1940. She left this job to become a machinist in the defense industry. There she met Ruth Uckerman and the two soon moved to rural Woods Cross in Utah. Berry never completed writing up her research, but fortunately it was preserved by her partner; it eventually came into the hands of the Bulloughs, who published part of it. Her actual interviews have not survived, only her summaries of the case studies.

She objected to much of the scholarship available about lesbianism and homosexuality at the time, but her studies nonetheless were much influenced by them anyway, indicating just how much societal attitudes affect the perspectives of people. Her highest compliment to a woman was that she had a "masculine mind." The fact that her summaries did survive, however, was enough for interested Utah gays and lesbians to construct a real history of the underground lesbian and gay movement, centered in the Bohemian Club of that city (which dated back to the 1880s). The surviving membership lists have been combed to reconstruct the relevant history, and the study of Berryman's life and that of her partner have become a small cottage industry. However, neither she nor her partner could be said to be closeted lesbians.

In fact, the home of Berry and Ruth served as a center for many lesbians in Salt Lake City and for many traveling through. They were accepted in their community as eccentrics, and apparently many of their neighbors never even surmised they were lesbians. In fact, one of the complaints that Berry often made was that after Radclyffe Hall's *Well of Loneliness* came out, it was more difficult for lesbians to hold hands while walking down the street because people were more suspicious of close women. Since Berry's partner was the mother-in-law of the author of this brief biography, one of her main contributions was also encouraging and supporting my own research into gays and lesbians, and early introducing me into the life and culture of the gay community. Her life emphasizes how rich and varied were the lives of gays and lesbians in a time when it was not polite for many in society to inquire more deeply into unorthodox living relationships. She thought long and often about what it meant to be a lesbian, and one result of her activity as communicated to me was to open up the study of same-sex relationships in the intermountain west and in Mormon country in particular.

BIBLIOGRAPHY

Bullough, Vern and Bonnie Bullough, "Lesbianism in the 1920's and 1930's: A Newfound Study," *Signs,* 2 (summer 1977).

Quinn, D. Michael, *Same Sex Dynamics Among Nineteenth-Century Americans: A Mormon Example* (Urbana: University of Illinois Press, 1996).

PART II:
ORGANIZATIONAL ACTIVISTS

Until gays and lesbians could have a voice of their own to put forth their own collective ideas, to give aid and comfort to each other, and to effectively challenge misinformation, they were victims of what others said and thought about them. To be their own advocates, they had to become public, but how could any group that reported on and even advocated what in essence was an illegal activity survive? Homosexuality was denounced by the medical profession as pathological, by religious groups as immoral and sinful, by the laws and courts as criminal, and by society in general as a perversion. Inevitably and unfortunately, many if not most of those who were labeled as homosexuals felt ashamed of what they were doing. To change this situation ultimately entailed a many-pronged attack; and in retrospect, there were radical societal changes in the latter half of the twentieth century. Few who began the organizational efforts in 1950 would have predicted such change. The early proponents for change simply wanted to have their voices heard and their sexual activities decriminalized. Although, as pointed out earlier, informal social groups had long existed, probably most of them were known to police and law enforcement officials who more or less tolerated their existence. There was, however, never any guarantee that this would always be the case; often out of the blue the police would one day suddenly intervene and charge individuals with crimes against nature or, more likely, with lesser crimes such as indecent behavior, creating a public nuisance, or any number of greater or lesser crimes dependent not so much on what an individual did or was doing but what particular law enforcement officials decided to call them. The whole process was not only demoralizing to the gays and lesbians involved but highly dependent on police corruption and lying. Entrapment was common; the policeman's word was usually believed, so much so that most of those arrested simply pleaded guilty to minor charges such as lewd vagrancy, hoping against hope that they might be simply fined and their arrest would escape the notice of the public. Since the sexual activities involved were between consenting individuals, police had to resort to entrapment and other dubious procedures to make the arrests. The methods were corrupting to police forces because their judgment could be influenced not only by bribery but by their own basic attitudes. Some law enforcement officials went on what can only be called moralistic crusades, while others adopted a more "live and let live" attitude. However, even this was a gray area because when officialdom felt the need to make arrests, they had to decide whom to arrest. Some were victimized more often than others.

Not everyone who engaged in same-sex activities was arrested, but it is also true that not all of those who were arrested regarded themselves as homosexuals. Laud Humphreys, in his pioneering study of what was called the "tea room trade," i.e., sex in public toilets, found that a significant number of the men he observed regarded themselves as heterosexual, were married, had children, and simply found this an easy way to achieve orgasm, cheaper than going to a prostitute, better than solitary masturbation, and much less involved than the bargaining that many had to do with their spouses who for one reason or another were regarded by them as unresponsive to their sexual needs.

The complexity of the issues makes for a difficult organizing task of how to present the biographies of the individuals in this book. One way is to simply do so alphabetically, and let the reader decide. This is the policy that was adopted in Part I. In this section, however, rather than continue the alphabetical listing, it seemed wiser to try to cluster individuals, but this poses problems because some individuals seem to fall into more than one group. Still it seems that, at least in the early stages, organization was the key, and thus this section is devoted to the many individuals involved in organizing activities. Yet people involved in organizations also did other things. Because organization is such a large category, not all those involved in organization are included here because their contribution in other areas seems even more important. Readers should look upon the book's parts as a helpful organizing principle, not the only known contribution of the individual to the gay and lesbian cause.

A second point also must be made. Contradictions in the biographies in some cases remain unresolved, particularly regarding who did what and when in any particular group. This is natural because different individuals (and their biographers) saw their roles in different ways than did others. No attempt was made by the editors to change these sometimes conflicting claims or views except when such easily verified questions about dates or events were corrected. These differences became greater as the movement grew and individuals who had basic differences found they could go their own way or establish their own organizations. Many of the differences early made their appearance in organizational strategies, which the reader should note.

The two major centers of early organizational activities were in California, namely in Los Angeles and San Francisco. Although New York City, Chicago, Philadelphia, Boston, and other metropolitan cities attracted large numbers of gays and lesbians and informal groupings, it was in Los Angeles that the original Mattachine Society appeared and where ONE, Inc. got its start. Although both of these organizations included males and females, and a few women were in important positions, many women felt they were misunderstood by the men. The common complaint often heard was that the men involved looked upon the women as best suited to making and serving coffee at meetings. It was in San Francisco that the Daughters of Bilitis began, and for all of its national history, San Francisco has remained the headquarters.

This section includes biographies of Harry Hay, who conceived the idea of a secret society; Dale Jennings, whose arrest and trial resulted in a dismissal of the charges and brought an influx of new members to the struggling Mattachine; W. Dorr Legg and Don Slater, who wanted something more than the Mattachine Society offered and went on to found a more public organization, ONE, Inc., which became the dominant organization in Los Angeles and its magazine, for a time, was the voice of the gay and lesbian movement. Some individuals were not organizational founders but are important because they were simply there, always when they were needed. Jim Schneider is the organizational man who strove to keep competing groups and personalities in Los Angeles working together, not always successfully. Billy Glover, who unintentionally split the ONE organization, is also included in this section. Another person who was always there was Jim Kepner. He was active in the organizations but was more important as a writer, a collector of data, an archivist, and an idea man. Also included in the Los Angeles contingent in this section is Stella Rush, a woman activist in ONE as well as in the DOB who often wrote under the name of Sten Russell. Her co-worker and life partner Helen Sandoz has been written up by Stella herself. Important also were the lawyers who cooperated with ONE and other groups. Several did so, but in this book Herb Selwyn is representative.

San Francisco soon disputed with Los Angeles for the title of the most important gay activist center in the country. One of the reasons for this was the presence of Hal Call, who was instrumental in moving the Mattachine Society headquarters to San Francisco. Call is another one whose category might be debated: he was seemingly everywhere and doing many things, but because of his importance in the San Francisco-based Mattachine we have included him in this section. Also putting San Francisco on the map were Phyllis Lyon and Del Martin, the founders of Daughters of Bilitis who began publication of *The Ladder*. The two seemed to be everywhere in the gay and lesbian movement, but because of the importance of DOB we have included them in this section. Also important on the San Francisco scene was Billye Talmadge, as were Cleo Glenn (Bonner) and Pat Walker, whose activities are covered in briefer biographies.

A different kind of organization person was Bob Basker who might be regarded as the traveling salesman for the movement during the 1960s and 1970s, assuming activist roles in Chicago, New York City, south Florida, and even in Cuba before settling in San Francisco. Shirley Willer similarly established a number of DOB chapters in the country, but her plans for radically changing DOB failed, and the organization more or less ceased to exist. Not mentioned in this section are Frank Kameny, Jack Nichols, and several others who were everywhere and are included in the next part of the book.

REFERENCE

Humphreys, Laud. *Tearoom Trade: Impersonal Sex in Public Places*. Chicago: Aldine, 1970.

Harry Hay (1912-   )

Vern L. Bullough

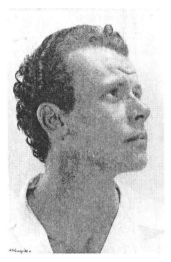

Photo by Hazel Harvey

Harry Hay is the Johnny Appleseed of the American gay movement, brimming with ideas, planting seeds for new projects and organizations, and then moving on. He is an unusual combination of the dreamer, the planner, the mystic, and the activist, who has devoted his life to trying to bring about change in the status quo. It was his determination to change things and his success in establishing the Mattachine Society that entitle him to be regarded as the founder of the modern American gay movement. He is, however, not the kind of person willing to devote himself to the administrative minutiae necessary to building a long-term organization. He has always been much too restless, too much the individualist marching to his own drum, to be an organization man.

His early dissatisfaction with the status quo led him to association with the Industrial Workers of the World and eventually to joining the Communist Party (CP), something that many radicals of his generation did. This identification with and eventual formal affiliation with the CP, however, was not as easy for Harry as for some others because he had been initiated as a young teenager into gay culture and identified with it, and the CP itself was antihomosexual.

It was his experience with communist organizing activities among minorities that led him eventually to consider organizing homosexuals. For Harry, homosexuals were the "androgynous minority," a term later abandoned since it ignored the existence of lesbians. Harry argued that homosexuals met the four Stalinist principles for definition of a minority in that they had a common language, a common territory, a common economy, and a common psychology and culture, although his definition of these terms was quite different than those Stalin had conceived.

73

In spite of his various plans and organizational activity, Harry never held leadership for long in the organizations in which he was involved. His was the work of agitator, the organizer, the idea person, and in a sense the gadfly, the burr under the saddle. He has always been a kind of mystical utopian; the early Mattachine Society reflected this, as did his later efforts such as the Circle of Loving Companions and the Radical Faeries. Increasingly he also emphasized the need for a separatist gay identity instead of being assimilated into mainstream America.

His rugged independence often got him into trouble with mainstream gay organizations. In the 1986 Los Angeles Gay Pride parade, for example, he insisted on wearing a sign on his back reading "NAMBLA [North American Man/Boy Love Association] walks with me," an action he took because he remembered his pleasure in coming out as a teenager with a man who initiated him to the gay world. Getting him to agree to simply wear a sign rather than carry a banner took considerable negotiation by the parade organizers, who wanted to distance the gay and lesbian movement from pedophilia, yet wanted Harry to participate.

Like most communists of the 1930s and 1940s, he left the CP, but he continued to regard himself as a leftist and progressive, struggling to help those whom he felt did not receive a fair shake in life— African Americans, Native Americans, women, and, of course, gays and lesbians.

Henry Hay Jr., as he was officially named, was born on Easter Sunday, April 7, 1912, in Worthing, an exclusive seaside resort near London, England, the son of Margaret Neall and Henry Hay. His mother had met his father in South Africa where his father, usually called Harry (as was his son), managed the Witwaterstrand deep mine for Cecil Rhodes. Shortly after their marriage in 1911 the couple moved to what is now Ghana, where Harry was to open a new mine. Since there was no real hospital available there, the pregnant Margaret was sent to England to have her baby. Shortly after young Harry was born, his father moved to Chile to help develop a new Anaconda copper mine. There Harry, his mother, and his recently born sister joined him in 1914. They lived there until 1916, when his father lost part of a leg in a mining accident. The family then moved to California where Harry spent most of the rest of his life.

Harry's family was well-to-do, but his father believed in discipline and work, demanding that even his children work. Harry, however, did not conform as a child to what his father thought a boy should be and, in Harry's words, his father was fearful that he had "spawned" a big sissy. Harry says he was much more interested in music and literature than most boys his age and spent much time in the library. As a precocious eleven-year-old he had run across Edward Carpenter's *The Intermediate Sex* (1912); while reading it, he realized for the first time that love was possible with a person of the same sex. He later wrote:

> Suddenly my world was transformed into a whole wonderful, different place because my night-dream and day-dream fantasies from then on would always include HIM—the one who was going to be everything to me, as I naturally would be to him. (Timmons, 1990, p. 29)

Harry matured early. When he entered Los Angeles High School at twelve, he was already six feet, two inches (eventually he passed the six feet three mark). At the end of his first year, Harry's father sent him off for the summer to work in the hay field of a relative in western Nevada in order to be toughened up and become a real man. Three things in that summer had great influence on young Harry. First was meeting and talking with Wobblies, miners who belonged to the Industrial Workers of the World and who worked off and on in mines and as farm laborers. This experience made him a socialist determined to change the working conditions of the ordinary man. Second, while there, he was also invited to an Indian fandango where he was blessed by a medicine man known as Jack Wilson whose Indian name was Wovoka. Wovoka had founded a mystical Indian religion known as the Ghost Dance religion. Harry felt certain he had been invited because the Indians recognized he was different, i.e., homosexual, and he later continued to believe that there was a kind of mystical brotherhood of gays and that Wovoka, the holy man, might well be one.

A third experience took place on his return trip to Los Angeles. Instead of traveling by train, Harry, through the influence of his IWW co-workers, and his own height and brawniness from the summer work, managed to get a union card, which allowed him to work on a tramp steamer going to Los Angeles from San Francisco. Even before the ship departed, Harry had his first sexual experience with an adult, a fellow "merchant marine" who told him they were members of a "silent brotherhood" that reached around the world, emphasizing Harry's own feeling of a mystical union with fellow gays. Harry later reported that as a child of fourteen, "I molested an adult until I found out what I needed to know" (Timmons, 1990, p. 36).

After his graduation from high school in the class of 1929, he briefly became an apprentice in a downtown Los Angeles law firm. He often visited Pershing Square during his free time (already known as a place for pickups) where Harry allowed himself to be picked up by a number of partners. One of his contacts told him about Henry Gerber who in the 1920s in Chicago had tried to set up homosexual groups but was closed down by the authorities after a few short weeks. Harry never forgot this.

Although Harry's father had been willing to send him to college if he would study engineering or become an oil geologist, Harry, after a year in the law office, decided to go to Stanford and study international law even if his father refused to pay for it. At Stanford, he soon became active in the drama group and at the same time began exploring the San Francisco gay scene. In his sophomore year he declared his homosexuality to nearly every student he knew, and this action cut him off from most of his peers, although at least one became a lover for a brief time. Unfortunately for Harry, his attention-drawing action led Stanford officials to question some of his friends about "his complex." As pressures mounted on Harry, he fell ill and left Stanford for the ranch he had worked at in Nevada. He never went back to Stanford. Returning to Los Angeles in 1932, he became very active in gay life and met many of the more famous closeted gays, although some were fearful of being seen with him because they felt he was too obvious or flamboyant and was therefore a threat to their desire for anonymity.

Although he still lived in the parental home, he led an independent life, supporting himself by acting or working at studio-related jobs, wrote poetry that occasionally got published, sang either solo or in groups, and cruised in his spare time. He later recalled that he sometimes had two or three mostly anonymous contacts a day, although he also established some long-term friendships as well. One of his friends was Will Geer who introduced Harry to the left-wing community of Los Angeles and eventually to the Communist Party. Increasingly Harry became a hard-core activist in the radical community, often joining with Geer in what was known as agitprop, acting out scenes at picket lines to keep spirits of the strikers high, or doing planned demonstrations or scenes at large meetings to keep audience attention focused. The final step in his radicalization occurred during the San Francisco general strike of July 1934, which he and Will Geer traveled north to join. On his return to Los Angeles, Harry became even more active in Communist Party activities although he had not yet formally joined.

The problem for Harry was that the Communist Party was hostile to homosexuality. As he moved more and more in party circles, he realized that the active sex life which he carried on without the party officially knowing about it posed a dilemma for him. Although other homosexuals and lesbians had ignored the communist prohibition and joined the party, Harry, the utopian idealist, felt unable to do so. The conflicts between his gayness and his left-wing ideology led him to seek psychiatric help, and out of one such session came a decision to marry and to leave the gay life. In 1938 he and Anita Platky, a fellow activist, were married. They set up housekeeping in the Silver Lake district, the first time Harry had ever formally moved out of his parents' house. One of the first actions the couple took was to officially join the Communist Party. Although they never had children of their own, they eventually adopted two girls.

In spite of the best of intentions, Harry soon found himself again cruising and in conflict with the communist ideology about homosexuality and his own belief in the correctness of being gay as well. He never discussed such matters with his wife, however. Several times he came close to leaving both the party and Anita over a more-than-casual love affair with another man, but each time he drew back. Later, in recollecting this aspect of his life, he regarded much of the 1940s as a lost decade: "I missed the forties, because I was being married and a Communist." Increasingly he threw himself into party work, for a brief time in New York City but mainly in Los Angeles, where he became known as an extremely effective teacher of communist ideology as well as more topical and party-approved courses such folk music.

The conflict between his gayness, the party, and his family came to a head during the Wallace campaign of 1948. Henry Wallace, Franklin Roosevelt's vice president during his third term, had been replaced on the ticket by Harry Truman in 1944 when Roosevelt sought his fourth term, and it was Truman who succeeded to the presidency on Roosevelt's death. Wallace had eventually broken with the Democrats as had many other "progressive groups" because of what was regarded as a rightward shift in the party. The discontent led to the formation of the Progressive Party and the nomination of Wallace as its presidential candidate in the 1948 election. Communists exercised a great deal of influence on the Progressive Party, although Wallace himself was not a communist. To publicize the campaign and gain support, there were attempts to organize special interest citizens' groups for Wallace. Some of these groups had hundreds or thousands of members; others were little more than letterhead committees with a handful of members. It was the endorsements and publicity that counted for the Progressive Party and not the total membership. One of the paper organizations that appeared was the Harry Hay-originated Bachelors for Wallace. The committee is important not for it what it accomplished, which was very little if anything, but because it set off a train of thinking in Harry's mind that resulted both in the formation of the Mattachine Society in 1950 and in his divorce from Anita in 1951. Harry was also expelled, at his request, from the Communist Party, because he no longer felt that he could cope with the communist prohibition of homosexuality and his own sexual orientation. His wife also resigned, although on her part it was because of a growing disillusion with the party.

The excitement generated in the discussion about the potential Bachelors for Wallace committee motivated Harry to refine and develop the concept of a gay organization. He started by drawing up a potential plank for the Progressive Party platform on homosexuality and from there began to develop an idea for a postelection organization to fight for homosexual rights. Nothing came of this on-paper concept, which went through several drafts until two years later when he met Rudi Gernreich, a man who later became a prominent fashion designer, and with whom Harry Hay fell in love. The two had met on July 8, 1950, and Gernreich was very excited about Henry's plan. Within a week, the two had begun to plan how to bring such an organization about. They circulated petitions for such an organization and made individual contacts with little response until November 1950, when the two were joined by Robert Hull, Charles Dennison Rowland, and Dale Jennings in the formation of the Mattachine Society. Both Hull and Rowland had also been communists but less concerned about the party's prohibition of homosexuals than Harry.

The term *Mattachine* was Harry's. He had hit upon it while doing research on the historical development of folk music for his classes. The Mattachine Society had been an all-male society that had grown out of the medieval "Feast of Fools," and which, among other things, developed a special dance form. In Harry's euphoric description the Mattachine troupes conveyed vital information to the oppressed of the countryside in late medieval France and elsewhere. It was his hope that modern homosexual men, living in disguise in the twentieth-century heterosexual world, could do the same thing for the current generation of oppressed queers.

The solution to building an organization, the Mattachine founders believed, was to keep the actual organization secret but carry its message to the gay public through public discussion groups on topics of interest to homosexuals, such as the Kinsey report and its data on the existence of a significant number of gays. Hay, fearful of police intervention as had been the case with Gerber's early Illinois organization but also enamored of romantic ideas about earlier male societies, and perhaps also influenced by the communist experience of secret cells, had insisted on secrecy. This was also the time that the government itself began to mount campaigns against homosexuals as being subversive, and if the organization was to grow he felt it had to protect its members. The original five members constituted themselves as the steering committee which they called the Fifth Order. The very romantic Hay wanted to call the steering committee the Parsifal Group after the Wagnerian operatic knight who searched for the Holy Grail, but agreed to the Fifth Order. The first open discussion of the group was held in December 1950 with about eighteen people in attendance, both men and women, and other meetings were soon held. The public meetings served as recruiting grounds for future Mattachine members, and the Fifth Order carefully selected other individuals to join with them in the society itself. Two other individuals, Konrad Stevens and James Gruber, joined the Fifth Order in April of 1951, as others soon did, including Ruth Bernhard, who became the first and most active woman. A Mattachine mission statement was drawn up stating that the purpose of the society was (1) to unify homosexuals isolated from their own kind and unable to adjust to the dominant culture, (2) to educate and improve and add to the information about homosexuality through further research, and (3) to lead those who are regarded as socially deviant to achieve the goal of unification and education.

In an initiation ceremony developed by Harry, members stood in a circle with hands joined, intoned a solemn oath, and pledged to work for a reborn social force of immense and simple purpose aimed at equality of security and production—all to proper musical accompaniment. The ideal Mattachine group was regarded as about twenty with new groups splitting off as old ones grew. Sometimes as many as 150 people attended a public meeting and those in the Fifth Order invited the most enthusiastic participants to join the Mattachine Society itself. The Fifth Order produced a simple guidebook on how to lead a discussion group with suggested topics. Social events were also held for members that featured same-sex dancing, among other activities, at that time something that was forbidden by the Los Angeles police but which could be carried out by a private group.

The society grew slowly until it took up the case of Dale Jennings. Jennings, a founder of Mattachine, had been arrested for "lewd and dissolute" conduct by a vice officer whom Jennings had ignored and who insisted on following him home and who pushed his way into Jennings' house. While Dale went to get coffee, more vice officers raided and charged him. Rather than copping a plea, as happened regularly at that time, Jennings decided to fight it with the help of the Mattachine Society, urged on by Harry. Jennings admitted that he was a homosexual but that he was not lewd nor dissolute and that the policeman was lying. Rather than appearing publicly as an organization, the Fifth Order set up the Citizens Committee to Outlaw Entrapment to defend him. This strategy received the backing of a significant portion of the gay community. In the trial, the jury deadlocked, in part because the police had been caught in a lie, and the case was dismissed. There was an immediate jump in attendance of discussion groups and new groups, known as circles of friends, were established in Whittier, Laguna, Capistrano, San Diego, Bakersfield, Fresno, Monterey, and San Francisco. Since no central membership records were kept, membership is hard to estimate, but it might have ranged from 2,000 to 5,000.

Although the Matttachine remained a secret organization, it was recognized that there was a need for a more public dissemination of information, and discussion on this issue led to the formation of a magazine, *ONE,* and a separate organization. Since the term *homosexual* could not be listed in the telephone book or even mentioned very publicly, the title *ONE* was picked from the writings of Thomas Carlyle who had written that "A mystic brotherhood makes all men one," an obvious extension of the mythic fraternity of the Mattachine Society. The Mattachine foundation provided *ONE* with its mailing list and its first subscriptions.

As the success of the Mattachine grew, it became difficult to avoid public notice. It was a period of virulent anticommunism, and Harry Hay had been publicly named as a Marxist teacher in one of the Los Angeles newspapers. Fearful of the consequences of this on the Mattachine, Harry agreed to retire from public association with the Mattachine Society and Foundation. The press, however, had begun to suspect that something was happening in the gay community, and not too long after a separate story on the Mattachine Society itself was published in the *Los Angeles Daily Mirror,* the evening paper owned by the *Los Angeles Times.* The article stated that homosexuals in the Los Angeles area (the first time the paper had used the term) had a voting block of 150,000 to 200,000 people and thus had to be regarded as important. The writer of the story had apparently tried to contact some Mattachine members, but the only publicly identified person was the group's attorney. The writer then stated that the attorney was a well-known subversive, i.e., an unfriendly witness before the House Un-American Activities Committee, and indirectly implied the potential menace in such an organization. Although the article was not necessarily hostile, it certainly was not friendly and the reaction was quick. There was a demand that the Mattachine go completely public since remaining secret caused all kinds of speculation. Many members had apparently long felt that a homosexual organization should be public, although its mailing list and members might be kept secret. At a convention called to discuss the issue over two weekends in April and May of 1953, there was a determined effort by some to get rid of the so-called communists in the leadership and the red-baiting was intense. The result was a restructuring of the society, with the original Fifth Order resigning and handing over the name to the members. The result was the end of what Harry called the First Mattachine, and the appearance of the Second Mattachine, a much-sanitized organization which spread throughout the country over the next two decades. The new Mattachine moved its headquarters to San Francisco and became what Harry called a "white glove" assimilationist group.

THE AFTERMATH

Harry dropped out of sight, cut off both from the mainstream gay community and from his former friends in the Communist Party. He joined with his new lover Jorn Kamgren in establishing a millinery shop in Los Angeles. His communist past, however, was not forgotten and when the House Un-

American Activities Committee appeared in Los Angeles in May 1955, Harry was summoned to appear. Rather than refusing to testify as many had done, he told about his family and his life, and when the inevitable question was asked as to whether he was a communist, he said no, adding that he had resigned four years before. For some reason, his answer incensed the chief counsel of the committee who, in attempting to stand up, knocked over the desk behind which he sat, and this in turn led to the court reporter's transcript ending up in a jumble on the floor. In the ensuing commotion and laughter, Harry was dismissed without having to say more.

After this appearance he again went into hibernation, feeling rejected by both gays and communists. He spent much of the time studying and researching homosexuality. One result of this research was published in the *ONE Institute Quarterly* in 1963, namely the report of the U.S. surgeon general who had observed *mujerados* or "made women" among the Pueblo Indians of New Mexico. He also traveled extensively around the United States, camping out, look for surviving remnants of *mujerados* or similar groups.

After breaking with Jorn, he had a brief relationship with Jim Kepner, one of the old Mattachine members who had kept his contacts with the gay community and wrote extensively on it and for it. After this ended, he established a relationship with John Burnside who had invented and manufactured a kaleidoscope-like machine which did not rely on the traditional glass chips to color the view. The two moved in together and Harry founded the Circle of Loving Companions, a gay collective that emphasized love of comrades. Although it occasionally had several members for long stretches, the only long-term members were Harry and John Burnside. Harry periodically made public appearances to join or help publicize other organizations, such as the Council on Religion and the Homosexual, the Committee to Fight the Exclusion of Homosexuals from the Armed Forces, and the Southern California Gay Liberation Front. He also became active in the American Indian movement through the Committee for Traditional Indian Land and Life. In 1970 the two moved to northern New Mexico where they continued to manufacture kaleidoscopes and Harry pursued his investigations of homosexual roles among Indian societies. Unfortunately, the factory they had established burned in 1973, along with its inventory and most of its records. Their insurance company refused to pay on the grounds that since the factory was located on an Indian reservation and outside of state jurisdiction, they had no obligation to do so. Harry's attempts to establish a gay liberation stronghold in New Mexico also came to naught.

Turning inward again, Harry established the Radical Faeries, a group that he regarded as a flowering of the Circle of Loving Companions. It was a gay spiritual movement that rejected "heteroimitation" and redefined gay identity. He felt it essential for gays and lesbians to define themselves in their own terms instead of in reaction to the heterosexual world. There were many similarities in organization with the original Mattachine except instead of the Fifth Order it had a triad, originally composed of Harry, Don Kilhefner, and Mitch Walker. The new group debuted at the 1978 annual conference of the Gay Academic Union in Los Angeles and then later held a retreat attended by several hundred at the Sri Ram Ashram, a spiritual center near Benson, Arizona. A second retreat the next year attracted an even larger group and the result was an effort to incorporate and spread.

The founding of the new group also marked the return of Harry to Los Angeles. Inevitably there soon appeared disagreement among the founders and there was a split into two separate gay faerie organizations. A faerie-owned farm came about with the purchase of a Magdalene Farm in 1987, near Grant's Pass, Oregon, but Harry had very little official connection with it.

Harry has continued to push his vision of a gay community, different than the heterosexual one with all gays coming together. He planted seeds for gay organization far and wide and some grew into trees, although not always in the way that Harry had expected or anticipated. Although the world has changed, Harry has not. He remains a gay visionary who has kept his faith with himself, although not always with his followers or his friends.

BIBLIOGRAPHY

Coates, Paul. Column. *Los Angeles Mirror,* March 12, 1953.
Hay, Harry. "The Hammond Report," *One Institute Quarterly,* winter/spring, 1963.
Hay, Harry. *Radically Gay: Gay Liberation in the Words of Its Founder,* edited by Will Roscoe, (Boston: Beacon Press, 1996).
Timmons, Stuart. *The Trouble with Harry Hay* (Boston: Alyson Publications, 1990).

Dale Jennings (1917-2000):
ONE's Outspoken Advocate

C. Todd White

Dale Jennings is frequently mentioned in the annals of gay American history, but the references are often pointed and brief. He is listed as one of the founders of the Mattachine Society, a cohort of Harry Hay. At his death he was lauded as the "Rosa Parks of the gay rights movement" for having prevailed in the first court case in the United States in which a man admitted in court to being a homosexual yet successfully fought charges of lewd conduct in a public space. He helped found *ONE,* the first successful magazine in the United States dedicated to equal rights for homosexuals, and was briefly senior editor as well as a significant contributor under his own name and various pseudonyms.

Not much has been written of Jennings' personal life, but it is hard to encapsulate the history of a man who never really settled down. He was born in El Paso, Texas, October 21, 1917, grew up in Denver, Colorado, and traveled extensively as a child as a violin prodigy (Legg, 1994). He moved to Los Angeles in his late teens where he developed a passion for sailing. He rented an old stable and launched a traveling theater company, Theatre Caravan, for which he reportedly wrote and produced an estimated sixty plays. Unfortunately, he earned very little money in the process. During World War II, Jennings was stationed at Guadalcanal, but after the famous battle that had been fought there. When he was discharged, he returned to Califor-

I would like to thank Walter L. Williams, Vern L. Bullough, Stephen O. Murray, Jim Schneider, Joseph Hansen, and George Mortenson (Fred Frisbie) for their comments on prior drafts of this article.

nia and studied cinema for two years at the University of Southern California. Not about to be "tagged as a fag," he played it straight and pursued relationships with women. He tried the married life—three times. Each was brief and annulled. He began to explore sex with men and learned that a lot of "straight" guys enjoyed sexual play with other guys from time to time. He began to visualize sexuality as a spectrum of possibilities and thought that rigid labels such as "homosexual" or "heterosexual," "gay" or "straight," were illusory—and dangerous.

Although often referred to as among the great queer pioneers of the gay or homophile movement, Jennings frequently stood counter to the culture-forming "minoritizing" tendencies emerging within the early days of Mattachine. He was a steadfast libertarian who stood up for the right for same-sex love and eroticism, but he refused to the end of his days to don the "gay" mantle. He repeatedly wrote in later essays that to do so would be like tattooing a target on one's chest; it would be the equivalent of suicide. Jennings perceived the homophile movement to be caught in a paradox: although the rights of those who practiced homosexuality needed to be protected, to stand fervently in favor of something was the surest way to incite those most adamantly against it.

Nevertheless, Jennings stepped into the gay movement one November night in 1950 when he met Harry Hay and Rudi Gernreich, two active members of the Communist Party in Los Angeles. Hay was a teacher for the California Labor School. With Gernreich's blessing, they had given Bob Hull, a student in his music history class, a prospectus he had written that called on the "androgynes of the world" to unite (Hay, 1996). Hull was thrilled with the document, so he asked Hay if he could bring two friends over to discuss the matter. These were his lover-turned-roommate, fellow communist Chuck Rowland, and Hull's current boyfriend, Dale Jennings.

According to Hay, "These five 'sexual outlaws'" had "gravitated to the Left because . . . they found themselves in total empathy with the programs and goals of our Hetero outlaw friends in labor and politics" (Hay, 1996, pp. 315-316). Hay recalled that Jennings had not been active within the party, but he referred to him as "one hell of a fellow traveler" (Timmons, 1990, p. 144). However, in an undated (c. 1984) Christmas card Jennings sent to his friend Don Slater, he had written, "When I was a loud-mouthed commie, people fled the Mattachine in the thousands; now that the prevailing shade this season is red, my conservatism is worse than damned: it's ignored." A letter to Don Slater dated July 16, 1990, also indicated that he had once been in "the local red cell." Indeed, Jennings was eventually cast out of ONE in 1954 by a zealous Dorr Legg, due to Jennings' communist activities and associations.

Gay journalist/historian Jim Kepner (1994) explained that the communist background "gave them a starting philosophy with strategic applications . . . analyses which suggested specific courses of action, the experience and chutzpah to tackle what seemed hopeless, and the idea of a minority community, which must learn to respect itself, to build its own institutions, resources and sense of fraternity/sorority." It was these five comrades who met to discuss the prospectus on November 11, 1950, and again two days later. A larger, semipublic "discussion group" convened the following month, on December 11. By early 1951, Mattachine had recruited another five members, including their first woman, Ruth Bernhard, although other women had attended the public meetings. That summer, they adopted official missions and purposes, which proclaimed homosexuals to be one of the largest minorities in America. Hay designed an elaborate initiation ceremony reminiscent of the Masons. Jennings seems to have appreciated the importance of this ritual, for he later wrote, "To many a homosexual, who may have lived out years of loneliness or bitterness, believing that his lot in society was a miserable one and without hope, the whole proceedings, the sense of group fellowship, the joining of hands in solemn oath, bespoke something so new, and of such dazzling implication as to be well-nigh unbelievable" (Timmons, 1990, p. 155).

This does not mean, however, that Jennings agreed with the "cultural minority" impetus that was driving Mattachine. As the others sifted and sorted through names trying to find one that aptly described them, Jennings grew frustrated, wanting simply to work toward freedom of choice in sexual preferences and behaviors. As Joseph Hansen, another early member of Mattachine, wrote, "You can't start a society of people with nothing in common but what they do in bed" (Hansen, 1998, p. 19). While other members droned on about "the pain and sorrow, the desperate loneliness of being homosexual and afraid, always having to lie and hide," Jennings stood aloof and "struggled not to laugh aloud" (Hansen, 1998, pp. 19-20). Writing under his pseudonym Jeff Winters, he commented that when Hay proposed that the group call itself Mattachine, after a troupe of masked bachelors who led the festivities in the medieval French Feast of Fools, Hay hadn't noticed "the sniggers of the rest of us." Yet it was also Jennings who wrote, as Hieronymous K., "It would be the Mattachine Foundation commemorating the fools and jesters of legend who spoke the truth in the face of stern authority" (1953, p. 19).

It is somewhat ironic that, through the course of events, it was Jennings who galvanized the Mattachine. The precipitating event was his arrest in the spring of 1952 for allegedly soliciting a police officer in a toilet in Westlake Park (now MacArthur Park). Jennings left his Echo Park apartment in search for a good movie. After passing on the first two shows, about 9:00 p.m.

he stepped into a public restroom on his way to a third theater. He soon left, "[h]aving done nothing that the city architect didn't have in mind when he designed the place," only now he was followed by a "big, rough looking character who appeared out of nowhere." Jennings proceeded to the theater to find that the show there was one he'd already seen. So he headed for home, still followed by the burly stranger (letters, not yet catalogued).

Jennings now became afraid that the man had set out to rob him, so he "walked fast, took detours and said goodbye at each street corner." Upon arriving home, however, the man persisted and, before a witness, he pushed past Jennings and into the apartment. Jennings describes what happened then:

> What followed would have been a nightmare even if he hadn't turned out to be vice squad. Sure now that this big character was a thug, I—as the prosecutor described it—"flitted wildly" from room to room wondering how to get rid of this person sprawled on the divan making sexual gestures and proposals. I was almost relieved when he strolled into the back bedroom because now I could call the police . . . Then he called twice, "Come in here!" His voice was loud and commanding. He'd taken his jacket off, was sprawled on the bed and his shirt was unbuttoned half way down. . . . [H]e insisted that I was homosexual and urged me to "let down my hair." He'd been in the navy and "all us guys played around." I told him repeatedly that he had the wrong guy; he got angrier each time I said it. At last he grabbed my hand and tried to force it down the front of his trousers. I jumped up and away. Then there was the badge and he was snapping the handcuffs on with the remark, "Maybe you'll talk better with my partner outside." (Jennings, 1953d, p. 12)

The partner, Jennings wrote, was nowhere to be found when they left the apartment. Cuffed, he was paraded all the way back to the park, where he was ushered into the waiting patrol car. The arresting officer sat in the back seat beside him, and he and two other officers in the front seat asked baited questions, such as "How long have you been this way?" The officers "repeatedly made jokes about police brutality, laughingly asked . . . if they'd been brutal and each of the three instructed me to plead guilty and everything would be alright" (1953, p. 12). Jennings feared that he was in for "the usual beating," probably out in the country somewhere, but they eventually made it to the station, where Jennings was booked at 11:30 p.m., although he was not allowed to make his phone call until after 2:00 in the morning. That call was to Harry Hay, to ask for fifty dollars bail. Hay posted the bail by 6:30 a.m., and the two went for breakfast at the Brown Derby. It was there decided that Mattachine would help contest the charge. That night Hay called a meeting, and Mattachine convened, back in Jennings' apartment.

Hay hired Long Beach lawyer George Sibley to take the case and, under his advisement, Mattachine organized the Citizens Committee to Outlaw Entrapment, which raised funds and promoted Jennings' case through use of leaflets and flyers. The trial began on June 23, 1952, and lasted for ten days. Jennings admitted to being a homosexual, but he adamantly denied any wrongdoing. The jury deadlocked eleven to one for acquittal, and the charges were dismissed by the judge.

Hay's later recollection of the arrest somewhat contradicts Jennings' story. This account by Hay was related to journalist Stuart Timmons:

> Dale had just broken off with Bob Hull and was not, I know, feeling very great. He told me that he had met someone in the can at Westlake Park. The man had his hand on his crotch, but Dale wasn't interested. He said the man insisted on following him home, and almost pushed his way through the door. He asked for coffee, and when Dale went to get it, he saw the man moving the window blind, as if signaling to someone else. He got scared and started to say something, when there was a sudden pounding on the door, and Dale was arrested. (quoted in Timmons, 1990, p. 164)

As to what really happened that night, none can know save Jennings and the arresting officer. Jennings knew that even some of his supporters did not believe the story, and he wrote in the first issue of *ONE Magazine:* "To be innocent and yet not be able to convince even your own firm constituents, caries a peculiar agony" (Jennings, 1953d, p. 11).

The controversial case drew national attention to Mattachine, and through the summer following the trial, membership in the organization ballooned. Mattachine-like discussion groups immediately sprang up in Long Beach, Laguna, and Fresno. By early 1953, groups had formed as far away as San Diego, San Francisco, Oakland, Berkeley, and Chicago.

As for the original founders, Hay was becoming disturbed by what he felt to be the increasing belligerence of Jennings, and Jennings grew disdainful of Hay's visionary theatrics. Like a Judas, Jennings was continually in vocal opposition to anything Hay favored (Timmons, 1990, p. 178). Hay believed that gays were a unique and specially talented folk who had been an integral part of tribal societies and needed to unify to reclaim those sacred and traditional roles. Jennings thus compared Harry Hay to a surly Moses bearing "that dratted Decalogue" (Hansen, 1998, p. 23). Jennings and others maintained that there was no essential difference between males who preferred sex with women and those who preferred other men. Hay wanted visibility;

Jennings wanted privacy. Hay wanted publicity; Jennings wanted the right to be left alone. "Homosexuality is today's great irrelevancy," he wrote in one of his first articles of the nation's first successful homosexual magazine, "Homosexuals Are Not a People" (Jennings, 1953b, pp. 2-6, as Jeff Winters). He was not alone in his discomfort. Even before the entrapment incident, several other members, such as latecomer Don Slater, had complained that Hay's secret organization was not doing a satisfactory job of reaching the general public and of taking legal/political action to protect and defend the rights of homosexuals. "We wanted more action than weekly symposia," wrote Mattachine member George Mortenson (2000).

No one seems to recall who came up with the idea of publishing a monthly magazine at a meeting in the home of George Mortensen, but the idea immediately sparked interest. In October of 1952, a small cadre met in Martin Block's bookshop on Hollywood Boulevard and decided to separate from Mattachine and form ONE, Incorporated. Block was elected president, with Dale Jennings as vice president, and Don Slater as secretary. These three formed the editorial board of ONE Magazine, with W. Dorr Legg as their business manager, Bailey Whitaker, a.k.a. Guy Rousseau, in charge of circulation, and Joan Corbin as "Eve Elloree" as the primary artist. George Mortenson and Ann Carll Reid also assisted as needed (Legg, 1994).

By the second meeting, much had been accomplished. Jennings and Slater had secured an office at 232 South Hill, Suite 302, and somehow managed to pay the first and last months' rent. They had also contacted over a dozen attorneys, which they then narrowed down to two. With the blessings of Legg and others, Jennings and Slater appeared the next day in the law office of Eric Julber. The Articles of Incorporation were signed on November 15, 1952, by Tony Reyes, Martin Block, and Dale Jennings.

Never before had Jennings been so animated to the homosexual cause. A seasoned playwright and budding author, he had at last found his niche in the movement as editor in chief and writer. George Mortenson, an early president of ONE, Inc., recalled:

> Dale Jennings was the only one who had been exposed to the process of pamphleteering in the process of helping his sister issue broadsides and advertising matter in her sewing business. So Dale Jennings was busy from morning till night coaching we novices, in this and that nicety from scribbled notes to properly formed "Dummies" ready for the printer—to be set in type, how to indicate the position of artwork relative to text, etc. Don Slater designed the cover. (Mortenson, 2000)

The first issue of ONE was odd looking: nearly square, with a gray cover and logo reminiscent of a cross, in purple ink. Hansen (1998) recalls that it was printed by Jennings' sister and brother-in-law in their basement, and distributed by hand in the streets and bars of Los Angeles.

Jennings' narratives were pointed and angry, and the personas he wrote under invited controversy. For example, in the second issue of *ONE*, as Jeff Winters, he scathingly chastised Christine Jorgensen, equating her much-discussed sex change operation with eunuchism: "You're not a woman you know . . . those expensive scalpels only gave you the legal right to transvestitism" (Jennings, 1953a, p. 13, as Jeff Winters). Winters assured his audience:

> [H]omosexuals are not a third sex, personalities in the body of the wrong sex, biological confusions of nature. Most neurotic symptoms they display—and there are plenty—can just as easily have been caused by society refusing to adjust to them as the reverse. Their vast number in both history and present makes it impossible to label them freaks and so unusual as to be called abnormal. (Jennings, 1953a, p. 13)

With Jennings at the helm, *ONE Magazine* launched against the winds of culture. Through its thought-provoking essays, daring social commentary, and sharp, consistent design, *ONE* tacked its way into history, serving "as one of the unofficial voices of the homosexual rights movement" until 1972—covering forty years of queer history (Licata, 1981, p. 172). But Jennings did not get to stay editor in chief for very long. Early in 1954, their business manager, Dorr Legg, pressured him to leave. Jennings later admitted in a July 16, 1990, letter to Don Slater that his bullying tactics and maverick manners were to compensate for his own low self-esteem. He confessed to having been overly divisive, and he felt that his bullying approach had backfired on him. He did not contest Bill Lambert's (i.e., Dorr Legg) decision to cast him from the editorial board of *ONE* and found it ironic that he had been evicted from *ONE* and the "red cell" simultaneously:

> Bill Lambert got rid of me at almost the precise time that the local red cell took my [communist party] membership card away from me for being a carnivore and hence a security risk. Naturally both organizations were quite correct and should have been more circumspect about letting me come near them in the very beginning. (letter to Slater, July 16, 1990)

In the years after he had left *ONE*, Jennings wrote and published his first novel, *The Ronin* (1968). Jennings had once studied tai chi in China and Zen in Japan, and this book is a homage to Japanese culture. In *The Ronin*, he recast an old Buddhist myth into his own poetic encomium on manhood. He was proud that the story had been published in Japan, but he lamented that it did not sell as well as he'd hoped: "I'm afraid my erotic passages were a little too much for them," he wrote to a fan in June 7, 1983. In this letter, Jennings' described his Ronin as a man of mythic stature, "with three balls . . . and a permanent erection," whose "pretty damned big" manhood/sword gets him into all sorts of trouble. Tuttle Books of Japan secured the copyright for *The Ronin* in 1968, and the book has been reprinted several times since. *The Ronin* was Jennings' first and most successful novel.

Jennings' second book was based on a film treatment he had sold to Warner Brothers, called *The Cowboys* (1971). Warners had purchased the motion picture rights to *The Cowboys* in 1970, for $150,000. At that time, *The Cowboys* was a three-page plot summary in which an aging rancher named Anse, an old cook, and nine boys drive a herd of cattle across Montana, replacing Anse's original crew who had gone to fight in the Civil War. Through the drive, each boy would become a heroic man: "The fat boy outshines everyone in calming the cattle at night with his soft singing—and the one they started out calling sissy turns out to have the coolest head in a crisis" (letter to Slater, July 16, 1990). The group encounters rustlers, pure "prairie scum" who "grab-ass" with the boys and beat Anse to a pulp, nearly killing him. The boys reap revenge by tricking and exterminating the prairie-vermin rustlers, and Anse recovers in the end to berate the boys lovingly. In the movie itself, however, Anse is shot and killed.

Jennings worked with Irving Ravetch and Harriet Frank Jr. to create the screenplay for the film. Jennings received a separate credit, "Based on a novel by," though plans for publication were still being drawn. Mark Rydell produced and directed the movie, with John Wayne starring as the rancher, who was renamed Wil. The movie was a great success. It is one of John Wayne's last movies, and one of the few in which his character dies.

Besides the aging rancher, *The Cowboys* featured another wave-tossed hero, a boy named Cimarron, a Mexican word for "an animal that runs alone or a man who is wanted; in combining the sense of being both wild and solitary, it is one of the beautiful words in the language" (Jennings, 1971, p. 227). In the introduction to the novel, Jennings advises readers to read the glossary before delving in to the text, in order to "bone up on the West a bit." Be wary of double entendre and euphemisms, he winks. How, then, is one to interpret the description of Anse as he coyly eyes young Slim and slaps his leg with "that long, stiff riata of his" (Jennings, 1971, p. 65)? The sight of the boys scrambling under their blankets to get dressed in the cold, early morning suggests to one of the boys an orgy, an idea elaborated on "until many of the boys stumbled off into the darkness too stimulated to irrigate the plain" (p. 83).

Jennings defended such passages as portraying a historic reality. The publishers, however, would have none of it. According to a September 25, 1970, memo, one editor at Bantam demanded that all glimmers of homo-eroticism be deleted if the book was to be published:

> Sure there was sex in "them days," and for all I know this story may depict it accurately. It gets in the way, however, and it weakens the story unnecessarily. Judicious cutting would make a big difference, and I think the real taboos have to do with masturbation and the way in which the author has suggested adolescent homosexuality without really describing it. Such stuff is out of place in a book for adults.

This same editor advised that Jennings turn up the intensity, so to speak, on the heteroerotic: "I rather like the scene of the floozy walking naked through the town with a gun in each hand." Let's kill the circle jerks, but bring on the femme fatale!

In a formal letter from editor Bob Silverstein of Bantam Books, Jennings was formally entreated to make substantial changes to *The Cowboys:* "The intimations of adolescent homosexuality are distracting. Either they should be more clearly spelled out or considerably toned down. And frankly I urge the latter." Jennings submitted a revision in January 1971, but it was clearly not enough; Silverstein replied in March that Bantam had submitted *The Cowboys* to Putnam. "No word yet," he wrote, "but very high hopes all around." The book was again rejected, however, and finally published by Stein and Day in 1971, but Jennings never let go of the copyright.

With the financial success of *The Cowboys,* Jennings was able to purchase a ranch outside of Los Angeles, where he lived for a time. According to his friend Jim Schneider, he moved for a time to northern California, after he lost his home and most of his possessions in a lawsuit brought on by an ex-lover. When he returned to Los Angeles, he found he had been forgotten by both Hollywood and the gay movement. He eventually reconnected with the gay movement in February 1985, when he wrote to his old friend Don Slater to ask for a job. Slater had separated from ONE and founded HIC, the Homosexual Information Center, in 1965. Jennings came to Slater hoping that the HIC would accept and protect his scripts and books, and perhaps even hire him: "The time has come to send out signals. Those in need of the services of a life-guard must advertise."

Thus began a correspondence with Slater that would last until Slater's death in 1997. Jennings greatly admired Don Slater, and he believed wholeheartedly in the goals of the HIC. They agreed, as Slater wrote in a letter to Jennings dated July 5, 1991, that the protection of privacy in sexual relations is the key to sexual freedom. It is the only centralized control necessary or acceptable in a democratic society. . . . It is the individual not the state that should make decisions that touch so directly on the freedom and dignity of people. . . . The sexual act and all its variations belongs to everyone.

The 1990s were not great years for Jennings. He remained isolated and alone, a surly and reclusive old man who drank too much, who felt befuddled by technology and haunted by regret. He grudgingly allowed others to care for him, but he hated having live-in guests and feared that someone might throw away or destroy his archived pictures and writings. He worked diligently on his writing every day, but more than a few times he lost a day's efforts by turning his word processor off before saving his work. By 1996, he realized that his memory was slipping. He wrote vexedly of losing his scissors and not being able to remember names of objects or recent events. Concerned, he made final arrangements that his works and property would go to the HIC, which would be housed within ONE Institute and Archives in Los Angeles. He wrote of his relief that his words would be preserved—but swore to haunt from the grave anyone who should dare to edit him.

To the end of his days, Jennings never stopped writing, and his legacy to the HIC consists of hundreds of articles, including unpublished books, plays, film treatments, and stories, which he called "invaluable treasures of the heart." He has also left to the HIC a collection of thousands of pictures of men that he had cut out of magazines, a "pictorial record of America's most beautiful men" from the 1950s through the 1980s that had brought him great joy in his solitude. He hoped that HIC could preserve his writings and his collections, and perhaps it might even profit from them.

William Dale Jennings died on May 11, 2000. He was eighty-two years old. His friend Jim Schneider had taken care of him and was with Jennings at his death. His memorial service, held June 25, 2000, was the first public event held in HIC's new home in the ONE Institute and Archives, near the campus of the University of Southern California at Los Angeles.

In method and manner, Jennings was indeed, as Timmons wrote, "[o]pinionated, intelligent and aggressively virile" (1990, p. 144). In a way, Jennings lived a life similar to that of Cimarron, whom he had so admired—his had indeed been the way of the maverick. But solitude did not seem so heroic to Jennings as an old man, when he had to pay penance for the crimes of his youth. So, like his Ronin, he tunneled through a mountain to secure the safety of others only to find, after years of effort, that he had miscalculated from the start and had created a path to a ledge he judged more lethal than the one he had sought to avoid.

BIBLIOGRAPHY

Hansen, Joseph. *A Few Doors West of Hope: The Life and Times of Dauntless Don Slater*. Universal City, CA: HIC/Homosexual Information Center, 1998.

Hay, Harry. *Radically Gay: Gay Liberation in the Words of Its Founder*. Will Roscoe, Ed. Boston: Beacon Press, 1996.

Jennings, Dale, writing as Jeff Winters. "As for Me. . . ." *ONE Magazine* 1:2, February 1953a, pp. 11-13.

Jennings, Dale, writing as Jeff Winters. "Homosexuals Are Not a People." *ONE Magazine* 1:3, March 1953b, pp. 2–6.

Jennings, Dale, writing as Hieronymous K. "The Mattachine." *ONE Magazine* 1:1, January 1953c, pp. 18-19.

Jennings, Dale. "To Be Accused Is to Be Guilty." *ONE Magazine* 1:1, January 1953d, pp. 10-13.

Jennings, Dale. *The Cowboys*. New York: Stein and Day, 1971.

Jennings, Dale. *The Ronin*. Japan: Charles E. Tuttle, Co., Inc., 1968.

Katz, Jonathan Ned. *Gay American History: Lesbians and Gay Men in the U.S.A.: A Documentary*, Revised Edition. New York: Meridian, 1976/1992.

Kepner, James. "Goals, Progress and Shortcomings of America's Gay Movement." Self-published lecture, July 1994.

Licata, Salvatore J. "The Homosexual Rights Movement in the United States: A Traditionally Overlooked Area of American History." *Journal of Homosexuality*, 6:1-2, pp. 161-189. Binghamton, NY: The Haworth Press, 1981.

Legg, W. Dorr, Editor. *Homophile Studies in Theory and Practice*. San Francisco: GLB Publishers and ONE Institute Press, 1994.

Mortenson, George Henry. "Random Notes About the Pioneering Movement of Gay Rights." ONE Institute and Archives, HIC collection. Unpublished essay dated June 22, 2000.

Timmons, Stuart. *The Trouble with Harry Hay: Founder of the Modern Gay Movement*. Los Angeles: Alyson Publications, 1990.

Timmons, Stuart. Personal communication: Eulogy for Dale Jennings, at ONE Institute and Archives in Los Angeles, July 25, 2000.

The personal papers of Dale Jennings are housed in the Homosexual Information Center within ONE Institute and Archives in Los Angeles.

W. Dorr Legg (1904-1994)

Wayne R. Dynes

One of the founders of the modern American gay movement, W. Dorr Legg served the cause until his death. Legg's experience had an extraordinary span, for he lived in every decade of the twentieth century. He witnessed World War I, the Great Depression, World War II, and the profound social changes that began in the 1950s, including the civil rights movement. From his base in Los Angeles, he tenaciously fostered the rise of the American gay movement, guiding its most durable organization, ONE, Inc., through many unanticipated storms and discouraging setbacks.

Once he got started no one could challenge Dorr for dedication and stamina. Yet he was a late starter. Only in his forties did Dorr Legg take his place as a leading pioneer in what he preferred to term "homophile" activism and scholarship. At the height of his career in the 1970s he was a lanky, balding man who, apart from his height, would scarcely attract attention in a crowd. He refused to "send up flares," as he termed the extravagance some displayed to announce their homosexual identity. Yet he remained clear and forthright about who he was and what he was doing. For the shy and retiring, his stalwart and unstereotypical persona tacitly attested that participation in the movement was open to everyone.

Beneath the veneer of blandness lay a core of steel. In the little world of homophile activism Dorr Legg's life recalls the career of the founder of a small nation-state. One might think of Syngman Rhee (1875-1965), for example, first president of Korea, or Hastings Banda (1905-1997), who exercised the same office in Malawi. They began with a tiny band of followers, sticking to their task through thick and thin. For long years their endeavor seemed quixotic. More conventional personalities would have given up. Yet when the time came they were ready to play a major role, but the sequel was less glorious. Clinging imperiously to power, Rhee and Banda wore out their welcome through their rigidity and arrogance.

Although it came to occupy a four-acre estate in west-central Los Angeles, the ONE, Inc., of Dorr Legg was never an independent country. Still, Dorr maintained his position at the helm through policies not unlike those of Rhee and Banda. Rarely venturing beyond his office, where he received visitors with an almost imperial assurance, Legg was without question a "control freak." As a leader he showed exemplary courage and dedication; he was incorruptible and unswerving, but ultimately he failed to change with the times.

A serious intellectual, Legg crafted an original strategy of homophile activism and scholarship. Repeatedly he found himself obliged to defend his approach, which he did with steadiness and application. Gradually, almost imperceptibly, though, steadfastness modulated into rigidity. ONE seemed to many to be an anachronism in the post-Stonewall world despite continuing accomplishments.

At ONE, Inc., Dorr Legg encountered not one but two challenges that tested his mettle. The first began in 1965 when a group of dissidents attempted to take over the organization. The second crisis stretches through the 1980s until 1993, as the adventurism of a former benefactor threatened to deprive ONE of its headquarters.

A founder of what was to become the Log Cabin Club, the gay Republican group, Dorr Legg sometimes seemed intent on polishing his retro image. Yet in some respects he was ahead of his time, for he anticipated the rise in the 1990s of the nonleft gays such as Bruce Bawer and Andrew Sullivan.

At the core of Legg's Republicanism was a libertarian distrust of government. This distrust led him to throw two FBI agents out of the ONE office when they sought to intimidate him. He also reversed the efforts of the United States Post Office to keep *ONE* from the mails. Unfortunately, however, toward the end of his life, his antigovernment instincts led him to refuse to fill out forms needed to secure the continuation of the status of ONE Institute. In following this principle of resistance, and in other ways, he sometimes went too far.

Dorr Legg also ranks as a pioneer of interracial understanding. The Knights of the Clocks, his first organization, was biracial, black and white. As a rule his partners were either African American or Asian. He established his credentials in this realm long before it became fashionable, and long before militancy and infighting took their toll.

Fulfilling his duties at ONE, Inc., Dorr demonstrated fidelity for forty years, six days a week. Running ONE was like riding a bicycle; you had to keep going so as not to fall off. At the price of a certain rigidity, he resisted volatility in the movement, a problem which has, if anything, increased in recent years.

The future homophile leader came into the world as William Lambert Dorr Legg in Ann Arbor, Michigan, on December 15, 1904, the second son of Frances C. Dorr and Frank E. Legg. His father had settled in the university town as a manufacturer of pianos. From the lively family circle the boy learned to take pride in his forebears, for his family roots in North America stretched back to pre-Revolutionary times. One of Dorr's ancestors was reputedly involved in Shays' Rebellion (1786-1787), an antigovernment rising in western Massachusetts.

In Ann Arbor the family circle kept up with national issues, including the tragedies of lynching in the South. From these discussions Dorr developed a concern with discrimination against Americans of color. His commitment gradually converged with his sexual interests which included, although were not limited to, African Americans.

When he was ten or eleven his father began to take him on his rounds to collect rents from the small properties he owned. This experience prepared him for his later role as financial monitor of ONE, which he proudly asserted had never been accused of fiscal irregularity—a common problem with many gay and lesbian organizations.

In those years Michigan glowed in a general sense of prosperity and accomplishment. The state's farmers, generally of northwestern European stock, struggled with the difficult climate to produce bumper crops. Alongside agriculture, industry flourished, famously in the manufacture of automobiles, with Henry Ford as its standard bearer. Michiganders took pride in their universities, arguably the finest of the state-supported institutions in the Midwest. At the age of sixteen Dorr enrolled in the University of Michigan where he took a double major in landscape architecture and music. The music studies involved memorization of intricate compositions of Johann Sebastian Bach. To this training Dorr attributed his remarkable power of memory, which proved crucial in reconstructing the membership lists of ONE, Inc., after a dissident group made off with the organization's records in 1965.

Like many other young people in quest for self-knowledge, he recalled cautiously straying from the beaten path—in his case it was reading in the library. Before it was translated into English he read Marcel Proust's novel *Remembrance of Things Past* in the original French so as to learn something of homosexual life in Europe.

Taking several years off to participate in the real estate boom in Florida as a landscaper, Dorr was graduated from the University of Michigan in 1928. He settled at once in New York City, where he worked for an architectural firm. He found the manners of the "queens" circles to be fussy and pretentious: in his mind they were still trying to keep alive the manners of Oscar Wilde's set without adjusting to the times. He did take the opportunity to read Radclyffe Hall's then notorious lesbian novel, *The Well of Loneliness,* shortly after its American publication, and to frequent the Broadway theater, where productions then could be quite daring. There were speakeasies and, above all, drag balls in Harlem. It was at such places and events that Dorr began to explore the link between gay social life and the almost equally taboo world of black-white friendships.

In 1935 he was appointed an assistant professor of landscape architecture at the State University of Oregon in Eugene. The following seven years saw a quiet but satisfying round of teaching and small social gatherings. During World War II, though, the college shrank as the draft siphoned off many if not most of its students, and the program he was in more or less collapsed.

Rather than hanging on in Oregon, he chose to return to Michigan, settling for a time in Detroit to be close to his aging parents. There he developed a relationship with a young black man and, to his dismay, he found that the pair, even though they appeared reasonably "straight," could not walk down the street together without eliciting hostile questioning by the police, who regarded any kind of black-and-white friendships as an anomaly, suspecting such relationships as having criminal overtones. Perhaps the fact that Dorr's lover, Marvin E., was strikingly handsome further piqued the officers' attention.

Such reactions precipitated Dorr's resolve to find another place to live. But where? After extensive research, he concluded that Southern California would be best, not only for the racial aspect and its climate, but he also believed that the postwar boom would fuel the economy and jobs in his field would be plentiful. Accordingly, he and Marvin set out for Los Angeles by car in 1948 and, following instructions of friends who had been there before, they drove straight down Wilshire Boulevard to the gay beach at Santa Monica which was thronged with happy bathers. Repeatedly over the years Dorr recalled his astonished pleasure at the joyfulness and camaraderie of the scene. For him this was indeed "the place."

While conditions in black-white relationships and socialization in Los Angeles surpassed those in most parts of the United States, they were still far from ideal. To be sure, a bar, the Piccadilly on Pico Boulevard near Western Avenue, fostered contacts between black and white gay men. Other bars flourished at the beach itself, where the special atmosphere of the Tropical Village (or "TV" as insiders called it) still enjoys a fond place in recollections of many older gays. There was always a diverse crowd gathered to be entertained by jazz pianists, drag entertainers, and comedians. Dorr and Marvin also visited predominantly black nightclubs on Central Avenue in East Los Angeles, the Los Angeles counterpart to Harlem.

As Dorr began to put down roots in his new city, he developed a number of gay black friends. One of them, a young accountant named Merton Bird, suggested that they form a social organization. Meeting for the first time, apparently in early 1950, they took the name Knights of the Clocks, attracting blacks and whites. Attendance, however, rarely surpassed ten members and the aims of the group were not political.

Later in the same year Dorr learned of a gay group that was decidedly political, the Mattachine Society, which had been founded by Harry Hay and four colleagues. In keeping with the Masonic principle of organization favored by the group, Dorr soon garnered an invitation to join the Fifth Order. Two years later, on October 15, 1952, a group of mostly Mattachine members attended a private party where the participants decided to start a monthly magazine, *ONE*. Although he did not realize it then, this event was to determine the rest of his life. In April 1953 he quit his job to become a full-time business manager of the newly organized ONE, Inc., at a salary, when it was paid, of twenty-five dollars a month.

A number of talented people joined in editing the managing including Eve Elloree, Jim Kepner, Ann Carll Reid, Sten Russell (Stella Rush), Dale Jennings, and Don Slater. They worked in offices on the third floor of a rickety old building on Hill Street in the decaying downtown area of Los Angeles. The door always stood open for people to drop in and, after overcoming their initial trepidation, many did.

ONE Magazine had to surmount an early challenge when the postmaster of Los Angeles declared it unmailable. After considerable legal maneuvering, the United States Supreme Court ruled in *ONE*'s favor in 1958. The case ranks as the first gay success before that august body, and the opening wedge for the distribution of much more sexually explicit material.

Similar to many contributors to the magazine, Dorr sometimes published work under pseudonyms, giving the impression that more writers participated than was actually the case. Dorr's monikers included Hollister Barnes, Richard Congar, Marvin Cutler, W. G. Hamilton, William Lambert (an abbreviation of his full name), Wendy Lane, Valentine Richardson, and Sidney Rothman. Under the name of Marvin Cutler, Legg edited a landmark survey of the international gay movement titled *Homosexuals Today: A Handbook of Organizations and Publications* (1956). When the American gay movement began in Los Angeles in 1950 its founders knew little of their European counterparts, but six years later *Homosexuals Today* demonstrated that *ONE* was up to speed. In due course the group organized a series of European and Asian trips for gays and lesbians, allowing direct contact with movement figures and groups in other countries.

ONE, Inc., was also conceived by Dorr as an educational institution, and he and others began offering classes on homosexuality. These were given wide publicity but the overall response was disappointing and few students actually came. Legg preferred the term "homophile studies" and emphasized an interdisciplinary methodology. He believed that the approach prevailing at universities, in which homosexuality was often included as part of a course, only fragmented the subject by dividing it along conventional departmental lines. Moreover, universities, he believed, could not be relied upon to study homosexual behavior and culture both fairly and comprehensively and institutions such as ONE, maintained by homosexuals themselves, were essential.

Finances remained a chronic, often urgent problem, and appeals were made for private donors. Most of the donations were small in scale. In the summer of 1964, however, Dorr received an urgent request that ONE, Inc., send a representative to Louisiana to discuss funding. Finding that no one else would go, Dorr borrowed a suit and flew to New Orleans at the donor's expense. At the airport he was met by a young man who introduced himself as Reed Erickson, who took him to his home near Baton Rouge and told him that he must first meet Henry before any real discussion could ensue. Assuming that Henry was Erickson's lover, Dorr blanched when he found that instead Henry was a leopard. After wrestling for a bit with his animal companion, Erickson invited Dorr to touch the beast's head, which he did with some trepidation. Later, after some informal conversation with his host, Dorr was told that ONE would get some money. Erickson said he made a fortune in the oil business and had set up the Reed Erickson Educational Foundation to give out money to gay and other causes. This foundation became the main financial support of ONE.

Only in the course of time did Dorr learn that Reed Erickson had been formerly Rita Alma Erickson and had been one of the first to undergo surgery to change from female to male. Later Erickson moved to Mexico and finally to Ojai, north of Los Angeles, from which post he sought to exercise a more direct influence over the organization he had benefited.

For several years during the early 1960s ONE, after moving to new and commodious headquarters on Venice Boulevard, had a fairly placid existence, only disturbed from time to time by the need to oppose police raids and other hostile acts from the straight world. Trouble, however, was brewing from within. Some members of the staff had come to resent what they regarded as Dorr's authoritarian style and feared that he might use the ONE elections scheduled for 1965 to extend his power over the organization. Although most members were prepared to tolerate Dorr's attitude because of his unflinching dedication to the cause, Don Slater, one of the most active editors, was not. On Easter Sunday of 1965 the dissidents, headed by Slater, who had a key to the premises, hired a truck and removed every file and the entire library from the Venice Boulevard headquarters to a new location in

Hollywood. When Dorr appeared for work on Monday morning, he found almost everything gone, including the full membership list with its addresses. Dorr turned his ability to memorize great chunks of information to his advantage and reconstructed many of the names and addresses, informing members through mail and phone calls that a palace revolution had taken place, and that ONE was still in business. The ensuing legal proceedings were protracted. Dorr proved tenacious and unyielding, so much so that his tactics alienated the judge who might have been expected to rule in his favor. Instead, the judge ordered that the material be divided. Dorr's group could keep the name ONE, while the dissidents who had been publishing *ONE* during the trial changed their publication's name to *Tangents,* and adopted the official name of the Homosexual Information Center. Los Angeles now had two competing groups and magazines, and animosities only gradually died down. In a petty act of spite, one of the things not returned to ONE was Dorr's draft of his master's thesis on the sociology of homosexuality, and he never did get his degree.

To return to the comparison with leaders of emerging countries, Dorr found that although he had turned back the invaders, his domain was not what it had been. It proved impossible to keep publishing *ONE Magazine,* which sputtered out and disappeared in 1972, along with its scholarly twin, *ONE Institute Quarterly of Homophile Studies.* One of the landmark studies the group did complete and publish in 1976 was a project several years in the works, the two-volume *Annotated Bibliography of Homosexuality.* The 13,000 items included constituted a landmark in the gathering of information on the subject.

Drawing conclusions from his experiences, Dorr resolved never again to be dislodged from control of ONE. Each year he obtained from the board of directors a signed statement of wages due him—which he declined to collect. As these IOUs piled up, his position became more and more secure, as no one could raise the money to redeem them. His defense might have been that having been labeled an autocrat, he might as well behave as one. But the tactic exposed an enduring character trait, a kind of libido dominandi, whereby he sought to control his surroundings, not always with the proper sensitivity to changing circumstances. Gradually, the membership became older and more rigid, mirroring the leader himself.

For many years ONE functioned out of its second floor office in an increasingly shabby building on Venice Boulevard in central Los Angeles. The depressed neighborhood undoubtedly discouraged some visitors, but ONE was open during business hours for consultation with staff and visitors to make use of the large but uneven Blanche M. Baker Memorial Library. This availability also characterized the rival Tangents group, which for some years maintained an office on Cahuenga Boulevard in Hollywood, and later on Hollywood Boulevard itself. In the latter place, however, the office hours were more irregular.

Some events continued to take place: regularly monthly meetings with lectures, occasional conferences, and classes. These last, some observers felt, had a certain Potemkin village aspect. The classes tended to attract only two or three persons, but figures given out to the public suggested considerably more. In public relations, Dorr sought to put the best face on things, hoping that better times would eventually come. In the 1970s and 1980s such an advance seemed unlikely, as Dorr and his associates did little to assimilate themselves to the headier currents of gay liberation. In his speech and writing Dorr continued to prefer the term "homophile" rather than "homosexual" or "gay." It goes without saying that he shunned the 1990s fashion for "queer studies."

It was the continuing connection with Reed Erickson, the wealthy transsexual philanthropist, that opened the possibility of breaking the log jam. Concerned that the Venice Boulevard premises were increasingly shabby and inadequate and in a neighborhood perceived as unsafe, Erickson encouraged Dorr to seek a better location. The result was the purchase of a turn-of-the-twentieth-century estate in Los Angeles on Country Club Drive. Erickson bought the property outright with bags of South African gold coins and announced his attention to give it to ONE. The staff moved the library in, made plans for a museum, and considered creating quarters for resident research scholars. Attendance at the monthly lectures increased. Even before the move, Legg and his associates had obtained authorization from the state of California to award the PhD degree, and Dorr himself had assumed the post of Dean of the ONE Graduate School. Several dissertations were written and degrees granted, but again disaster struck.

A falling out with Reed Erickson, in part because of Dorr's intransigence about sharing part of the property with transsexuals, caused the benefactor to withdraw his de facto donation of the Country Club Drive property. Because there was no written agreement, legal proceedings became unavoidable. It was in retrospect a vicious battle; at one point Dorr was locked in at the premises for a week because Erickson had the gates welded shut. In 1993 the courts ruled that the estate be divided. ONE received two of the four acres and the smaller of the two houses. It was something of a Pyrrhic victory, for of necessity the school and research facilities had been neglected during the years of legal wrangling.

But the neglect was scarcely total. During those hectic years, Dorr Legg and his associates—David G. Cameron, Walter L. Williams, and Donald C. Paul—found time to compile and publish a major volume, *Homophile Studies in Theory and Practice,* which Dorr fortunately lived to see published. This book is both a detailed record of the academic achievement of

ONE Institute of Homophiles Studies and a statement of the underlying philosophy. It is one of the rare comprehensive documents of a gay and lesbian organization that has been produced by its creators and sustainers themselves.

Dorr died peacefully in his sleep in his Los Angeles home on July 26, 1994. He was survived by his partner, Japanese-American John Nojima, who had faithfully supported him financially and morally for thirty years. Appropriately, the Los Angeles City Council observed a moment of silence.

Shortly after Dorr's death ONE merged with the International Archives that had long been valiantly conducted by Jim Kepner, who had originally deposited much of his material with ONE and later withdrawn it after a falling out with Legg. The new group, termed ONE/IGLA for short, enjoys the support of the University of Southern California.

As Dorr might have predicted, the experiences of the enlarged group have been neither easy nor smooth. But with dedicated workers the enterprise is under way, continuing and expanding Dorr's legacy. His motto, and that of his beloved ONE, would fittingly be Latin, *Per ardua ad astra*—through difficulties to the stars.

BIBLIOGRAPHY

Bullough, Vern, Barrett W. Elcano, W. Dorr Legg, and James Kepner, (Eds.), *An Annotated Bibliography of Homosexuality*. 2 Volumes, New York: Garland, 1976.

Cutler, Marvin (W. Dorr Legg), (Ed.), *Homosexuals Today: A Handbook of Organizations and Publications*. Los Angeles: One, Inc., 1956.

Legg, W. Dorr. "Exploring Frontiers: An American Tradition," *New York Folklore*, 19 (1993), 217-236 (autobiographical account).

Legg, W. Dorr, David G. Cameron, Walter L. Williams, and Donald C. Paul, (Eds.), *Homophile Studies in Theory and in Practice*. Los Angeles: ONE Institute Press and San Francisco: GLB Publishers, 1994.

Don Slater (1923-1997)

Joseph Hansen

In January 1953, sixteen long years before the much-ballyhooed drag-queen rebellion at the Stonewall Inn on New York's Christopher Street, Don Slater, with the help of a handful of friends with more idealism than good sense, quietly launched from a modest side-street bungalow in Los Angeles the first openly publicly sold magazine for homosexuals in the United States, *ONE*.

This was the true spearhead of the American homosexual movement. It awakened homosexual men and women all across the country to a sense of who they were, that they were not alone but everywhere, and were not outsiders, not criminals, but citizens with equal rights under the law, deserving decent treatment from the society in which they lived and to which they contributed.

So bringing *ONE Magazine* into existence and by whatever means possible getting it out into the world was Don Slater's first towering achievement. His second, at least as important, was to gain for us all the right to send through the U.S. mail printed matter dealing with homosexuality.

No, I don't mean pornography. The mind-set of postal authorities and the courts in the reactionary 1950s was that the very concept of homosexuality was pornographic, nasty, disgusting, repugnant, unacceptable, un-Christian, and un-American. Freedom of the mail (and of the press) was for nice, normal people—not homosexuals. Don Slater turned this around. And no, this is not a myth.

Don Slater was born August 21, 1923, at Pasadena Hospital, in the staid, tree-shaded California town of that name, at one minute past 2 a.m., the firstborn of twin boys, the second being Harvey. Their father was Warren Steven Slater, age thirty-nine; their mother Katherine Fairen Slater, age thirty-five. The couple had come to California from Connecticut in 1920, and were already the parents of a son and a daughter when Don and Harvey arrived.

Warren Slater made his living as an athletic director at YMCAs and Boys Clubs in Pasadena, Glendale, Los Angeles, and Oceanside. Although never out of work during the Great Depression, he moved around a lot and all those moves from town to town, job to job, make it hard to trace which schools Don attended. He ended his public education in Capistrano Beach at Chaffey High as a member of the class of 1942.

To be a young man graduating from high school in that year meant only one thing: Uncle Sam wanted you. Whether in the Army, Navy, Air Force, Marines, or Coast Guard, your future was laid out for you, in a nice, neat uniform. That Don ended up at Camp Hale, Colorado, as a ski-trooper trainee suggests that Coach Slater, as his father was known, must have done some telephoning to friends in high places. Warren Slater owned a ski lodge on Mt. Baldy, and Don had skied from an early age, so what branch of the armed services could have suited him better?

Don was inducted in February 1943 among snow-covered Rocky Mountain Peaks. He had what looks from snapshots to have been a lively and louche time with his buddies, then developed rheumatic fever, was put to bed in the infirmary with his "heart beating double-time," and after a few weeks was honorably discharged. This was October 19, 1943, and rifleman Private Don Slater had served his country for exactly eight months and three days.

Whatever went on in those very temporary-looking barracks after lights out between Don and his frisky young friends, evidently the officers didn't know or didn't care about. One has written in the blank labeled Character on Don's discharge papers, "Excellent," which, of course, it was, and would always remain.

Maybe Don chose the University of Southern California as the place to enroll in February 1944 because the campus sprawls through the heart of old Los Angeles, and Don loved old Los Angeles, the more run-down and ragged the better. There was then nothing distinguished about the college. Anyway, Don didn't pay a lot of attention to his studies. He worked in the library, but he also spent riotous nights with Hal Bargelt and other members of the university's "gay underground" boozing in the bars on sleazy Main Street. "He enjoyed the transvestites," Bargelt recalls, and was as friendly with them and the other lost souls adrift in the gritty shadows of Main Street's gaudy neon as he was with his fellow students by day.

Always impish, in college Don's devil-may-care attitude got him into frequent hot water. All his life he would love thumbing his nose at authority. At USC, he collected traffic tickets like trophies, then decided to act like Thoreau, refuse to pay the fines, and go to jail for civil disobedience. His position was that the state had no business telling him where he could park. Far graver was his naive mistake in letting someone photograph his trim swimmer's body naked and sexually aroused. The photos fell into wicked hands, and for the next half-dozen years Don paid blackmail to keep his sexuality from harming his father's reputation. Don had bought a brand new shiny Ford convertible about that time. He loved it, and his friends couldn't understand why he kept it only a month. Now at this later date they know it was because of blackmail.

Rheumatic fever revisited him in 1948, causing him to miss classes. He was a "high senior" and didn't want to flunk out, so he asked for time to rest, recover, then start the term over. As anyone who knew Don Slater would expect, he chose an unlikely means of rest. A friend, Ernest Carter, found a newspaper ad offering young men a chance to see the world at no cost by signing on as hands aboard a freighter. Don jumped at it, an action which did not sit well with Tony Reyes.

Tony had been a baby-faced, slim-hipped, Tex-Mex high school student of sixteen who dreamed of being a dancer when he and Don met in the shaggy tree shadows of nighttime Pershing Square in the heart of downtown Los Angeles, where each of them was on the prowl for sex. The year was 1945. Twenty years later Don told it to me this way in a conversation I had with him:

> We kept skulking around in the underbrush and, AAGH! bumping into each other. "What, you again?" Finally, we couldn't stop laughing, and we decided we must be meant for each other, and we never changed our minds.

Still, Don did take off with Carter on this very different sort of cruise, and although Tony was hurt, their relationship survived. "Our love affair was just beginning." Actually, it was three years old by this time, and he and Don, after living for a spell in Don's parents' ski lodge, had settled into rented rooms in a refurbished Victorian mansion on Bunker Hill, "a few doors west of Hope"—a statement he often used because of the nearby Hope Street, a main north-south thoroughfare. It had originally been part of a triad of streets, Faith, Hope, and Charity, of which only Hope had survived.

However, in 1948 Don had his *Wanderjahr* in the best Eugene O'Neill style, going ashore to explore the waterfronts of Oslo, Stockholm, Bremen, Le Havre, Marseilles, and other fabled ports of call. How long was he gone? Six months, at least, maybe nine. Whenever he returned, he was soon back in college.

After graduating with a BA in English literature (he specialized in the Victorian novel; whenever later in life I would ask him if he'd read my newest book, he would protest that he still hadn't gotten through the collected works of Edward Bulwer-Lytton), Don took a job at Pasadena's stuffiest bookshop, Vroman's. He had to wear a tie. The pay was fifty cents an hour. Tony, meanwhile, danced at the El Paseo nightclub on Olvera Street, a crooked, humpy brick lane between eighteenth-century houses lined with vendors' booths selling everything from serapes and huaraches to tortillas and beans. Mariachi bands, tooting trumpets, and strumming guitars wandered through in huge sombreros. In those days, Olvera Street not only drew tourists but the movie crowd. El Paseo was their main watering hole, and Tony became a favorite of many of these tinsel types who invited him to parties at their showy Hollywood Hills mansions. Lonely women of a certain type seemed to idolize Tony, and paid the management to have him join them at their tables for a drink, and to have their photos taken with him. As Tony said: "Don didn't like it, but the extra money was nice. And Don used to bring his friends to see me dance. That made me happy. My heart lifted, and I always danced my best on those nights" (Hansen, 1998, p. 17).

Among the friends he brought was tall, lanky Bill Lambert (W. Dorr Legg), then in his late forties, who fascinated Don with his erudition and his way with words. "He had charm and poise and manners," Tony remembers, "and was clever." He was an initiate of a circle of homosexuals that called itself the Mattachine, after a troupe of medieval mimes. Lambert took Don and Tony to a meeting one night. "A sewing circle," Don said afterward. "The Stitch and Bitch Club." More formally, and forty-odd years later, he wrote in a letter dated May 3, 1995:

> I had gone to a few of the Mattachine meetings and was disappointed. We were only talking to ourselves. I was perfectly content with my sexual conduct, had always been. I was not interested in self-serving self-pity. We needed to address the general public. *ONE Magazine* [became] our medium.

ONE came into being on a November night in 1952, and by January 1953 the first issue was printed by Dale Jennings' sister and her husband in their basement. Finding a professional typesetter-printer willing to risk association with the magazine was difficult. At the place they finally found, Don told me years afterward, "the linotypist was a frail little old man with thick glasses. And we all roared when we saw the first galleys. Every time he'd come to the forbidden word, his skills had failed him. Over and over again he wrote 'homoseeeeeexual!'"

Newsdealers were just as shocked: "A what-kinda magazine? What are you—trying to get me arrested?" So Don Slater, Bill Lambert, Tony Reyes, Martin Block, and a brave handful of others took a deep breath, squared their shoulders, and did what they had to do. Each to a different section of the sprawling city, they trudged the empty night streets from one gay tavern to the next, peddling copies from bar stool to bar stool, from the sober to the drunk, from the business-suited john to the muscle-boy hustler, to the drag queen, to the wispy, bespectacled closet case with a picture of his mother in his wallet.

It seems a safe bet that none of their customers had entered his or her favorite gay bar that chilly January night looking for something to read. Still, this brand of reading had never been offered before. If nothing else, it had curiosity value. Copies were twenty-five cents each, the price of a beer. And Tony Reyes swears that the amateur peddlers all came home with pockets jingling.

"Listen to me, Don," *ONE*'s consulting attorney had said, "you can't print fiction. Your charter says you're education. You give anybody the idea that you're printing entertainment, you're dead. Catering to the perverted, that's what they call it" (Hansen, 1998, p. 29).

Don chafed under this restraint. He loved fiction. What kind of magazine didn't print fiction? After a few months, he couldn't stand it any longer and in the July issue printed what Ross Ingersoll (*ONE,* January 1962) called a harmless little tale, "But They'll Outgrow It," by David Freeman.

Wouldn't you know, with the very next (August 1962) issue of the magazine came the first hint of trouble. The magazine was held up at the post office, and Don had to hire a lawyer to get the copies released, which took three weeks. Next time the post office acted, it would take three years!

ONE at least found offices they could afford to rent: two seedy rooms in a ratty old building of garment sweatshops on Hill Street in one of the sadder sections of downtown Los Angeles. Desks, chairs, and shelving were donated, and as sand ran through the hourglass, typewriters, a mimeograph, and other equipment were procured as well, and the two seedy rooms expanded to six as the library, which took up a lot of space, kept growing.

Under a dozen pen names, to make readers believe the magazine had many writers, Don, Bill Lambert, and other stalwarts turned out all sorts of copy. Energetic staffer Jim Kepner was Lyn Pederson and Del MacIntire as well as himself. Robert Gregory was a name kept for random use when imagination flagged. Gregory was on the staff; Gregory was this, that, and the other functionary. He didn't exist.

Determined to keep in the background although the dominant force, Don put witty New Yorker Martin Block into the editor's chair first. When Block quit after six months, the sardonic playwright-novelist Dale Jennings stepped in. When he quit in February 1954, Ann Carll Reid, who took the post seriously, worked hard and well, and kept at it until 1958 when her health failed. Don, with a sigh, took on the job that fate had meant for him from the start.

ONE was consistently supported by women, not only Ann Carll Reid, but Eve Elloree, for many years its art director. Other women included the poet Helen Ito and writers Elizabeth Lalo, Geraldine Jackson, Alison Hunter, and Sten Russell (Stella Rush). In February 1954, an entire issue, "The Feminine Viewpoint," appeared, written by, for, and about women and thereafter a column with that title was a frequent feature of the magazine.

"Meantime," wrote Ross Ingersoll (ONE, January 1962), "the going was rough. There was never enough money, never enough good publishable material [magazines that cannot pay contributors are prone to this problem] and there was never enough help [ONE depended on volunteers], which meant there was never enough time. The October 1954 issue notified readers 'there would be no August or September issues that year. All subscriptions would be extended for two months.'"

That October issue turned out to be a historic document. Assertedly because of a lukewarm lesbian love story and some crude comic verses, "here was the issue which Otto K. Oleson, the Los Angeles postmaster," according to Ross Ingersoll (ONE, January 1962), "felt he could legally refuse and safely label 'obscene.'"

Had Don Slater asked for it? On the cover is the screamer, "You Can't Print It," plugging an article inside by ONE's legal counsel detailing the "laws of mailable matter." To read it today is to be flabbergasted at how little freedom Americans had at that time, but it was a red flag to Postmaster Oleson. He impounded the issue and sent a copy to the solicitor general in Washington, DC who had found in ONE's favor last time, but not this time.

A keen young attorney, Eric Julber, went to bat for ONE, bringing a court action against Oleson, enjoining him from interfering with the mailing of the magazine. After a year's delay, U.S. District Court Judge Thurman Clarke ruled that the October 1954 issue was nonmailable because it contained "filthy and obscene material obviously calculated to stimulate the lust of the homosexual reader" (Hansen, 1998, p. 37). Julber, fully aware that ONE could not afford to pay him but sensing a landmark civil rights case was involved, appealed the verdict. And after another year, in March 1957, the Ninth Circuit Court of Appeals in San Francisco affirmed the lower court verdict, adding some colorful language of their own. ONE's board of directors grew restive. Some at ONE were ready to give up, but not Don Slater and not Eric Julber. Julber bought his own plane ticket to Washington and filed a brief with the U.S. Supreme Court. "Maybe they'll look at it," Eric told Don, "and maybe they won't. They only handle about one in a hundred of the cases submitted for review."

"You know how to cheer a man up," Don said.

"It's all right," Julber said. "They'll love this one. It's a chance to write law" (Hansen, 1998, p. 37).

It was, and they did. On January 13, 1958, without hearing oral arguments, by unanimous decision the United States Supreme Court reversed the lower court findings, concluding that the October 1954 issue of *ONE Magazine* was not in fact obscene, but was an exercise of American free speech. Ross Ingersoll wrote in *ONE* (January 1962),

> *ONE*'s own victory was tremendous, but it pales alongside the overall gains which came with this decision. The real, the basic, the honest and fundamental issue resolved was that the mention, the treatment, in fact and in fiction, of homosexuality was not in and of itself obscene.

Commented *The New York Times,* "The decision means that the Supreme Court is insisting on a rigorous, narrow definition of 'obscenity.' It means, as one lawyer put it, that 'the court is going to keep a weather eye out itself, to prevent censorship of anything, but what might be called hard-core pornography' " (Hansen, 1998, pp. 37-38).

ONE, if it ever would, now had that destined fifteen minutes of fame of which Andy Warhol spoke. Subscriptions increased, and in more and more cities the modest little periodical began perching on news racks like a sparrow among peacocks. Dare we think there was even a little income? Probably not much. Still, luck had not run out. In 1962, Morgan Farley, the actor, located (and I expect, knowing Morgan, paid the first month's rent on) a large, sunny office space for ONE, Inc., above a neighborhood tavern on Venice Boulevard.

The magazine and all the accumulated trappings of its first ten years were hauled downstairs from the gloomy, crowded old Hill Street place, loaded into moving vans, and trucked southwestward and upstairs again into its new quarters on May 1, 1962. Bill Lambert waxed ecstatic and wrote an editorial about the crowning of the May Queen. Did he mean himself? Certainly Don believed that Lambert's delusions of grandeur set in about this time.

ONE was always a penny-ante operation. Money had never been the object. The object had been to make the world a better place for homosexuals. Rarely was anyone paid at *ONE.* If they had an extra dime, they were expected to put it in the pot. The rent, the light bill, the printer's bill were always a problem. If the printer was not paid, the magazine did not appear. There were scary moments. Would there ever be a next issue?

At the same time, Bill Lambert was "magicked" by the new place with its wonderful large central room. He could hold seminars in it. Conducted by himself. With famous guest speakers. Some of the surrounding cubicles could be converted to classrooms where he could teach. He visualized these rather stark accommodations as ivied halls, a new university—a new university devoted solely to "homophile studies." (Lambert loved that word: it got rid of the nasty "sexual" part that so put off the, uh, heterophiles.)

The charter had specified that the main function of ONE was to publish a magazine. Now, Lambert decided, that would change. When a list of ONE's functions was painted on the door at the new place, education came first. With no money to pay instructors, where would the staff come from? Why, he would teach socioscientific courses; Morgan Farley could teach theatre; Don Slater (listed in the prospectus as having "traveled widely in Europe and the Orient") could teach literature; tireless Jim Kepner and other volunteers could be roped in to make a faculty. For the fact that the magazine had been the sole excuse for ONE's existence, had brought it friends and supporters all across America, had alerted the establishment that homosexuals were part of the warp and weft of society and had rights the same as everyone else, and were now, not unreasonably, asking for those rights—Bill Lambert suddenly cared nothing. He would build his hallowed Institute of Homophile Studies above that dusty saloon on Venice Boulevard, and teach the Truth to a happy few (and few they always would be), expenses be damned.

Strangely, Lambert's dream would soon come true, financed by Reed Erickson, a transsexual oil millionaire. In the meantime, Bill Lambert destroyed *ONE Magazine*. With so little money to go around, a trade-off was inevitable. At first, Lambert simply resigned from the editorial board, leaving Don Slater in sole charge of the magazine, while he, now dropping his pseudonym of Lambert, became W. Dorr Legg, Dean of the Institute.

Don shrugged. If Lambert could find the nickels and dimes to make his dream a reality, he didn't mind. I had been writing stories regularly for *ONE*, and Don brought me into replace Legg on the editorial board. I was pleased, because I felt the magazine needed to liven up its contents, to slick up its looks, and to reach a general readership, not just a gay one. Don agreed. He just hadn't the steam to handle all the work alone.

I began coming to the office to help out in early afternoons, before I went to my job. There were stacks of manuscripts to be read and responded to. There were letters weeks old that had to be answered. There were accepted manuscripts to be edited. There were proofs to be read; dummies to be pasted up. No one else was around to do these things, so I did them.

Usually the only other being in the vast bare-walled reaches of ONE's headquarters would be Bill Lambert, and I would give him a cheerful

"Hello," when I arrived at the top of the stairs. He never answered me. He never even looked my way. Later, I understood why. My desire to breathe new excitement into the magazine was for him at best a nuisance, at worst a threat to his private plans. He wanted *ONE Magazine* to die.

To recount the details here exactly how he managed to kill it would take too long, and the details would bore you silly. But by the time Don realized that Lambert wanted total control of the organization the two of them had built and always (he thought) comfortably shared—it was too late. By foxy parliamentary maneuvering, Lambert had won. Not only had Don's friends on the board of directors been dumped and replaced by Lambert's lackeys, but Lambert then, on Easter eve, 1965, barged in on a work session of the magazine's editors and fired us all.

Don, after talking to a lawyer to be sure he was within his rights, staged a midnight raid and hauled off everything worth taking from ONE to quarters he had rented in Cahuenga Pass in Hollywood. Lambert went to court, but the judge impatiently calling this a "squabble between a couple of hysterical queens" gave the name ONE to Lambert and instructed Don to divide up the library and files with Lambert. The division began amicably until Lambert issued some letters calling "Queen Don" a thief, and then all bets were off.

The magazine was the important thing. Using *Tangents,* the name of the most popular feature of *ONE,* Don, Ross Ingersoll, Billy Glover, and I got the first issue out to subscribers of the old *ONE* and newsstands as fast as we could. The cover design by Jane Hansen showed a phoenix rising from the ashes. In a flurry of subpoenas and like nuisances, Don Slater, hardly stopping for breath, pressed on with his mission in life.

He was exhilarated to be out of the range of Bill Lambert's droning, "No, we tried that once, and it didn't work" negativity. One of the first actions was a motorcade through Los Angeles to protest the military's antigay policies. *The New York Times* took notice. Don formed a corporate basis for the Tangent Group called, with his usual matter-of-factness, Homosexual Information Center. He began counseling service people who had been unfairly discharged, even finding them defense lawyers. He kept this up doggedly for years, although he rarely won a case.

Bill Lambert's intemperate letters to *ONE*'s subscribers had divided them. Some stuck with Dorr Legg who soon ceased to publish a magazine altogether. Some others favored Don. Some said, "A pox on both your houses." Circulation dropped for *Tangents* and money, always a problem, became even more of a headache. I suggested we advertise. New people who needed us would subscribe, but first they had to know we existed.

Right away we hit a snag. While the *Nation,* a liberal New York-based magazine rather bemusedly accepted our advertisement, the *Los Angeles Times* refused it because they were a "family newspaper." Don, Billy

Glover, and I, along with Morris Kight, a gay community ombudsman, met with the paper's top brass and tried to convince them to change. They wouldn't budge. So we said we would have to picket them, and picket we did. The picketing was fun, but the paper ignored it.

This was the era of the hippies, the flower children, love-ins, the sexual revolution. While Lambert gasped in shock and firmly closed ONE's doors and pulled the shades down, Don invited even the rowdiest leaders of gay liberation to speak at *Tangents'* headquarters. I interviewed them for the magazine. We joined them at Griffith Park on summer Sundays where guitars and bongos played, and the young danced half-naked with flowers in their hair.

At the magazine, we began having lively exchanges with *Playboy*'s Hugh Hefner and other trendy editors who began treating sex behavior openly in their pages. When they showed prejudice or misunderstanding, Don was quick to send them his viewpoint, to straighten out their thinking. Leo Skir sent lively reportage and photos from New York and Fire Island on the youthful gay life there. Lee Atwill, a young film buff I'd met, agreed to write us a multipart history of Hollywood's treatment of homosexual themes in the movies with accompanying stills. Barbara Grier, writing as Gene Damon, reviewed stacks of current books each month, never missing a significant title. Sol Hirsch, our designer-printer, gave the magazine a sleek exciting appearance. Jane Hansen continued to provide stunning cover designs.

But *Tangents* remained a quiet, thoughtful voice, and quiet was no longer in style. The new-style gays were protesting, demonstrating, clowning, making a noise in the streets. The newspapers noticed, television noticed. Our subject was no longer our subject. Magazines such as *Cosmopolitan* that had never before dared to speak our name discussed homosexuality constantly, seriously, and with increasing balance and good sense.

Splashy color collections of photographs of naked young men hit the news racks. Neither *ONE* nor *Tangents* had ever offered such fare. In 1968 along came *The Advocate,* an inky tabloid for gays, with a thick advertising section selling sex, classified and unclassified, that paid its bills, even its staff. *Tangents* stopped selling. Copies came back from distributors by the carton full. It was time to pay off our long-suffering printer and close up shop, which we did in 1970.

"The day will never come when serious thinking and writing about homosexuality aren't needed," Don said. After moving from Cahuenga Boulevard to smaller and cheaper cramped upstairs offices on Hollywood Boulevard and later from his house, Don continued until his death to issue the *HIC Newsletter,* with his own relentless essays and scathing comments on the passing scene, and book reviews and others pieces by some of us who had written for his magazines.

He was interrupted in 1979 by his damaged heart and he had an artificial valve implanted at the veterans administration hospital. The transplant was successful but somehow during the surgical procedure Don was infected with hepatitis B, which nearly killed him. To aid in Don's recuperation, Norman Kelly, a retired interior decorator who had supported *Tangents* financially, took Don along with him on a cruise of Europe. An acquaintance Don made on that voyage insisted he accompany her to South Africa, where the apartheid policies then in force depressed him. Don made one more sea trip, a brief one to Brazil, seemingly on his own.

Then, three years later, leaving his office late one night, he was attacked in the dark parking lot in Hollywood, savagely beaten, and robbed. "Every bone in his face was broken," said Charles Lucas, the friend who found him that night. After that episode, Don moved HIC and its library and archives to his and Tony's house near Echo Park. Tony, to add to his income as an entertainer, was now working as a warehouseman for a book publisher.

For very little money he and Don bought a mountain cabin in Colorado with land around it and a stream running through. Don enjoyed the place thoroughly, rustic as it was. Sometimes alone, sometimes together, sometimes with friends, they spent a lot of time there every year, a part of it skiing. At home in Los Angeles, Don added to his menagerie of beloved cats and dogs a rooster named Calhoun. He liked gardening at home, and was often seen clambering around on his rooftop, patching it against the rains.

His doctors urged him that it was past time to replace his frayed heart valve, but he said that he felt fine. In fact, he was fearful that another surgery would mean another infection, so he kept putting off the procedure until it was too late. In December 1996, he suffered a massive heart attack and was carted off to the hospital. He tried to leave at Christmas but could not. Too run down for surgery, he lay in the hospital, visited often by Tony and other lifelong friends, dying on the night of February 14, 1997.

BIBLIOGRAPHY

Joseph Hansen, *A Few Doors West of Hope: The Life and Times of Dauntless Don Slater*. Universal City, CA: HIC, 1998 is the main source.

Other printed sources are back files of *ONE* (1953-1965), *Tangents* (1965-70); *HIC Newsletter* (1972-1996); and the booklet *Don Slater Remembered by His Friends,* Universal City: HIC, 1997.

In addition, Don's personal papers served as a source as did long conversations with William Edward "Billy" Glover, Don Slater's longtime aide-de-camp, now living in Louisiana. Tony Reyes, Don's life partner, now living in Colorado, shared letters and evocative photographs, as did his sister Marion S. Grandall, who now lives in northern California. Others who contributed were Hal Bargelt of Palm Springs and Howard Russell of Malibu, Ross Ingersoll, and Martin Block. I would like to dedicate this article to the memory of Martin Block, 1920-1995, a founder and first editor of *ONE*.

Jim Schneider (1932-   ):
ONE's Guardian Angel

C. Todd White

Historians of gay and lesbian history have often overlooked the more quiet heroes, the ones who kept their fingers on the pulse of the movement but guided its fate from outside the spotlight. Yet the key players of early gay history, namely Harry Hay, Jim Kepner, Don Slater, Dorr Legg, and Dale Jennings, ould not have accomplished their historic feats without the assistance of many diligent and dedicated workers. One of the first and most constant of those workers was Jim Schneider, whose involved commitment to the movement now spans forty years.

James Vernon Schneider was born on a family farm in Nebraska on April 4, 1932. He was second of seven children. His father was a dedicated worker who supported his family well through the depression. When Jim was thirteen, tragedy struck. His father was injured in a farm accident and was never able to walk again. A year earlier, his sister had been born mentally retarded. Much of the responsibility fell upon Jim and his elder brother who kept the family together until their father died in 1954.

Schneider grew up close to his family, but he often felt very isolated from the world. He sensed that something was wrong with him but couldn't quite place what it was. After his father's death, he moved to Oakland at a brother's invitation. Finding he had no tolerance for Oakland's perpetual fog, he moved after three months to Fresno and, after a year there, he settled

Acknowledgments: Gratitude is due to Jim Schneider for his help in compiling this history. I also wish to thank Jim Kennedy and Vern Bullough for their comments on previous drafts of this chapter. Much of the information is based on personal interviews with Schneider during the year 2000.

in Huntington Park, a suburb of Los Angeles. Alone, he tried meeting women through a dating agency, but nothing "clicked" with any of them. Schneider became increasingly aware that he enjoyed watching guys. This awareness did not set well with him.

One night, after a particularly enjoyable evening of dinner and conversation with a young woman from North Carolina, she seemed surprised when Schneider prepared to leave without having made a pass at her. "Is something wrong?" she asked, and the question echoed in Jim's mind for a few days. He called the Los Angeles Medical Association and for the first time in his life stated, "I think I'm a homosexual." The respondent on the phone, clearly uneducated on the topic, suggested that he call a urologist. He did so, and after the obligatory wait in the magazine room, he told the man in the white jacket that he was a homosexual. The doctor laughed. "Who sent you here?" he asked. "What you need is a psychologist!"

So Schneider returned home and called the recommended clinic. Here he met a young psychologist named Richard Timmer. The two met weekly for a period of months, and rapport gradually developed. Breakthrough came when Timmer introduced Jim to a novel, *The Price of Salt,* by Patricia Highsmith writing as Claire Morgan. Jim read the book about two women who fell in love with each other, and, tearful at the happy ending, he reconciled himself to his sexuality and set about to learn what it meant to be "gay." Timmer told him of ONE, Incorporated, and their magazine and suggested he contact the group.

Sometime around Christmas in 1959, Schneider called ONE, and editor Don Slater answered the phone. Schneider asked where he could find a copy of ONE's magazine, and Slater recommended the Florence and Pacific newsstand near Jim's home in Huntington Park. Schneider found the magazine and was moved by the image portrayed on the cover: two young men sat beside a campfire, one reaching toward the other with a burro in the background looking on, seeming to smile. Schneider again contacted Slater, and a few weeks later he attended a discussion group at the office where *ONE* was published, on Hill Street, where he met Slater and Dorr Legg, ONE, Inc.'s, business manager, then known to the public as William Lambert.

Schneider was not particularly inspired by his first encounter with ONE. He had expected more people than the scant few he met that evening. The building itself was old; the office shabby and unkempt. Still, he became active in the organization. In 1962 he helped ONE move to larger quarters on Venice Boulevard, west of downtown Los Angeles. About this time, Schneider had placed a carefully phrased personal ad in the *Los Angeles Times* that resulted in a roommate situation with a school teacher, which developed into a long-term relationship. Soon, both were helping on the Friday Night

Work Committee at ONE, doing odd jobs and distributing the magazine. Jim became the leader of the committee and in 1964 he was nominated and elected onto the board of directors.

Apart from ONE, Schneider had secured a job in the Los Angeles plant of Bethlehem Steel, where he was head of the clerical division, managing 600 employees. In his twenty-year association with the company he proved himself to be an excellent administrator and organizer. He once designed and conducted a two-day seminar in safety that reduced the occurrence of accidents in the electrical/mechanical department by 80 percent. He was commended for this, but his heroism was forgotten in an altercation with a newly hired superintendent. Jim left and started his own computer and office supply business, which he still manages today.

In those early days of ONE, his organizational talents and experience with business went largely untapped and unrealized. The organization's energy and resources were continually divided between conflicting goals and personalities as the conflict between Slater and Legg began to escalate. Legg wanted to use the space for a series of seminars in which he and others could lecture so the One Institute of Homophile Studies, founded by Legg and Jim Kepner, could be expanded. Slater, on the other hand, remained dedicated to the magazine and desired to use ONE's scanty assets to fight for the rights of homosexuals in the courts and legislatures. Schneider and the board were caught in the middle.

In the January meeting of 1965, the situation came to a head over whether Billy Glover should be allowed onto the board. Glover had first volunteered and then worked as a gofer for ONE, and he shared Slater's commitment to the magazine. Legg knew that with Glover on the board, his influence would be lessened. Legg prevailed, and Glover was not elected to the board. Frustrated, Slater consulted with an attorney and planned his retaliation. Under the advice of his council, Slater, Glover, Slater's lover Tony Reyes, and a friend of Slater who owned a moving van met at ONE early on Sunday morning, April 18, and emptied the office of everything, hauling it off to another location on Cahuenga Boulevard (Hansen, 1998).

Legg was furious when he discovered what had happened, but he did not call the police. In a confrontation later that day, Slater told Legg that if he would "restore the legally-elected board, and resume ONE's activities on the old footing," everything would be returned (Hansen, 1998, p. 58). Legg opted to take the matter to court. Schneider felt obligated to try to repair the schism. He wrote a letter to all board members in which he called for both Legg and Slater to step down from the board so that ONE would not be divided. When he talked to Slater about the letter, Don admitted the idea had merit, but he added that his plan was not likely to work. Indeed, Legg responded by having Jim cast from the board—and the corporation. The news came to Schneider in a letter dated May 18, 1965, signed by ONE's secretary, Manuel Boyfrank.

When Slater heard Schneider had been cast out, he called and invited him to be a part of his group and to help with the magazine. Schneider wrote a letter to author Joseph Hansen dated May 19, 1998, recalling the incident and his feeling: "If I find myself joining Don's revolution, it will only be because (1) I was kicked into it by Lambert, and (2) I will not be restricted from speaking my mind freely, or from asking questions and seeking factual answers" (Hansen, 1998, p. 59). Schneider also felt Slater's group "seemed more willing to engage in activities that would benefit the gay movement at large, such as the motorcade [protesting the ban on gays by the military] and the court fights that were ensuing by individuals who were charged with crimes against nature" (personal interview January 7, 2001). Slater's group continued to produce *ONE Magazine,* although for three months each group published its own version of the magazine. Schneider had the advantage of the mailing list, but Legg's group held firm to the title *ONE.* As a result, in the fall of 1965, *Tangents* was born, getting its name from a popular column in *ONE.* Although the title was different, *Tangents* on the copyright page of each issue stated it was published by "the majority of legally elected voting members of *ONE.*" The issue was resolved two years later by the courts, who denied the use of the term, ONE, Inc. Slater, Glover, and Schneider formally signed articles of incorporation creating the Homosexual Information Center, or HIC, in 1968.

After twenty years of incredible success and numerous historic triumphs, ONE, Inc., and the HIC began to fade in the early 1970s. The thrust of the movement had left Los Angeles, although a wave of activism rolled out from there, spawning similar movements in San Francisco, Kansas City, Chicago, and New York. By the time of the Stonewall riot in 1969, many gays and lesbians had forgotten all about *ONE* and the history that had been made in Los Angeles. The archival materials that had been gathered by Kepner, Slater, and Jennings remained boxed and divided, scattered around Los Angeles in various basements, warehouses, and garages.

When Slater closed his office on Hollywood Boulevard (the Cahuenga office had been closed earlier), he moved the materials belonging to HIC to his home in Echo Park. When he died February 14, 1997, there was some dispute about what to do with the collection. Two men approached Schneider, Jennings, and Reyes and offered to protect the collection. One was Vern Bullough, who hoped to archive the materials in a gay and lesbian collection at California State College, Northridge. The second was John O'Brien, executive director of ONE Institute, a surviving offshoot of ONE, Inc., which in 1994 had merged Jim Kepner's International Gay and Lesbian Archives with Dorr Legg's Blanche Baker Library collection. In that same year

ONE, through the efforts of Walter Williams, had become affiliated with the University of Southern California and after considerable negotiation was given a building near campus that was then being occupied by a fraternity. The two-story brick structure with its pyramidal skylight showed much promise but was in need of refurbishing and remodeling.

O'Brien invited the board of HIC to tour the new facility and there, a few days after Don's death, he promised that if they would agree to house their collection within ONE, it would remain autonomous and not be merged into the general collection. Moreover, when the renovation was complete, HIC could move in to its own office in the building. This offer appealed to the HIC board, though board member Dale Jennings in particular was leery of the deal. He and Slater had met with O'Brien before Don's death, and both had felt that if ONE wanted to join the collections, HIC should at least be offered a seat on ONE's board. This had not happened while Slater was alive but such a position was offered after his death, and because of this, but also because Slater had been a USC alum and Jennings had studied cinema there for two years, the group decided to cast its lot with ONE.

Schneider became the custodian of the materials until the renovations were completed. He purchased ten large filing cabinets for the clippings, correspondence, and newsletters, and these he stowed in his company's warehouse. The remaining 280 boxes of books and materials had to be stored in a separate facility, which Schneider paid for. The board of ONE expressed its gratitude, and Schneider was voted back onto the board in the fall of 1997—thirty-two years after he had been dismissed by Legg. But all was not well in O'Brien's organization. Schneider watched as money was wasted and the building went unfinished. The monthly board meetings dragged on, although little was resolved or accomplished. Schneider believed that O'Brien continually thwarted the efforts by the USC facilities people to get the job done. He became frustrated and worried.

Finally, after a heated discussion during the October 1998 board meeting, Schneider asked O'Brien if he would resign as director if so asked by the board. O'Brien agreed that he would. So Jim made that motion, which carried five votes to two, and O'Brien stepped down. Schneider then stated that he was willing to deal directly with USC to get the building finished, and he immediately set about the task. When Dale Jennings died, Schneider, who had been his caretaker during the last years of his life, added the forty boxes of Jennings' personal archives and his seven filing cabinets to the HIC collection then stored in his company's warehouse. Schneider and fellow board member Stuart Timmons organized a memorial service for Dale that convened on June 25, 2000—the first public event held at the new facility. Schneider emceed the service.

In the fall of 2000, the HIC collection was at last transferred to its new location on West Adams. Immediately, however, the HIC materials spawned new controversy as some librarians sought to merge the books and magazines with ONE's general collections. Whether the separate identity promised by O'Brien's will be kept remains to be seen. What is clear, though, is that Jim Schneider managed to bring together long-competing groups and though the smoldering rivalries continue, he kept them quiescent enough to establish a world-class library, one of the major goals of the original ONE, Inc.

In an age when people expect instant results for their work, when day trading and serial monogamy have supplanted long-term investments and lifelong commitments, it is difficult to relate to those who stick to allusive if not impossible goals. But the story of Jim Schneider is not like that of the scurrilous jackrabbit bounding over obstacles, moving from this task to that in an opportunistic race for money and fame. Rather, Schneider knows the wisdom of Aesop's tortoise, who persevered through methodical plodding, sheer determination, and a steadfast will. His motto is familiar to those currently active with ONE: "It is better to try and fail than to fail to try." His lesson to us all is that patience is the fulcrum by which one might move the world.

BIBLIOGRAPHY

Hansen, Joseph. *A Few Doors West of Hope: The Life and Times of Dauntless Don Slater*. Universal City, CA: HIC/Homosexual Information Center, 1998.

Kepner, Jim. *The House that Found a Home*. Bell, CA: Rancho Southeast Press, 1971.

Legg, W. Dorr, editor. *Homophile Studies in Theory and Practice*. San Francisco: GLB Publishers and ONE Institute Press, 1994.

William Edward (Billy) Glover (1932-   )

Vern L. Bullough

Billy Glover, as he is known to his friends, was a dedicated volunteer at ONE who, without any intent to do so, was a precipitating force in the division of ONE into two competing groups. He then became the loyal supporter and volunteer to Don Slater at the Homosexual Information Center in Hollywood, and was a decisive influence in eventually merging the Slater collections into the new united library of gay and lesbian materials at the University of Southern California. His activist life emphasizes just how much individual personalities played in the struggle for gay and lesbian rights.

Born in Shreveport, Louisiana, September 16, 1932, and named William Edward Glover, Billy now still lives in the house in Bossier City, Louisiana, that he was raised in. He attended Bossier schools, and after graduation from high school in 1950 he entered Louisiana State University in Baton Rouge. There he was active in Methodist and YMCA/YWCA student groups, which struggled to initiate some form of racial integration in the south. His activity was such that his father's employer, Dow Chemical, cautioned him about the activity of his troublemaking son. It was in a psychology class at LSU that Billy realized he might be homosexual and soon decided he was. After graduating from LSU he joined the army where his protests about the army's slowness in paying First Division troops returning to the United States from Germany got him transferred to another post. Angry at what he felt was unjust treatment, he said, "I flaunted my sexuality" with the result that he was kicked out of the army with an undesirable discharge. He found that this did not interfere at all with his ability to get employment at major companies, at one of which he was transferred to San Francisco. While in California he made contacts with Hal Call in San

Francisco and Jim Kepner in Los Angeles, volunteering his service first briefly with the Mattachine in San Francisco and then with Don Slater and Dorr Legg with ONE in Los Angeles. Since Billy had an independent income, he could choose and do what he wanted, and mainly he enjoyed acting as office manager and doing the essential staff work at the 232 South Hill Street office of ONE, and later at the new headquarters at 2256 Venice Boulevard.

Increasingly there was disagreement between Don and Dorr over potential programs made possible by the new headquarters. When an opening on the board of directors of ONE appeared, Billy was nominated by Don to fill the vacancy. Dorr opposed the nomination. Don Slater, feeling that the annual election had been rigged against Billy, seized the opportunity to move the library and most of the files to a new headquarters on Cahuenga Pass in Hollywood. Billy emphasizes that the intention of Don and his colleagues (they had a majority of the legally elected members to the board) was not to destroy ONE but to see that its work was not stopped, and the move was regarded as a bargaining tool to force Dorr to agree to changes. Certainly there was an outburst of activity from the Cahuenga group, which sponsored a motorcade through Hollywood demanding that gays be drafted, picketed the *Los Angeles Times,* participated in a gay love-in in Griffith Park, produced an all-male cast of Clare Boothe Luce's play, *The Women,* and cohosted a week of discussions on homosexuality on a popular radio show. After the legal suit between the two contending factions was settled, the Homosexual Information Center, as it was called, continued to publish *Tangents,* a continuation of *ONE,* for several years until other publications came to the fore. Billy continued to work with Don until he returned to Louisiana in 1989 for family reasons. There he decided to create a new center for homosexuality. Unfortunately, because of political opposition and a series of unforeseen circumstances, he was unable to do quite what he planned to do, but he continued to maintain a Los Angeles address and telephone message center where he could remain active.

Billy had a fairly long-term relationship with Melvin Cain but mainly he lived alone or with others in groups and he said he always avoided intimate contact with his fellow workers. As he told me, his advice to later generations of gays is to get involved in a cause they believe in.

> You don't have to know anything at first. You don't even have to become a "leader" or "expert" but just being there to help and support each other is the main benefit to you and the cause. And when you look back years later, as I have, you will see that by luck you seemed destined to do what you have done, and you can have no regrets for what you didn't risk doing since you took a chance and followed what

seemed like a dream. As one of ONE's founders said in the fifties, to actually someday see people like us marching down Hollywood Boulevard proudly and to have lived to see that day multiplied around the nation is enough.

Billy adds that while Don and Dorr insisted that "we should honor the organization and goals" and not "worship the people doing the work or make them celebrities," it is clear that our lives and work were in fact done better because of the people we met and with whom we worked. Moreover, "we won."

Jim Kepner (1923-1997)

Lewis Gannett
William A. Percy III

When Jim Kepner died unexpectedly on November 15, 1997, at the age of seventy-four, he left a legacy to the gay and lesbian cause that stretched from the early 1950s through the entirety of his life. Moreover, he contributed in a remarkable number of ways. Cofounder of many activist initiatives and organizations, he decried the movement's tendency to splinter into ego-driven antagonisms. Journalist, archivist, bibliographer, essayist, and chronicler, he insisted that knowledge of history, both distant and recent, is vital to homosexual self-awareness. Mentor, sage, and, above all, educator, he strove to promote understanding.

With Dorr Legg and others in 1956, Kepner created the first gay studies program in America—indeed, one of the first anywhere worldwide after the Nazis torched Magnus Hirschfeld's institute in Berlin twenty-three years earlier. To complement the program's classes he started the first American reference library for gay and lesbian issues, about which there is much more to be said. In 1958 he launched yet another first, the *ONE Institute Quarterly of Homophile Studies,* the debut in this country of scholarly journalism devoted exclusively to gay and lesbian topics.

At a time when the production or even the possession of frank writing on homosexuality was illegal, Kepner published prolifically in such journals as *ONE Magazine, Mattachine Review,* and *ONE Confidential.* Kepner exhibited an intellectual daring quite rare in the 1950s, to which he added an

The authors thank Wayne Dynes and Charley Shively for their assistance in preparing this chapter.

equally rare political daring. For a sense of what it was like to live in this repressive climate—an era that young people of today scarcely can imagine—Kepner's *Rough News, Daring Views: 1950s' Pioneer Gay Press Journalism* (The Haworth Press, 1997), a collection of his early articles and essays, is a bracing eye-opener. It's also an excellent testament to the breadth and prescience of Kepner's thinking. Unlike many of his fellow pioneers, however, Kepner did not have a domineering personality. "He just hung in there," Vern Bullough remembers. "When the library opened in Hollywood, he slept in the basement. His needs were not many."

Kepner's greatest achievement was the creation of an open-access library and archive for gay and lesbian history, a project that grew out of the gay studies library already mentioned. For many years he had placed his own substantial library at the disposal of scholars; he encouraged these men and women to peruse the collection at his cramped Hollywood apartment. In 1979 he incorporated his library as the National Gay Archives (after 1984 known as the International Gay and Lesbian Archives, or IGLA). Drawing mostly on his own meager funds, Jim rented a building of 2,500 square feet at 1654 North Hudson Street, just off Hollywood Boulevard. Here the collection grew to more than 25,000 volumes; it also included photographs, sound recordings, a huge clipping file, posters, calendars, banners, and buttons.

The truly remarkable thing about Kepner's archives is that they were directly accessible from the street, where the exhibits in the big plate-glass window invited even the hesitant to drop in. One seasoned gay activist, perhaps jealous of Kepner's accomplishment, sniffed that it was the equivalent of a Christian Science reading room. Be that as it may, Kepner's operation was a joyous beehive of productive energy. As volunteers struggled to cope with the constant inflow of new material, Kepner took time, as much as was needed, to guide researchers and freely share his sage advice. No appointment was needed.

Eventually the landlord raised the rent on the Hudson Street premises, forcing Kepner to move out and place the precious material in storage. Before his death, though, he made sure that the archives, strengthened with the addition of other collections, would have a permanent home on the campus of the University of Southern California.

Kepner's activist career grew out of a struggle he began in his youth. James Lynn Kepner Jr. was born in Galveston, Texas, sometime in early 1923. The exact date is not known because he was abandoned when he was about eight months old under an oleander bush in an empty lot, where a passing nurse found him on September 19. That date thus stands as a kind of birthday, although August 19 was made his legal date of birth, and, years later, an astrologer friend divined that he most likely had been born in the early hours of February 17. Apparently the abandonment did not leave permanent scars, for Kepner was able to regard it with humor. He wrote in the March 1996 issue of his newsletter, *Jim Kepner's Song and Dance,* "With three possible birthdays, it's no wonder a friend once called me 'the man with a grasshopper mind.' It took years for me to stop apologizing for not having a straight mind."

The rendezvous with the oleander bush may have stemmed from the fact that the foundling had deformed legs and club feet, problems that required the childless couple who adopted him, James and Mary Christian Kepner, to arrange for an operation and years of ongoing therapy. The care that young Kepner received from his new parents came with a downside, however. Mary, raised a Catholic, suffered from the psychological burden of having been prostituted by her own father during her youth, and Kepner *père,* although a hard worker, was an aggressive, loudmouthed alcoholic. Nonetheless, Kepner recalled that he "remained basically cheery" throughout his childhood. He did quite well at school, devoted himself to Bible study at various churches, planned to become a missionary, and prayed for harmony between his fractious parents.

Despite a growing awareness of his sexual interest in other boys, Kepner's piety stayed with him until his late teens, when realms of a different sort began to capture his imagination. After graduating magna cum laude from Galveston's Ball High School in 1940 (nearly the sum of his formal education) and fulfilling a ROTC commitment, his growing adherence to pacifism inspired him to reject both a lieutenant's commission and religious fundamentalism. Another alternative way of viewing the world also changed his outlook: He found refuge in science fiction; he found idealistic fantasy lands far preferable to the repressive reality of homophobia.

Kepner's father moved from Galveston to San Francisco in 1942 to seek better work opportunities in the booming wartime economy. Shortly thereafter he sent for nineteen-year-old Jim and his daughter, Ella Nora, but not for his wife Mary, from whom he had permanently separated.

Life in the Bay Area afforded young Kepner his first glimpses of gay life. He joined the Golden Gate Futurian Society, a science fiction fan club, through which he met other closeted men, and began visiting used bookstores to collect material on homosexuality, the foundation of his legendary library. His first find was Radclyffe Hall's *The Well of Loneliness;* later, he became renowned for the zeal with which he gathered up every sort of pamphlet or flyer related to lesbian and gay organizing, no matter how obscure.

Sometime in late 1942, Kepner made his first foray to a gay nightclub, the Black Cat, but was steps from the door when a police raid shut the place down. Kepner withdrew into the shadows and watched the proceedings with fascinated horror. For the rest of his life he would recall a startling difference in the reactions of the bar's patrons: while the butch types shame-facedly acquiesced to being hustled into police vans, the "outrageous queens" resisted, struggling with and savagely cussing out the cops. The experience later prompted Kepner to defend the more flamboyant elements of the queer world whenever conservative gays denounced them for attracting the wrong kind of attention. "Who," he would ask, "first stood up to our oppressors?"

Wartime San Francisco was swarming with horny servicemen, and Kepner quickly learned to pick up men both in bars and on the streets. That thrilled him, of course, but he was dismayed to find that almost all of his tricks exhibited a visceral antipathy to the idea of organizing against mainstream homophobia, or even the homophobia of gays themselves. Thus one can well imagine Kepner's reaction when, in early 1943, a gay sci-fi pen pal named Wally wrote from Wisconsin to disclose the bombshell that a secret group called "The Sons of Hamidy"—led by senators and generals, no less!—was fighting for gay rights. Kepner immediately tried to recruit new members for this organization. Wally, however, did not elaborate on how one could join. Kepner eventually realized that SOH was a figment of Wally's fertile imagination, but not before other pen pals had told him that they'd heard rumors, apparently spread by Wally, that Kepner himself was the formidable group's "national secretary." It is both poignant and telling that Kepner's first stab at organized activism emerged from such wishful fantasy.

The SOH episode raised Kepner's profile as a gay man, with destructive results. Homophobic criticism of him circulated in San Francisco sci-fi circles. Dispirited, Kepner moved to Los Angeles to seek a fresh start.

But Los Angeles proved equally disappointing. The tone of its gay scene (he was told that gays should "act like queens") made Kepner question his place among his sexual peers. Over time he came to realize that he sought a gay community, not one-night stands or even a lover. Adrift and alone, he put his energy into work for the Los Angeles Science Fantasy Society, first as its secretary and later as president. Although most of the members did not share his interest in activism and social issues, five did, and in 1945 they split off to form the Futurian Society of Los Angeles. For inspiration the group turned to one of the very few ideologies that then seemed capable of charting a politically progressive course: Marxism. In due course Kepner and four co-Futurians decided to join the Communist Party. The move backfired when one of the comrades turned out to be an FBI plant.

Shaken but undeterred, Kepner hitchhiked to New York City, got a job at a cafeteria, and threw himself into Communist Party activities. He supported efforts to have meat packers hire blacks, fought for rent control, and wrote a column for the *Daily Worker*. While making a delivery for that paper he met the activist Richard Wright, whom he greatly admired and believed to be bisexual. Aware of communist hostility toward homosexuals, however, Kepner remained closeted, to no avail because a fellow Communist party member discovered the truth and informed on him. This led to his expulsion as "an enemy of the people," a devastating setback. Nevertheless, Kepner's party affiliation provided valuable experiences: marching in May Day parades and organizing for causes fanned his desire to work for a similar community of gays. He honed skills that he would later need to pursue that goal.

Kepner moved back to San Francisco with one of his original Futurian comrades, Mel Brown, with whom he opened an avant-garde bookstore on Telegraph Hill. Although stimulating, the venture was a business failure. Close friends but not lovers, Kepner and Brown moved on to Los Angeles, where they settled into a house on Baxter Street in Echo Park. Kepner would live there from 1951 to 1972, and later from 1989 to 1991.

The Baxter Street house soon became the locale of twice-weekly meetings, which Kepner described as "half-parties/half-discussions," of a small group of gay friends that included clergymen and blacks. At the meetings Kepner pushed for starting an organization. Although the others were interested, they didn't want to commit themselves. In mid-1952, however, Kepner started to hear tales of a covert gay group called the Mattachine Society that restricted its members to a select few—an entity reminiscent, perhaps, of the Sons of Hamidy, but which on further investigation proved to be real.

Mattachine's closed nature, and the night job that Kepner was working, prevented him from attending meetings until January of 1953, when a friend, Betty Perdue, took him to a Mattachine gathering at a private Hollywood house. At a subsequent Mattachine meeting Kepner met Dorr Legg. He told Legg he would like to work for *ONE Magazine,* the beginning of Kepner's long, productive, and at times contentious affiliation with the various offshoots of Legg's pathbreaking activist enterprise, ONE, Incorporated. The two men developed rapport at a Mattachine Society conference convened in April of 1953 to write a new constitution for the organization, which quickly degenerated into a fracas. Like Kepner, a number of Mattachine's founders came from working-class, Marxist-oriented backgrounds, whereas newcomers tended to be middle-class and politically much more conservative. The delegates arrived with "bounding optimism, anxious to solve our problems fast," Kepner later recalled, but about "100 of us ripped one another to shreds."

Kepner and Legg repeatedly rose to protest the handling of the same issues, including the parliamentarian's threat "to report us all to the FBI if the idealistic preamble, which [Dorr] and I had worked all night on, wasn't removed." San Francisco delegates charged that one preamble passage, which called for a commitment to "build a high ethical culture among homosexuals," amounted to "communist propaganda." Harry Hay, presiding, did not handle the dissension well.

> Hay was remote, enmeshed in abstract theory, so a counter-revolution was inevitable. . . . [He] regarded any compromise as a sell-out of *his* dream—forgetting that each gay has had a dream or two, and not all identical.

In the end Hay "astonished and disappointed most members by surrendering Mattachine to the insurgents—in a long, rousing, but impenetrable speech." (All quotations either from Kepner's August 1993 address to the American Historical Association or from the July 1995 issue of *Song and Dance.*)

The turmoil rocked Mattachine's California operations, but solidified Kepner's relationship with Legg. Kepner's first articles for *ONE Magazine,* "The Importance of Being Different" and "England and the Vices of Sodom," grew out of long conversations between the two men in late 1953, often held in Legg's tiny one-room office at the South Hill Street Goodwill building (the first known gay organization office in the United States, Kepner noted).

Kepner and his fellow activists understood that the vast majority of gay men lived in ignorance of their history, both distant and recent, and of their rights as citizens. To address the problem, ONE Institute developed educational strategies: classes at the institute, symposia sponsored by the institute, and *ONE Magazine.* Kepner participated in each, as can be seen from the meticulous records reproduced in Dorr Legg's *Homophile Studies.* He wrote myriad articles for *ONE,* often under several different pseudonyms (Lyn Pederson, Dal McIntyre, Frank Golovitz, and others) as well as under his own byline. In classes and symposia he taught Americans about the homophile movement in Germany, exposed them to the essential writings of Freud on human sexuality, and led discussions of such topics as "Religious Doctrines Down Through the Ages." However familiar these subjects may seem today, a further measure of the pioneering nature of the work done by Kepner and his ONE colleagues was their astonishing ability to focus on issues whose topicality remains undiminished.

At a time when the legal status of homosexuals was just beginning to receive serious consideration, Kepner devoted an entire issue of *ONE Institute Quarterly* (winter, 1960) to the right of association, and to the argument, eventually upheld by the California Supreme Court, that "homosexuals have a civil right to congregate in bars." His writings reveal no less a desire to educate in a way that would uplift, hence his relentless campaign to attack the misinformation about homosexuality long disseminated by religion and science. As early as the August/September 1957 issue of *ONE Magazine* he composed a pointed rejoinder to the argument, first found in Plato and repeated insistently by Christian authors, that homosexuality is "against nature." Nature, Kepner declared, does not always conform to the storybook conception of family life, "The male as a good provider and protector of the family and the female having all the maternal instinct and blessed fidelity." In truth, "Examples of this idyllic picture are somewhat rare—only a few birds and such disreputable animals as the wolf, the fox, and the weasel."

ONE Institute's symposia routinely involved members of the Daughters of Bilitis and the Mattachine Society. In 1958 the Institute sponsored a discussion of "Homosexuality—A Way of Life." Roundtables were held on such topics as the "The Older Homosexual" and "The Lesbian Partnership." The 1959 sessions included progress reports on "Homophile Movements in the United States Today," given by Del Martin of the Daughters of Bilitis, Rick Hooper of the San Francisco Mattachine Society, and Kepner of ONE. However, when the institute chose "A Homosexual Bill of Rights" as its topic for the 1961 symposium, the Daughters of Bilitis introduced at the very first session a motion to cancel the program. The motion failed, but during the closing banquet the DOB president again denounced the very notion that had been at the heart of the symposium: "It would make us laughable to claim any rights other than those guaranteed in the Bill of Rights" (interview, 1996).

Recurring battles between those activists who saw a need for confrontation to wrest legal protections for homosexuals and others who preferred to seek respectability and establish good relations with the power structure in order to influence it led Kepner to break with Dorr Legg and ONE in December 1960. Later, similar tensions put him at odds with fellow activists in several other gay organizations. But activism always remained at the center of his life. After leaving ONE, for example, he drove a cab and took courses at Los Angeles City College in black studies, which he understood to be analogous to gay studies.

During this time he became very close to Harry Hay. They lunched almost daily with each other in the backseat of Kepner's taxi, theorizing "about every aspect of the homophile movement," Hay recalled in an April 1998 video interview taped at his home (transcript published in *ONE IGLA Bulletin,* #5, summer 1998, pp. 14-16). In 1963, Hay moved in with Kepner "to further cement our loving friendship," Hay stated in the same interview, adding, however, that they were not sexually compatible. In a poem titled "Harry Hay" from Kepner's unpublished manuscript, *Loves of a Long-Time Activist* (the poem appears in the same *ONE IGLA Bulletin,* p. 16), Kepner included the lines:

In 1964 I often parked my cab
An hour where he worked
We shared lunch, held hands
Eyed each other soulfully for a year
Discussing the state of the movement . . .
We never had sex . . .

Interestingly, historians such as John D'Emilio and Neil Miller have had little to say about Kepner. Kay Tobin and Barry Adam make no mention of him at all. Despite this lack of acknowledgment, his dedicated pursuit of an enlightened and enfranchised gay community earned him a place in the gay rights movement second to none. From the movement's earliest days until his death, he indefatigably advanced a radical liberation agenda.

A 1967 episode illustrates Kepner's willingness to confront authority with deeds as well as in print. The Los Angeles police had raided its Black Cat bar (no connection to the San Francisco bar of the same name) on New Year's Eve. Kepner helped organize a rally outside the bar on February 11, 1967, to protest the raid; about 200 supporters showed up, as did an equal number of gun-wielding cops, whose commander ordered the protesters not to utter the word "homosexual." Kepner would have none of that. To the crowd he declared, "The 'nameless love' will never again be silent!" This may well be the first instance in which the famous phrase associated with Oscar Wilde was adapted to the purposes of gay lib rhetoric. In ways both inspiring and amusing, it foreshadowed the oft-heard (to the point of cliché) gripe of conservative 1980s' commentators: "The love that dared not speak its name now won't shut up."

The rally galvanized PRIDE, Los Angeles' nascent street-militant group, and boosted PRIDE's modest Kepner-edited newsletter into *The Advocate,* for which Kepner was a major writer for many years. He went on to participate in countless other rallies, marches, and parades. To give but some examples from a very long list, he marched with Los Angeles' Gay Liberation Front, which he cofounded in 1969; he contributed to the founding of the Los Angeles Gay Pride parade of 1970 and to the Southern California organizing committee for the 1987 March on Washington; and in 1994, along with the Radical Faeries, ACT UP, NAMBLA, and nearly 7,000 others, he protested the commercialization of Stonewall's twenty-fifth anniversary. Kepner, Harry Hay, and John Burnside led a countermarch.

Kepner's belief in the importance of gay history—so graphically evidenced by the archives he created—ran counter to the tendency of many homosexuals to reject the past as part of their break with family and tradition. Kepner characterized their position as follows: "Don't bother me with what happened 20 or 200 years ago, just you get Tilly Law off my back so I can enjoy myself today." He riposted by comparing the past to memory. In the same way that memory is necessary to guide individuals and protect them from repeating old mistakes, so history can inform and direct groups (*In Touch,* June 1973, p. 22). But Kepner admitted that reconstructing the past is difficult. Moreover, he pointed out:

> To many homosexuals the sole value of historic study is the search for heroes. . . . Our job is not to glorify or apologize but to understand homosexuality and make it understood. This demands rigorous honesty. Along with Plato, Alexander, and Caesar we might have to exhume less savory skeletons from the closet. (*Mattachine Review,* September/ October 1956, in Kepner, 1997)

As always, understanding remained his chief goal.

Splendid educator though he proved himself to be in so many ways, Kepner wasn't a scholar in the traditional sense, for he lacked the training, a fact he freely acknowledged. His *Becoming a People: A 4,000 Year Chronology of Gay and Lesbian History* (self-published, August 1995), while lively, fun to browse through, and full of fascinating facts, hardly was the work of a professional historian. But then, the readership he wanted to reach—everyday gays and lesbians unaware of homosexuality's significance since ancient times—is an audience that professional historians rarely manage to reach. With *Becoming a People,* Kepner sought to bridge that gap, a wholly admirable goal. There were times, however, when his eagerness to uncover history's hidden homosexual threads took him into shaky territory.

One of this chapter's authors, William Percy, for a time served as chair of the Gay and Lesbian Caucus of the American Historical Association. It was a position I didn't particularly want, but which Charley Shively persuaded me would become extinct if someone didn't take it. A 1990 symposium I convened in New York City, "Gay American Presidents?", promised to be controversial. But my straight friend and colleague, Michael Chesson, a "reputable" historian, agreed to chair it, which imparted some gravity to the proceedings. I read a paper that outed Presidents Buchanan and Garfield (the latter's great-nephew rose from the audience to confirm that Garfield was indeed homosexual), and Shively discussed grounds for believing that two far more hallowed presidents, Washington and Lincoln, also preferred sexual relations with men. Shively's presentation shocked some in the audience—which, of course, we expected. But we didn't expect a contribution from Jim Kepner that elicited general astonishment. To my own embarrassment, and that of Vern Bullough, a longtime Kepner mentor also in attendance, Kepner rose from the front row to announce that he had unearthed proof of the homosexuality of no less than *sixteen* American presidents!

That anecdote notwithstanding, Kepner wasn't the kind of gay activist who clung to doctrinaire views. On the contrary, one of his greatest virtues was his tolerance, for this veteran of so much disagreement over the aims and methods of the homophile movement never wavered in his respect for diversity among homosexuals. We have noted Kepner's defense of queer-dom's more flamboyant elements, and his policy, dating from 1953, of dis-closing harassment of gay men to readers who demanded other fare. Forty years later, in his 1993 address to the American Historical Association, he was still insisting that failure to understand our legitimate differences re-garding goals remains a major obstacle:

> The biggest problems in our movement, next to the fact that we've tended to be more reactive than pro-active, is that most activists have been inflexibly single-minded. Whether they were conformist or revo-lutionary, they usually tried to channel the entire movement into their narrow aims: right to privacy, law reform, social revolution, sexual freedom, assimilation, education, litigation, dancing in the moonlight, focus on identity, or social service—all worthy concerns, but their struggles have jerked our movement from one narrow focus to an-other.

Kepner also reminded us that, by the same token, as Jews in Hitler's Ger-many discovered, assimilation and access to the powerful do not guarantee that our struggle is won (Kepner, 1993). The fight must go on, he ceaselessly declared, always with the hope that the process will deepen our appreciation of the communality we share.

BIBLIOGRAPHY

"Harry Hay Remembers Jim Kepner," transcript from a video interview with Harry Hay, April 11, 1998, transcribed and edited by Ernie Potvin, *ONE IGLA Bulletin,* summer 1998, #5.

Jim Kepner's Song and Dance, a personal newsletter for associates and friends: #3, February 1995; #4, April 1995; #5, July 1995; #6, October 1995; #8, March 1996; #9, March 1997; #10 (version 2), August/September 1997.

Kepner, Jim. "Homophobia Is Not Just a Straight Disease." *In Touch* 1:5 (February) 1973, pp. 22-23, 60-62.

Kepner, Jim. *Rough News, Daring Views: 1950s' Pioneer Gay Press Journalism.* Binghamton, NY: The Haworth Press, 1997.

Kepner, Jim. "Goals, Progress and Shortcomings of America's Gay Movement,"
    from a 1993 presentation to the American Historical Association.
"Kepner Remembered," by Ernie Potvin, *ONE IGLA Bulletin,* summer 1998, #5.
Personal interview with Jim Kepner, by William A. Percy. January 1996.

Stella Rush a.k.a. Sten Russell (1925-   )

Judith M. Saunders

The formation of the Mattachine and of ONE was not an all-male affair. Women from the first played important roles and among these Stella Rush stands out. Interestingly, the contribution of these women is sometimes overlooked because several women writers also used male pseudonyms.

Stella Rush published her first article in *ONE Magazine* under the pseudonym Sten Russell in 1954, at the height of the witch hunts and government purges that were backed by Senator Joseph McCarthy and the executive order of President Eisenhower. Rush continued to publish in *ONE* until 1961 and in *The Ladder* until it ceased publication. Her writings and those of other brave pioneers provided isolated gay men and women throughout the United States with a community to which they could belong. In these early publications, gay men and women read accounts of conferences (held by ONE, the Mattachine Society, and Daughters of Bilitis), scientific studies, police oppression activities, fiction, poems, and more. Always lively were the letters to the editor, which provided a forum of dialogue otherwise unavailable to these readers.

Stella, an only child, was born in Los Angeles on April 30, 1925. She spent her childhood and school years migrating between Los Angeles and Kentucky. Not only was Stella's childhood marked by unending geographic upheaval but also by family disruptions and losses. Stella lacked the stability so important to the developmental years of childhood: Stella's beloved father died before she was two years old, and when she was five her mother developed a serious illness that recurred throughout her life. The illness

---

I would like to thank Del Martin and Phyllis Lyon for their assistance.

drained her mother's energy, leaving her irritable, unstable, and emotionally inaccessible to her daughter. Stella feared her mother's fragility. This fear placed constraints on the closeness that she and her mother shared, causing the relationship to be defeated by an inherent estrangement.

Stella took refuge in her studies, and developed a reputation as a "brain." Having begun her education in California, she had to start first grade over in Kentucky when she and her mother moved back to live with Stella's maternal grandmother. When she returned to California, she was advanced early from the second to the third grade. She was back in Kentucky for her fifth year at school, but halfway through the fifth grade, Stella's grandmother, fearing Stella was ill, told Stella's mother to take her back to California for medical treatment. Stella explained, "Grandmother thought I had tuberculosis, but really, I had just curled up inside myself dying of depression from the impossibility of my situation." This ebb and flow between Kentucky and Los Angeles continued throughout Stella's grade school and junior high school education. She graduated from high school in Los Angeles shortly after the United States entered World War II, after having had the luxury of going to one school three years in a row. She was fortunate to get a trainee aircraft draftsman job at North American Aviation for two years where she worked and saved money for college. She completed three years of college at the Universities of California at Berkeley and Los Angeles, with majors in math and public speaking.

Stella explains that although reserved, she always felt free in her schooling. Contrary to popular belief, her schooling in Kentucky was more advanced than California, such that teachers in her second grade in Los Angeles promoted her early to the third grade. Stella was fortunate in having several teachers along the way who were very special and helpful to her. Stella remembers, "I fell in love with almost all my teachers."

From her relatives in Kentucky, Stella learned to value family, religion, and duty; whereas Los Angeles, for Stella, was the land of liberty. Exposure to such differing values and lifestyles was as broadening as it was confusing. Stella credits being raised in a family with a strong tradition of a fundamentalist religion as contributing to her difficulty in working through her denial about being gay and in reaching an acceptance of herself. Los Angeles contributed to Stella's sense of a right to fairness, regardless of skin color—what Stella calls "the race thing." This core belief has remained a steadfast value guiding Stella's actions in life.

Responding to the question, "How did you get into gay life?" Stella answered, "That makes me smile. It took a lifetime, it seems—seventeen years to see it (being gay) standing there in front of me—another six-plus years to accept it on a beginning basis, another five years of going to gay bars in order to meet gay women and men, and to find out about a small magazine named *ONE*." Stella couldn't discount these feelings as she had with her earlier crushes on teachers and schoolmates.

In high school, Stella became good friends with one schoolmate. This time, Stella was aware of a difference in her feelings: she wanted more than friendship, she wanted to kiss this wonderful, beautiful girl. One day, overcome with feelings, she tried to kiss her friend; she soon realized that her girlfriend did not return her feelings. Embarrassed, Stella passed the whole incident off as a joke, and successfully repressed this incident for many years.

When World War II ended in 1945, men returned to reclaim their jobs and to seek women to fulfill traditional roles, "just like the gal who had married dear old Dad." Stella was working at Firestone Tire and Rubber as an aircraft draftsman. She also was attending the First Unitarian Church of Los Angeles and singing in the choir. Unique among Unitarian churches at that time, their humanist minister welcomed people of all races and creeds. It was noted for its "radical beliefs" in a society that was increasingly vigilant about perceived threats to the American way of life. The most powerful threat to this American way of life were "commies," then "queers," with "niggers" prominent among the third wave of threats. The Unitarian Church was open-minded and attracted rebels of all sorts. The church and its activities were central to Stella's social life as a young woman. Around the corner from the Unitarian Church was the If Club, a gay bar where Stella and others went after choir practice to visit, talk, and have a beer.

One night Stella was at the If Club alone when two women approached and invited her to join them in a trip to a gay bar at the beach. They finally persuaded her to go, and Stella was surprised to find other women there she knew—a gal from college and another woman from her night drafting class. Two people came up to Stella and asked, "Well, Stella, what took you so long?" Stella later learned that many people over the years had seen her as gay but realized that Stella hadn't discovered that she was gay for herself yet. Stella tried to find books to read that would help her but was often confused by what she read. She didn't want to get married and have kids, then find out she was gay. Still, a door to her identity had been opened for her that couldn't be closed again. The books she read convinced her that the lifestyle of gay men and women meant living a series of lies. The primary social life for meeting other gay women and men during this time was at bars, where the risk of police raids was constant. Stella was involved in several police raids at gay bars. Stella reported,

> I was in a raid down at a Venice Beach gay bar. Came out in December of '48, so it was probably early part of '49, when I was alone—before I started living with anyone. The bar was mixed, and it was a dancing

bar. Wham, all of a sudden the police were there and made all of us go outside. The raid seemed to be aiming mainly at the guys, although if a woman gave them lip she could also go to jail. The police were very democratic about that. I had been warned ahead of time, probably because I belonged to a church where we were in political hot water over the communist thing—loyalty oath thing, And so we had some counseling [by the minister] to give only name and address when asked, but don't tell them where you work. Let them think you are unemployed or whatever. So you don't end up on the front page. I was scared to death, standing there shaking. This cop asked me to identify myself, so I hauled out my driver's license, and said that's me. "Where do you work?" I don't have a job. You don't know. You don't want to argue with a policeman or anyone who has a gun and a billy stick. I didn't give them any reason to take me down to the station. At the same time, I wasn't going to help them. The whole thing with me was not to argue with them about anything if I could help it. . . . The police officer told me, "You should cooperate with us." And I answered, "I would, sir, if I knew what you wanted." Actually there were about four times I had to talk with cops, and most of the time there was a good cop/bad cop scene. The most difficult ones were not the gay bar raids, but were being stopped by the police about race, like the time my partner, Bea, and I were taking a black man home from choir practice. I was ready, if I had to, to go to jail for the right of free association with others and to take a stand against race discrimination. I was a member of ACLU and could see what the ACLU could do about it—that is, for the racial discrimination. I wasn't prepared to go to jail about the homosexuality issue, because, as far as I could see, gays didn't have any civil rights and ACLU didn't have anything to offer. It took a lot of work and education before the ACLU took us on—they had to get to know us and to read a lot of our stuff.

After a few years of reading, and going to gay bars to meet women and men, Stella entered a four-year relationship with a lesbian who was twenty years her senior. This relationship had many points of strain, but it was through this relationship that Stella met women who were involved with *ONE Magazine*.

After Stella learned about *ONE Magazine,* she didn't rush to them to offer her services. Stella explained, "At first, I hung out around the edges of the organization and gave it gifts of what money I could afford anonymously. I had a civil service job as a civil engineering assistant. I didn't want to lose it." She had differentiated knowing she was gay from the lifestyle associated at that time with being gay. She believed of herself and of the gay community, "We are just people. Not any better or any worse than other people." Stella believed strongly in a vision of normalcy for gay men and women, and this included being able to live within a context of human and civil rights. ONE brought together men and women in order "to publish and disseminate a magazine dealing primarily with homosexuality from the scientific, historical and critical point of view, and to aid in the social integration and rehabilitation of the sexual variant." ONE battled with the U.S. Post Office for the right to mail the magazine to their subscribers. The U.S. Post Office declared the magazine to be obscene literature. ONE responded with a lawsuit that found its way to the U.S. Supreme Court before being vindicated.

The values reflected in ONE's purpose drew Stella to their work, but crossing the line from anonymous supporter to active participant was not an easy transition. "It took going through waves of fear before working on this stuff." Like so many others in the early 1950s, Stella had a lot to lose.

One of the first things Stella wrote for *ONE* was "Letter to a Newcomer" in 1954. Stella explained, "I wrote this because it had finally gotten to me in my heart and mind, that people, including me, shouldn't have to live like this. Shouldn't have to be using pseudonyms (e.g., Sten Russell), or lying all the time just to make a living or just to get along in society." Stella calls this a simple article, but admits that "some people got a great deal out of it and seemed galvanized to activity by it." The staff at ONE heard often from many people about how much this magazine meant to people throughout the country. People subscribed to the magazine, but often one individual's magazine would circulate to dozens of friends.

Stella was a reporter, later also an assistant editor and a corporate member for ONE. As a reporter she was assigned to report on conferences held by organizations such as the Mattachine Foundation (later the Mattachine Society) and ONE, Incorporated. Her reporting of the papers presented at conferences was so thorough, so complete, that it prompted Don Slater, editor, to remark, "You wrote more than I remember hearing."

She also was assigned to explore the "butch/femme phenomenon" among gay bar lesbians. Stella found that opinions were strong and expectations firmly held that role distinctions needed to be sharply drawn. Not being distinctly butch or femme was courting disapproval as strong as that usually reserved for the practicing bisexual individual.

Although Stella participated in ONE's corporation and publications from 1953 to 1961, she also became active in the Daughters of Bilitis and their publication, *The Ladder,* in 1957. Stella believed that she had found a very good fit between her beliefs and the values reflected in the Daughters of Bilitis's purpose: A women's organization with the purpose of promoting the integration of the homosexual into society by education of homosexuals and the public at large, participation in research projects, and investigations of the penal code as it pertains to the homosexual.

Stella resigned from the *ONE Magazine* editorial board in 1961 and explained her resignation in an article in *The Ladder:* "I resigned from ONE seven months ago, mainly due to great policy difference between myself and the rest of the editors of *ONE Magazine*. It is dismally depressing to be a minority of one person most of the time" (Russell, 1962). As her explanation continued, she affirmed her continuing support of *ONE Magazine* because its importance as a publication was greater than the ideological differences that existed.

Stella attended One's Midwinter Institute in 1957 so she could report the proceedings and discussions in *ONE Magazine,* and there she met the love of her life, Helen Sandoz, whom everyone called Sandy. Sandy was the president of Daughters of Bilitis, a group in San Francisco that had been founded in 1955 by Del Martin, Phyllis Lyon, and other women. Stella believed Sandy to be one of the most noble, courageous women she had ever met. Not only was Sandy one of the original signers of the Daughters of Bilitis Charter, she also was a good executive and had published her own newspaper in Oregon. Soon Sandy and Stella had overcome all obstacles to their relationship and began a life partnership that ended only when Sandy died June 7, 1987.

Stella made her debut as a reporter for *The Ladder* in March 1957, and she continued to use the protective, necessary pseudonym, Sten Russell. In 1958, Stella also assumed the responsibility of publications director for the Daughters of Bilitis. Her first assignment was to report for *The Ladder* at ONE's Midwinter Institute at which had been assembled a lively panel of psychologists, psychiatrists, clergy, attorneys, and members of ONE to debate the issue of whether homosexuals should be coerced into heterosexual practices. The panel concluded that (1) if homosexuals are neurotic, it is due more to negative attitudes toward society and their position in society, and (2) no one believed homosexuals could or should be coerced into heterosexual practices.

As the Los Angeles reporter, Stella was kept busy throughout 1957 reporting on conferences and attending a specialized course (thirty-six hours over an eighteen-week period) that surveyed the social and biological sciences and the humanities as they pertained to the homophile. Stella, as Sten Russell, reported discussions in depth, so that readers learned who spoke and what they said. Some of her reports were up to seventeen pages long because the discussions required that much space for accurate reporting and audience understanding. The dialogue was rich at the conferences and seminars that brought together scientists, gay activities, police officers, medical staff, and clergy. The topics that focused the dialogue were the social and philosophical concerns of the gay men and women in the 1950s, and in many instances, concerns that continue to live today.

Sten Russell reported on the Fourth Annual Mattachine Society's Convention, and its broad range of topics. A prominent panel addressed the topic, "Must the Individual Homosexual Be Rejected in Our Times?" Dr. Harry Benjamin, endocrinologist and sexologist, began by saying he was ashamed that the question had to be asked. In his opinion, no one knows what is "normal," only what is "customary." Leo Zeff, clinical psychologist, rephrased the question to, "Can the individual homosexual be accepted in our time?" "No," he said, "this is not an antihomosexual society; it is an anti-sex society." With this reshaping of the discussion, he brought the problem to heterosexuals as well. Julia Coleman, social worker, spoke of "the price of rejection" to society, and that society must ground its actions in facts, not myths. William Beher, social worker, suggested that the homosexual must first accept himself or herself, thereby paving the way to being accepted by others. Alfred Auerback, clinical professor of psychiatry at University of California, San Francisco, believed that change could not be brought about in present attitudes by force or pressure, only by evolution. Sam Morford, moderator, wrapped up the panel discussion by saying, "It didn't seem to him that anyone could be rejected unless he (or she) accepted the rejection."

Although Stella's reports of conferences, seminars, and research were welcomed by both *ONE Magazine* and *The Ladder,* she struggled as other writers had before her to have her poems published. A common response was, "They aren't gay enough." Stella wondered: if the poem was good, and if it was written by a gay woman (or man), why wasn't it gay enough? Her poems were good enough that her stance eventually prevailed. Consequently, readers were able to discover and enjoy yet another dimension of Sten Russell, reporter. Although her poems spoke of passion and love, she combined humor and love in, perhaps, her best known poem, published in *ONE,* in 1961:

PYEWACKET

Love poem to a Lady Cat
"Cherchez la femme."
Oh, tiny Siamese lady cat
—beautiful kitten—
The wisdom of a thousand
Years shines from your
Bright, mischievous eyes.
Oh, loving little soul—

Such feminine grace
—and only eight weeks old:
How I love you!
We are betrothed.
You have snored on my sleeve.
Arched your back
And crossed your paws (all four).
My heart is gone
As I contemplate the
Mysterious infinitude of
Womanhood!

Sten Russell

In addition to conferences and seminars, Sten Russell also reported results of scientific studies that examined homosexuality in a variety of dimensions. The controversial Kinsey statistics were reported from a review of three programs that had been taped when presented by WRCA-TV in New York City. This same taped series in 1957 included the report of a study by the noted anthropologist, Margaret Mead, "Male and Female in American Culture." Mead, so Russell reported, discussed cultural institutionalization of an ordinary variation of sex drives, and that the problem arose with attempts to define sexual identity in terms of occupation and temperament. Mead believed that this was the basic mistake any society could make and it led to curbing and warping of the great human potential for variety and adjustment to changing conditions.

Russell also reported the results of a study by Virginia Armon, PhD. The study found no significant difference between homosexual and heterosexual women when their Rorschach tests were compared. Although Armon indicated that it had been a tremendous amount of work for a relatively meaningless result, Russell reported she was not sure . . . "the significance of insignificance is quite meaningful."

From ONE's tenth anniversary annual meeting, Russell reported the taped presentations that featured two prominent clinician/researchers of the time: Blanche Baker, MD, psychiatrist, and Evelyn Hooker, PhD, psychologist. Baker said that homosexuality was a product of many factors. She believed every human being was a mixture of femaleness and maleness. Baker was convinced that the neurotic conflict of most homosexuals existed because they did not accept themselves. Hooker said that she did not believe that homosexuality and pathology are necessarily connected. This position is hallmark of her pioneering research. Hooker continued to assert that homosexuals, even with the most compelling motivation, would find change (to heterosexual) well nigh impossible in the vast majority of cases. From this same conference, Russell also reported on Suzanne Prosin's observation, as a result of her independent research on lesbian couples, "The homosexual minority is the reverse of most minorities, since those comprising it come from the majority to the minority. Therefore, its values started with those of the majority, and its values may still be the same."

Stella continued her reporting and working conscientiously at her other, varied positions with both *The Ladder* and Daughters of Bilitis through 1968. Her life-partner, Helen Sandoz, a.k.a. Helen Sanders a.k.a. Sandy, was even more involved in the activities of Daughters of Bilitis and *The Ladder*. Sandy designed many of the covers of *The Ladder,* reported on conventions, organized the Los Angeles chapter of Daughters of Bilitis, and typically was an officer of either one of the chapters (San Francisco or Los Angeles) or the national group. Their combined contributions in building gay organizations and publications were significant in establishing the groundwork for a major gay rights movement. Perhaps people who build major movements, such as gay rights, are known in the same manner that major architectural structures are known—by the visible structure that emerges, not by the foundation that provides the structure with its strength and shape. Stella and Sandy were two pivotal people who helped to shape the sound foundation of the gay civil rights movement that we know and enjoy today.

During the foundation years (1950 to 1970) for the gay civil rights movement, a lot had been accomplished. By the end of the 1960s other organizations had appeared and provided gay men and women with more choices about how to direct their energies. Many lesbians struggled with these choices of directing their energies toward integrating lesbians into society through the feminist movement or to continue with organizations devoted exclusively to the welfare of the homosexual. Many leaders of the Daughters of Bilitis and publishers of *The Ladder* believed they could accomplish the purpose of "promoting the integration of the homosexual into society" by joining forces with the emerging feminist organization, National Organization for Women founded in 1966.

Stella and Sandy found the rhetoric of the early feminist movement too strident. They were particularly concerned that fighting for rights of women, which they strongly supported, was being waged against men. Both Stella and Sandy believed fervently in rights of all women *and* men, and were reluctant to give their efforts to groups that aimed to elevate one group at the expense of another group. They had relegated their private and personal interests to the background for many years, and they decided the time had come to place their private and personal goals and activities more centrally in their lives.

Stella and Sandy lived a quiet life together until Sandy died in 1987. They had been together thirty years. Stella continued to work and remained in touch with old and new friends. She retired in 1997 and lives in Southern California.

BIBLIOGRAPHY

Much of the information in this biography is based on interviews with Stella Rush conducted between June and December 2000.

LeVay, S., and Nonas, E. *City of Friends: A Portrait of the Gay and Lesbian Community in America.* Cambridge: MIT Press, 1995.

Russell, Sten, "Letter to a Newcomer," *ONE,* 1954, pp. 18-19.

Russell, Sten, "Mattachine Looks at Life—Life Talks Back," *The Ladder,* September 1957.

Russell, Sten, "The Open Mind," *The Ladder,* November 1957.

Russell, Sten, "The Personality Variables of Homosexual Women," *The Ladder,* May 1959.

Russell, Sten, "PYEWACKET: Love Poem to a Lady Cat," *ONE,* 1961.

Russell, Sten, "The Searchers Probe the Homosexual Neurosis," *The Ladder,* March 1957.

Russell, Sten, "Ten Years of History," *The Ladder,* March 1962.

Helen Sandoz a.k.a Helen Sanders
a.k.a. Ben Cat (1920-1987)

Stella Rush

Helen Sandoz was born November 2, 1920, and grew up living on a farm at the edge of a small town in Oregon where her mother lived and worked as a maid. Somewhere along the way, her friends gave her the nickname Sandy, and it stuck with her for life. After she earned her bachelor's degree, she moved to Alaska for a time, then moved back to the lower forty-eight and held supervisory positions in department stores in Washington and Oregon. While doing a bank errand for her mother in Oregon, she rear-ended a farmer's truck transporting a pregnant cow. Thinking the accident was minor, Sandy was so focused on reaching the bank that she was unaware how injured she was. The bank teller asked, "Miss Sandoz, did you know that there is blood trickling down your chin?" Sandy had not been aware of any personal injury, but left the bank to seek medical treatment and learned that she had broken her neck. She had to spend a year in a full-body cast and never again was able to sit in a chair or remain immobile for any length of time. Never one to waste time or unnecessary energy in self-pity or meaningless activity, Sandy decided to shift her career goal to one in which she did not have to sit for any length of time.

Since she had artistic talent and some graphic art experience, she decided to build a career on these assets and became a sign printer by trade. Although it was physically demanding, it did not involve much sitting down. She soon left Oregon and settled in San Francisco and discovered the Daughters of Bilitis. When DOB legally organized with a state charter in 1957, Sandy was one of the courageous and far-sighted women who signed her real name in the state documents for chartering DOB as an educational and social organization for gay women. For some fifteen years, Sandy worked devotedly for the Daughters of Bilitis and its publication, *The Ladder.*

Under her "public" pseudonym, Helen Sanders, she became president of the DOB in February 1957. Sandy's competence in so many areas quickly made her indispensable throughout DOB and *The Ladder.* When she decided later that year to move to Los Angeles to continue the personal relationship that she and I had recently formed, DOB regarded her as a missionary for DOB activities in Los Angeles. The following excerpt, "Time Out for Tribute" in *The Ladder* says it best:

> The feud between the cities of San Francisco and Los Angeles is one of long standing, but it would appear that there will soon be a liaison officer in the person of Helen Sanders. Come the first of the year she will be taking up residence in "smogland."
>
> Sandy, as she is known in DOB circles, has served as past president of the Daughters, as production manager last year for THE LADDER. She is presently serving on the Board of Directors as publications director. She has also proved most valuable in public relations, having represented the DOB at ONE's Mid-Winter Institute and the Mattachine Convention last year—to say nothing of her numerous appearances on panels at Mattachine and DOB public discussion meetings.
>
> But aside from her usefulness (which we have taken full advantage of), we just kinda like the gal! And we hate to lose her . . .
>
> *However,* if she's determined to make the move, we aren't above cutting out a big job for her in Los Angeles. For there is the matter of a chapter there, and she's just the gal who can swing it.
>
> With warmest regards and best wishes, the Daughters say So long, Sandy! (*The Ladder,* December 1957, p. 15)

Sandy arrived in Los Angeles with a list of names of women, some provided by others and some from her own acquaintance, who might be interested in a chapter of DOB. She took me driving all over Los Angeles County. She kept track of those who were interested and got us all together at our home. She was the first president of the Los Angeles DOB. An important function of the chapter was to give the women a place to meet and get to know each other and to talk about their common problems, and to learn how to eventually accept themselves.

Many of the women eagerly came to the DOB meetings where there were no men present, but were reluctant to attend a public meeting where there would be a male speaker or gay men. Under Sandy, the Los Angeles DOB worked to help its members become comfortable at public meetings with speakers from the scientific and medical communities. The group thrived.

Sandy also continued to work with *The Ladder.* Although her roles and titles changed over the years, Sandy was a major contributor to the look and substance of this publication. She designed some of the most memorable covers and in 1966, for a brief time, became editor of *The Ladder.* Sandy made clear that what happened in the name of the homophile community also happened to lesbians, even though men dominated the homophile community. Because of this belief, she felt it obligatory to print extensive reports of programs and surveys that might not, at first glance, be pertinent to lesbians, but could have considerable effect on them if not reported, and sometimes challenged.

Although Sandy used her Helen Sanders pseudonym for most of her writing and public persona, she occasionally wrote under the pen name Ben Cat, writing from the perspective of the beloved housecat that Sandy and I had. As Ben Cat, Sandy was free to explore topics and perspectives that she would never have written in public print as Helen Sanders or herself, Helen Sandoz. For example, Ben Cat puzzled over the meaning of Christmas and the frantic pace of that holiday.

Sandy and I decided not to follow others in *The Ladder* and Daughters of Bilitis in joining forces with the new organization, National Organization for Women. Although she believed in NOW's goals, she did not approve of much of the rhetoric, and she wanted to concentrate on getting rights for both gay men and lesbians in the homophile movement. She died June 7, 1987, in Anaheim, of lung cancer.

Herb Selwyn (1925-   )

Vern L. Bullough

Serendipity played an important role in Herb Selwyn's involvement with the gay and lesbian community. A devoted member of the American Civil Liberties Union, Selwyn was, in a way, a typical member of his generation. Born and raised in West Hollywood, a community which is surrounded by the city of Los Angeles, he entered UCLA and left for military duty in World War II, serving in the Air Corps in England, France, and Germany, returned to UCLA, went onto the University of Southern California law school, set up a law practice, married, and eventually had four children.

He was not, however, typical in his defense of gays and lesbians, a cause in which he became involved because his father, a doctor, had a patient who was known to him to be a lesbian. On one of her visits he mentioned that his son was a lawyer. She turned out to belong to the Mattachine Society and was hunting for a lawyer to speak at a society meeting, but, as an indication of the stigma and fear which many gays and lesbians lived, rather than approaching Selwyn directly, she asked his father to query him about whether he would be willing to talk to such a group. Selwyn remembers his reply was that his concept of a lawyer was a person who could help others and certainly he felt that gays and lesbians needed help.

The meeting itself was held in a private home with between twenty-five and thirty men and women in attendance, none of whom were lawyers. This lack of lawyers in attendance was understandable simply because those who were lawyers for the most part were fearful of being exposed, since they could in fact be disbarred. With such official hostility to gays and lesbians, it was perhaps inevitable that many of the public advocates for the community came from the straight community. Selwyn's talk led to various members of the Mattachine coming to him for legal advice. He handled the incorporation of Mattachine in 1954 without fee, the first gay organization to be incorporated. He also became involved in various legal cases in the community and appeared on various radio and television talk shows. One of the most traumatic involved a television appearance with a judge who claimed that all male homosexuals had become gay because they had been seduced by sailors when they were twelve or thirteen years old. A fellow panel member, a psychiatrist, Dr Frederick Hacker, disagreed with the judge. The judge, who had a violent temper and was particularly abusive when individuals disagreed with him, became greatly agitated and suffered a stroke on camera. He was taken from the television studio to the hospital and died a few days later. Selwyn reported that several members of the district attorney's office, who had often suffered from the temper of this particular judge and who were rather pleased that they would no longer have to face him in court, congratulated him on his great success.

Some of Selwyn's activities were also done anonymously. He wrote a wallet-sized card entitled "Know Your Legal Rights," for the Mattachine Society, which distributed it to members and at gay bars. It apparently aroused the ire of at least one member of the city attorney's office who showed the card to Selwyn and said, "Isn't this awful? Isn't it horrible?" Selwyn simply inquired, without claiming authorship, whether any statement on the card was incorrect. Even such a response upset the attorney who then walked away.

One of his cases involved a man who challenged his unfounded arrest in a public rest room. An undercover cop had approached and said, "I'm just down from Sacramento and I'm a lather [someone who puts up lath and plaster], and I don't know anybody down here." After some additional conversation, his client allegedly propositioned the man, who then arrested him. At the trial the policeman admitted he had lied about his identity; he wasn't a lather and he wasn't from Sacramento. The jury acquitted the client. The trial is significant not only because of the acquittal but because the accused person was willing to go public to fight the case.

Another one of Selwyn's cases dealt with an attempt to revoke the license of a cosmetologist who had a lewd conduct arrest for propositioning an undercover policeman. Selwyn pointed out that the arrest was a misdemeanor, not a felony, and should not be used to revoke a license. Selwyn also made fun of the prosecuting attorney's case by requesting that the judge ask his own wife how many hairdressers she knew who she thought were gay and what would happen to the women of America if all their licenses were revoked. The client's license was not revoked.

Selwyn worked with Vern Bullough and others to establish the first gay rights policy of the American Civil Liberties Union in 1964 and with publicity more cases came to the ACLU as more and more gays were willing to go public to challenge what they regarded as unfair laws. As they did so other lawyers in Los Angeles also began to take cases, many of them gay or lesbian themselves, and Selwyn was called upon less and less by the gay community. As he looked back upon his career in the year 2000, Selwyn felt that his handling the criminal cases or affiliation with gay and lesbian groups did not hurt his career at all. Rather, it caused considerable admiration from some of his fellow members of the bar who were impressed by his willingness to defend those most in need of defense, something that Selwyn has done all of his life. He later came to realize, as gays and lesbians came out of the closet, many of his friends, acquaintances, and fellow professionals were gays and lesbians. Still, when he entered the field, there were few lawyers of any sexual identity willing to deal with the topic, and that is what made him a pioneer in the movement. He was there almost from the beginning because, as he says, it was the right thing to do.

Hal Call (1917-2000): Mr. Mattachine

James T. Sears

Only when police chased Chicago advertising salesman, Hal Call, out of the windy city in 1952, did San Francisco get its first permanent gay activist.

Randy Shilts, *The Mayor of Castro Street*

"If the priests controlled sex," the lanky man with cobalt eyes bellowed to me, "they knew they could control man." Sitting on his worn gold casting couch and surrounded by 7,000 gay erotic videos, eighty-three-year-old Harold Leland Call has devoted a half-century to the gay movement. Applauded by some and disparaged by others, all would agree that the Missouri-born Call was a prominent figure during the pre-Stonewall era. From the *Mattachine Review* to Bob Damron's *Address Book,* from physique magazines to hard-core erotica, from the Black Cat to the California Hall, from *Life* magazine to *CBS Reports*—Hal Call furthered homosexual rights at a time when there were few activists and even fewer willing to lend their real names.

Harold Leland Call was born in September 1917 to a fervent Baptist mother, Genne, and her freewheeling twenty-four-year-old husband, Hal's

 father, Fred. In Grundy County, the sharp-eyed Call quickly became aware of the contradictions between religious belief and everyday life. His father's extramarital exploits eventually led to a divorce when Hal was ten. As Call entered puberty, "I knew I had a fascination and attraction for male genitals. I was hungry for information about sex, anxious for sexual experiences. I was fascinated by other men's penises" (Kepner interview).

Hal also developed a love for writing in addition to an interest in sports. At age eleven, he printed "The Daily News" with

151

a rubber lettering set and writing skills acquired in a one-room schoolhouse. Later, his eighth-grade schoolteacher at Smith School wrote for his graduation: "Congratulations and best wishes to the best student I ever had in school. The future is yours." And, for Hal Call, it was.

Receiving a scholarship to the University of Missouri in 1935, Hal studied journalism while supplementing his income by publishing a weekly flyer, "Theater News," with local movie listings and advertisements. He also worked at the *Columbia Missourian.*

As war neared and the draft began, Call enlisted as an Army private in June 1941; within a year he had been promoted to sergeant. Originally expecting to serve only one year, Pearl Harbor changed that and the realities of war and Army life altered the Missourian's worldview: "I am being taught to kill in battle," he wrote his mother. "I do not like that part, although I am not a conscientious objector, nor am I a coward" (letter to his mother, March 15, 1941). Call became a lieutenant after completing officer candidate school in the summer of 1942, before seeing combat in the Pacific theater. Call saw the worst of the war two years later. Writing his family after the intense fighting where much of his battalion was cut to ribbons:

> I'm safe. I've seen 14 continuous days of hell! 14 nights of hell, fear and prayer on the battlefront here on Saipan Island. Fourteen front line days without a letup. No man who sees and knows it will ever forget it. Dead everywhere. Shells, snipers, and enemy machine gunners shooting at you; I can smell and feel death every minute. . . . Rain, sun, land crabs, and giant snails all add to the misery of shells, dead Japs, and the stench and destruction of the battlefield to make life dreary, dull and yet keenly exciting. (letter to mother, July 6, 1944)

Earning a purple heart from taking a shell fragment and later appointed regimental battalion commander, Captain Call returned to the United States in the fall of 1945. And, at the beginning of the New Year, he returned to the University of Missouri to complete his degree. One of his courses was country newspaper production. One week the entire class helped assemble the edition of the *Eldon Advertiser.* Call worked in the shop casting stereotype plates for advertisements. "When the owner saw me back there using the printer's tools, sawing and cutting plates, and setting type, he went gaga! He offered me one-quarter of interest in the newspaper." Call traveled the sixty miles three days a week from Columbia working as a printer, editor, and advertising salesman. Graduating a year later, Call continued to work at the paper until the owner retired. When the paper was sold, Call's modest investment had yielded him a handsome financial return.

Postwar gay life in Missouri—except in Kansas City—was far from liberating. J, a friend from Brookfield, wrote Hal about problems in his former college town: "Naturally you know about all the nastiness in Columbia. Neither I, fortunately, nor Jack, were involved—that to me is typically amazing! But the scare of the witch hunt was a little too much for us" (letter from J, September 23, 1948). In another letter, addressed to the "Scarlet Whore of Babylon," J described the aftermath:

> There was a "clean up" on here and all sorts of grotesque rumors, fantastic terrors, etc., are floating from pillow to nameless post. . . . There was a small article in one of the St. Louis papers several days ago saying that EK had been let off scot-free after his last week's trial but was on probation for a period of time. (letter from J, 1949, no date)

Call received this letter in Walensburg, Colorado, a once-affluent mining community where he had purchased the *World Independent* in 1948, after a brief stint editing a daily newspaper in Brookfield, Missouri. As one of the emerging community leaders, Hal engaged in a relationship with a daughter of a prominent family. And, like most closeted homosexual sons, he fended off letters from his mother, who fretted:

> You said in your letter you could never afford being married with all your expenses you have, well, there are thousands of married men not making what you are and have lovely families and nice homes. You come in contact with them each day and so do I. Harold, it isn't our prestige that gets us along in this world—I know from experience. Just simply be what you are and live it. You remarked in your letter you'd be in a mess if you had a family to care for. Well, dear son, that is a mistake. You're missing the dearest thing in your life by not having a dear wife and little ones to care for. (letter from mother, November 13, 1949)

Similar to other small-town homosexuals during this lonely hunters' era, Hal experienced problems living the dual life. His friend J philosophized at the time: "You mentioned something about 'us who have such a difficult time finding happiness' well, my view on that one is that any life has its share, rather evenly distributed, of happiness and its contrary" (letter from J, March 28, 1950). Hal found solace with gay men who were generally his junior with respect to Hal's war and work experience: Bill, an archaeology student in Alamosa; Terry from Durango; Jack, another student who would eventually follow Hal to Chicago.

Following a declining financial base for his paper and realizing the importance of being earnest with the woman he was dating, Hal placed the *World Independent* on the market. As he awaited the July sale, he wrote Bill in the spring of 1950:

> The way is still cleared for my own getting out of here on schedule. . . .
> Oklahoma City and St. Louis, I see, have just finished local vice clean-up campaigns, although the word is they only scratched the surface.
> . . . I find it [Denver] matches the worst I saw in Kansas City—and I thought that the limit. I've met many persons there one way or another in the past few weeks, and I am more convinced than ever that the axe is about to fall.

After working for the *Kansas City Star* for a year, Call secured a transfer to the newspaper's Chicago office where he joined several of his Missouri gay friends, including J. Then, on a hot night in August of 1952, Hal and three companions were arrested for "lewd conduct" in a parked car at Lincoln Park. He paid an $800 "fee" to get the charges dismissed. "I had to borrow the money from my mother and told her what it was all about. I told my boss at the *Star;* I was one of those people that didn't know that to be accused was to be guilty—as all of us have learned since" (Kepner interview). Hal resigned from his job, packed everything in his 1945 Buick super sedan, and departed for San Francisco—accompanied by his lover, Jack.

When Hal and Jack drove across the Golden Gate Bridge in the mid-October 1952, there was no inkling that the City by the Bay would become America's gay Mecca or that Harold L. Call would play a major role in its transformation. Although the city had long enjoyed a tradition of "mixed bars" filled with returning soldiers, police harassment was common and much of the homosexual scene remained underground. Hal and Jack frequented the Black Cat on Montgomery Street, where on Sundays José Sarria sung operas while Jim McGinnis (known as Hazel) played the open-front piano. They also spent time at a few bars on Post or Taylor Streets. "We were always weary and on the lookout. With hands, arms, and elbows on the bar at all times. We were always afraid a cop would come in and sweep the place out as they did on some occasions."

Working for an insurance trade magazine, Hal's thinking was profoundly influenced by two odd groups that had taken root in the area. The Prosperous Society, whose cornerstone was the "only thing in any individual is his consciousness," challenged Call's intellect. His gay political consciousness was activated by the Mattachine Foundation.

Founded a year earlier by a handful of Angelinos, the Mattachine Foundation sponsored clandestine ongoing discussion groups mostly in California metropolitan areas. At the beginning of 1953, Hal attended a discussion group held in a Berkeley student's room. About fifteen men were in attendance. Recognizing the importance of this effort but dismayed by its lack of organization, he formed another group across the bay. In the spring of that year, the former Army captain helped lead the charge against Mattachine's secretive Fifth Order. "They all had communist backgrounds," remembers Call, "every damn one of them!" (interview by Paul Cain, July 27, 1994). Two years later, he observed

> the original founders of the movement had built better than they knew. . . . Gone were the "secret" orders, the questions of who was behind it all, and the possibility of alternate motives. Established was an association of persons who knew and trusted the others within the group and shared the zealous desire to alleviate a pressing social problem. (*Mattachine Review,* March-April, 1955, p. 39)

Mattachine chapters soon expanded to New York, Chicago, Denver, and Boston, among other cities. As secretary of the San Francisco Area Council, Call began publishing the region's newsletter in the fall of 1953. Two years later, Call was director of publications for the Mattachine Society. The Society entered an agreement with the newly formed Pan Graphic Press (partly owned by Call) to produce *The Mattachine Review.* This monthly magazine informed the heterosexual as well as the homosexual with questions posed on its cover such as: "How would you face the problem if a member of your family is found to be a homosexual?" Nevertheless, the magazine was hardly a bastion of reactionary political thought as alleged by some contemporary commentators (e.g. Streitmatter, 1995, p. 89). The *Review* advocated disclosing one's homosexuality to others, published excerpts from England's *Wolfenden Report* and articles from the liberal *Der Kreis,* a European gay journal. There also were cover stories such as "Police Roundup Jails 69" and "Intolerance, Hate, Prejudice, Fear, Ignorance," as well as thoughtful essays on bisexuality and pornography. Further, Call's Dorian Book Service offered readers—many living in towns lacking progressive bookstores—the opportunity to order books such as André Gide's *Corydon* and Jeannette Foster's *Sex Variant Women in Literature.*

Politically, the *Review* argued against the ghettoization of homosexuals or their elevation as a "special people" and generally veered away from the more political and separatist stance adopted by *ONE Magazine*—although activists such as Jim Kepner wrote for both and Dorr Legg, ONE's founder, was treasurer of the Mattachine Society. "I wanted to live in the general society," stresses Call, "not create a homosexual subculture."

As a journalist from the Midwest, Call was sensitive to the role the media (and society's professionals) could play in advancing homosexual rights. His public appearances stressed reason and common sense as he sought to educate a sexual illiterate citizenry. In a 1958 radio show, for example, he explained:

> Homosexualism is just one of the things that exists in nature. It always has been with us, as far as we know, and always will be as far as we expect. It seems that no laws, no attitudes of any culture that we have looked into in the past have ever been able to stamp it out or even essentially curb it. (KPFA program, November 24, 1958)

Later in the show, when confronted with the "problem" of the nelly homosexual, he again offered a radical response—couched in common sense:

> We hear so many homosexuals who urge us to please preach that the flamboyant individual should not show off and shouldn't be obvious so that he receives the ridicule and scorn of his fellow man. . . . However, we feel that there is a more basic problem to get at, that will in the long run—if it can be solved—take care of this. That is to educate the public so that its attitude toward these people who are displaying these mannerisms will be changed. Then, the mannerism will no longer be of any significance and whether they are recognized or not, it won't amount to anything.

In private, however, Call's blustery outbursts and bawdy style coupled with his political conservatism and business acumen annoyed some homophile activists who generally were less able to translate ideas into the "nitty-gritty." Throughout the 1950s and into the 1960s, Pan Graphic Press was the Alyson Publications of its time, publishing booklets on transvestism, West Coast bars, and the sexual continuum. Other services included *Dorian Book Quarterly* with reviews of books on "sexual variance and related themes." The Press also printed the lesbian periodical, *The Ladder,* edited by Del Martin and Phyllis Lyon, for most of its first year, as well as legal briefs for the bohemian Black Cat club, which was constantly under siege by state officials.

During one visit back to Grundy County, Hal sat his mother down and explained "the facts of life." Putting her on the Mattachine mailing list, he said: "If I come back home and find that little magazine hidden and not read, you'll never see me again. Mom, you're gonna learn something!" And she did—as did others.

Ground zero for sexual liberation during the 1960s was San Francisco. It had begun, however, a year earlier during the city's mayoral election when Russ Wolden sought to unseat Mayor George Christopher. Although ahead in the polls, Wolden sought to link Christopher to a city becoming a "national headquarters" for perverts based on information released from the Mattachine Convention that was hosted by the chapter in Denver. The gambit, however, backfired as the city's newspapers roundly condemned Wolden's tactics and Christopher won handily. Meanwhile, local homophile groups benefited from the publicity and soon after the election, Call recalls, "our first real meeting with top police officials came to pass after that."

Call was influential in moving city government—particularly the mayor's office and the police—away from its antihomosexual stance. He was also active in many of the city's gay milestones, providing financial support and printing services to José Sarria's 1961 campaign for city supervisor (the first openly gay man to run for public office in the United States), lending a hand (and designing its logo) for the Tavern Guild (the first gay business association in the country), assisting ministers in forming the influential Council on Religion and the Homosexual, identifying subjects for Alfred Kinsey's further sexuality studies, facilitating *Life* magazine's 1964 cover story of "The Homosexual," bailing out customers arrested at the Tay-Bush Inn and helping to organize the California Hall New Year's Eve Party, at which a police raid resulted in a public relations disaster for the city.

Cliff Anchor, an activist who had been introduced to the gay movement when he saw a newspaper article that featured Mattachine and Call, observes:

> Call was a great strategist. Sarria got away with it since he was in the entertainment business. But Hal was out in front and conservative. He attracted people and money into the gay community who wouldn't have been involved otherwise. (interview by author)

By the summer of love, there had been a dramatic change in the San Francisco homosexual scene thanks to the efforts of groups such as Mattachine, the Tavern Guild, and the Society for Individual Rights, a new group that merged the social with the political. Although conservative politically, as a fierce defender of free speech Call found himself at odds with both federal authorities and some homosexual leaders. He asked: "What's the use in battling for sexual freedom without having any?" Hal Call's most pivotal role was in an obscenity case that forever altered the American homosexual landscape.

From his early sexual experiences as a Missouri teen paging "one-handed readers," Call recognized that to be human was to be sexual. But a seismic cultural and legal shift was occurring during the mid-1960s as evidenced in the popularity of *Playboy* and the use of "the pill." For the homosexual, however, the legal climate had changed little even though images of men in athletic poses, wearing G-strings, often appeared, and homosexual acts were illegal in every state except Illinois. In Minnesota, during the summer of 1967, a trial was held with defendants Conrad Germain and Lloyd Spinar facing a twenty-nine-count federal indictment for producing and distributing "obscene materials." Their company, Directory Services, produced full-frontal-nude men's magazines. Interspersed among the thirty- to fifty-page nude spreads in publications such as *Rugged* (butcher-than-thou men wearing little more than leather motorcycle jackets and boots) and *Tiger* (muscled or thin twenty-somethings) were essays espousing gay liberation as well as comic strips with gay political sensibility.

Call "was instrumental" in connecting the defendants with key expert witnesses such as Wardell Pomeroy, who had been associated with Kinsey's Institute for Sex Research and in developing their legal strategy. In July 1967, the court ruled these materials did "not exceed the limits of candor" and "the right of minorities expressed individually in sexual groups or otherwise must be respected" (p. 11). The homosexual revolution moved into high gear as the landmark decision thwarted the federal government, who smugly had assumed a quick guilty verdict (*Butch*, 1967).

"We opened Pandora's box," confesses Call, who soon opened Adonis Bookstore with partners Robert Trollop, Jack Tennyson, and Bob Damron. The city's first gay venue sold bold magazines such as *Golden Boys* (from Calafran Enterprises owned by Damron/Trollop) and homosexual literature. The storefront also was a good recruiting ground for male models as well as Mattachine activists. In 1967, Call also began Grand Prix PhotoArts Films which produced slides of male stars such as Tony Rivers and Peter Decker. Hal worked with many of the leading erotic photographers of the day such as J. Brian, Toby Ross, and David Hurles (The Old Reliable), and he knew or filmed male models, including John Holmes, Joe and Sam Gage, Casey Donovan, Scott O'Hara, Jack Wrangler, Gordon Grant, Kip Knoll, and Ray Fuller. He also collaborated with major West Coast adult filmmakers such as Chuck Holmes at Falcon, Bill Higgins of Catalina Video, and Manco videomaker Bill Wyman.

During this "golden era of gay sexuality," Call perfected video techniques beginning with his first fifteen-minute loop film, "Let's Beat Off," in his Adonis, Halcyon, Zante, and Cockpit film series. "I had the capability of talking to these people and putting them at ease so they didn't feel embarrassed about jacking off. I had the knack." As the new decade of the 1970s dawned, Call opened CineMattachine on Ellis Street, the first live jack-off stage show in the city.

With the new decade, another generation of leaders arose and a different homosexual agenda emerged. Polk Street and the Tenderloin area fell on hard times as the gay population and businesses migrated to the Castro area. As gay power segued into gay rights and "Silence = Death" aborted "Free Love," tales of the homosexual city seldom included Mr. Mattachine, except for his efforts in promoting safe-sex practices as city health officials threatened closure of the movies houses and sex clubs.

In July 1999, six months before his death, Call sat in front of ten video screens in a cramped office above the Circle J Theater. There he entertained a dwindling number of friends and lectured to a drying stream of admirers or writers. From cybersex to queer nation, Hal admitted, "I'm not in step with them; they're not in step with me." A spectator to the movement he helped engineer, he was at ease with himself and his accomplishments: "I'm off center stage now. It's another generation."

BIBLIOGRAPHY

Primary Sources

Unless otherwise noted, all quotes are taken from interviews with Hal Call by James Sears, May 1998-July 1999. Copies of this are in the Call papers, International Gay and Lesbian Archives, in Los Angeles. Additional sources used in Call's direct quotations are from an interview with Jim Kepner and another from Paul Cain, both located in the Call papers. His correspondence is also located there.

The article on the history of the Mattachine Foundation is in *Mattachine Review* (March-April 1955). For other details see my *Calling Shots: The Life and Times of Hal Call, the Homophile Movement, and Male Erotica,* New York: The Haworth Press, forthcoming.

Background Materials

D'Emilio, J. *Sexual Politics, Sexual Communities.* Chicago: University of Chicago Press, 1998.

KPFA. *The Homosexual in Our Society: Transcript of a Program Broadcast on November 24, 1958, by Radio Station KPFA-FM* (1959). San Francisco: Pan Graphic Press, 1959.

Loughery, J. *The Other Side of Silence.* New York: Holt, 1998.

Marcus, E. "Gay Sexualist 'Hal Call,'" in *Making History: The Struggle for Gay and Lesbian Equal Rights.* New York: Harper Collins, 1992, pp. 59-69.

Shilts, R. *The Mayor of Castro Street: Life and Times of Harvey Milk.* New York: St. Martin's Press, 1982.

Streitmatter, R. *Unspeakable: The Rise of the Gay and Lesbian Press in America.* Boston: Faber and Faber, 1995.

Del Martin (1921-   )

Phyllis Lyon

Del Martin is determined, positive, combative, loving and caring, a stubborn Taurus, always right but also ready to admit if she is wrong. An activist and lifelong Democrat, first energized by Franklin Delano Roosevelt, she is passionate about human rights and politics and a rabid champion who insists that the lesbian's place in history be written as it happened, not as some men have assumed it happened. Growing old has not changed her. She has continued to fight for new causes, not sitting back and waiting for others to act. She's Del Martin, and she has been the love of my life for the almost-fifty years we have been together.

Del Martin is a writer. Her piece, "If That's All There Is," written in 1970 after particularly egregious actions by a group of gay men, was published and widely reprinted, and made quite a stir. Male historians uniformly attribute the piece to her—and that is all! But she has written much more than that—articles and essays and editorials which have had a definite impact on the lesbian and gay movements from the 1950s to today. Her reporting tells what actually happened. Her more reflective pieces often wonder what would have happened if, or when, or if not.

Born in San Francisco on May 5, 1921, she was raised by her mother, Mary, and her stepfather, Jones Taliaferro. Mrs. Jones Taliaferro, who had only a grade school education and had worked as a waitress, spent her life trying to keep up with the Joneses, an ambition her daughter did not share.

Early on, Del discovered her attraction to other girls but had no words for what she felt. Somehow she knew enough not to say anything about it to anyone. Eventually, like so many others, she discovered Hall's *The Well of Loneliness*. It gave her some sense of who she was although she never could relate herself to the main character in the novel, Stephen Gordon. (Many years later Del realized she was a "sissy butch.")

In Presidio Junior High School she took her first class in journalism and starting writing for the student page of the *San Francisco Chronicle*. She met, talked with, and was inspired by *Chronicle* reporters at weekly after-school meetings. One such meeting happened on Election Day, and Del was invited to stay and witness the excitement of election returns in the newsroom. She later reported that this "experience melded my two top interests: politics and journalism. It had an indelible effect on the direction of my life."

Del was very shy. She admired a student a year ahead of her, Gertrude Kirsch, but did not know her personally. It was Gertrude, however, who prompted Del to take the bold step and sign up for debating. The easy part was going to the library to research the topics—first to reinforce arguments for the side she was assigned; second to understand and anticipate arguments of the opposition. The hard part was learning to speak in front of an audience and respond spontaneously in rebuttal. Judy Turner, a Presidio cheerleader (later to become Lana Turner, the movie star), stepped in to help Del overcome her stage fright. Thanks to these two girls, Del acquired a tool that would come in handy in her life as an activist.

She continued her journalism career at George Washington High School, editing the yearbook and the school newspaper. After graduation she enrolled at the University of California at Berkeley and worked on *The Daily Californian*. Finding the commute to Berkeley onerous, she decided to transfer to San Francisco State College, now University, where she became managing editor of the student paper, *The Golden Gator*. It was there she met James Martin, who was the paper's business manager. Some time later, probably because she did not have a particular girlfriend and also wanted to get away from home, Del and James were married. Two years later they had a daughter, Kendra, and several years after that Del divorced James.

Del was given custody of Kendra, whom she adored, and received child support and mortgage payments from James on the house they owned. Still, as a single mother she had trouble making ends meet even though she took numerous jobs. Child care was also a problem and eventually she put Kendra in a boarding school and brought her home on weekends. Life remained a struggle.

James, who had remarried, and his new wife were unable to have children. They came to Del and pointed out that they could give Kendra a traditional home with a mother and a father. Jim, Del felt, was a good father, and she bought into the concept of mom and dad and allowed Jim to take her. She had Kendra in summers when possible, and Kendra was with her when Del and I first set up housekeeping. When Kendra graduated from high school her dad said college was a waste of time if a girl did not have a clear-cut major in mind. We thought otherwise and put her through University of

California, Berkeley, supported her decision to marry and financed the wedding. She, her two children, and both of her husbands have been a wonderful family to us as well as advocates for lesbians, gays, and others needing support.

Del, even before her marriage, had been struggling with her lesbian feelings, trying to find out who she really was. She told neighboring women friends she thought she was a lesbian. They said they did not think so, but told her about the lesbian bars in the North Beach section of San Francisco. Knowing there were others like herself helped, as did falling in love with another woman friend with whom she had a short affair.

At that time (1948-1949) Del was a reporter for a construction daily, *Pacific Builder,* in San Francisco. A job on a similar paper in Seattle opened up and in 1950 she was hired as editor of *Daily Construction Reports* published by Pacific Builder and Engineer. It was there she met me. I was working as an associate editor on magazines also published by PB&E. Word that this "gay" divorcée (gay in those days had a different meaning from San Francisco was coming to Seattle created quite a stir among the women employees, especially me, since I was also from the Bay Area. I remembered seeing Del when she first arrived at the office, an attractive, short, stocky woman with dark hair wearing a gaberdine suit, heels, and carrying a briefcase. It was the latter that caught my attention—I had never seen a woman carry a briefcase before.

The first weekend after she arrived, I hosted a welcome party in my apartment. Del spent most of the evening in the dinette with the men, smoking cigars, while they tried to teach her to tie a tie. (She never learned.) The next morning she called me. She had run into Washington state's blue laws closing bars on Sunday, and she needed some "hair of the dog that bit her" for her hangover. I invited her over, and from that day we forged a close friendship. I, at that time, had no knowledge whatsoever about lesbians and knew very little about homosexuality. Sometime during that first year Del, another woman co-worker, and I were at the Washington Press Club having drinks. Somehow the subject of homosexuality came up and Del was holding forth. "How come you know so much about it?" one of us asked. "Because I am one," Del replied.

That evening opened up a whole new world to me. Del and I continued our friendship (she thought of me initially as her good straight friend). In 1952 I prepared to leave Seattle to meet my sister in San Francisco in order to take an automobile tour of the country. The trip had long been planned to coincide with her graduation from the University of California at Berkeley. My pending departure moved Del to action. One evening, sitting on the couch in my apartment, she made what I considered a half pass at me—I completed the other half. We had sex together for the first time.

We drove to San Francisco together (her parents lived there) and visited the lesbian bars and other attractions. We even managed a night together. Then she went back to Seattle and Tricia, my sister, and I started on our grand adventure. I found I missed Del a lot, and managed to phone her, collect, frequently. I told Tricia about Del being a lesbian and about my feelings and confusions. My baby sister was very helpful and understanding. Unfortunately, Tricia came down with polio when we reached New Orleans, and we were there for a month until she was strong enough to travel again. That was a time when I really ran up Del's phone bill.

On our return to San Francisco, I stayed with my parents while Tricia was in the hospital in Berkeley. Del visited several times and finally asked me if I would live with her. I was in conflict, but after we exchanged numerous letters and about the time she had decided it was a lost cause, I answered yes. I began looking for an apartment while she wound down her obligations in Seattle. I found a furnished one-bedroom apartment on Castro for sixty-five dollars a month (which Del thought was too much) and moved in. She arrived around 11 p.m. on February 14, 1953 (Valentine's Day), and our life together began.

Del found a job and I, while collecting unemployment insurance, played at being a housewife, although not very successfully. We did not know any lesbians in San Francisco and spent a lot of time trying to meet some. We went to the lesbian bars but all the women seemed to be in groups and/or cliques. We just sat and watched, too shy to approach them, and they did not approach us. Eventually we met two gay men who lived around the corner from us, and the four of us hung out together. Jerry, the older of the duo, was a bartender at the 299 Club in North Beach and encouraged us to start a restaurant, rent free, in an empty room behind the bar. We became partners, and Ricky and I were the "waitresses" while Jerry cooked. Del was still working. We were the first to offer a single menu of steak, baked potato, and salad for $1.19. The restaurant, however, did not make it since we could not afford to advertise. The idea was picked up by another group, which made a big success of it downtown on Powell Street.

We toyed with the idea of moving to New York for a while to get away from our parents, both sets of whom lived in San Francisco. Since we had to save money for the move, we settled down to pass a year at least before going. The people in the apartment above us made such a racket that we decided to look for another place to live and serendipitously found a house we simply had to have (and still have).

Eventually we met another lesbian, Noni, at a party we attended with Jerry and Ricky. One day in September 1955, while we were housecleaning, we got a call from Noni: "Would you like to join me, my partner, and two other couples in starting a secret club for lesbians?" Of course we would—

that meant we would know five additional lesbians! The "secret society" turned into the Daughters of Bilitis, a name which we adopted from Pierre Louys writings. DOB was the first national organization of lesbians and marked the start of Del Martin's lifetime of activism on behalf of the lesbian, gay, bisexual, and transgender communities, the women's movement, and civil and human rights for all people.

Del was the first president of DOB's San Francisco chapter and, when the organization went national, she was the first national president. She was the second editor of *The Ladder,* DOB's magazine.

Shortly after DOB began, we discovered two other organizations, the Mattachine Society, now in San Francisco, and ONE, Inc., in Los Angeles. Both were 99 percent male. Associating with members of the two groups was often very helpful, but the male attitude toward women was a problem—for us. At the Mattachine's convention in 1959 in Denver, Colorado, Del addressed the delegates.

She said that at every one of the conventions she had attended, year after year, she found she had to defend the Daughters of Bilitis as a separate and distinct organization:

> What do you men know about lesbians? In all of your programs and your *Mattachine Review* you speak of the male homosexual and follow this with—oh yes, and incidentally there are some female homosexuals, too. . . . *ONE Magazine* has done little better. For years they have relegated the lesbian interest to the column called "Feminine Viewpoint." So it would appear to me that quite obviously neither organization has recognized the fact that lesbians are women and that this twentieth century is the era of emancipation of women . . .

Still, finding Mattachine helped us meet others, including the two Bobs— a gay couple who lived just around the corner from us. Through them we met Sala Burton, wife of Phillip Burton, then a California assemblyman, and this precipitated our first and only foray into electoral politics. In the late 1950s, the two Bobs suggested that the four of us run for the San Francisco Democratic County Central Committee. Since they were printers, they made up a colorful folder listing our names and backgrounds as nominees of the Franklin D. Roosevelt Democratic Club located at our address. No mention was made that we were homosexuals and the only members of the club. We did not win, but Del received the most votes because her name appeared ahead of the rest of us on the ballot.

At the Mattachine convention in Denver, we had become acquainted with two members of the Prosperos, a metaphysical group that taught translation (straight thinking in the abstract) and "Releasing the Hidden Splendor" (how to psych yourself). The teaching, based on ontology, a sense of being in the world but not of it, transformed Del's concept of self in relation to universal truth, and she became a convert. Like most converts she became a preacher, a position she had always despised. In fact, she had been criticized by members of DOB and readers of *The Ladder* for being too preachy. Rightly too; as Del looks back at some of her essays, she feels embarrassed not by the message, but by the tone.

As the years went by Del became a cofounder of the Council on Religion and the Homosexual in 1964, and among other things served on Episcopal Bishop James A. Pike's Diocesan Commission on Homosexuality in 1965-1966. She has often said that learning the politics of the church helped her to understand the politics of other groups and of the country. In 1965 she helped found Citizens Alert, a coalition of civil rights groups and affected minorities to respond to police brutality, and served as its chairperson 1971-1972.

In 1967 we heard about the advent of the National Organization for Women and immediately joined the budding Northern California Chapter. In 1968 we discovered there was a couple membership. We did not want to go back in the closet, so we sent our check and a note as to why we were applying as a couple. Inka O'Hanrahan, the national treasurer who lived in San Francisco, not only accepted but said "There must be more of you. Bring them around." When she informed NOW's executive committee of this lesbian couple, National President Betty Friedan expressed her displeasure and the "couple membership" soon vanished.

Friedan, in fact, tried to purge lesbians from NOW and when Aileen Hernandez, who had served as NOW's Western Regional Director, succeeded Friedan, she inherited the controversy. She asked us to convene a workshop on the role of lesbians in the feminist movement at the NOW national conference in Los Angeles in 1971. We thought we would have to act as referees, but to our surprise the grassroots membership was way ahead of the East Coast national leaders who were so afraid of the media. A positive resolution was a shoo-in, and by the 1973 convention Elaine Noble and Sidney Abbott convened a lesbian caucus, and Del was elected the first open lesbian to NOW's national board of directors.

Our organizing activities continued. We helped found the Alice B. Toklas Memorial Democratic Club in 1972. In 1976 San Francisco Mayor George Moscone appointed Del as the first open lesbian on the Commission on the Status of Women, and she served as chair in 1976-1977. Del had become increasingly prominent on the San Francisco political scene and many candidates for office asked for her endorsement. She had to make a radical change, however, when one candidate wanted her to sign her sponsorship papers and Del realized she would have to sign the name under which she was registered to vote—Dorothy L. Martin. No one in San Francisco would know who Dorothy was, so she reregistered as Del Martin. Although she later initiated paperwork to change her name legally, she never completed the process.

In 1977 she was elected a delegate to the International Women's Year Conference held in Houston, Texas. This was an incredibly important conference as its purpose was to adopt a National Plan of Action to advise the president and congress on the needs of women for the future. The Sexual Preference plank called for legislation to ban discrimination against lesbians and gays and, among other things, to repeal laws restricting private sexual behavior between consenting adults. The plan passed overwhelmingly, triggering a deluge of balloons with the slogan "We Are Everywhere" from the balconies full of nondelegate lesbians. It moved the delegates on the floor of the huge auditorium to hug and dance together in joy, regardless of sexual orientation. It was also a message to gay men (although few probably noticed) that the women's movement was concerned with discrimination against them as well.

In 1978 Del cofounded the Lesbian Lobby and San Francisco Feminist Democrats. From 1980 to 1983, she served as the only lesbian (or gay) on the California State Commission on Crime Control and Violence Prevention. She also served on the board of advisors to Senior Action in a Gay Environment, and in 1984 she joined the Advisory Committee for Gay and Lesbian Outreach to Elders (now New Leaf's Outreach to Elders). After seventeen years of service she resigned.

In 1971, Del traveled to Washington, DC for the annual meeting of the American Psychiatric Association to participate in a panel of "nonpatient" homosexuals. The impetus for the panel had been an invasion of the 1970 APA meeting in San Francisco by gay liberationists. In her speech, Del chastised the psychiatrists and their "science" for thinking of homosexuals only by their sexuality, not as a whole person. She challenged them:

> I have heard you allude to such lofty ideals as "improving the quality of life," of offering individuals "choice" and helping them to attain "selfhood." And I have heard such terms as "social justice," "mental health," and "humanitarian concern." But nowhere did I hear these ideals or terms applied to homosexual men and women—only to heterosexuals. . . . Somehow we must convey to you how your subjective value judgments deny homosexuals a part in the good life and how, to the contrary, you have become the guardians of mental illness rather than promoting the mental health of homosexuals as a class of people in our society.

This assault was part of a campaign that resulted in the 1973 revocation of listing homosexuals as mentally ill in the *Diagnostic and Statistical Manual of Mental Disorders*. But Del did more. She and Nanette Gartrell, the first lesbian psychiatrist to come out during her internship, joined forces to teach the "staid" women psychiatrists how to protest against their male counterparts, who voted to hold a conference in a state that had not passed the Equal Rights Amendment.

Del went on in 1976 to publish *Battered Wives,* a book that acted as a catalyst for the battered women's shelter movement and Del increasingly moved toward center stage not only as an advocate for lesbians but for women in general. The number of speeches she gave and the workshops she was involved in at universities and colleges, mental health associations, women's groups of various kinds, and law enforcement agencies increased at a rapid pace. She was cofounder of the Coalition for Justice for Battered Women and chaired NOW's Task Force on Battered Women and Household Violence. She served as a member of the California Alliance Against Domestic Violence, the Police Liaison Committee of the San Francisco Human Rights Committee, and the Women's Advisory Council to the San Francisco police chief.

All the time, she continued to write magazine articles and book chapters. In 1987, Del and I heard about a conference of older lesbians (age sixty and up) to be held in Southern California. Since we were beginning to admit we were aging, we went. It was a wonderful experience that taught us the values and rewards of growing old. In 1989 a similar conference was held in San Francisco and Old Lesbians Organizing for Change was born. Our focus of activism shifted to include ageism and other "isms" that made life difficult for old people. When we heard about the 1995 White House Conference on Aging, we decided there should be a representation by lesbians and gays, and Senator Dianne Feinstein responded by appointing Del as her delegate, while I was appointed by Congresswoman Nancy Pelosi. When we arrived in Washington, we found that Lisa Hamburger, a young gerontologist who went to the conference to convene a workshop on senior housing, had put Del's name down as a speaker for California for the scheduled Speak Out. Del was told she had fifteen minutes to prepare a three-minute speech. When she stepped to microphone she said: "I am Del Martin. I am seventy-four years old, and I am a proud, old lesbian." There was a gasp from the audience as if all 1,000 in attendance had gasped at once. Del was instrumental in placing "sexual orientation" in the general nondiscrimination resolution that was later adopted. Some 10 percent of the delegates, under our leadership, managed to get Resolution 69 on the agenda, which delineated many demands and needs of lesbian and gays. It did not pass, nor did we expect it to. But it served its purpose as a consciousness raiser, and it was part of the conference record. More references to older gays and lesbians appeared in the final report; as of this writing we are both working to get a large and strong delegation to the next White House Conference on Aging in 2005.

Del has received many awards and honors, but the one she treasures most is her induction into the George Washington High School Alumni Hall of Merit in 1990 as an open lesbian. She was interviewed for the school paper she once edited. The induction ceremony took place in the school auditorium that had not yet been built when she graduated in 1937. Her proudest moment, Del says, was when the alumni president introduced her and her life partner, me, to the student assembly. In her speech she began, "When I was a student, I didn't have a clue." Times have certainly changed.

As she has moved into her eighties in this new millennium she has slowed somewhat in her physical actions but not in her passionate work for human and civil rights for all. She is still a consummate caring lover, worker, counselor, woman, and a committed lesbian.

BIBLIOGRAPHY

The personal details have come from my long association with Del.

Books

Martin, Del, *Battered Wives*. San Francisco: Glide Publications, 1976; revised Volcano, CA: Volcano Press, 1981.
Martin, Del and Phyllis Lyon, *Lesbian/Woman*. San Francisco: Glide Publications, 1972; revised New York: Bantam Books, 1983; updated Volcano, CA: Volcano Press, 1991.
Martin, Del, Daniel Jay Sonkin, and Lenore E. A. Walker. *The Male Batterer: A Treatment Approach*. New York: Springer, 1983.

Selected Articles

Martin, Del, "If That's All There Is," *Vector,* November 1970.
Martin, Del, "Lesbian Mothers: Legal Realities," *GPU News,* April 1975.
Martin, Del, "About Censorship," *On Our Backs,* September-October 1990.
Martin, Del and Phyllis Lyon, "Reminiscences of Two Female Homophiles," In *Our Right to Love,* edited by Ginny Vida, Englewood Cliffs, NJ: Prentice-Hall, 1978, pp. 124-128.

Phyllis Lyon (1924-   )

Del Martin

Phyllis Lyon is not afraid of the L-word, whether it be lesbian or liberal—or even lipstick. In fact, L-words best describe her life. "I am a singular Lyon," she protests when people persist in adding an "s" to her name. She has the largess, pride, and roar of a lion. She is distinguished by her laughter. She loves light and bare windows. She is loquacious, but she also listens. She is loving, loyal, learned, logical. She loves literature and is an avid reader. She is a lover, a leader, a liaison. She lives up to her ideals. She also likes to live it up. Her concerns are limitless, as are her talents. She hopes to win the lottery so she can support all her causes more lavishly.

I met Phyllis Lyon fifty-two years ago on the job in Seattle. She threw a welcoming party for me as a new addition to the staff of a trade publication. That led to a lasting friendship. We found we had much in common. I am a native of San Francisco and California and Phyllis, although born November 10, 1924, in Tulsa, Oklahoma, spent much of her youth in the San Francisco Bay Area and identifies herself as a Californian. We both grew up during the Great Depression and were greatly influenced by President Franklin Roosevelt's "fireside chats" and by Eleanor Roosevelt's compassionate advocacy for social changes. I had seen FDR from a street corner when he came to San Francisco to promote what would be the birth of the United Nations in our city. Phyllis one-upped me. As a reporter for a newspaper in Chico, California, she had been assigned to interview Eleanor Roosevelt on one of the train "whistle-stops" nearby. Phyllis was so awed to be in the presence of her idol that she was speechless. Graciously, Mrs. Roosevelt conducted the interview herself. In our childhood we were both exposed to racism—Phyllis by her mother, a Southern belle, who said Negroes were okay in their place, being subservient; my mother,

also from the South, thought Negroes were okay as long as they kept themselves clean, and my stepfather, a veteran of World War I, deplored Krauts.

We also discovered that we had both gone to the University of California
at Berkeley, majored in journalism, and worked on *The Daily Californian*.
Our experience with the diverse population on campus and as reporters was
contrary to the experiences of our parents. It made a very deep impression
on both of us. We both became champions against discrimination. Phyllis,
who initially had spoken vehemently against allowing Negroes in her dorm,
had early on been forced to examine her racist attitudes and she soon found
she could not justify them. A person's skin color had nothing to do with a
person's worth. She went home and told her folks, "I believe Negroes are
just as good as we are." They had a fit. Phyllis also wrote a scathing editorial for the *Daily Cal* about the internment of Japanese-Americans during
World War II.

We both like martinis and often spent cocktail hours after work at Seattle's Press Club. Coincidentally, we both had a sister who was six years
younger and who had fallen in love with her college professor, and both
married a man with the surname Rowe. Neither of us identified with a religious denomination. According to Phyllis, although her father, William
Lyon, had been raised as a strict Presbyterian and her mother, Lorena, was
the daughter of a Southern Methodist preacher, her parents never went to
church. Nor did they require her and her sister, Patricia, to do so. When
Phyllis was in high school she went on a skiing trip with a church youth
group. A boy in the group invited her to come with him to the church Bible
class. Out of curiosity, she accepted. When the class ended, they were asked,
"Do you believe Jesus Christ was the son of God?" Phyllis was pressured to
say "yes'" with the others, but she could not. Although trained not to question adult authority, she could not lie. She had just wanted to learn about the
Bible.

While most of her schoolmates observed a weekend Sabbath, Phyllis and
her sister Tricia went bicycle or horseback riding. They started the latter as
soon as Tricia was old enough to sit on a horse. In Sacramento, with a stable
nearby, Phyllis became a proficient equestrian and collected many ribbons
for horsemanship and jumping. As a nonbeliever Phyllis thought she had escaped any power that religion had over her life. Wrong!

In 1961 after Illinois adopted the prestigious American Law Institute's
Model Penal Code proviso that sexual activity between consenting adults in
private should no longer be a concern of the law, it gave hope to those of us
in the Daughter of Bilitis, the organization that we had cofounded (as indicated in the biography of Del),[1] that it would happen in California too. We
talked to Phillip Burton and John O'Connell, San Francisco's state assem-
blymen, about the possibility. They said there was no way for this to come

about without the support of the churches. DOB had established a foot in the door when the San Francisco Council of Churches filled our request for a clergyman by sending Episcopalian priest Fordyce Eastburn to speak at our first National Lesbian Convention in 1960. Attempts with other denominations brought the same negative response of "love the sinner, hate the sin" and "celibacy" party lines. The Mormons and Catholic Churches were the worst.

In 1964 when the Reverend Ted McIlvenna, a Methodist minister at Glide Urban Center, invited us to participate in a retreat/consultation between clergy and homosexuals, Phyllis reluctantly agreed to attend. Little did she know that this retreat would be the genesis of a whole new career and partnership that lasted until she retired in 1987. McIlvenna was the founding president of the Council on Religion and the Homosexual, the first organization that dared to use the H-word in its title. It was formed in San Francisco as the "test" city, as suggested by the clergy participants at the retreat. The police harassment and arrests at the New Year's 1965 Costume Ball in San Francisco to raise funds for the fledgling organization prompted seven very angry ministers to hold a press conference the next day in protest of the police actions. The international wire services picked up the story and McIlvenna was deluged with mail from around the world. Phyllis volunteered to help him answer the letters and he hired her as a temporary secretary. The two worked together so well that she began to take on more responsibility and was elevated to a permanent position as his administrative assistant.

After the notoriety of the infamous New Year's ball, a couple of gay men appeared on Jim Dunbar's early morning show on KGO-TV. Later, Phyllis, as DOB's public relations director, was invited to appear. She was eager to have the opportunity but not eager enough to cross the picket lines outside the studio by its employees involved in a labor dispute. In past years she had tried to persuade her fellow workers to join the Newspaper Guild. While in Chico she had lost her battle by one vote. In Seattle the issue was getting the women comparable pay. She lost there by a larger majority because married women whose husbands belonged to unions said their families were already covered and they did not want to pay dues twice.

After the dispute at KGO was settled, Phyllis was again invited to appear. I went with her to the studio. One could expect a little stage fright on her part, but the panic we witnessed at the studio over having a "les-bian" on the air surprised us, since they had already interviewed gay men and the roof had not fallen in. But the attitude seemed to be that lesbians were independent of men, even men haters and contrary to America's "mom and apple pie" tradition.

The interview went fairly well. Phyllis wasn't frightening to the radio audience. There were some negative and positive telephone calls from the listening audience. What Phyllis remembers most was when she returned to Glide. The woman at the switchboard exclaimed: "I'm so glad you're back. The switchboard has been overloaded with calls." Most of them were from married and single heterosexual women who were weary of their husbands and boyfriends and wanted to know how and where to meet a lesbian (presumably to have an experimental sexual encounter). Phyllis explained it did not work that way and offered some general information. She quipped later, "If we'd had a lesbian whorehouse then we'd have made a mint."

During the latter half of the 1960s Phyllis was on a roller-coaster ride. McIlvenna, a catalyst for change, came up with idea upon idea and moved rapidly from project to project. Her job was to help implement them. She was Glide's liaison to the homophile community, coordinating activities of the Council on Religion and the Homosexual (CRH) and in effect acting as the lesbian/gay switchboard. For clergymen who came to the Glide Urban Center for training in how to cope with the changing urban scene, Phyllis was often the first "homo-sexual" they had ever met.

In 1965 the CRH published *A Brief of Injustices,* an indictment of our society in its treatment of homosexuals; then *Churchmen Speak Out on Homosexual Law Reform* in 1967, and *CRH 1964-1968* in the following year. Then the Daughters of Bilitis, Society for Individual Rights, and the Tavern Guild of San Francisco collaborated with CRH to prepare and publish *The Challenge and Progress of Homosexual Law Reform in 1968* and *Homosexuals and Employment* in 1970. CRH also organized a symposium on the "lifestyle" of the homosexual. Thanks to CRH, lesbians and gays assumed the role of experts in training clergy, attorneys, nurses, therapists, teachers, physicians, social workers—anyone who might counsel homosexuals.

McIlvenna, noting how uptight most ministers, other religious professionals, and most helping professionals of whatever persuasion were about the topic of sex, realized it was impossible to deal with homosexuality without first dealing with human sexuality itself. To be a good pastoral counselor one needed first to overcome personal sexual hang-ups. So he, Phyllis, and Laird Sutton, another Methodist minister, began developing multimedia teaching techniques.

Both Phyllis and I were active in politics and, after we came out, we realized the political potential of the lesbian and gay movement. We began to endorse candidates and held our first candidate's night in the sanctuary of Glide Church in 1965, where we endorsed attorney Robert Gonzales, who wanted to be the first Hispanic on the board of supervisors. The campaign tactics we used, however, were unusual. We feared that our public endorsement might not be helpful and we decided to conduct a "water closet" campaign. We displayed Gonzales' posters behind closed doors in the rest rooms of gay bars. Gonzales came in sixth in an election of the top five candidates and at an election postmortem with his supporters Gonzales gave the gay community credit for 20 percent of his vote. We had arrived as a political force.

Phyllis' greatest triumph in DOB was in her role as public relations director. By 1966 the seven homophile organizations in the city had gained enough clout that the San Francisco chapter, host of the DOB Convention, decided the theme should be "San Francisco and Its Homophile Community—A Merging Social Conscience." Although it was a national convention, members chose to use San Francisco once again as the test city, as had been the case with the Council on Religion and the Homosexual. CRH had opened up channels of communication with newspapers, police, armed services, suicide prevention, politicians, ethnic minority groups, civil rights organizations, and the chamber of commerce. CRH board members had appeared on radio and television programs, both locally and nationally.

In the course of her preparation for the meeting, Phyllis noted that DOB had not been included in the list of conventions the San Francisco Convention and Visitors Bureau had given to the newspapers and other media. As public relations director she sent a letter to the Bureau charging "discrimination" and demanding "a public statement of apology for this oversight." She also sent copies to the two daily newspapers and the major television and radio networks. She got her wish—and then some.

The *San Francisco Chronicle* came out with a four-column story and a big bold headline, "S.F. Greets Daughters." The on-the-hour news summaries broadcast on radio stations KEWB and KSFO featured DOB. Phyllis was interviewed by KEWB about the convention and on other radio and television stations. On August 20, the day the convention opened, the Convention Bureau sent two young women to help with registration. A bevy of reporters were in the sound booth of the hotel taping speakers and sessions.

The morning panel was devoted to "The Homophile Community and Civic Organizations—How They Relate" and the afternoon explored "The Homophile Community and Governmental Agencies—Can They Relate?" Mayor John Shelley sent a message of welcome and best wishes for a successful meeting, and designated the director of the San Francisco Health Department as his official representative. Also in attendance were representatives of the district attorney's office, the police department, the public defender's office, Center for Special Problems, San Francisco Council of Churches, Suicide Prevention, the Council of Religion and the Homosexual, and the Mexican-American political association. Municipal Judge Joseph Kennedy was the luncheon speaker and part of his speech was broadcast. Dr. Evelyn Hooker, psychologist and researcher at UCLA, moderated a roundtable discussion featuring all speakers to close the afternoon session. Dorothy von Beroldingen, a member of the San Francisco board of supervisors, was the banquet speaker.

Following the convention Phyllis was interviewed on *Spectrum 74,* a CBS radio call-in show. She also spoke at the Sirtoma Breakfast Club and appeared on various radio programs. Even Herb Caen, legendary *Chronicle* columnist, ran a blurb about the Daughters featuring the banquet where DOB gave out SOB awards (Sons of Bilitis) to men who had helped the lesbian cause.

Critics of Daughters of Bilitis, especially gay males, had belittled DOB for being a separatist organization and tended to treat DOB as a women's auxiliary. Even though lesbians were front and center at the convention, more attention was paid to gay male civil liberties than lesbian civil rights— only emphasizing that lesbians understood and supported their gay brothers who were more apt to face beatings and entrapment than women and to be arrested for public sex and/or perceived effeminate behavior.

A more intense focus on lesbian issues came with the rise of the feminist movement in the 1970s. In the later 1960s, Phyllis, as a member of the National Organization for Women, joined in demonstrations which focused on desexing employment want ads in the newspapers, equal employment opportunity for women, equal membership rights for women at the Press Club, and for putting an end to male-only restaurants. She added another dimension to Glide's focus on the changing urban scene: feminism.

In 1966 our family (including our pregnant daughter and our granddaughter) joined the picket line at the gates of the Sacramento State Fair for denying CRH a booth. It brought far more attention to our four-page tabloid, headlined "Every Tenth Person Is a Homosexual," than being in a booth would have. On Armed Forces Day we joined the first national demonstration in major U.S. cities protesting discrimination against gays in the military. The action (in San Francisco in front of the Federal Building) had been initiated by the North American Conference of Homophile Organizations.

In 1968 the National Sex Forum was founded by Glide and the Sexual Attitude Restructuring process (SAR) was introduced. It began as training for clergy, later expanded to helping professionals and their referrals. In the end the Forum accepted anyone who wanted to know more about human sexuality. McIlvenna and Phyllis wrote articles for religious magazines and professional publications to spread the word. They participated in a *Playboy* symposium on homosexuality with psychiatric, legal, and sociological experts and researchers. Phyllis found working with McIlvenna was a continuous adventure. There was never a dull moment. Between her job there and her work with DOB, increasing contact came about with Paul Gebhard and

Wardell Pomeroy of the Kinsey Institute for Sex Research, and the growing profession of sexologists.

The feminist movement of the 1970s sparked a lesbian rebellion against gay male domination and chauvinism in the gay movement. Lesbians came out in droves to claim their identity, their bodies, their lives, their spirits. In the process, the lesbian liberation movement became so diverse that it was unidentifiable by traditional standards. The 1970s was a freeing, exhilarating, inspiring, and empowering decade for lesbians. It was evolutionary and revolutionary. A lesbian/woman culture and a lesbian national counterculture brought about a renaissance of lesbian music, performing, literary, and visual arts. Contradictions in experience, ideology, and organizing techniques often gave the appearance of irreconcilable differences among lesbians, but the result was an unrelenting advocacy for lesbian visibility and freedom. Phyllis Lyon was right in the middle of it all.

She helped with the lesbian struggle to pass policy resolutions at the 1971 and 1973 NOW national conventions which recognized that oppression of lesbians was a feminist issue and which pledged support for legislation to end discrimination on the basis of sexual orientation. NOW's national board, in an effort to deal with both racism and homophobia within its ranks, invited Aileen Hernandez, the African-American former NOW president, and Phyllis Lyon to be the keynote speakers at the 1974 convention. Phyllis recalls that most members had assumed that the "lesbian issue" had been resolved and wondered, what do lesbians want? The answer, she stated, was simple: implementation and personhood. "Lesbianism is not just an aspect of human sexuality or an alternative lifestyle," she pointed out, but rather "a fundamental way of being in the world." She concluded that lesbians want "the language and behavior of every person to bespeak a consciousness about, and affirmation of, lesbian existence. That means *now* in NOW."

In 1972, after the book *Lesbian/Woman* Phyllis and I wrote was released, we went on the road to publicize it, speaking, doing television and radio interviews. Among other things we appeared on the Phil Donahue show as well as a number of college campuses, usually as a duo, but also with researchers and others attempting to dignify sexology as a profession. Back in San Francisco, Phyllis worked with McIlvenna to move the Sex Forum from Glide to its own location, established the International Museum of Erotic Art, giving Phyllis and Eberhard Kronhausen a home for their art collection. Phyllis also worked with the Sex Forum to produce a series of booklets which together made up what was called the Yes Booklets of Sex. They were "how to" books designed to help the average person understand, accept, and value human sexuality. Our contribution, *Lesbian Love and Liber-*

ation ran photos of real live lesbians and used real names of lesbians who braved suffering through court suits over their jobs or child custody rights.

In 1974 we went to Europe nominally to participate in a SAR seminar in Paris, but we also took the opportunity to go to the first British Women's Conference held in Edinburgh, Scotland. Lesbians, hoping to pass a resolution similar to the one NOW had adopted, had set aside a workshop period before the plenary for simultaneous encounter groups between lesbian and nonlesbian women. Although we had attended with some trepidation about what might happen, our fears were groundless. The lesbian resolution passed unanimously.

We met with Sappho members in London, and visited with Holland's lesbian and gay organizations, which predated the American ones. The highlight of our Paris presentation was when we mentioned that lesbians in England were engaging in artificial insemination in order to get pregnant. A man jumped up, identified himself as the director of a French sperm bank, and exclaimed, "No lesbian is going to get any of my sperm!"

On our return to San Francisco, Mayor George Moscone appointed Phyllis to the Human Rights Commission, and she chaired the Commission's Lesbian and Gay Advisory Committee for ten years, and the Commission itself in 1982-1983. In 1976, the Erotic Art Museum closed its doors. Shortly thereafter McIlvenna founded The Institute for Advanced Study of Human Sexuality as a graduate school to offer doctoral degrees in sexology. Phyllis served as registrar, trustee, professor, and dean of lesbian and gay studies until 1987.

In 1978, Phyllis broke new ground when she and Pat Norman, a black lesbian activist and a community health worker, decided that employees in the mental health field needed in-service sensitivity training on "gay, lesbian, and bisexual lifestyles." After some pressure the city's Community Health Services contracted with the National Sex Forum to offer such training and mandated that its 400 employees attend.

Phyllis' political skills were called upon again in that same year when State Senator John Briggs put an initiative on the ballot to ban homosexuals, or anyone who publicly supported homosexual rights, from teaching in California schools. Phyllis chaired San Franciscans Against Proposition 6, part of a statewide campaign which defeated the resolution by a whopping 75 percent to 25 percent vote.

In the 1980s and 1990s "Wonder Woman" Lyon continued to serve on numerous and diverse committees and boards of community, government, political, and charitable causes, although she admits she might have slowed down a bit. She keeps saying that we both need to learn to say no. But when the telephone rings and a new problem is posed, Phyllis the activist is always raring to go. Her latest issue might be called self-serving—ageism and advocacy for an invisible constituency. Our generation of lesbians and gay men are still mostly in the closet, making lesbian, gay, bisexual, and transgender elders a most underserved population. Through prodding by Old Lesbians Organizing for Change, of which Phyllis is an active member, national LGBT legal and health organizations are beginning to address this oversight.

Phyllis Lyon has won respect and love from many quarters and has received many honors. The one she is most proud of is the 1996 Society for the Scientific Study of Sexuality Public Service Award "in recognition and appreciation for her pioneering work in the lesbian movement which forced the world to pay attention to lesbian and gay activists."

And that's the truth.

In 1999 during the campaign against Proposition 22, a California initiative denying LGBT couples the right to marry, we decided to take advantage of the new domestic partners ceremony at City Hall. Beforehand, we saw it as a political statement. Afterward, we knew it was really a declaration of love.

NOTE

1. Phyllis Lyon was DOB's first secretary, the first editor of its magazine *The Ladder,* peer counselor, and host at social and fundraising events.

REFERENCES

Most of the information in this chapter is based upon my long association with Phyllis Lyon.

Books

Lyon, Phyllis, with Toni Ayres, Ted McIlvenna, Frank Myers, Margo Rila, Maggi Rubenstein, Carolyn Smith, Laird Sutton. *SAR Guide for a Better Sex Life.* San Francisco: National Sex Forum, 1975; revised, 1977.
Lyon, Phyllis, with Del Martin. *Lesbian Love and Liberation.* San Francisco: Multi Media Resource Center, 1973.
Lyon, Phyllis, with Del Martin. *Lesbian/Woman.* San Francisco: Glide Publications, 1972; revised New York: Bantam, 1983; updated, Volcano, CA: Volcano Press, 1991.

Selected Articles and Chapters

Lyon, Phyllis, with Del Martin, "A Lesbian Approach to Theology," in *Is Gay Good? A Symposium on Homosexuality, Theology and Ethics,* edited by W. Dwight Oberholtzer, Westminster Press, 1971, pp. 113-220.

Lyon, Phyllis, with Del Martin. "The Old Lesbian," in *Positively Gay,* edited by Betty Berzon and Robert Leighton. Millbrae, CA: The Celestial Arts, 1979; updated and edited by Betty Berzon, 1992, pp. 158-178.

Lyon, Phyllis, with Del Martin. "The Realities of Lesbianism," originally appeared in *Motive,* March-April 1969, republished in *The New Women.* New York: Bobbs-Merrill, 1970.

Lyon, Phyllis, with Del Martin. "Reminiscences of Two Female Homophiles, Part II," in *The New Our Right to Love, A Lesbian Resource Book,* edited by Ginny Vida. New York: Touchstone, 1996, pp. 121-126.

Billye Talmadge (1929-   ):
Some Kind of Courage

William Fennie

Times of crisis often cause courage to be drawn from unexpected places. During wartime, unimposing individuals can demonstrate capacities far beyond what seems possible. During natural catastrophes, ordinary citizens often behave with astonishing self-sacrifice. When commended for their actions later, they often say, "I just did what had to be done." The struggle for sexual freedom and liberation certainly continues in this new millennium, despite years of effort by countless numbers of individuals. The toll of the struggle is rarely tallied, except among those closest to the fray, because the battlefield does not exist in real space but in the interior landscapes of millions of people. For many, the rivers there run red from injury, denial, defiance, confusion, and every form of abuse. For Billye Talmadge, each and every casualty of that invisible conflict was and is a personal affront.

Plain-spoken, straightforward, and dedicated to personal and sexual freedom, Billye has always called herself a teacher. It might be more correct to say that she has made a career of taming wild animals. By the age of thirteen she had no less than seventeen stray dogs depending on her at her mother's house in (then) rural Bethany, Oklahoma. She frequently refers to the people who find their way to her as "one of my little foxes," referring to Antoine de Saint-Exupéry's story *The Little Prince*. During the mid-1950s and early 1960s she made it her business to learn the law and to educate others like herself—lesbian women—so that they could live with dignity in a society that did not want to admit their right to exist.

Born December 7, 1929, Billye Talmadge grew up in Bethany and for a time in Joplin, Missouri. Her parents were separated before she was born and she did not know her father. Growing up in Oklahoma posed unique challenges: Billye found that she could not agree with her family's position on race and many other issues. At age sixteen she set out on her own. Intellectually precocious, Billye completed her educational training a year early and began teaching eighth-grade English at the age of twenty-one. The short-lived foray into conventional academe left her emotionally bruised and dissatisfied. For six years she worked other jobs in Takoma, Seattle, and Oakland before finally finding her true calling teaching special education.

179

During her college years, on a brief visit home in 1949, one of Billye's closest friends told her that she was in love with a roommate at a local girls' school. Billye was dumbfounded. Never shy about asking for help, she took her confusion to the dean of women at her university, who provided her with materials on the subject, including *The Well of Loneliness,* by Radclyffe Hall. Reading it was "like coming home." She knew the course her life would run.

Five years later, when she became deeply involved in the Daughters of Bilitis, Billye would contribute to a publication that would serve the same purpose. *The Ladder,* for many women of the era, was a lifeline that reminded them that they were not alone, not crazy, and that there was nothing wrong with them. Its circulation grew to be worldwide. As a dedicated member, officer, volunteer, and peer counselor with the Daughters of Bilitis, Billye touched the lives of thousands of women and many men. She had an eye for the strays, the lost souls, the rebels, and the abused. Over time she accumulated a suite of tools and expertise which allowed her to help the people who came to her to find their way to wholeness.

In tandem with this work, she gave her unique love and encouragement to many youngsters as a special education teacher with the California school system. Noting bluntly that she enjoyed being able to teach without anyone else telling her what to do, Billye experimented, innovated, and introduced new methods. For more than twenty years Billye was not only a teacher but a healer to many physically or mentally handicapped children. The state saluted her efforts with recognition as Teacher of the Year in 1971.

When she became conscious in the late 1940s of her love and affection for other women, she suddenly realized that she probably would not be settling down with a husband and a crop of children as so many of her peers had. Billye took a characteristic choice, i.e., the direct approach: not knowing, really, what to do, even though she knew her preferences, she shadowed "the biggest butch on campus" for a week before getting up the courage to ask for some direction. "I asked her name, to make sure she was the right person, and then I said, 'Are you a lesbian? Because I think I am and I need to know what this is all about.'" As was to be the case so often in the future, Billye was well rewarded. The woman answered every question and treated her with thoughtful consideration. It is doubtful that, had this woman been interested in taking advantage of the situation, Billye would have succumbed without a fight.

Even before she became involved in the Daughters of Bilitis, Billye found herself counseling and caring for others. To begin, she was an inveterate matchmaker with a sure eye. She had suggested to an acquaintance from Oakland that she might enjoy meeting a woman Billye knew in Seattle. The two met, and the Seattle friend, Bonita, wrote to Billye for advice. Billye wrote back while she was at work, putting her response on the letterhead of the company she was working for at the time. Bonita read the letter and, in a hurry to leave, accidentally dropped it outside her door. Her postman found it, read it, and proceeded to blackmail her, threatening to expose Billye.

The risks were enormous. To be exposed as a "deviant" could cost a person one's job, often one's career. Billye recalls reading about a raid on a place in San Jose—a men's room in a bus station. Police arrested about forty, and the newspaper listed all of their names in a story with huge headlines. Included in those listed as arrested was a man who had been using the pay toilet without paying for it. He had had no small change in his pocket and had simply crawled under the door. In Billye's word, he was "tagged, snagged, and fired." He did fight the charges and eventually won, but it took him a long time and a lot of money—and although he got his job back, the public exposure remained. "He had the balls and the means to fight, whereas most women did not."

When Billye found out about the attempted blackmail, she was consumed with rage, and got in touch with authorities in Oakland who directed her to the post office inspector general's office. Because the laws about pornography were as yet very vague, the inspector general first asked Billye if there were anything in the letter "that my sixteen-year-old daughter should not read." She replied that there was counseling but nothing untoward. "I was too angry to be afraid. I had been violated, threatened, blackmailed, and my friends had been involved, and I was just furious." About a year later she learned that the postman had been arrested, had lost his job, was fined, and had spent two years in jail.

Billye came to believe that many gay people had built-in guilt about their sexuality which made them victims of intimidation when they had done nothing illegal. Thus her primary purpose became to educate not only the gay community but society at large. In spite of the very real potential cost of public exposure, Billye participated in conferences, was interviewed on the radio, and was never very secretive simply because, in her own words, she "didn't have sense enough to be afraid."

The Daughters of Bilitis had been organized in 1954. By the time Billye arrived all the founding members had moved on except for Del Martin and Phyllis Lyon, who were thinking about throwing in the towel unless things turned around. Billye and her friend Jaye Bell, affectionately known as "Shorty," attended a meeting with the two women, along with another couple. The six women talked through the night and into the morning and succeeded in initiating a new beginning for the DOB. Billye remained involved for five or six years until the time when "the Daughters had pretty well accomplished what it needed to do."

Billye believes that the DOB represented her greatest contribution to the movement; Del and Phyllis report that Billye was "very sensitive about people. . . . She was intuitive about somebody who might have a problem." Not only that, "She was fun to have around," they said. Some of the women who came to the "Gab'n'Javas" that Billye organized through the Daughters were truly troubled and had been victims of abuse; these were the ones that Billye was there for. "It was not unusual to get a call at 3 a.m. saying that we had somebody who was trying to commit suicide," she recalls.

Realizing that in many cases they were out of their league, the DOB leadership sought professional psychiatrists to help with some of the severe cases. They found one, a man, who was willing to help, but he turned out to be a lemon. His "therapy" consisted of curing a lesbian by attempting to seduce and rape her. Eventually, they found an excellent female psychologist who put Del and Phyllis and Billye through rigorous training in counseling and crisis management. As with so many things in Billye's life, the training was not taken for its own sake but because it was dearly needed to meet the challenge of so many people who were in pain.

Things were changing slowly. One of the turning points that eventually sparked the rise of gay electoral power was the mayor's race in San Francisco in 1959. Incumbent mayor Christopher was being challenged by a city official named Wolden. By this time, word had gotten around that San Francisco was something of a haven for gay men and women. In fact, at a meeting of the Mattachine Society in Denver, Colorado, the San Francisco Police Department had asked for, and received, a resolution commending it for its tolerant response to the gay community. Most people ignored the resolution even though it was printed on the inside pages of the local newspapers—but not Mr. Wolden, who believed he saw an issue that would define him as the clear choice for the mayor's office. He accused Mayor Christopher of allowing the city to become a hotbed of deviants.

It was one of those crisis moments that defines a movement. Afraid that their membership would take to the hills, DOB put together an emergency meeting to determine how to respond. It was a question, Billye says, of either "stand up and fight for being gay, and for your right to be gay, or hide— hide for the rest of your life." The group voted to fight and did so by organizing politically. "We got people registered to vote who hadn't voted in their lives," Billye recalls. The strategy was simple: vote as you please, but abstain from voting for mayor. The idea was to defeat the antigay candidate without explicitly supporting the incumbent. Herb Caen, one of the most influential columnists in San Francisco, picked up on the idea and plugged it in his column. "In that particular election, for the city, it was a tremendous number that came out to vote—and the number who abstained was just fantastic. . . ." Suddenly, the political world was forced to sit up and take notice of a new voting bloc. "From that moment on, any politician out of San Francisco really wooed the gay vote. It was not too long after that that they got an openly gay person on the council, Harvey Milk," Billye recalls.

Yet the atmosphere was far from tolerant. She remembers that DOB then had a couple of members who while walking down the street in Chicago in the late 1950s had been picked up for impersonating men. They had been dressed in fly-front jeans. Planning for a national convention DOB and with this Chicago experience in mind, DOB wrote in a requirement that every woman in attendance wear a skirt. "One woman hadn't been in a skirt in seventeen years, but she bought a skirt for the convention! That's how much they believed in what we were doing."

Then there was Halloween. In the 1960s October 31 was always the drag queen's big night out, but laws about impersonating a person of the opposite gender were still on the books and still enforced at the time. So planners for the big Halloween ball made arrangements for taxis bringing the men in drag to the hotel to deliver them close enough to a door that they could step directly from the cab to the hotel, a private establishment, without "being on the street."

Hair-splitting tactics such as these—successful ones—came from knowing the law and, in knowing the law, finding power. These people needed all the help they could get from whatever loophole they could find. The law was not imposed with any consistency. Billye asserts that,

> a lot depended on the arresting officer, how much he hated queers. We had one of our members who was picked up drunk, and she was drunk. But she was dressed butch, and the officer damn near beat her to death. He kept calling her a dyke, and a queer, and a son of a bitch, all this type of stuff. I was called and I went down and bailed her out. . . . I could hardly recognize her she was so badly beaten.

These events happened many decades before suing police departments became a viable option for anyone and, frankly, a queer didn't stand a chance. "She'd just be marked by every cop in the joint. So there was all that fear that you had to help people go through. It was justifiable fear; it wasn't like they were being paranoid."

Much more needed to be done, and to do it gay leaders knew they needed help. The goal was to get homosexuality out of the domain of the criminal justice system. With that in mind, in the mid-1960s, the Daughters conducted an informal survey of members and their relationship with their religion. They found that once a woman discovered she was gay it was difficult to reconcile herself with church beliefs. Rather than fight it, many dropped away from their faith. "That doesn't mean they she dropped away from God," Billye is quick to point out. "[A woman] ceased going to church because they would not accept her as the homosexual she was, or the lifestyle she had."

According to the survey the ones who had the most difficulty were Mormons. In that faith

> the woman was not considered a whole person—nor even to have a soul—unless she were consummated in marriage. So, you lay that on top of being gay . . . It was a heavy trip. The Catholics had it easy because they could be reconciled and forgiven [in confession] and do their penance. . . . There was a priest over in Fresno that most of the gay guys went to because he was an understanding person who would give them absolution so that they could participate in the sacraments of the faith. . . . The Jewish woman had it the easiest because as long as she fulfilled her responsibilities as a woman, which were wife, mother, or sister, she had no problem. Plus, it was the Jewish belief that it was the man whose sin was spilling his seed on the ground; the woman didn't have any seed to waste.

To deal with this problem, the Glide Urban Center organized a three-day weekend retreat that included ten gay men, five lesbian women, and fifteen clergymen from many different religious organizations. A remote Marin County location was chosen specifically to make it impossible for anyone to leave. "The first night we had absolute segregation: the men here, the women there, and the ministers over yonder. Bit by bit by bit the divisions broke down. Out of this meeting came the Council on Religion and the Homosexual." With ministers behind them, DOB and others began to see some success in changing the laws and moving the issue of homosexuality out of the criminal justice domain.

> At the end of the conference we took these ministers on a tour of the gay bars, from the god-awfulest, filthiest dive to some of your better restaurants. We said, "because of the laws this is what we have to go through to meet and congregate." We had to work like crazy, but we accomplished it.

Part of the work was building bridges between gay men and gay women.

> When I first came out [during the late 1940s and early 1950s], gay men and gay women were miles apart—it was as unusual as can be for a gay woman to have a friend who was a gay man . . . [mostly] out of sheer ignorance. Through a great deal of work we were able to break down some of those barriers.

This included inviting two gay men to a women's discussion group. They were "bombarded with hostility, questions." Billye had told the men what they would be up against and they were prepared. Little by little, distrust and suspicion were replaced by mutual respect and friendship.

In some ways, discrimination helped to forge the movement. Certain beer distributors, for example, refused to service gay bars. The owners of the men's and women's establishments got together and formed the Gay Tavern Guild and started cooperating. They boycotted the brands involved and made a significant economic impact, which added to the growing political clout of the group.

During these years, Billye volunteered uncounted hours while working a full-time job teaching in Berkeley. She would drive over to the city after her classes. During a typical week she would open and handle communications with the many women who wrote or called DOB from around the world. A great deal of the correspondence came from teenagers. Responses had to be very carefully thought out because one wrong word could put the Daughters in court faced with charges of contributing to the delinquency of a minor.

It is a simple fact that great movements are born of long, tedious hours that are given freely from the hearts of individuals who care deeply about the issue. No matter how events may be dramatized later, the core of the movement can be found in the hearts of individuals, and in the willingness of these individuals to work together despite their intrinsic differences. "We were all of us a bunch of rebels," Billye says. But there was a cause, a reason, a goal, and an aim.

> We had disagreements—not on the major issues. Our disagreements were always about the means. Sandy [Helen Sandoz] and I went head to head lots of times but never on the goal. I was always for the educational approach; Sandy was always for the political approach. They were simply two ways of achieving the same goal.

Politically, the Daughters of Bilitis made good neighbors. After the Denver meeting of the Mattachine Society, when the issue of "deviants" started to heat up again, the San Francisco police checked out the DOB office by interviewing the landlord. He simply stated that they were good, quiet tenants who paid their rent on time. "We blundered along," although as Billye admits, "sometimes it was scary." One raid had picked up about ninety-seven people, including four women. Del and Phyllis felt DOB should be involved and called Billye, who agreed. They arranged for a lawyer for the women, who advised them to plead innocent and ask for a jury trial. All the men ahead of them had pled guilty and were each fined eleven dollars. Only later did these men realize that pleading guilty to being in a house of ill repute gave them a police record. The four women, who pled not guilty, soon found their charges dismissed and no mark added to their records. This incident forcibly reminded Billye that most gays and lesbians did not know their rights.

Other groups also became involved in the struggle. The closing of "Mary's First and Last Chance," a gay club in Oakland, attracted the attention of the American Civil Liberties Union in the late 1960s. The ACLU filed a suit which found its way to the California Supreme Court. The Court found that laws prohibiting public establishments based on the character of their clientele violated the constitutional right of people "to peaceably assemble."

This revolutionary period, from 1959 to 1969, saw great strides in the decriminalization of homosexuality. "It became part of the medical domain," Billye notes. "Now we had to be cured, but at least we were not criminals anymore." In 1959, San Francisco's Mayor Christopher could not even bring himself to use the word "homosexual" in political discourse. Ten years later the seeds of what would become a strong gay pride movement were well planted. The dedication required to accomplish these gains had costs. "It was rough on relationships sometimes, because a couple would meet us and one would become very interested while the other was not," but Billye believes, "the rift had to be there to begin with."

> We had many couples who were clearly a couple and went through everything together as a couple. We didn't make too many glaring errors. We were very good about talking things over and trying to figure out which was the best way to try to approach something. We worked very hard to have a membership vote—not just those of us who were the leaders.

Does Billye have any regrets? "None, I really don't. I think the Daughters just sort of dissipated because the need for it had been met." Gay women, she believes, had begun a movement that others would carry into the mainstream as "women's liberation," a movement that would transform the face of American society and lead to a new identification for men as well. Gradually Billye moved on to other things.

While still in the Daughters she had met women associated with a group called The Prosperos. As she explored this new organization, she found that many of its goals vis-à-vis education spoke to her ever-present interest in social change. From 1965 until 1979 Billye dedicated herself to helping people of all kinds—gay, straight, man, woman, old, young—to strip away the conditioned roles that imprisoned them. The Prosperos was dedicated to "revealing the true identity of man as consciousness." Due largely to the insight and erudition of the school's founder, Thane Walker, several of the leaders in the lesbian movement found themselves involved in this new project. Helen Sandoz and Stella Rush became very involved, as did Del Martin and Phyllis Lyon, who maintained cordial and cooperative relations over many years. The Prosperos' fundamental idea, drawn strongly from the philosophy of Aristotle, held that the spiritual identity of every person is beingness, or essence, and that beingness is male and female. In their view, every person has access to both sets of capacities and cannot be separated from either. This viewpoint was, at the time, unique in according a spiritual justification for any person's sexual preference. To put it perhaps too simply: God as male and female beingness was present in and as every person, and it really didn't matter which set of plumbing was involved in a social or sexual encounter. "The Prosperos had wooed us from the Daughters," Billye relates. "It was an educational group, primarily. Sexuality was one of major topics. I got involved and became a teacher, with the goal of helping people to find themselves: not what I want them to be, but to find themselves and to express whatever that self is."

By the late 1970s, Billye came to believe that she had made whatever contribution she could to The Prosperos and turned her energies to her relationship with Marcia Herndon, which began in 1974. Marcia was a professor of ethnomusicology, and Billye put in many hours editing, typing, and organizing materials for Marcia's seven books, two of which are still in use as instructional texts. The twenty-three-year relationship did not alter her commitment to being there for others. Her involvement in the gay community

> diminished in numbers but not in intensity. Marcia was a healer in her own right, and we each drew to us people who needed our help. We were different in so many ways, but when it came to counseling or teaching we could end each other's sentences.

Before Marcia's death in 1997 Billye had begun gathering materials for a book of her own, a work of fiction. She is just now rekindling her efforts in that direction. She stated, "I'm rereading my ideal writer, Rita Mae Brown; I love her humor. I'm not sure I can sustain my energies for a book, but I can for short stories." Billye has not tried to build up her counseling practice again, although she feels she has a lot to say. Perhaps that will be done through the written word.

After all that has happened, what she hopes for most is that Del Martin and Phyllis Lyon are recognized in a different way.

They are [already recognized] in many ways, but I would like to see them recognized as the steadfast friends they have proved to be to me and to others. . . . In some ways they have been idealized as a couple, but in other ways the trueness of their friendship has not really been touched.

Billye Talmadge could be described as the antithesis of the "quiet desperation" that so many are said to be living. She has reached out with both hands and grasped her life, striving to solve its puzzles and sharing the fruits of her insights willingly with anyone interested. She cannot stand the sight of any creature experiencing pain. Faced with the pain of others, she struggled, found help where she could, and made mistakes, but always she was there. Her unique courage surfaces and raises great indignation when human beings act in ways that bring pain upon others. She is vigorously spiritual and refreshingly earthy. She does not suffer fools lightly; yet her advocacy has always been tempered with compassion.

One can almost imagine that after a long and event-filled life, on the verge of entering the next world, Billye will look at some close friend and say, "Is that some kind of spot on your forehead? Promise me you'll get that looked at." After which she will move on to another place, another challenge, and a plenitude of interesting times. Today, on her own again after Marcia's death, Billye maintains her connection with life through the several feral cats and numerous woodland critters that crowd the deck of her rural Maryland home each night for dinner at Chez Talmadge. She remains ebullient and optimistic, a relentless advocate for the disadvantaged.

REFERENCES

This chapter is based on a series of interviews with Billye that took place in July and August 2000. There was also a telephone interview with Del Martin and Phyllis Lyon in August 2000.

Cleo Glenn (Bonner) (Dates Unknown)

Phyllis Lyon
Del Martin

Some of the activists in the gay and lesbian movement seem to come from nowhere to take a dominating role and then, after a period of intense activity, disappear. Somehow, they manage to keep much of their private lives from their activist colleagues, and it is only later that we find out they dropped out because they were ill or had died. Some made such a strong impression and were so important that they deserve a brief mention. Cleo Glenn (Bonner) was such a person.

Cleo was a tall, attractive African-American woman with an aristocratic and assured manner. She was in a conflicted interracial relationship, not so much about racism as about her son. Her lover was adamantly opposed to having children cross the threshold of their home. Cleo solved the problem by renting a duplex. That way she could share one unit with her lover and the other with her son. Anyone who could juggle such a home life and hold down a job at Pacific Bell had to be strong and determined.

We first met Cleo in 1960 at a brunch held by a closet group of lesbians whom we were attempting to recruit to the Daughters of Bilitis. Cleo was the only one who responded. She assumed the surname Glenn and took on the job of circulation manager of *The Ladder,* DOB's magazine. She soon became manager (without the title) of DOB's national office, assumed the job of acting national president in November 1963, and in 1964 was elected national president in her own right. In May 1964 she represented DOB at a retreat where lesbians and gay men met with members of the clergy, a meeting which ultimately led to the formation of the Council on Religion and the Homosexual. In June of that same year she delivered the welcoming address at DOB's national convention in New York City.

We had traveled together across country to go to New York and we had registered at a strange hotel in the Village, one recommended by a gay man. We had just entered our room when Cleo phoned us, practically in tears, over the accommodations—unclean paper peeling off the walls, holes in the carpeting—and all three of us marched down to the desk asking if we could get something better at the same price, as the three of us were paying (money was a problem) for our separate rooms. We wound up in the building's penthouse, which included a sitting room and two bedrooms.

The convention went off without a hitch, despite efforts of the FBI to catch up with us as a result of a tip that lesbians were going to meet at the New Yorker Hotel. That plan had fallen through; instead, we met in the Barbizon-Plaza across from Central Park, and *The New York Times,* which had previously refused to take any advertisements for books with "homosexual" in their titles, deigned to cover the public forum. Despite the publicity, the FBI never did find us—or at least they never publicly accosted us.

Cleo continued as president of DOB, but at the 1966 convention in San Francisco, she was nowhere to be seen at the public forum. Although she did not say so, it apparently was one thing to be "out" in New York and another to be "out" in one's home state, only emphasizing the courage it took for many DOB members to be open about their homosexuality. When she stepped down as president, she dropped out of her activist role and we lost contact. She must have been ill, for the next time we heard about her was in a call from her lover who announced that Cleo had died of cancer. She is symbolic of the many lesbians who demonstrated the courage to speak out and be themselves, but she is also emblematic of the difficulties that such action entailed not only in the community at large but in segments of the lesbian community itself.

Pat Walker (1938-1999)

Del Martin
with assistance from Leslie Warren

Pat Walker was nicknamed Dubby because she was short, but she was ever long on memory. Pat could literally see in the dark and saved on her electric bill by cooking, doing dishes, sewing, and cleaning house in the dark. Most of us had two strikes against us as lesbians and as women. She was discriminated against on four counts—because she was also blind and an African American. None of this stopped her from being an activist and making the world better for women, lesbians, African Americans, and the blind.

She made up for her inability to see by developing her memory and her senses of hearing, touch, smell, and taste. She could tell who was approaching by their steps or voice. She didn't want a Seeing Eye dog. "They get all the credit," she quipped. She spent a year at the Independent Living Center learning how to survive, how to use a cane, and how to use her other senses to "see" her way on downtown traffic-filled streets. Her independence was very important to her.

Pat took over a telephone wake-up call service to support herself. Later she ran a snack bar in a Berkeley public office building. If people tried to rob her, she tackled them. She was known as a tough little lady who shouldn't be messed with.

Pat joined the Daughters of Bilitis in the early 1960s. With her humor, her sensitivity and warmth, her caring and patience with people, and her funny stories, she became very popular. Pat was elected president of the San Francisco chapter and proved to be a strong leader who had no trouble delegating authority. Besides her work with DOB Pat donated some time answering the night help line run by San Francisco's Suicide Prevention Agency.

In 1964 she was one of the representatives of DOB at a retreat in Mill Valley arranged by Reverend Ted McIlvenna of the Glide Foundation. He brought together fifteen lesbian and gay leaders and fifteen clergymen for a consultation on "The Church and the Homosexual." Living together for several days and breaking down stereotypes brought results. Out of that meeting came the establishment of the Council on Religion and the Homosexual in San Francisco, a combination that was to have an indelible impact on society that continues today.

Pat loved to read (by Braille) and listen to music. She was a devoted fan of Joan Baez and was thrilled when she got to meet her in person at a concert. In a poem published in *The Ladder* in July 1962, Dubby wrote:

> Burning, blistering sand,
> Desolate desert all around me.
> I seek the sanctum of an oasis
> Where in the cool of sheltering shade
> By a pool of life-giving water I may be revived once more.

In her later years, Pat Walker found her beloved "sanctum" in the desert near Lake Elsinore. An aunt had left Pat her home in Los Angeles. Pat sold this property and used the money to purchase five acres in the desert. Although she usually lived alone, she was resourceful and gutsy, stubborn, and funny. When friends warned her about rattlesnakes and tarantulas, she retorted, "I could get killed walking across the street in Los Angeles." It did not matter to her either that she had to walk five miles to get groceries. She had a dog and two cockatiels. She could listen to her records. She could play her musical instruments (sax, piano, flute, piccolo, and guitar) as loud and as long as she wanted without interruption.

During her final years, Pat lived her dream. She died surrounded by friends and family, who prompted the hospice volunteer to observe, "You are all so different. She must have been quite a person." That she was, demonstrating that lesbian activists can come in multiple forms and with multiple handicaps and can make major contributions.

Bob Basker (1918-2001):
Selling the Movement

James T. Sears

Courtesy of Jim Sears

Bob Basker, a native New Yorker, was a traveling salesman for the movement during the 1960s and 1970s, assuming activist roles in Chicago, Cuba, New York City, and South Florida before settling in San Francisco. He seemed for a time to go everywhere and meet everyone in the movement.

Basker's parents were from a *Fiddler on the Roof*-type community in pre-Revolutionary Poland. Immigrating to America, they operated a grocery store in East Harlem, where Bob, then named Solomon, the youngest of five boys, was born in 1918. After losing the store because of hard times, his family was dispossessed of its home on 109th Street. Forced to sell newspapers, there were times when they could not afford even tenement rent and were put "out on the street."

Basker, who would be lauded by *The Advocate* as "Dade County's chief salesman for gay rights" forty years later, first demonstrated his activist bent at the age of fourteen. In 1932, he defended his mother in a New York City court for selling newspapers without a license. While awaiting the hearing, Solomon read Paul de Kruif's recently published *Microbe Hunters: Fighting Foes Too Small to See*. He also thought about how the owner of the speakeasy, across from the subway at 193rd Street and Bennett Avenue, had set up his "cook" with a newspaper stand three weeks after the Baskers had begun selling papers. Soon the number of papers they sold dwindled, while the competition, now with a license in hand, informed the police of the illegal operation of Solomon's mother.

After being informed that his mother was in violation of the law, Solomon asked the judge: "What would you rather we should do? Break a little

193

one-sided ordinance and sell papers so we can eat or observe this law and go away, not to make any money, to starve, and then, out of desperation, to steal?"

The judge dismissed the case and offered to write a letter to the licensing commissioner asking that Basker's mother be given some help in this matter. The magistrate then looked down on the young lad and asked: "What do you expect to be when you grow up?"

"I would like to be a doctor, your Honor," Solomon replied.

"No," said the judge. "You should be a lawyer."

Growing up within a staunchly religious family (he had been a cantor at the Uptown Talmud Torah), Basker remembered the German-American bund leaders in the mid-1930s making speeches against Jews, "looking forward to Jewish blood flowing into the streets." As a sixth grader, he recalled being beaten by Italian students, who rationalized, "Jews killed Christ; we're going to kill you!" Basker's political views were also shaped by Abraham Lincoln Brigades of youth fighting fascism in the Spanish Civil War and populist culture, from union songs such as "Solidarity Forever" to novels such as Steinbeck's *The Grapes of Wrath*. As a budding activist at Morris High School, located in the Bronx, Basker was suspended for "arrogance, insolence, and insubordination" for organizing the American Students' Union, a coalition of student peace groups united against "the forces of reaction." Later, as a City College of New York night student, he led student peace strikes and distributed pamphlets published by the Workers Library, again facing the opprobrium of school authorities. While studying accounting, Basker also served as president of the Marxist Study Club and joined the George Washington Carver Negro Cultural Society, becoming a delegate to the National Negro Congress. Before his death, he lived in San Francisco and remained active in progressive causes. Basker sang me one of the songs of that day when I spoke with him:

> City made a Marxist out of me who me
> I came up a petty bourgeoisie
> I came up to study some courses
> Now, I'm shouting down with the bosses
> City made a Marxist out of me

As a teenager during the mid-1930s, while selling newspapers on the trains, Basker discovered various men's rooms on the Lexington Avenue and Broadway subway stations where he would go to "be serviced or service." He also encountered "bushwhackers" (masturbating men in Central Park bushes) near 59th Street and Fifth Avenue when he attended the city's brass band concerts. At the time, "I didn't think about being gay or straight," but a few years later he would go "camping" with gay kids at the park and enter the sexual underground: gay or mixed bars on 52nd Street between Fifth and Sixth Avenue; the Cerutti's Waldorf Astoria on Lexington Avenue where Billie Holiday performed, and Bar 13 on Third Avenue where he found "great social relationships and after-hours private parties." There was also cruising outside of clubs such as Sardi's on Theater Row or going to the 181 Club that featured drag. Some of the men he met schooled him in the opera, ballet, literature, and classical music. Although Basker had heard of raids on the gay bars, the only incident he witnessed was one early evening when a policeman slammed "this sissy-boy into the back of his car" and slapped him around. "He was just beating the hell out of this kid. It was at that point that I became very antagonistic to the police because of this injustice." There was little, however, that homosexuals could do at the time. Efforts to organize the country's first homosexual group had failed a decade earlier in Illinois, and the Nazis had crushed the homosexual emancipation movement in Germany, destroying Magnus Hirschfeld's Institute for Sexual Science.

Basker was also brought "in the life" of Harlem's homosexual community where he frequented the Paradise Club on 135th Street and Seventh Avenue—a straight nightclub downstairs and an upstairs bar for men—and he visited the Mount Morris baths. He became the only white member of the clandestine JUGGs ("Just Us Guys and Gals"). This group of fairly well-to-do black lesbians and gay men included professionals such as a Methodist homosexual minister and his lesbian wife who, after a late night of partying, would meet their congregation for all-day Sunday services. With them, Basker—dressed like the other tuxedoed men—frequented black drag shows and Saturday night house parties as well as straight supper clubs with a lesbian "date."

Similar to his Harlem friends, Basker faced discrimination. He experienced difficulties finding a job because of his first name, Solomon. When he enlisted in 1941, he informed the sergeant that his name was Robert: "I figured I might as well use a name that is more accommodating to getting by." Nevertheless, when Robert was recommended for officer candidate school by his commanding officer, Colonel Richardson Bronson, he was turned down by a panel of officers. "Colonel Whittington told my commander, Colonel Bronson, that he didn't like the shape of my nose or the way I parted my hair. In other words, he was not going to allow a Jew to go to Officer Candidate School."

Following the war (Bob saw service in England, France, Belgium, Holland, and Germany) and a brief stint in the import-export business, Basker became a salesman for *Encyclopedia Britannica*. He moved from New York

City to Chicago on a management promotion in 1952, after breaking up
with Francis Galkin, a dress designer from Staten Island:

> I was undergoing psychotherapy in New York for the purpose of try-
> ing to get to the point that I might be able to find successfully the right
> woman and raise a family. In New York it was impossible because I
> was so integrated into the gay life and my phone was constantly ring-
> ing.

After only being in the Windy City for a week, however, Bob spotted a
young man on the street who was in the company of several other gay men.
Basker followed them into an art gallery and "little by little nursed my way
into their group," becoming lovers with the young man, Bobby McDowell.
Nevertheless, he continued his psychotherapy as he sought to qualify as "a
good husband and father." In 1953, he and his psychiatrist agreed that
Basker was ready. Bob proposed to a woman named Hedda, whose family
had come from Germany following the war. "I realized I was still gay, but I
also wanted to have a family. My fiancée knew I was gay and about my
friends, but we had a heterosexual relationship."

By the 1950s, Bob was living the quintessential lifestyle in a Chicago
suburb with his wife and three children. However, he had not abandoned his
socialist convictions nor his homosexual inclinations. During this Cold War
era of loyalty oaths, the House Un-American Activities Committee, atomic
bomb spy trials, and blacklists, Basker was active in many subversive and
not-so-subversive groups, including the Chicago Council for American Soviet Friendship, American Veterans for Peace, the Civil Rights Congress,
the Women's International League for Peace and Freedom, the American
Committee for Protection of Foreign Born, and the American Civil Liberties Union. Among his fellow activists was the blacklisted actor and
singer Paul Robeson and "fellow travelers" Scott Neering, a long-time Chicago activist and writer, and Henry Noyes, then regarded as a spokesperson
for Red China. Bob and Hedda supported Chicago families who were Smith
Act victims, hosted Russian dancers during their Chicago tour, held fundraisers for Helen Sobell. Helen's husband, Morton, had been convicted in
1951 and sentenced to thirty years for conspiracy to commit espionage for
the Soviet Union. Bob and Hedda also wrote letters to local newspapers in
support of racial integration.

Such activities did not escape the attention of Hoover's men. The FBI
visited the Baskers' Skokie home, where Bob recalled that an agent stroked
his four-year-old son's head. He remembered Hedda, who had been in a
concentration camp, observed contemptuously: "The way you're doing that
reminds me of the Gestapo doing that to me when they visited my mother in

Germany." The agent responded: "Oh! Then you're a communist." The FBI also visited Basker's workplace at *Encyclopedia Britannica* headquarters and he soon found himself out of work.

During the first spring of the so-called Camelot administration of John F. Kennedy, when freedom riders challenged the South's Jim Crow laws, Bob agreed to help bring about the racial integration of his Skokie neighborhood. Through the assistance of the American Friends Service Committee and the Catholic Interracial Council early in 1961, he and Hedda bought and immediately resold a newly constructed split-level home to a Hyde Park black professional couple. Basker's suburban home was firebombed. There was an unending stream of obscene phone calls. Menacing protesters marched and leaflets were distributed, asking: "Is communism infiltrating our community through the guise of integration?" Bob suffered a heart attack. Within a year, his wife—unwilling to live with a sick and sexually troubled husband—filed for divorce.

During the divorce proceedings, Basker was represented by civil liberties attorney, Pearl Hart. Hart was a founding member of the National Lawyers Guild and had collaborated with Jane Addams, the founder of Chicago's legendary Hull House. Similar to Addams, Hart was a closet lesbian and a lifelong activist in feminist and leftist causes. After the divorce, Baskers' wife quickly remarried and moved to Cuba with their children. At the end of his seven and a half years of marriage and no longer with a family to worry about, Basker had little to hold him back. In 1961, he became involved in the fledgling homophile movement.

Now working for a travel company, Basker took advantage of the job to visit "different gay communities around the country getting a sense of how groups were organized." He spent time with Mattachine leaders such as Frank Kameny in Washington, Dick Leitsch in New York, and Hal Call in San Francisco. He also spent considerable time in Los Angeles at the ONE Institute overseen by Dorr Legg. He subscribed to the *Mattachine Review* and *ONE Magazine* and attended national homophile conferences. Locally, he tried to organize in Chicago's gay bars, which were subject to erratic raids—including one that resulted in mass arrests, names published in the newspaper, and several suicides. "I'd ask the bartender if I could talk to different people around the bar. It was very difficult to get the customers to understand the usefulness of the movement. On the contrary, the reaction I got was: 'You're creating waves and just going to get us into trouble.' "

Meeting little success in bar recruitment, Basker found his first breakthrough through his contact with Hart, who had defended homosexual men arrested through police entrapment and who gave Basker occasional client names as potential members. He also got names of Chicago residents from national groups such as Mattachine and ONE. Through these efforts, Basker, under the alias Robert Sloane, eventually revived the "moribund" Chicago Mattachine Group founded in 1954 into a new Mattachine Midwest, a name suggested by Craig Rodwell, the founder of the nation's first gay bookstore. In that summer of 1965, Basker, as founding president, was helped by Ira Jones, prominent in the Episcopal church, Chuck Renslow, a gay bar and bathhouse owner (who would later begin the Mr. International Leather Contest), and the minister of a Park Ridge church that hosted the regular Mattachine meetings and helped produced a monthly local homophile newsletter—a rarity in the pre-Stonewall era. Basker also faced down Chicago red-baiting gay members who argued for "loyalty oaths" as a condition of membership. "I told them: 'If we do that I'll have to resign. These oaths are designed to break groups up, not keep them together.'" After his "consciousness-raising lecture" the issue was dead.

Within a year, the group had a functioning organization that included a telephone referral service (attorneys, clergy, bail bondsmen, psychologists) and regular guest speakers including visiting homophile activists such as Dorr Legg. The group also successfully challenged arrests in court. In 1966,

> Detective Benjamin, who had quite a record of arresting gays in T-rooms, organized the random arrest of some fifteen young men crossing the street in the area of Clark and Diversey. One or two weren't even gay. Mattachine Midwest got them out on bond and had legal representation for them the next morning in court, together with a legal stenotypist. Our attorney was Rolla Klepack [a closet lesbian]. Benjamin didn't show up. The judge had him tracked down, and when he was asked why he hadn't shown, he replied: "I didn't think it was necessary. They usually plead guilty, anyway." Our defendants made a nice appearance, all freshly shaved, and in coats and ties. Charges were dismissed; Officer Benjamin reprimanded. We nicknamed the incident "the harvest of fruits." (letter to John D'Emilio, February 8, 1979, Basker papers)

The successful court case, as it had earlier done in Los Angeles, raised the homophile banner and attracted new members.

Shortly after this success, Bob Basker moved to Miami, hoping to visit his family regularly in Cuba. This gregarious salesman who was working again for *Encyclopedia Britannica* stood in sharp contrast to Richard Inman, who, as the founder of the South's first state-chartered gay organization, the Atheneum Society, preferred the solitaire of political intrigue. The two had corresponded when Bob was organizing Mattachine Midwest, but Inman, a wiry cab driver with ties to the intelligence community, was troubled by Basker's leftist background. A staunch anticommunist, Inman had supported the failed Bay of Pigs and labeled Bob a "pinko of the worst kind" (letter to Warren Adkins, September 28, 1965, in Inman papers).

Within a few months, Bob was on his way to Cuba to be reunited with his children. Teaching English and serving on the board of the Norteamericano Amigos de Cuba, Basker promised to make "as much of a contribution to the Revolution as I can" (letter to Campanero Hugo Garcia, March 25, 1967, Basker papers). However, he soon proved less helpful to the Cuban government when he organized support for two Cuban teachers who were accused of being lesbians and fired from the Escuela Nacional de Idiomas de John Read:

> I was outraged! I didn't want to scandalize my children and ex-wife, but how could I allow this to go down without anything happening? I got together with several other teachers in the school . . . to complain about these teachers being fired without having any due process. Within two weeks, the two teachers were reinstated—again without any due process.

On an island where the revolutionary goal is producing "the new socialist man," Basker realized that he would likely feel the wrath from authorities who seldom countenanced dissent. He soon relocated to Greenwich Village where he began attending Tuesday night discussion groups at which a new generation of homosexual youth talked about a gay revolution. Unlike homophile leaders such as Dorr Legg and others, wars of liberation, civil rights organizing, and student strikes linked Basker across the gay generational divide.

Several months after Stonewall, he returned to Miami and was reunited with his children. There, from time to time he'd also run into the former Mattachine Florida leader, Richard Inman, with whom he would discuss the prospects of bringing Stonewall south. Inman was then running his one-man organization, the Florida League for Good Government, and for a time also operated the Atheneum Bookshop, an X-rated bookstore on Miami's southwest side. The frequent subject of vice raids, Inman successfully fought them in the courts; when the 1960s ended, Inman moved to California.

The 1970s were marked by the growth of greater sexual freedom, elevated political consciousness, and the emergence of lesbian and gay communities in the South. In this atmosphere Basker found "more receptivity" in South Florida than he had before. In his speeches and his action he "married" individual self-interest to like-minded groups. "You don't widen your influence by being sectarian," he argued. "For coalition purposes, you *always* have open arms." At local gay bars, "I wouldn't talk about me. I'd talk about *you* and your needs." Merging Saul Alinksy-style organizing with the

positive thinking of Dale Carnegie, Bob strategized: "When you get somebody with a resonance that sounds empathetic, you latch on to them. *And,*
you use them for gathering others." Rejecting the single-issue position that
was the hallmark of the New York-based Gay Activist Alliance, Basker
preached "cross-pollination" in movements:

> I still remember pushing memberships at gay meetings for the Ameri-
> can Civil Liberties Union: "If we want their help, we got to help them!
> Don't limit your issues to just your own situation. Do you want people
> to come and support you? You're not going to get them to support you
> if you don't do something to help them on issues that are not contra-
> dictory to your own.

Basker practiced what he preached, laboring across sundry groups ranging from Citizens Against the Death Penalty to those working for migrant
workers' rights. As chairman of the legislative committee for the Florida affiliate of the ACLU and a board member of the Dade County's Concerned
Democrats, Basker "worked slowly, individually perhaps, to bring them
along to make sure that the issues you believed in became common issues
for the entire board." He also invested significant time as vice president of
Transition, a program for soon-to-be released inmates, and was active in
support of Haitian refugees.

Activities in Miami began to gel as the twin national political party conventions appeared on the city horizon. A small but determined group advanced "tactics toward the strategy to get the law changed," according to
Basker, "setting all of the pawns in place for the grand move." In the late
evening of November 6, 1971, the game began in earnest when law enforcement officials intervened.

Posing as patrons, Miami undercover agents entered the Bachelor II
Lounge on SW Twenty-Second Street. Among other things they observed
thirty-six-year-old Enrique Vela serving a drink to a fifty-something homosexual. A short time later police stormed into the Coral Way bar, arresting
six, four of whom were employees. A disappointed sergeant later told a
news reporter that "about fifty customers took off through the doors. Otherwise we would have had more homosexuals" (Patrus, 1971).

Unlike other bar raids that occurred as regularly as the winter migration
of Yankee snowbirds, those arrested at the Bachelor II refused to retreat into
their invisible subculture. They entered "not guilty" pleas in municipal
court. Their attorney, Rose Levinson—like Pearl Hart in Chicago, a closet
lesbian—had long represented gay men charged with various offenses.
Levinson challenged the constitutionality of the ordinance.

Two weeks before Christmas Judge Donald Barmack tossed out the cases, declaring: "You cannot label a person a homosexual or a lesbian or a pervert and refuse to serve him or her a drink." Noting that neither Plato nor Oscar Wilde could legally visit a Miami bar, he continued: "You pass a law like this and pretty soon you can refuse to serve somebody because he's a Democrat or Republican or blue-eyed"(Glass, 1971). Later, the city quietly repealed the ordinance, and the Florida Supreme Court struck down the state's 103-year-old "crimes against nature" law for its "vagueness and uncertainty in language." A new era had begun.

Basker was the ringmaster for community organizing, starting and encouraging groups, networking with individuals, laboring across movement groups. By 1973 there were several Basker-organized or -inspired groups, ranging from Gay Activist Alliance—Miami which successfully had fought a local cross-dressing ordinance to the Miami chapter of the Metropolitan Community Church. Basker set his sights toward another goal: passage of a local ordinance barring discrimination against homosexuals similar to the one just passed by his ally Frank Kameny in Washington, DC.

Although similarly dressed gay men discoed at the Lost and Found just as they did at the Warehouse VIII and similarly undressed men cruised the Olympic Baths just as they were doing at Club Baths—Miami, South Florida was not the District of Columbia. Dade County, home to "Cubans and New York Jews on the retirement plan," was still held hostage by

> good ol' boys [who] have Bible-totin' wives. Their religion, steaming in Florida's heady mixture of sunshine and swamp gas after 200 years of slow fermentation in the backwoods South, gets kid-glove treatment at all times. (Rose, 1977, p. 46)

Nevertheless, in 1973, Basker called for a "rebirth of activity and commitment" among South Florida activists. "Power concedes nothing without a demand," Basker quoted Frederick Douglass in the GAA Newsletter. "Find out just what people will submit to and you will find the exact amount of injustice and wrong which will be imposed on them." Four years later, the boy who read *Fighting Foes Too Small to See* as he waited to confront the injustice of his mother's arrest would confront forces of biblical proportion and, in the process, usher in the second wave of the modern gay rights movement.

Bob Basker died on April 6, 2001, at a home for the aged in San Francisco. He was eighty-two.

BIBLIOGRAPHY

Interviews and Unpublished Sources

Most of the quotations are from the following sources: an audiotape interview with Bob Basker by James T. Sears, June 14-15, 1997, and available in the Sears papers, Perkins Library, Duke University; a videotape interview with Bob Basker by John O'Brien, circa 1995, and available in the Basker papers, International Gay and Lesbian Archives, Los Angeles, hereafter referred to as IGLA, which includes correspondence, diary, FBI file, and other personal papers; Mattachine Chapter Minutes and Correspondence, Hal Call papers, IGLA; correspondence with Richard Inman, Inman papers, Stonewall Library and Archives, Fort Lauderdale, Florida.

Published Sources

Baker, J. "Gay Establishment Activist," *The Advocate,* June 15, 1977, p. 10.

D'Emilio, John. *Sexual Politics, Sexual Communities.* Chicago: University of Chicago Press, 1983, pp. 115-117, 173.

Gay Activist Alliance of Miami, *Bulletin,* November 23, 1973.

Glass, I. " 'Gay Bar' Law Here May Get Test in Court," *Miami News,* November 8, 1971.

Loughery, J. *The Other Side of Silence.* New York: Holt, 1998, pp. 53-55.

Patrus, A. "Police Start Crackdown on Homosexual Bars; Arrest 6." *Miami Herald,* November 17, 1971.

Ramirez, P. "Law Upset Forbidding Serving Homosexuals," *Miami Herald,* December 10, 1971.

Rose, F. "Trouble in Paradise," *New Times,* April 15, 1977, p. 46.

Sears, J. *Lonely Hunters: An Oral History of Lesbian and Gay Southern Life, 1948-1968.* New York: Harper Collins-Westview, 1997, pp. 24-33, 44-47, 252-253.

Sears, J. *Rebels, Rubyfruit, and Rhinestones.* New Brunswick, NJ: Rutgers University Press, 2001.

Frank Kameny carrying a sign with the slogan he coined, "Gay Is Good," in the first Gay Pride march, New York City, 1970. (Photo by Kay Tobin Lahusen)

one

THE HOMOSEXUAL VIEWPOINT

JANUARY 1958
FIFTY CENTS

SIXTH YEAR

A cover of *ONE Magazine*, 1958.

THE LADDER

Adults Only .50

Jan. 1966

A LESBIAN REVIEW

The Ladder, 1966. Only a few years later, *The Ladder* pioneered in using real gay individuals as cover subjects. (Photo by Kay Tobin Lahusen)

Randolfe Wicker (at left) and Barbara Gittings in demonstration on July 4, 1966, at Independence Hall in Philadelphia. This was the second of five annual "Reminder Day" demonstrations. (Photo by Kay Tobin Lahusen)

"Hug-a-Homosexual" booth run by Task Force on Gay Liberation of the American Library Association/Social Responsibilities Round Table at ALA annual conference in June 1971, Dallas. Barbara Gittings (left) with Isabel Miller, author of *Patience and Sarah*, winner of the first Gay Book Award (1971). (Photo by Kay Tobin Lahusen)

Frank Kameny (right) breaking the barrier with Philip Johnson at the psychiatrists' ball at the American Psychiatric Association conference, 1972.

Dr. H. Anonymous listens while Barbara Gittings explains to the American Psychiatric Association audience why he must wear a mask and why all his gay peers remain in the closet. Dallas, 1972. (Photo by Kay Tobin Lahusen)

Del Martin (left) and Phyllis Lyon receiving the second annual Gay Book Award for their book *Lesbian/Woman* from the Task Force on Gay Liberation at the American Library Association annual conference, June 1972, Chicago. (Photo by Kay Tobin Lahusen)

Lige Clarke, Barbara Gittings, Kay Tobin Lahusen, and Jack Nichols at the first Philadelphia Gay Pride rally/march in 1972. (From the collection of Kay Tobin Lahusen)

Morris Kight (at left, back seat of car)

Phyllis Lyon and Del Martin (photo by Jane P. Cleland)

Caricature of Sten Russell on the cover of *ONE Magazine,* June 1960.

Jack Nichols and Harry Hay, 1998.

Harry Hay, c. 1934.

W. Dorr Legg, 1938.

Dale Jennings, 1994.

Activists who gathered in Los Angeles in 1998 during a celebration of Jim Kepner's life and the fiftieth anniversary of the current gay and lesbian rights movement. From bottom left: Lisa Ben, Harry Hay, John Burnside (early 1960s' activist), José Sarria, Del Martin, Phyllis Lyon; (second row) Fred Frisbie (president of ONE, Inc., in mid-1960s), Bob Basker, Frank Kameny, Florence Fleischman (Los Angeles DOB, Council on Religion and the Homosexual), Hal Call, Robin Tyler (entertainer and activist); (third row) Philip Johnson (founded first activist group in Dallas, Texas), Eddie Sandifer (1960s' Mississippi activist), Vern Bullough, Malcolm Boyd (activist, priest, writer); (fourth row) Barbara Gittings, Kay Tobin Lahusen (activist, photographer), Jack Nichols, Mark Segal (1969 founder of first youth group), Unidentified; (fifth row) Cliff Anchor (1960s' San Francisco activist), Leo Laurence (1960s' San Francisco activist), Eldon Murray (founder of Gay People's Union, Milwaukee, 1969), John O'Brien (founder of New York City Gay Liberation Front), Jerome Stevens (founder of National League for Social Understanding). (Photo by Fred Camerer)

Shirley Willer (1922-1999)

Del Martin
Phyllis Lyon

Shirley Willer was a heavyset woman who wore mannish attire and a short haircut. The clothes, she claimed, fit her ample figure better than standard women's clothing. She had a deep voice and the commanding demeanor of a leader. As a nurse she exhibited the caring and nurturing manner of her profession. She objected to being called "butch," which to her was stereotypical role-playing. She was fated to take on the role of Robin Hood during her stint as national president of the Daughters of Bilitis—a role that led to her downfall and the downfall of the organization and its magazine, *The Ladder*.

Shirley was born in Chicago in 1922. Her father was a judge, a heavy drinker, and a wife beater. In 1931 her mother packed Shirley and her younger sister into the family car and fled. In order to make ends meet her mother had to work split shifts and strange hours, leaving Shirley to run the household.

Eventually Shirley managed to get into nursing school where she learned that some women, called lesbians, were attracted to other women. When she told her mother she might be one, her mother got a copy of *The Well of Loneliness* for her to read. She was grateful for her mother's understanding. All hell broke loose in the family, however, when Shirley's first love turned out to be her cousin. Her aunt took her daughter home and told her never to see Shirley again.

In 1962 Shirley moved to New York because she had learned that the Daughters of Bilitis had a chapter there. At her first event she met Marion Glass (Meredith Grey), a founding member, and they soon became a couple. Marion was a reserved, intellectual type who found her voice through Shirley. With Marion as mentor Shirley soon became president of the chapter and by 1966 the national president of DOB.

Shirley had become a friend, confidante, and therapist to a wealthy, closeted lesbian who wished to contribute to DOB anonymously. The two devised a plan whereby Shirley, acting as a conduit, named individual members to receive checks for $3,000. Initially the donations were used to make *The Ladder* a slick paper magazine, professionally typeset, with a distributor to get it on newsstands. Shirley planned also to increase the membership of DOB and to improve the structure of the organization. To this end Shirley and Marion began to travel the country organizing more chapters for DOB, but they failed to provide anyone with their itinerary and did not keep in contact with the national office in San Francisco. The vice president, who was supposed to be in charge of the national office, was unfortunately not functioning. Efforts to communicate with other national officers also proved elusive. Del Martin and Phyllis Lyon, who had come to the rescue in previous DOB crises, felt they had enough and both resigned in 1968.

The August 1968 issue of *The Ladder* ran an article titled "Changing Times" by Meredith Grey introducing a plan to decentralize DOB in which there would be no need to elect a national president or hold national assemblies anymore. No mention was made of where or when the DOB Convention of 1968 would be held.

When Shirley finally surfaced she announced she had made arrangements for the convention to be held in Aurora, Colorado. On such short notice only fifteen members showed up. It was here that Shirley and Marion formally introduced their plan to decentralize DOB, giving autonomy to chapters to establish their own policies. The new United Daughters of Bilitis, Inc., a separate corporation, would undertake publication of *The Ladder.* They also urged DOB to become a member organization of the recently organized North American Conference of Homophile Organizations. The DOB members present felt the drastic new plans needed more consideration and deferred action until the next scheduled convention in New York City in 1970.

Upset at the refusal of DOB members to follow through on their recommendations, Shirley and Marion quit both the DOB *and* the national homophile movement. Rita Laporte succeeded Shirley as national president. She and Gene Damon (Barbara Grier), editor of *The Ladder,* felt that drastic action was necessary to save the magazine. Rita then took the mailing list as well as some of the properties and records of DOB to Reno, Nevada. The move was perceived as a theft. DOB members in San Francisco consulted attorneys who advised that any suit to recover the magazine would end up in federal courts and would take years (and large quantities of money and energy) to settle. The August/September 1970 issue of *The Ladder* did not mention DOB. With this fait accompli, Shirley, even after her resignation, had achieved her goal to decentralize DOB. At the 1970 convention in New York the national board, whose principal responsibility had been *The Ladder,* dissolved itself. The chapters were set free. Only one chapter still exists, in Boston. *The Ladder,* without the backing of the organization or the "anonymous donor," ceased publication in 1972.

Shirley and Marion spent the last years of their lives in Key West, Florida, where they opened and ran a rather profitable "rock shop" and became involved with the growing lesbian and gay community there. On reflection it was realized that Shirley, as the first non-California president of DOB, was caught in the middle of East-West conflicts and power struggles in the homophile movement at that time. She and Marion had their roots and loyalties in New York and the East Coast way of operating. What had started out as a grandiose plan to reorganize DOB, with Shirley's guaranteed source of financing, ended up destroying it.

Shirley died on New Years Eve 1999. Shortly before, Manuela Soares had interviewed her on videotape for the New York Lesbian Herstory DOB Project. By then Shirley had come to terms with her anger and feelings of betrayal. She realized that all the participants in the struggle had probably done what they thought was best. She did not want to put anyone down. Shirley's good deeds and intentions and her deep disappointment reflect the feelings and ideals of the pre-Stonewall movement.

PART III: MOVERS AND SHAKERS ON THE NATIONAL SCENE

There is a tendency among Californians, of which I am one, to think that everything in the gay movement began in California. Although the organizations mentioned in the previous section certainly had their origin in California, activists in other parts of the country were encouraged by developments in California and either joined in or went off on their own.

One of the most significant figures in the movement was Franklin Kameny who, beginning in 1957, spearheaded a new period of militancy in the homosexual rights movement. As founder and president of the Washington, DC Mattachine Society, he promoted the slogan "Gay Is Good," and launched a systematic challenge to the U.S. government's exclusion of gays and lesbians. Joining with him was Jack Nichols, who later moved on to New York City where he and his partner, Lige Clarke, began publishing a column in *Screw* entitled the "Homosexual Citizen." Jack and Lige became the most celebrated and recognizable gay male couple in America. Together they were involved in the launching of the first homosexual weekly, *GAY*. After Lige Clarke was murdered in Mexico in 1975, Jack carried on without him and remained one of the leading advocates for gays and lesbians in the country.

Also included in this section is Barbara Grier who was active in DOB, wrote for and later edited *The Ladder,* cofounded the largest lesbian press in the world, and has continued to be a major spokesperson for the lesbian cause. Quite a different personality is Barbara Gittings, who in her search for her own identity found the gay movement. For a time she too edited *The Ladder* and, though not a professional librarian, was a major figure in changing attitudes in the American Library Association about gays and lesbians.

Some people became activists early in their lifetimes. Stephen Donaldson, for example, founded the first gay student organization in the world. He was also gang-raped while in jail, while being detained for protesting at the White House with a group of Quakers. Rather than avoid the issue of rape, Stephen used his experience to campaign for greater public awareness of male rape.

There was a wide divergence in personality and approach of those in the gay movement. Randolfe Wicker, for example, was the leading counterculture force in the movement: a radical hippie, ever pushing the gay cause forward, taunting the authorities to change. Different folks make different strokes, and the exact opposite of Wicker was Arthur Cyrus Warner. An early member of the Mattachine Society in New York, Warner's real interest was in changing the legal status of homosexuality. His legal briefs, his consultations, and his behind-the-scenes activity brought about changes often without people knowing he had been involved.

Almost inevitably there was burnout in the movement. An example of this is Richard Inman, an early advocate of homosexuality in Florida; in fact, he was nearly the only voice to speak out for gays in that state in the 1950s and 1960s, even founding his own organization to carry on the battle. He, however, was too much of a loner to be a leader in the movement; after unsuccessfully suing the city of Miami in 1966, he became disillusioned with the chances of progress and gradually withdrew from the battle, feeling he had too little support among the gay community to continue his crusade.

Franklin E. Kameny (1925-   )

David K. Johnson

Photo by Kay Tobin Lahusen

In October 1957, Franklin E. Kameny's life was forever changed. Fired from the federal civil service for his homosexuality, that month Kameny began a Herculean struggle with the American establishment that would transform the homophile movement. As historian John D'Emilio has noted, Kameny spearheaded a new period of militancy in the homosexual rights movement of the early 1960s. From his base in the nation's capital, he brought traditional reform movement tactics—publicity, lawsuits, lobbying, public demonstrations—to the homophile movement. As founder and president of the Mattachine Society of Washington, DC, Kameny showed that gays, similar to other minority groups, could stand up for themselves and demand equal rights as "homosexual American citizens." One of the first gay leaders to proclaim that homosexuality was neither sick nor immoral—a philosophy he eventually refined into the slogan "Gay Is Good"—he persuaded gays and lesbians to move beyond the strategies of 1950s' self-help groups and to adopt the political strategies of the civil rights movement. A victim of the federal civil service's antigay purges, Kameny launched the first systematic challenge to the government's exclusion of gays and lesbians, attacking the Cold War era notion that gay men and lesbians posed a risk to national security. A tireless advocate for other purge victims and a persistent critic of government security officials, he more than any other individual deserves credit for the federal civil service's 1975 decision to abandon its antigay exclusion policy. As the first gay activist in the United States to take on the

---

Portions of this essay are reprinted with the permission of David DeLeon, editor, *Leaders from the 1960s: A Biographical Sourcebook of American Activism* (Greenwood Press, 1994).

federal government, Kameny inaugurated many of the tactics and strategies that have since become standard in the gay and lesbian rights movement.

Kameny was born in Queens, New York, in 1925 to a modest, middle-class Jewish family. His Polish-born father worked as an electrical engineer for an automotive parts company; his mother, born on New York's Lower East Side, had been a secretary for the famous lawyer Max Steuer. A precocious child, Kameny took an early interest in science and by the age of six had decided on a career in astronomy. After skipping several grades and graduating from Richmond Hill High School at the age of sixteen, he studied physics at New York's Queens College. With World War II came nightly blackouts, which made for prime stargazing for the budding astronomer, but the war eventually took Kameny away to Europe, where he served as a U.S. Army mortar crewman. His knowledge of the German language also made him the unofficial company interpreter. Until then, Kameny had been painfully shy, but, according to his mother, his service in the war brought him out of his shell. After the war, he finished his undergraduate education and won a scholarship to Harvard to study astronomy.

Early on, Kameny developed an absolute belief in the validity of his intellectual processes and habit of challenging accepted orthodoxies. As a teenager, he announced to his parents that he was an atheist. As a teaching fellow at Harvard, he refused to sign a loyalty oath without attaching qualifiers: "If society and I differ on something, I'm willing to give the matter a second look. If we still differ, then I am right and society is wrong," Kameny declared. "And society can go its way so long as it doesn't get in my way" (Johnson, 1991). But Kameny was less sure about his sexual orientation. At Harvard he spent most of his nights at the observatory gazing at the stars. It was not until he was researching his doctoral dissertation in Arizona that Kameny fell in with a gay crowd. After his first night in a gay bar in Tucson, Kameny thought to himself, "I've come home." Similar to many gay men who come out later in life, Kameny spent the next several years making up for lost time.

After completing his PhD at Harvard, Kameny moved to Washington, DC to accept a position as a research and teaching assistant in the astronomy department at Georgetown University. In the 1950s the federal government, engaged in the arms race with the Soviet Union, was sponsoring much of the nation's scientific research. Within a year Kameny transferred to the Army Map Service, where Cold War pressures promised fast advancement. In his new position, Kameny traveled to observatories around the country to calculate distances between points in the United States and overseas using astronomical observations, helping the Army more accurately target its growing arsenal of nuclear weapons. In October 1957, the Soviet Union launched the first artificial satellite, and the space race was off and running. As one of only a handful of astronomers in the country, Kameny looked forward to working in the U.S. space program and contemplated serving as an astronaut.

But along with the government's scientific patronage came demands for political and sexual conformity. In 1957, while on assignment in Hawaii for the Army Map Service, Kameny was suddenly called back to Washington for an interrogation by government investigators. "Information has come to the attention of the U.S. Civil Service Commission that you are a homosexual," the investigators began, in a phrase that would haunt thousands of government workers throughout the Cold War. "What comment, if any, do you care to make?" When Kameny asserted that his private life was none of the federal government's concern, he was dismissed from his job and his scientific career ended. At the dawning of the space race, this skilled astronomer was jobless and dependent upon charity (*Kameny v. Bruckner,* 1960).

According to U.S. Civil Service policy, Kameny's homosexuality made him "unsuitable" for federal employment. Thousands of federal employees had been similarly dismissed or forced to resign since the McCarthy era, when Republican enemies of the Truman administration began insisting that gay federal workers posed a risk to national security because of their vulnerability to blackmail. In 1950, the U.S. Senate opened hearings on the "Employment of Homosexuals and Other Sex Perverts in Government," which highlighted, despite a lack of evidence, the claim that gays and lesbians were subject to coercion by foreign agents. To help ferret them out of the government, the U.S. Park Service administered a "Pervert Elimination Campaign" in the major parks in Washington, DC, arresting hundreds of gay men. One journalist called the hysteria that engulfed Washington at the time "the panic on the Potomac"; the officials behind the effort labeled it "the purge of the perverts." By the late 1950s, the Eisenhower administration's more restrictive security program diminished the hysteria while it institutionalized the purges as an intrinsic component of the national security state.

Most gay men and lesbians forced out of their jobs in this way quietly resigned. Kameny was among the first to challenge his dismissal. When administrative appeals failed and the U.S. Court of Appeals ruled against him, his attorney abandoned the case. Forced to write his appeal to the Supreme Court himself, Kameny outlined a strategy that served him for the next several decades. In the brief he charged that the government's antigay policies were "no less illegal and no less odious than discrimination based upon religious or racial grounds" (*Kameny v. Bruckner,* 1960). He asserted that because of his homosexuality he was being treated as a second-class citizen. Moreover, based on his interpretation of the 1948 Kinsey study finding that approximately 10 percent of the population is exclusively homosexual,

Kameny charged that 15 million Americans were subject to the same treatment. Deploying the language of the black civil rights movement, Kameny demanded that the court examine the entire history of antigay purges.

In 1961, when the Supreme Court refused to rule on his unprecedented claims, he decided to enlist others in the cause and founded the Mattachine Society of Washington (MSW). The first Mattachine Society was founded in California in 1951 as a sort of gay fraternal order, providing social services to gays and lesbians, but it moved beyond that. Kameny's group rejected the internal focus and secretive nature of the existing group and adopted a political activist approach. Mattachine of Washington dedicated itself, according to its constitution, "to act by any lawful means to secure for homosexuals the right to life, liberty, and the pursuit of happiness" (p. 3). Its goal was to change the homosexual's place in society. Elected the group's first president, Kameny was soon one of the few homosexuals in the United States willing to appear publicly and use his own name.

With an eye on the black civil rights movement, Kameny set about recasting homosexuality—traditionally considered a moral or a mental health problem—into a civil liberties issue. "It is time that considerations of homosexuality were removed from the psychoanalyst's couch and taken out of the psychiatrist's office," he argued. "The average homosexual . . . is far more likely to have employment problems than emotional ones" (Kameny, 1969, p. 20). Kameny lobbied the local affiliate of the American Civil Liberties Union (ACLU), eventually persuading it to take a stand against the federal government's antigay policies long before the national union would. Calling his group the "NAACP of the homosexual minority," Kameny championed the cause that gays were a political minority group. Although Donald Webster Cory had first advanced the idea that gays and lesbians constituted a political minority in 1950 in *The Homosexual in America,* Kameny was the first to put this notion into action. He continually reminded public officials that he and his constituency were not just homosexuals but "homosexual citizens," arguing that sexual identity and political rights were not incompatible.

Because they were fighting for what they believed were basic American rights, the Mattachine Society of Washington used traditional methods: distributing press releases, testifying before committees, lobbying government officials. Where earlier gay organizations had shunned publicity, MSW sought it out. Where earlier groups had brought various authorities in to speak to their membership, MSW sent speakers out to educate the nongay population about homosexuality. As Kameny argued, on issues of homosexuality, "*we* are the experts and the authorities" (*Kameny v. Bruckner,* 1960). MSW published a monthly newsletter and sent it to people they thought would be interested—such as FBI Director J. Edgar Hoover. When Hoover requested that his name be taken off their mailing list, the group told him that they would, as soon as he took them off of his list of subversive organizations. When Congressman John Dowdy (D-Texas) tried to rescind the right of MSW to solicit funds in the District of Columbia, Kameny requested public hearings on the matter and became the first openly gay person to testify before a congressional committee. He garnered much favorable publicity in the local press by eloquently defending his group's contribution to the welfare of what he called "the largest minority in the District of Columbia after the Negro" (testimony, 1963).

Kameny, convinced that antigay prejudice was based primarily on emotion, not reason, put little faith in attempts to educate or persuade. As he declared in a historic speech to the New York chapter of the Mattachine Society in 1964, "The Negro tried for 90 years to achieve his purposes by a program of information and education. His achievements in those 90 years, while by no means nil, were nothing compared to those of the past 10 years, when he tried a vigorous civil liberties, social action approach" (D'Emilio, 1983, p. 153). So when Washington police raided the Gayety Buffet and arrested and abused several gay men, "we demanded a meeting," Kameny remembered, "which was not the kind of thing they expected" (Johnson, 1991). Kameny got the men to sign affidavits concerning their treatment and got the local ACLU chapter to support them. At the meeting with the police, Kameny elicited an admission that gay people had the right to assemble in bars and a promise that this type of harassment would not be repeated. In the spring and summer of 1965, when efforts to meet with federal government representatives failed, Kameny—at the initial suggestion of MSW member Jack Nichols—organized an unprecedented series of gay pickets in front of the White House and other government buildings in Washington, DC. He also launched a series of test discrimination cases in the courts, all signaling a new period of militancy.

Kameny was convinced that the success of the gay movement hinged on debunking the psychiatric profession's assertion that homosexuality was a mental illness. Whereas earlier groups sponsored debates by medical authorities on the causes and cures for homosexuality, Kameny took strong, unabashed progay stands, proclaiming, "there is no homosexual problem; there is a heterosexual problem." As a scientist, Kameny pointed out the flaws in medical pronouncements based solely on the observation of psychiatric patients, not the millions of mentally healthy gay and lesbians beyond the medical gaze. In 1965, at the initial suggestion of member Jack Nichols, MSW was the first gay organization to declare that homosexuality was not a sickness but "a preference, orientation, or propensity, on a par with, and not different in kind from, heterosexuality" (McCaffrey, 1972, pp. 182-187). But with negative theories of homosexuality so pervasive, even among gay people themselves, Kameny realized he needed a more positive approach. By 1968 he coined the slogan "Gay Is Good"—consciously inspired by Stokely Carmichael's empowerment chant "Black Is Beautiful"—to help bolster the self-esteem of gays and lesbians.

Kameny spread his activist agenda through speaking engagements around the country, radicalizing existing gay organizations and helping myriad new groups get started in other cities. Kameny also succeeded in forming coalitions of gay organizations, first regionally and then nationally. He founded the East Coast Homophile Organizations (ECHO) in 1963 and was involved a few years later in the formation of the North American Conference of Homophile Organizations (NACHO), which in 1968 formally adopted "Gay Is Good" as the motto for the movement. Within his own group, however, Kameny's uncompromising positions cost him support. He believed that MSW's purpose was to advance the cause of gays and lesbians as a class, not to serve the needs of individual members. His dominance of the group and his single-minded focus on the enemy failed to inspire broad-based participation. Kameny was defeated in an election for the presidency of MSW in 1965, although he remained a member of its governing board.

With the rise of a grassroots gay liberation movement in the wake of the Stonewall riots in New York in 1969, much of the philosophical and legal groundwork laid by Kameny and other early activists began to bear fruit. Throughout the decade Kameny had orchestrated a series of test cases brought by fired gay civil servants. Several early victories were appealed or overturned. But in 1969, in *Norton vs. Macy,* the U.S. Court of Appeals demanded a proven connection between the off-duty sexual conduct of federal civil servants and their suitability for employment, establishing the "nexus criteria" later invoked in many federal employment situations. After several similar court defeats, the Civil Service Commission capitulated. On July 3, 1975, the Civil Service Commission's General Counsel personally telephoned Kameny to inform him that the Commission had expunged the term "immoral conduct" from the list of disqualifications in its new employment regulations. The battle Kameny inaugurated eighteen years before had been won. This change by the federal government, the nation's largest employer, set the tone for more liberal hiring policies throughout the private sector.

Around the same time the American Psychiatric Association (APA) began to reconsider its definition of homosexuality as a pathology. After appearing on numerous television debates with professional psychiatrists, Kameny succeeded in getting the APA itself to sponsor a panel of openly gay men and women at its 1971 annual convention in Washington, DC. To increase the pressure, Kameny, along with members of the Gay Liberation Front and antiwar protesters, stormed the convention, grabbed the microphone, and declared, "Psychiatry is the enemy incarnate. . . . You may take this as a declaration of war against you" (Bayer, 1981, p. 105). Under attack from gay activists and a growing number of psychiatrists, the APA voted in 1974 to remove homosexuality from its *Diagnostic and Statistical Manual of Psychiatric Disorders*. Frank was on hand at APA headquarters in Washington, DC to savor the victory and participate in a press conference.

If the 1970s gave Kameny several victories, it also offered new venues for battle. Prior to that time, the District of Columbia, Kameny's adopted home, was governed by a presidentially appointed city council. With no local political life, Kameny's early activism naturally focused on the national level. But in 1971, when U.S. Congress permitted the District to elect a non-voting delegate to the House of Representatives, Kameny ventured into local politics and became the first openly gay person to run for U.S. Congress. Although he came in fourth in the six-person race, he succeeded in using the election to increase publicity for his "personal freedoms" platform and to politicize the local gay community. In announcing his candidacy, Kameny declared, "I am a homosexual American citizen determined to move into the mainstream of society from the backwaters to which I have been relegated. Homosexuals have been shoved around for time immemorial. We are fed up with it. We are starting to shove back and we're going to keep shoving back until we are guaranteed our rights" (Tobin and Wicker, 1972, pp. 128-130). This was the opening salvo in a lengthy engagement in local politics in the nation's capital.

After the election, Kameny's campaign committee reorganized and expanded into the Gay Activists Alliance (GAA), a nonpartisan group dedicated to securing "full rights and privileges" of citizenship for the gay and lesbian community of the District of Columbia through "peaceful participation in the political process" (Tobin and Wicker, 1972, p. 132). Patterned after the Gay Activists Alliance in New York, GAA/DC was instrumental in securing passage of the DC Human Rights Law in 1973, one of the nation's first laws to ban discrimination against gays and lesbians in housing, employment, and public accommodations. Over the past twenty-five years, what is now the Gay and Lesbian Activists Alliance has been a powerful advocate for the gay community with local officials, the media, the police, and school systems. As its most consistently active and vocal member, Kameny has been instrumental in many victories, such as the elimination of funding for the vice squad in 1975 and repeal of DC's sodomy law in 1993.

Since his unsuccessful congressional campaign, Kameny has served the District of Columbia in a variety of appointed and elected positions. In 1975, after lobbying by GAA, he was appointed to Washington, DC's, Human Rights Commission, the first openly gay mayoral appointee in the nation's capital. After serving there for seven years, he was appointed to the city's Board of Appeals and Review. As an outspoken advocate of statehood for the District of Columbia, he was elected a delegate to the DC Statehood Constitutional Convention in 1981, where he helped draft a constitution for the proposed State of New Columbia. Since 1969 he has served intermittent terms on the Executive Board of the National Capital Area Civil Liberties Union.

After being fired from the federal government in 1957, Kameny held a number of temporary jobs using his scientific background, but he was never again able to work in the field of astronomy. Since the 1960s Kameny has managed to integrate his full-time activism and need to make a living by working as an independent paralegal, offering counsel to gay and nongay military personnel, civil servants, and contractors having problems with the federal government. In this capacity, Kameny has consistently attacked the government for running a "sexual-conformity program rather than a security program" (Kameny, 1969, p. 21), pointing to a lack of evidence that homosexuals are any more likely to pose a risk to national security than heterosexuals. His basic advice to people being interrogated by government officials about their sexuality never varies: "Say nothing. Sign nothing. Get counsel. Fight back." Using his knowledge of the federal bureaucracy, Kameny succeeded in 1974 in forcing the Department of Defense to conduct the first public security clearance hearing. His gay client, Otis Tabler, was eventually granted a clearance, marking a watershed in the Pentagon's program. Since then, gays and lesbians have been subject to special scrutiny and harassment, but they have generally been granted necessary clearances. Kameny has succeed in getting other federal agencies to liberalize their security clearance programs, including the highly secretive National Security Agency (NSA), which first issued a security clearance to an openly gay man in 1980. An executive order issued by President Clinton in 1995 banned discrimination based on sexual orientation in the granting of government security clearances, leading to a happy retirement for Kameny from paralegal work.

Kameny was also instrumental in beginning the first systematic legal challenge to the U.S. military's policy of discharging gay and lesbian service members. As early as 1965, Mattachine of Washington targeted the military ban by picketing the Pentagon and blanketing the building with flyers on "How to Handle a Federal Interrogation." Kameny also assisted in the much publicized case of Leonard Matlovich, whose 1975 lawsuit placed the gay Air Force sergeant on the cover of *Time* magazine. Although the suit eventually led to an out-of-court settlement in Matlovich's favor, the Pentagon responded by strengthening its ban on homosexuals in the military. As the Pentagon continued systematically to discharge openly gay and lesbian soldiers, Kameny, often acting as counsel, helped ensure that they at least received honorable discharges. Since the Clinton administration's aborted attempt to lift the ban on gays in the military and the rise of the Pentagon's "Don't Ask, Don't Tell, Don't Pursue" policy in 1993, a number of new, specialized organizations have emerged to monitor the situation and aid gay and lesbian service members. As with many other areas of gay and lesbian life, in the 1960s Kameny was one of the few people working on the military's antigay policy; today, it is the concern of a number of national professional organizations.

One of the few gay leaders from the 1960s still involved in the movement, Kameny's influence spans four decades. When Bruce Voeller and a group of fellow New Yorkers founded the National Gay Task Force in 1973—the first truly national gay organization—Kameny was one of two long-time national activists asked to sit on its board of directors, where he served until 1982. Despite his longevity in the movement, his philosophy and tactics have remained remarkably consistent. Although his brashness may have increased over the years as the cultural climate changed, Kameny has always preferred to work through established legal and political channels. Rather than just protest outside, Kameny goes inside and makes the bureaucracy work for him. His ability to use the legal system was recognized in 1988 when he received the prestigious Durfee Award for his contributions to "the enhancement of the human dignity of others through the law or legal institutions." Although he prefers to work on the inside, Kameny is not opposed to civil disobedience. His first dignified demonstration in front of the White House in 1965 has since led to numerous arrests defending the rights of homosexuals. In his fight to overturn the District of Columbia's statue outlawing consensual sodomy, he advocated and participated in sit-ins and other forms of direct action planned by groups such as ACT UP and Queer Nation. Ultimately, he is a pragmatist. "If society becomes intransigent, you escalate the battle as necessary. You plan a strategy using 'small guns' before 'big guns' in a calculated fashion" (Johnson, 1991).

His ultimate goal has always been to accord gays and lesbians the same rights and privileges enjoyed by all citizens. As an assimilationist, he has been criticized by more radical elements in the gay movement for participating in a system that is fundamentally oppressive to all minority groups. But Kameny feels he has forced society to change to fit his demands, thereby giving gays and lesbians the choice of participating in that society on equal footing without having to deny their sexuality. According to Kameny the gay movement's ability to "get things done" rests on not becoming "isolated in ivory towers of unworkable ideologies." Pointing to Kameny's "concrete ideas" and "willingness to be a martyr" for those ideas, fellow homophile leader Dick Leitsch, president of New York Mattachine, wrote in 1964, "A man like Frank is the most valuable single item the homophile movement possesses" (Kameny papers, December 28, 1964). Kameny's ability to combine the pragmatism of a bureaucrat with the indefatigable spirit of an activist succeeded not only in changing U.S. government policy but in transforming the movement.

BIBLIOGRAPHY

Bamford, James. *The Puzzle Palace: A Report on America's Most Secret Agency.* New York: Penguin Books, 1982, pp. 114-117.

Bayer, Ronald. *Homosexuality and American Psychiatry: The Politics of Diagnosis.* New York: Basic Books, 1981, pp. 81-111.

Constitution of the Mattachine Society of Washington, reprinted in U.S. Congress, House Committee on District of Columbia Charitable Solicitation Act, 88th Congress, 1st Session, August 8, 1963.

D'Emilio, John. *Sexual Politics, Sexual Communities: The Making of a Homosexual Minority in the United States, 1940-1970.* Chicago: University of Chicago Press, 1983, pp. 150-175.

Johnson, David K. Interview with Frank Kameny, October 19, 1991.

Kameny, Frank. "Civil Liberties: A Progress Report," *New York Mattachine Newsletter,* (X)1, January 1965, pp. 7-22.

Kameny, Frank. "Does Research into Homosexuality Matter?" *The Ladder, A Lesbian Review,* May 1965, pp. 14-20.

Kameny, Frank. "The Federal Government versus the Homosexual," *The Humanist,* (XXIX)3, May/June 1969, pp. 20-23.

Kameny, Frank. "Gay Is Good," in Ralph W. Weltge (Ed.), *The Same Sex: An Appraisal of Homosexuality* (pp. 129-145). Philadelphia: Pilgrim Press, 1969.

Kameny, Frank. "Gay Liberation and Psychiatry," in Joseph A. McCaffrey (Ed.), *The Homosexual Dialectic* (pp. 182-194). Englewood Cliffs, NJ: Prentice-Hall, 1972.

Kameny, Frank. "Homosexuals As a Minority Group," in Edward Sagarin (Ed.), *The Other Minorities* (pp. 50-65). Lexington, MA: Ginn, 1971.

Kameny, Frank. "Introduction," in John Alan Lee (Ed.), *Gay Midlife and Maturity: Crises, Opportunities, and Fulfillment* (pp. 1-5). Binghamton, NY: Harrington Park Press, 1991.

Kameny, Frank. Personal papers.

Kameny v. Bruckner, Petition for Writ of Certiorari, No. 676. U.S. Supreme Court, October 1960.

Marcus, Eric. *Making History: The Struggle for Gay and Lesbian Equal Rights 1945-1990: An Oral History.* New York: Harper Collins, 1992, pp. 93-103.

Testimony, U.S. Congress, House Committee on the District of Columbia, Subcommittee No. 4, Amending District of Columbia Charitable Solicitation Act, 88th Congress, 1st Session, August 8-9, 1963, and January 10, 1864.

Tobin, Kay, and Randy Wicker. *The Gay Crusaders.* New York: Paperback Library, 1972, pp. 89-134.

White, Edmund. *States of Desire: Travels in Gay America.* New York: Bantam Books, 1980, pp. 302-306.

Jack Nichols (1938-):
The Blue Fairy of the Gay Movement

James T. Sears

Jack was born during the year of the tiger, 1938. Mary Haliday Finlayson and John Richard Nichols, his parents, were high school sweethearts. "Mom was a Scottish-American beauty and Dad was a top-notch high school athlete. At the time of my birth he was in training with the Chicago White Sox, but he returned to Washington to get a 'responsible' job as a special agent for the FBI."

When Jack was three years old his parents separated and he went to live with his immigrant maternal grandparents (Nana and Poppop) in nearby Chevy Chase, Maryland. "Poppop was a Highlander; Nana, a Lowlander. Poppop had learned to read plans and began building." Jack's value system, like his grandfather's, was rooted in poetry. Murdo Graham Finlayson was for many years president of the St. Andrew Society, a Scottish fraternal order. Jack reminisced:

It was through Robert Burns that Poppop tenderly gave me the best of the Scotland he loved. . . . He wielded Burns like some unobtrusive patriarch who was satisfied to leave advice-giving to others if only he could first quote the poet aloud. Burns's portrait hung above our dining room sideboard. Sitting in my dining room chair, I faced the great poet daily. Poppop was never more bliss-filled than when giving a Burns recitation, something he did at the conclusion of every family discussion. . . .

From Poppop I learned that the constant repetition of themes laden with *values* turns those values into one's marrow. One becomes what one absorbs. From his love for Burns I absorbed a disdain for hierarchy and status. Burns's songs laughed at lords and nobles, celebrating instead the life of the common person. The poet had believed, and Poppop tirelessly communicated, that an honest man is far preferable to a rich one. Burns was extraordinarily conscious of universal welfare, worrying even about the plight of a field mouse.

The songs from the animated film *Pinocchio* complemented the poems of Burns. An exotic cartoon fantasy character easily outdistanced flesh-and-blood actresses:

> My goddess was the Blue Fairy. She explained to Pinocchio the essentials of what it means to be a "real boy": to be kind, to be truthful, to be honest, and to help others. Although the film premiered in 1941, it was 1944, when I was six, that I first saw it. I was just old enough to be captivated by her beauty. Electrified, in fact. She was to become a long-lasting childhood obsession. I got the record album and took it home. Fantasizing about Fairyland, which, I supposed, must be something like the Chevy Chase Country Club golf course, I traced her breasts over and over again on tracing paper. Identifying with the Blue Fairy, a stick for my wand, I traversed the golf course, aflame with magic.

After Jack's dad married for a second time, father and son saw less of each other. When they met it was more often for lectures and lessons than fun and frivolity:

> When I went on outings with Dad, he spent time trying to impose his awkward concepts of masculine deportment on me, giving me "butch" lessons: how to walk like a real man, how to talk like a real man, and how to be, if possible, as much like him as nature would allow. His concern was extreme. He feared I might become one of the *unthinkables,* which, not surprisingly, I did.

At the age of twelve, Jack met Feredoon:

> His father, a diplomat, was in the service of the Shah of Iran. I felt no physical attraction to Feredoon, but he beguiled me in a way I'd never thought possible. He was the first male of my age to show me how two boys can experience a passionate platonic love. He was more emotional than any of my American friends. He would kiss me full on the lips right in front of his mother and father saying "I love you." Hugging me close, he would whisper in my ear: "I never want to be apart from you. I wish you could come to live with me in Iran forever as my brother, which you will always be even if we're apart."

A short time later, Jack was stunned to learn that the Iranian government had ordered Feredoon's family to return to Teheran. Jack had decided he was gay. When he told the principal at Ardmore Junior High School near Philadelphia that he was gay, he found himself persona non grata. Soon after, Jack and his mother moved to Miami in 1952:

> Our front window looked out on a lawn that sloped to the water. My favorite spot, Bayfront Park, was the site of a spectacular library. There, browsing among books on comparative religion, I discovered several tomes on the Baha'i World Faith, a religion born in nineteenth-century Iran. Baha'i teachings emphasized planetary and racial unity as well as the equality of the sexes.
>
> The library books contained a Miami address where I could contact Baha'i converts. My initial interest in meeting these people stemmed from the fact that Baha'ism had had a Persian origin. The progressive principles seized my imagination.
>
> The first Baha'i meeting I attended was a "fireside" (Baha'i terminology for gatherings in the homes of the believers). It was conducted in a mansion on Star Island, a rich locale in the middle of Biscayne Bay. The speaker, later to become a mentor, was Ali-Kuli Khan Nabil, Iran's first envoy to America, and the first translator of the Baha'i writings into English.
>
> One night after a fireside meeting I got a ride home from an American Baha'i who struck me as effeminate. I decided he was gay. As we sat talking in front of my guest house, I told him about my homosexuality. He reciprocated, telling me that we were to be very secretive. Both of us decided that being gay was a real quandary. Explaining that he'd seen nothing in the Baha'i writings on the subject, he assured me that he was attempting to live a "moral life" and practiced celibacy.

In March 1953, Jack received a letter from his Iranian friends, now in Washington, DC, inviting him to live with them. Convincing his mother that he should move from Miami to DC was not difficult. Returning to Washington as the cherry blossoms came into bloom, Jack renewed his love for the capital and spent happy days with his Iranian friends. Attending Alice Deal Junior High School, though, was a loathsome chore. Jack, however, brandished a "weapon":

> Remembering how I'd made myself unwelcome in Ardmore's junior high, I asked for an audience with the principal of Alice Deal. Miss Bertie Backus was a sixty-five-year-old woman from West Virginia who looked exactly like Eleanor Roosevelt. Like Eleanor, she was a

liberal who was already planning a city-wide parade to be held during the centennial of the freeing of the slaves. Miss Backus's warm smile stood in marked contrast to the smug paternalism I'd noticed in the principal of Ardmore.

Well, I walked into her office and told her "I'm going to tell you what I told the other school principal: I am homosexual. You know, I would really like not having to come to school."

She asked me for a few days to think over the implications of what I'd said, especially with regard to feeling uncomfortable in my classes. When I visited with her again, she asked me to do my best at remaining in class, but if I felt unable, to make her aware of my comings and goings.

Well, that is what I did. I stayed out of class literally all the time. At the same time she invited me to dinner at her home. Over our first meal together I told her about my religious development, and she recommended that I read a poet, Walt Whitman, who, she said, had a universal outlook. In Whitman I stumbled upon the *Calamus* poems celebrating passionate love among men. I was startled.

Jack also began cruising Lafayette Park, located directly in front of the White House. But, as with most gay teens, Jack was not yet reconciled with his same-sex feelings:

The weight of the social stigma making homosexual feelings the worst thing that could happen to anybody bore down on me. I thought, a stunted life, one of self-denial, of turning away from a kind of love that seemed possible to only one lonely teen: me. I could envision always hiding my deepest longings to avoid those who saw homosexuals as ghouls or sickly vampires who wanted only to prey on them, to change them into sickly vampires. Queers were ugly night bats who'd suck the spiritual lifeblood from any careless male.

Only when reading the English poet and scholar Edward Carpenter during that summer of 1953 and the pseudonymous Donald Webster Cory a short time later did Jack "discover that I had ground to stand on." Jack recalls:

I rummaged through the basement of an old bookstore and found a rare, mildewed copy of *Love's Coming of Age* by Edward Carpenter. In 1896, it had been the foremost sex-liberation tome of its day. Turning the yellowed pages, I found myself mesmerized by the exquisite spiritual intonations of its author. His gentle sophistication was, for me, my first communion with a great gay thinker.

I was later to discover that this was fitting, since Carpenter had been, in fact, a kind of great-grandfather of the gay liberation movement. He was among the first such thinkers who acted to join his personal life, including his sexual/emotional leanings, with the world as he saw it, becoming a prophet of the perspective that one's personal life is a political statement. He saw far beyond the view that politics is only about elections, economics, and parliaments. He looked to women, gay men, and artists everywhere to plant the seeds of a new age he foresaw, a universal age that would celebrate the underlying unity of earth's peoples—and, he had elucidated this in the last century, as did Walt Whitman. Carpenter, in fact, described himself as "the moon reflecting the sun," Old Walt.

Later, in another bookstore, Jack stumbled across the classic *The Homosexual in America*. Written under the pen name Donald Webster Cory, Edward Sagarin's book had an enormous impact on Jack, as it did on a generation of lesbians and gay men:

> I studied this book at great length, memorizing many of its paragraphs, and focusing on parts which seemed to speak directly to my predicament. The "From Handicap to Strength" chapter gave me a very different viewpoint. Until then everyone around me had gone, "Oh! Poor Jack he's handicapped by being gay." Suddenly I had a strength! It was the "great democratic strength" inherent in the homosexual community.
>
> Cory made a powerful case for self-esteem under the most grueling circumstances. He helped me to see poor self-images not as a product of homosexuality, but as the result of the prejudices internalized. At that moment, I was determined to stand outside the condemning culture and, with the healthy pride of a teen, to claim my rightful place as an individual.

Jack shared his newfound book and his nascent enthusiasm with Miss Backus.

"What do you think of it?" he asked, hoping for her approval.

"It makes sense," she admitted. Jack was "overjoyed!"

Having Miss Backus's approval was important and the revelations from this book led to Jack's questioning of earlier ideas:

> I read and re-read it, marking sentences that lit up new avenues to self-acceptance. While this was happening, I began questioning Baha'i

thinkers about the homosexual question. None had a satisfactory answer, and, I noticed, some looked warily at me thereafter.

Attending Bethesda–Chevy Chase High School, Jack "cultivated" the comradeship of several classmates whom he suspected of being gay. Within a few months, he had come out to all of them, presenting each with a copy of *The Homosexual in America*. In addition to proselytizing among his high school comrades, Jack explored Washington's gay bars. Despite his age, most who spotted the six-feet, three-inch framed figure with short, curly, dark hair assumed—or chose to believe—that he was an adult:

> From boys I'd met at Dupont Circle I learned about The Chicken Hut, a quaint two-story restaurant/bar on H Street, three blocks from the White House and Lafayette Park. Upstairs sat Howard (affectionately nick-named Aunt Hattie), who played the organ and the piano, sometimes simultaneously. He'd held court in The Hut for over three decades. When I made my first entrance he was playing a Nat King Cole song "Somewhere Along the Way."

Much of Washington gay life, however, was "staid," as Jack describes:

> There was a stilted bourgeois mentality. In those days, people were pretty proper, enjoying drinking feasts peppered with dancing and inconsequential conversations. Those who ignored "proper" behavior were, if not openly scorned, at least privately criticized. In the bedroom oral sex predominated and anal sex was a subject for petty gossip. Not only was dancing in gay bars disallowed, but a peck on the cheek between men brought hysterical lectures from bar owners about endangered liquor licenses that couldn't survive such "lascivious" behavior.

By 1960, informal after-the-bar parties remained the norm in Washington's gay night life. At one such party, the twenty-two-year-old was sitting alone listening to the fashionable though less than fascinating conversations swirling around him. Preparing to bid farewell to his host with accolades of Southern gratitude, suddenly:

> I overheard a firm voice saying, "Donald Webster Cory, who wrote *The Homosexual in America,* has made an excellent case for our rights." I rose from the sofa and walked toward a group of five who were standing by the window, searching for the voice I'd heard. The man who spoke was animated by a peculiar intensity, each of his

words clipped, authoritative and academic in tone. As I approached he looked at me appreciatively, stepping back to make room in the semi-circle.

"I've read *The Homosexual in America*," Nichols told him. The other man's eyebrows did a little dance. "And what did you think of it?" he asked.

"I think every gay person should read it," Jack replied, "and that's why I came over to speak with you because I've never before met anyone discussing it in public. I wanted to say hello. My name is Jack Nichols."

"I'm Frank Kameny," he said.

"Ideas by themselves are fun," Nichols told him, "but what good are they if we don't put them into some sort of action?"

"That's exactly what I'm doing," Kameny said.

Kameny took Nichols' phone number. "I don't have a phone right now," Frank said, "because I haven't been able to afford one since beginning this struggle to get the government to reinstate me." The Harvard-educated astronomer explained: "I've been writing a brief to present to the Supreme Court about my case. It'll be the first time a homosexual has approached the Court to get his government job back. I'll call you, if you like, and you can come over to visit. We'll discuss these matters."

Frank telephoned Jack a few days later. Jack climbed the stairway to Frank's cramped, dingy apartment on Columbia Road. After a long discussion, the two decided to begin grassroots action. Jack met regularly with Frank throughout the remainder of 1960 and Kameny continued to develop and polish his written arguments for the Supreme Court. At the beginning of the New Year, he submitted his case; three months later, Kameny's petition for certiorari was denied. His efforts, however, were far from futile. The process streamlined Frank's thinking and politicized his agenda. With names provided by the New York Mattachine, Frank and Jack sought people willing to form another Mattachine group.

On August 1, 1961, the leaders of the New York Mattachine, Curtis Dewees and Al de Dion, met in Washington to discuss organizational strategies with Frank and company. "By the standards of the day," Jack recalls, "both were somewhat conservative and macho. Curtis was a quiet, dark-haired man, and Al was brown-haired and assertive." Meeting that evening in room 120 at the Hay-Adams Hotel, a group began to coalesce.

Jack, however, soon turned his energies toward assisting Frank in operationalizing strategies and crafting the purpose statement for the Washington Mattachine. Jack argued forcefully for the inclusion of a statement of cooperation among allied civil rights groups with parallel interests. Although Frank was initially troubled by "mixing causes," he eventually acquiesced and later embraced the position. On November 15, a group of a dozen or so women and men met to form the Mattachine Society of Washington, electing Frank as president; Jack would later become vice president. The group quickly assumed an aggressive stance. Within a year, letters were sent, demanding meetings with governmental officials from all three branches of the federal government. Meanwhile, Jack went in and out of the chapter as he pursued amorous adventures in other cities.

However, by January of 1963, "My experiment with irresponsibility and my flirtation with irrationality was at an end. A steady job, decent housing, and those free choices which only financial independence could bring now held special promise." As Jack recentered himself, pouring his energies into Mattachine, he became an able and dependable colleague for Frank, who continued to mentor the prodigal son.

Jack collaborated with Kameny in strategizing ways of breaking down antigay prejudices. "Kameny and I agreed we must plan challenges to the psychiatric establishment. This singular aspect of our cause united the two of us, perhaps, more than did any other issue." Doggedly, Jack assembled medical opinions and scientific research challenging the commonly held belief that homosexuality was an illness:

> As I helped develop such ideas, part of my passion, I knew, had been fueled by my early adolescent experiences. When my aunt-in-law had called me "sick," and my depression over this circumstance had led me at age fourteen to attempt suicide, I emerged from that depression inwardly furious that I'd been so deluded by the quackery around me. My disdain for organized religion, including Baha'ism, had, in part, similar roots. But it was psychiatric nonsense that infuriated me most. Kameny knew this and encouraged my anger. In autumn, he suggested that I approach the executive board of the Washington Mattachine, presenting my viewpoint.

A letter, dated October 14, 1963, represented a watershed for the fledgling movement as it contested the medical establishment's authority. Cogently and clearly, Jack argued that homosexuality was not a disease, concluding in Corydon language:

> It is often all too easy for us to sit in the comfort of a 20th Century apartment among certain enlightened heterosexuals and to imagine that after all our situation is not so bad. It is BAD. . . . The mental attitude of our own people toward themselves—that they are not well—that they are not whole, that they are LESS THAN COMPLETELY HEALTHY—is responsible for UNTOLD NUMBERS OF PER-

SONAL TRAGEDIES AND WARPED LIVES, and for poor self images. . . . By failing to take a definite stand—a strong stand—that is scientifically open, I believe that you will not only weaken the Movement 10-fold, but that you will fail in your duty to homosexuals who need more than anything else to see themselves in a better light. The question "Am I Sick?" is not an academic, drawing-room inquiry. It is an agonizing cry—and before you dare to give a drawing-room answer, I hope that you will give just a little more thought to the subject.

Doubt, disgust, and indifference greeted Jack's open letter. Movement conservatives of the past generation such as Call and Dewees gave little thought to it. Clearly, if change was to occur in the manner envisioned by Kameny, Wicker, and Nichols, then a new generation of activists would need to be recruited and educated. Within a few years this new generation would transform the fledgling homophile movement with rebellious chants of "Gay Power" and declarations that "Gay Is Good!"

A few months after he had penned the letter on the sickness issue, and on a typical sultry DC summer evening, with Lesley Gore scattering "rainbows, lollipops, and moonbeams" on the jukebox at the Hideaway, a Washington gathering place, Jack met the love his life. He spotted a lanky twenty-two-year-old spouting "hillbilly wisdom." He was a shapely Army man, wearing

a blue shirt that showed his absolute definition. His face had classic symmetry, his cheekbones high, his jaw strong, his eyes hazel with lips full. He was blonde, his hair styled in a civilian mode, a handsome wave directly above his forehead. I'd never seen anyone like him. The description penned by Old Walt in his *Leaves* came to mind: "Dress does not hide him / The strong sweet quality he has strikes through."

After stumbling into the bar the night before escorted by two Army buddies, this evening Lige Clarke was motivated by more than curiosity. "I was a little nervous, but before I could even order a beer, a guy came over to me and invited me to join him and some friends for a drink. . . . I said, 'Sure!' Later he asked me to dance, so we did and I loved it. Everything seemed so simple, so natural."

Lige fell into bed with Jack and into the homophile movement. The next day, the lanky serviceman, who worked at the Pentagon editing secret messages, was in the Mattachine basement mimeographing newsletters. Soon, he was lettering signs as his lover and the rag-tag group of homosexual militants picketed the White House, the Pentagon, and the State Department.

Four years later, the couple was living in New York City. Jack had secured a job at Countrywide Publications, where he helped to edit such magazines as *Strange Unknown* and *Companion;* Lige occasionally modeled
and wrote for Countrywide. At this busy production house, the two became
friends with Al Goldstein, an editor who dreamed of creating a magazine
that capitalized on the sexual revolution and liberalized pornography laws.

In November 1968 *Screw* hit the newsstands. Amid the photos of female
cleavage and assorted methods for achieving orgasm was a column, the
"Homosexual Citizen," featuring "two lively males who have spent some
very exciting years living and grooving together."

Capturing the spirit of the age, Lige and Jack wrote:

> To the homosexual the sex revolution means much more than greater
> freedom for sex relations. It means that we'll be able to build positive
> lives in our culture. . . . We need more of a sexual culture of our own. It
> does not need to be based on outworn heterosexual ethics, for these in-
> deed are crumbling fast.

Jack, now in his early sixties editing Badpuppy's *Gay Today,* remembers
their late 1960s' message of sexual liberation:

> Such calls hardly seemed outrageous or radical when, in fact, the
> counterculture had already greeted same-sex impulses with open
> arms. . . . [Men] in the counterculture were eager to show affection and
> tenderness—as part of the hippie ideology with its commitment to
> love-making on a planetary scale.

Writing to what was a mostly "straight" albeit largely supportive audience, the column "broke societal barriers just as the Gay Liberation Movement did" (Streitmatter, 1995, p. 89). Lige and Jack challenged the traditional male role. They observed that a major impact of the "hippie ethic"
was "its exposure and its attempted destruction of outworn 'masculinism,'"
arguing that "a truly complete person is neither extremely masculine nor extremely feminine."

The duo quickly became a fixture in the New York gay cultural scene, becoming the "most celebrated and recognizable" gay male couple in America
(Hunter, 1972). Just as quickly, the homophile activists turned gay liberationists distanced themselves ideologically from the older generation of homosexual leaders.

> In our discussion of the military, we took the counterculture's posi-
> tion, namely that any chewing gum we could put into its machinery

was gum well-placed. This stance was in direct conflict with Kameny, who hoped to see gay men and lesbians become a part of the Pentagon's schemes. . . . Perhaps our major departure from Kameny, Gittings, et al., was our conviction that homosexuality is not a minority condition, but, rather, a socially inculcated taboo. . . . Everyone, we began to say, would be capable of homosexual responses if only their abilities to relate to their own sex were not blocked by strict conditioning and abetted by the deliberate inculcation of fierce prejudice.

Spending the last weekend of June 1969 on Fire Island Pines, Lige and Jack returned Sunday night. Walking across Eighth Street, they entered the heart of Greenwich Village. On Christopher Street they spotted a few folks hanging near a partly boarded-up bar, the Stonewall Inn. Lige and Jack wrote their *Screw* column on July 8, the fifth anniversary of their fated rendezvous at the Hideaway. "Last week's riots in Greenwich Village have set standards for the rest of the nation's homosexuals to follow," they declared. However, the couple cautioned that the

> revolution in Sheridan Square must step beyond its present boundaries. The homosexual revolution is only part of a larger revolution sweeping through all segments of society. We hope that "Gay Power" will not become a call for separation, but for sexual integration. . . .

With the energies (and marketing potential) unleashed by Stonewall, Al Goldstein launched the nation's first homosexual weekly, *GAY,* in late 1969.[1] Jack and Lige were co-editors. The cover featured Lige wearing a white fishnet tank top and standing near an ocean vessel. The couple's first editorial quickly distanced these youthful veteran activists from the "homosexual as minority" approach held by the older generation of homophile activists. They wrote:

> *GAY* believes that there is only one world, and that labels and categories such as homosexual and heterosexual will some day pass away leaving human beings who, like this publication, will be liked and appreciated not because of sexual orientation, but because they are themselves interesting.

With Lige and Jack at the helm, "*GAY* became the newspaper of record for Gay America" with the largest circulation of any similar publication (Streitmatter, 1995, p. 121). As "journalistic prophets of the post-Stonewall Era," the couple shared editorial space with feminist writers such as Leah Fritz, Mary Phillips, and Claudia Dreyfus. There were regular features penned by Movement pioneers such as Virginian Lilli Vincenz writing a general/women's interest feature and Dick Leitsch, who wrote "History Facts Your Teacher 'Forgot' to Mention." Kay Tobin, formerly associate editor of *The Ladder,* was the paper's first news editor, and New York art critic Gregory Battcock attended museum art shows, lampooning "dorky tastes in clothes . . . mis-matched colorings, frumpy lines, and ugly buttons" in his column "The Last Estate." *GAY* attracted some of the best writers in Queer America. Vito Russo was *GAY*'s film critic, and the pseudonymous writer Ian J. Tree wrote on the black experience. There, too, were occasional contributions by historian Donn Teal and psychologist George Weinberg. In "The Editors Speak," Lige and Jack took issue with a variety of sacred cows: denouncing Uncle Sam as a Peeping Tom and taking African-American playwright Leroi Jones to task for urging blacks to avoid homosexuality as "the white man's weakness."

Irreverent in tone and brassy in style, *GAY* mixed controversial ideals with integrationist themes, becoming the *MAD* magazine for the new homosexual. "Although editors of such publications are generally thought of as radicals," Lige and Jack considered themselves neither "conservative" nor "crusaders." *GAY* "was not aimed at the middle-class, uptight, furtive homosexual," they reminded their readers. "[We] want to build bridges, establish a dialogue between homosexual and heterosexual . . . [and] to keep the paper free of the defensive tone which has been typical of so many homophile publications in the past" (*GAY,* February 1970, p. 12).

Resigning as editors of *GAY* in the summer of 1973, Jack began work on his groundbreaking *Men's Liberation: A New Definition of Masculinity* while Lige finished up their soon-to-be best-selling reflections on mores, *Roommates Can't Always Be Lovers.* Similar to Whitman's "We Two Boys," their comradeship helped to contour a movement as it transitioned from Mattachine chapters to gay liberation fronts. *Men's Liberation,* which Jack had dedicated to the Kentuckyian who had "taught me that a man can learn to bend like the willow," remains as timely today as it was a generation ago. In 1975, the partnership ended with Lige's murder. Three months later, a full-page sketch of Nichols appeared in the Washington *Star.* Describing the aftermath of his personal tragedy, the reporter observed:

> If he mourns his friend, he keeps it inside. He says Clarke is still alive because his values and dreams are alive. Nichols smiles at the memory of his friend "who lived his dream." Nichols' own dream is that of "human liberation." He says he's an optimist. "I'm not an alarmist. I think men are better than they think they are." (Flanders, 1975)

NOTE

1. Although *GAY* boasted the largest circulation of any gay newspaper in the country, several other liberationist publications emerged in New York City, including the GLF newspaper, *Come Out!, Gay Times,* and *Gay Flames.* The latter, produced by the Seventeenth Street GLF commune, declared: "Gay flames do not come from the matches of the church, the state, or the capitalistic businessmen. We are burning from within and our flames will light the path to our liberation" (Teal, 1971, p. 162).

BIBLIOGRAPHY

Unpublished Sources

Unless otherwise noted, quoted material is from the personal papers of Jack Nichols, Cocoa Beach, Florida. Some are included in the Sears papers, Special Collections, Duke University.

Published

Clarke, L., and Nichols, J. *The Gay Agenda: Talking Back to Fundamentalists.* Buffalo: Prometheus Books, 1996.
Clarke, L., and Nichols, J. *I Have More Fun With You Than Anybody.* New York: St. Martin's Press, 1972.
Clarke, L., and Nichols, J. *Roommates Can't Always Be Lovers.* New York: St. Martin's Press, 1974.
Clarke, L., and Nichols, J. *Welcome to Fire Island.* New York: St. Martin's Press, 1976.
Cory, Donald Webster. *The Homosexual in America: A Subjective Approach.* New York: Greenberg, 1951.
Flanders, J. "A Man Doesn't Have to Be Tough," *Washington Star,* May 18, 1975.
Hunter, John Francis (John Paul Hudson). *The Gay Insider, USA.* New York: Stonehill, 1972.
Loughery, J. *The Other Side of Silence.* New York: Holt, 1998.
Nichols, J. *Men's Liberation: A New Definition of Masculinity.* New York: Penguin, 1975.
Sears, J. *Lonely Hunters: The Oral History of Lesbian and Gay Southern Life, 1948-1968.* New York: Harper Collins-Westview, 1997.
Sears, J. *Rebels, Rubyfruit and Rhinestones: The Making of Homosexual Communities in the Stonewall South.* New Brunswick: Rutgers University Press, 2001.
Streitmatter, R. *Unspeakable: the Rise of the Gay and Lesbian Press in America.* Boston: Faber and Faber, 1995.
Teal, D. *The Gay Militants.* New York: Stein and Day, 1971.
Tobin, R., and Wicker, R. *The Gay Crusaders.* New York: Warner Books, 1972.

Lige Clarke (1942-1975)

Jack Nichols

In twelve days Lige Clarke would have been thirty-three, but he was murdered at a mysterious roadblock, his body riddled with automatic fire. He'd lived in whirlwinds of excitement during his short life, however, becoming the co-editor of *GAY,* America's first gay weekly newspaper and sounding on July 8, 1969, what historians note was the homophile movement's first "Call to Arms" following the Stonewall uprising:

The revolution in Sheridan Square must step beyond its present boundaries. The homosexual revolution is only part of a larger revolution sweeping through all segments of society. We hope that "Gay Power" will not become a call for separation, but for sexual integration, and that the young activists will read, study, and make themselves acquainted with all of the facts that will help them carry the sexual revolt triumphantly into the councils of the U.S. government, into the anti-homosexual churches, into the offices of anti-homosexual psychiatrists, into the city government, and into the state legislatures which make our manner of love-making a crime. It is time to push the homosexual revolution to its logical conclusion. We must crush tyranny wherever it exists and join forces with those who would assist in the utter destruction of the puritanical, repressive, anti-sexual Establishment.

Four years prior to the Stonewall revolt Lige had lettered nine of the ten picket signs carried by gay men and lesbians at the first White House protest held April 17, 1965. The young revolutionary had told me on several occasions that he had no fear of death. He'd seen it too many times in the mountains where he lived as a child. Following his murder I consoled myself thinking that he'd lived to see many of his dreams come true, traveling across the world—from Rio to Hong Kong, from Cape Town to the northernmost point in Europe.

Starting in 1966 Lige had begun discussing and writing about same-sex relationships, politics, and religious matters, showing an uncommon frankness. In an era when sexual repression and puritanical madness reigned, he hurled unsettling word grenades with unfailing good humor. He often experienced the satisfaction of watching these grenades blow gaping holes in fortresses of bias that had formerly been thought impregnable. Although a fierce warrior struggling to win basic freedoms, he regarded himself as a gentle person, and although he could express himself in memorable tones if angry, he most often opted to transform dull ignorance with his uproarious laughter. His targets were always ideas, however; he seemed little inclined to wax judgmental about individuals. People, he noted, don't remain the same. He maintained hope that they could change for the better.

I was often witness to his kindly treatment of others. He cared pointedly about what they were saying while he remained quietly aware of what their postures, expressions, and voice tones revealed. The inward ease he knew reflected in a posture that made him an unassuming master of entrances and exits. The first time I laid eyes on him he was twenty-two. I was immediately awed—as were many—by the classic symmetry of his face: cheekbones high, jaw strong; eyes hazel; lips full. He was lithe yet muscular, a soldier with a wide smile and top-level security clearances, editing secret messages from the Pentagon office of the Army Joint Chiefs of Staff.

Pentagon intelligence officers did not want to suspect that this smiling Kentucky youth might be involved, as he soon became, with challenging the "one true theory" of masculinity to which they subscribed. Inside the Pentagon he secretly passed out Washington Mattachine leaflets that explained to beleaguered gay soldiers how to handle a federal investigation of their sex lives.

I'd taken him to meet Frank Kameny on our first date, following a movie. It was about 10 p.m. and Kameny was mimeographing a press release, but gladly explained the nature of our Mattachine endeavors. He told Lige that because of his security clearances, he could, if he liked, use a pseudonym to join. "A semisecret society," Lige laughed to me on our way home. "This is really getting interesting." Our relationship developed with an undeniable passion against a backdrop of tunes by the Beatles and the Supremes.

In the spring of 1965 Lige reacted angrily to front-page news that Castro was imprisoning Cuban homosexuals in a concentration camp. Together we plotted what became the first gay movement march at the White House. Lettering the signs, he used slogans upon which he and I had agreed with Frank Kameny. The demonstration took place the Saturday before Easter. I carried the first sign, protesting federal treatment. Others showed how the governments of Cuba, the United States, and Russia had all persecuted gay men and lesbians.

Lige first marched in September's U.S. State Department protest as a representative of the Mattachine Society of Florida, Inc., which he'd cofounded earlier that same year with Richard Inman and with me. Meeting Inman while on a special Miami mission to persuade him to rename his Atheneum Society—Lige urged he use the Mattachine name in order to link an isolated realm—south Florida—with the homophile movement's groups in Washington, New York, and Philadelphia. It was the first time I'd ever witnessed Lige's diplomatic talents at work. He simply accessed his gentle, irresistible Kentucky manners.

It had been a snowy night, February 22, 1942, when Elijah Hadyn Clarke (Lige) was born in Cave Branch, a Knott County hollow in Kentucky's southeastern mountains, near Hindman (population 700) and twenty miles from Hazard. His earliest years were marked in part by his snow-white hair, later turning blonde, while he showed an earthy awareness that would soon begin to illuminate his concept of a more personal, self-aware approach to gay liberation. While World War II was winding down on another continent, Lige, the youngest of his mother Corinne's children, scampered through the surrounding hills and along the ridges with his sister, Shelbi, and his older brother George. The three Clarke children rode a pony each Sunday to Ivis Bible Church on the main road. When Lige's photo later appeared in a movie fan magazine, however, his Sunday school teacher warned him that he'd have to chose between Ivis Bible Church and Hollywood.

Portraying "Puck" in a Robert Porterfield summer stock production of *A Midsummer Night's Dream,* Lige, at seventeen, calmly demonstrated, without speaking a word to his Sunday school teacher, how Hollywood seemed to be winning in the struggle for his soul. Still, emphasizing how he owed much to the people in those steep hills, he often told how he'd seen raw nature's ways close at hand and that he'd learned about people—the wise and the ignorant—from the multifaceted behaviors of his Kentucky kin.

One day, after I'd known Lige eight years, he presented me with *Kinfolk,* a slim volume of poetry written in Appalachian accents by Ann Cobb, a pioneering educator. Inscribing the book for me, he chose a verse characteristic of himself, happy-go-lucky but determined, eschewing common comforts while climbing, climbing:

> Far'well bottom-land, with all the garden truck!
> Allus tol you hillside's the only place for luck!

Ms. Cobb had settled in Hindman with two other women friends. The three teachers had become a local legend because of their helpfulness, as had Lige's paternal grandfather, George Clarke, another educator honored by a historical marker at the Route 80 intersection. Lige recalled his mother Corinne advising him when he was still a toddler that he must not remain in Hindman after growing into manhood. "You mustn't hold on to your mother's skirt," she'd tell the little boy, "but you must learn to fly up and away from her—far far, away."

Although he wandered far from the hills, Lige never failed to access them in memory, putting hillbilly humor to work whenever city folk got too serious. Having enjoyed a surprising number of heterosexual sex trysts before he'd moved away from Kentucky, it hadn't occurred to him then, as it would later, that people's sex lives are often "chained," as he put it, "to wheels of despair whose spokes are society's conventional codes."

He told me how Sunday evening church revivals in Hindman—unbeknownst to the minister—had been "good cause for rejoicing." "While adults praised the Lord inside the church," he laughed, "we young'uns, more practical by far, enjoyed automobile orgies in the parking lot out back. There wasn't much else to do up in those hollows," he joked, utilizing Appalachian wordage.

Even so, Lige lamented, the Southern Baptists weren't about to let such good times last forever. By the time local males reached twenty, he noted, "life was almost over" for them. They'd marry. Their wives, following the advice of mothers, cooked to fatten their husbands during the first year afterward so that other women wouldn't lust for these men—much needed meal tickets—and cause them to wander. "Early marriages in Kentucky," he complained, had become "a must." At twenty-four, Lige remained the only member of his high school graduating class who hadn't tied the nuptial knot. "Thank God," he sighed.

Although he considered himself privileged by Kentucky standards, he carried with him a continuing passionate concern about the welfare of his country folk, hating the crushing poverty he'd observed among them during his formative years. When he returned home for visits, he wrote sadly of seeing "deep scars of frustration etched on the faces of boyhood friends." He noted that the sparkling eyes of their early years had vanished. He marveled at how those whose sexual company he had enjoyed on Sundays were now seated *inside* the church while their "young-uns" fiddled with each other in the parking lots outside.

A few locals regarded the handsome hometown visitor with suspicion. "How come you ain't fat? How come you ain't married?" Others said, "There something *quare* about that Clarke boy. Ain't natural for a man not to get married." A couple of old buddies took him aside to ask what they thought was a real "man-to-man" question: "Hey, Lige, did you ever do it with a colored woman?"

Before he moved away, Lige wrote that he assumed it was only the hills he'd escaped that were out of step.

> Little did I know that men and women—people from the middle, upper middle and upper classes were sad victims of the puritan heritage to even greater degrees. In the mountains, at least, we had learned to fuck *wildly*—at an early age, both heterosexually and homosexually. We were in touch with our bodies.

In big cities, Lige discovered, gloomy orthodox codes had "petrified sexual communication." These codes, he wrote, had created "an urban blight: an anally retentive population whose members find no relief." He noted that the

> message of sexual liberation falls hard on such ears: the Puritan mentality dies a slow death. It's hard for men and women to admit that their behavior codes are lies; that they have long been "controlling" themselves, "behaving" themselves and frustrating themselves for no good reason.

Lige explained that "jealousy, envy, and a thousand fantasies" people never have the courage to live "converge on them, exploding with an intense and fearful rage that a sexually sane person finds incomprehensible." Life, he observed, "has passed them by and they can't abide another's joy."

It was midsummer 1964 when I met him at a rathskeller, The Hideaway, directly across from FBI headquarters in Washington, DC. He struck me at first as an apparition, slyly seductive as only a smiling rural assurance can allow—earthy, wholesome, his serious side often hard to notice because of his Kentucky-bred joie de vivre. As he grew, Lige quickly learned to circumvent people's reactions to his good looks and somehow to touch them more meaningfully, with a few pointed words, a phrase, or perhaps as another biographer put it, "a whisper of poetry."

He was effective at presenting himself as significantly more than a stunning physical presence. He was often regarded as a very wise person, in fact. This was because he continually practiced a nurturing, empathetic awareness. He observed and listened well, and was often able to connect even with total strangers on an emotional level, making them feel somehow embraced or encompassed. Thus, he was beloved by shipmates and foreign nationals from every clime during his travels. He seemed to have embodied Walt Whitman's line, "I think whoever I shall meet I shall like."

He was, for me, my most beloved exemplar. He helped move my focus from abstract thoughts to a more profound physical self-awareness, increasing my enjoyment of living thereby. He taught me, as I noted in my books' dedication to him, which he saw three days before his murder: *a man must learn to bend like the willow.* This was simply hillbilly wisdom that his own mother had taught him. Lige clearly saw advantages to encouraging elasticity in men rather than their long-suffering old-fashioned macho rigidity. He said such elasticity—whether mental or physical—was a component of any hope for human survival.

Moving with me to Manhattan in 1968, Lige began working for the alternative press. The fact of sexual repression had struck with its unbridled force. He saw—as publishers and friends were arrested for "obscenity"— how the establishment refused to abide magazines and newspapers that celebrated sexual passion. "And the man in the street," wrote Lige, "is hungry, painfully hungry, for a taste of sexual freedom." Society, he noted, played cruel, heartless tricks on such people. Their alternatives to chaste dates and inhospitable spouses became "hideously painted prostitutes—nightmares in an upside-down carnival!" He believed that the average straight was "surrounded by an army of sex-starved gossips: 'Mary's boyfriend, John, is supposed to be true to her but he's been screwing Joanne on the side.' "

In Lige's small towns such gossip had seemed barely tolerable. If either the culprit or the victim were married, he knew, the gossip became even juicier. Husbands and wives, he believed, spent useless time worrying about each other's sexual fidelity. He reflected that society seemed to be forcing both the married and the unmarried to seek the pleasures of sex only under the most bizarre and tawdry circumstances.

Wary of procreation as the only proper excuse for sex, especially in the wake of church assaults on condoms, Lige insisted that "sex for pleasure" must replace sex for baby making as the sanest ideal. He called for an end to the commonplace use of sexual epithets and curses, hoping to see sexual organs and acts portrayed in affirmative terms. In gay terms, Lige Clarke was not, therefore, a cultural assimilationist. He looked instead to a day when humanity might free itself from the ancient taboos that have resulted in "heterosexual" bondage scenes. Petty jealousies, he wrote, butch/fem role-playing, and the concept of sexual ownership (I own your genitals and you may use them only with me) must be stampeded from our consciousness. Heterosexual patterns "must not be copied."

Lige believed that millions of unhappy slaves to the system were "waiting eagerly for such liberation." He felt they should be helped to turn away from common compulsive clutching and groping to joys that are informed by a "calm erotic awareness." Rushing toward some always-particularized goal, he insisted, interrupts the kind of spontaneous sensual flow wherein more satisfying and sexual experiences thrive best. These messages were part of what he brought to our "Homosexual Citizen" column, published over a period of four and a half years in *Screw,* the original sex tabloid that had become—in late 1968—an immediate sensation offering, for the first time, full frontal nudity. This groundbreaking column provided "Lige and Jack," as the byline read, with a degree of Manhattan minifame.

Lige, who taught Hatha yoga to Kay Tobin Lahusen, took her suggestion that he and I should start a newspaper. *GAY* was therefore born on November 15, 1969, and Kay became the newspaper's first news editor. Soon, in early 1970, *GAY* was turned into a weekly, which kept Lige busy writing letters, talking with columnists, and planning issues. Until he and I resigned in mid-1973 to write and travel, *GAY* faithfully chronicled the birth and growth of Manhattan's most effective activist groups, especially the Gay Activists Alliance. This particular group invented the "zap," providing colorful headlines and photos of surprise appearances of the activists at certain locales where they caused nonviolent distress to antigay zealots.

GAY was host to many writers who had helped found the gay and lesbian movement. It published the first-ever interview with Bette Midler; received the blessing of Allen Ginsberg, who contributed a poem titled "Jimmy Berman Newsboy Gay Lib Rag"; and served as the medium in which Dr. George Weinberg, who coined the term homophobia, first explained his understanding of the phobia itself.

Lige met his newspapering obligations zestfully. He appeared on Geraldo Rivera's first television special. He spoke at the twenty-sixth annual Conference on World Affairs at the University of Colorado. Together we appeared on numerous radio programs. We addressed gay liberation groups. Lige quoted Walt Whitman wherever he went. He was especially fond of the great poet's "Song of the Open Road." Having recited it as often as he did, he became increasingly eager to travel. In the meantime, he initiated and wrote two books with me, *I Have More Fun with You Than Anybody* and *Roommates Can't Always Be Lovers.* The first book was hailed as the first nonfiction memoir by a male couple. *Roommates* was subtitled: *An Intimate Guide to Male/Male Relationships,* and stood out as the first published collection of nonfiction letters from gay men. As the co-editor of *GAY,* Lige had received their queries seeking advice—and had taken meticulous care to reply.

With two more book contracts secured, Lige and I left Manhattan, although we still shared a Greenwich Village apartment there with Kay Tobin Lahusen and Barbara Gittings. I settled, for the winter, into an apartment on Cocoa Beach where I completed *Men's Liberation: A New Definition of Masculinity.* Lige worked aboard the *Vistajord* at this time, a Norwegian cruise ship that took him to the four corners of the earth. He wrote me passionate letters, asking me to join him, telling of the world's wonder. We met at Port Everglades, Lige leaving the ship for a day. Riding across Miami's freeways, a song of the time, "The Best Thing That Ever Happened to Me," was playing. "That's how I feel about you," I told him. Much later, shortly before his unexpected death, he asked me—uncharacteristically—if I still felt as I'd indicated on that day. "More than ever," I replied. In hindsight, I'm prouder of that timely reply than of anything I've ever said.

In the winter of 1974-1975 Lige and I took up residence again in Cocoa Beach, both of us writing, with Lige working to complete a book that would be called *Welcome to Fire Island.* Charlie, a new acquaintance we'd made, lived at the end of our outside corridor. He offered his Pinto as a mode of transportation should Lige wish to take a trip to Mexico. Finally, a two-week getaway was planned. At just that moment an old acquaintance, Juan, unexpectedly arrived and then offered to accompany Lige and Charlie on their jaunt. I felt somewhat assured by the fact that Juan could serve as a translator once they crossed the border.

Juan changed his mind in Houston, however, returning by plane to Washington, DC. Lige and Charlie crossed into Mexico at Brownsville, where they were searched for three hours by customs officials. Lige was carrying the two gay books he and I had written as well as his own worn copies of Walt Whitman's *Leaves of Grass, The Way of Life According to Lao Tzu,* and *The Prophet* by Kahlil Gibran.

The two journeyers entered the rich state of Vera Cruz, rich in sugar cane, bananas, vanilla, rice, and mahogany. They saw poverty everywhere, however, and laughed at how they had hurried to arrive at such a desolate locale. It was midnight, February 10, 1975, when Lige and Charlie ran into a roadblock on the Tuxpam-Tampico highways as they approached the city of Vera Cruz. According to Charlie's account, he had been asleep in the back seat and Lige had been driving. He'd awakened to bright lights shining on the Pinto and the sound of automatic gunfire. Lige slumped over the wheel and the car lurched across the highway, coming to a stop halfway up a hillside.

Charlie was shot too, a slight wound in his side. He pretended to be dead, he said. He later crawled into a passing bus going into the city and was taken to a hospital where he remained incommunicado for nine days. Mexican authorities were suspicious of him, accusing him of working for the CIA. They refused to let him speak to U.S. embassy authorities and informed him that Lige would be buried in Mexico. The intervention of Carl Perkins, a U.S. Congressman from Kentucky, was finally responsible for Mexican acquiescence in the transport of Lige's body back to his old Kentucky home.

Who killed Lige? I honestly don't know. There are four or five theories, but they are only that. I'm convinced, however, that he was a victim of machismo's homophobic influences. I attended Lige's funeral in the hills. One of his childhood's mentors, a woman he called Prudy, spoke: "Lige was truly a dreamer," she said,

> artistic, sensitive, and a chaser after rainbows. He was ever in search of new adventures and new places. His god was a loving god, one who met his children with a smile. If he were here, I feel he would say, "No sad faces: I am not dead. . . . Smile, for I am just away."

BIBLIOGRAPHY

Alwood, Edward. *Straight News: Gays, Lesbians and the News Media.* New York: Columbia University Press, 1996.

Bull, Chris (Ed.). *Witness to Revolution: The Advocate Reports on Gay and Lesbian Politics 1967-1999.* New York: Alyson, 1999.

Clarke, Lige, and Jack Nichols. *I Have More Fun With You Than Anybody.* New York: St. Martin's Press, 1972.

Clarke, Lige, and Jack Nichols. *Roommates Can't Always Be Lovers: An Intimate Guide to Male/Male Relationships.* New York: St. Martin's Press, 1974.

Hunter, John Francis. *The Gay Insider USA.* New York: Stonehill, 1972.

Kaiser, Charles. *The Gay Metropolis 1940-1996.* New York: Houghton-Mifflin, 1997.

Loughery, John. *The Other Side of Silence: Men's Lives and Gay Identities—A Twentieth Century History.* New York: Henry Holt, 1998.

Nichols, Jack. *Men's Liberation: A New Definition of Masculinity.* New York: Penguin Books, 1975.

Nichols, Jack. *Welcome to Fire Island: Visions of Cherry Grove and the Pines.* New York: St. Martin's Press, 1976.

Sears, James T. *Lonely Hunters: An Oral History of Lesbian and Gay Southern Life.* New York: Westview-Harper Collins, 1997.

Sears, James T. *Rebels, Rubyfruit and Rhinestones: The Emergence of Queer in Communities in the Stonewall South.* New Brunswick, NJ: Rutgers University Press, 2001.

Streitmatter, Rodger. *Unspeakable: The Rise of the Gay and Lesbian Press in America.* New York: Faber and Faber, 1995.

Teal, Donn. *The Gay Militants.* New York: Simon and Schuster, 1971; paperback by St. Martin's Press, 1995.

Thompson, Mark (Ed.). *Long Road to Freedom: The Advocate's History of the Gay and Lesbian Movement.* New York: St. Martin's Press, 1994.

Tobin, Kay and Randy Wicker. *The Gay Crusaders.* New York: Paperback Library, 1972.

Barbara Gittings (1932-   ): Independent Spirit

Kay Tobin Lahusen

Photo by Kay Tobin Lahusen

Barbara Gittings was standing tall as a gay activist long before Stonewall. She walked in the first gay picket lines and edited a national lesbian magazine in the 1960s. She went on radio and TV shows when producers first invited gay guests, and launched her public lecturing career at Bucknell University in 1967. She was an early consultant for the National Council of Churches and other religious groups. She helped challenge the federal government's denial of security clearances for gay people.

After the Stonewall uprising in 1969, she tackled psychiatrists for their gay-negative positions. For fifteen years she crusaded against "the lies in the libraries" and in the literature that commonly slandered gay people decades ago. Today she is still marching, still tackling bigotries and barriers, and still smiling!

I have been her life partner since 1961. She's a hero to me, as she is to many others. How did she get to be one of the pioneers who got the gay tide rolling?

Barbara was born in 1932 in Vienna, Austria, where her father was in the U.S. diplomatic service, so she was automatically a U.S. citizen. Her father was a strict Catholic and his three children attended Catholic schools in Annapolis, Maryland, Montreal, Canada, and Wilmington, Delaware, where the family finally settled for good. Their big old house was filled with books, which fed Barbara's natural bent for reading.

Barbara first felt different when she was attracted to other girls during her eighth to twelfth grades in public schools. Throughout four years of high school, she carried the torch for one particular girl and was too naive to hide her feelings even though she sensed that her attraction was considered wrong. There was a near-total taboo on mention of homosexuality. She first heard the word in her senior year when she qualified for the National Honor Society but was rejected on grounds of "character," and a sympathetic teacher explained that was probably because of Barbara's "homosexual inclinations."

In high school Barbara had enjoyed the concert, drama, and glee clubs. She chose to attend Northwestern University for its theater department. Upon delivering her daughter to her college dormitory in 1949, Barbara's mother left her with a warning to avoid certain kinds of women she might meet. Although Barbara didn't encounter other homosexuals in college, she herself was labeled a lesbian because of a close but platonic friendship she had with another student. She was the last to hear this rumor—from the dormitory director. Suddenly it made sense to Barbara. No, she didn't have homosexual feelings for "X" but yes, she was homosexual. She had to find out: What does this mean? What will my life be like? Meanwhile her "friend" rejected her.

With no one she could talk to, Barbara naturally turned to books for information. She began combing libraries at Northwestern and in nearby Chicago. That was little help. She struggled to dig up information under headings like "Sexual Perversion" and "Abnormal Psychology." She felt, "That's me they're writing about—but it's not like me at all."

While doing this research, Barbara neglected her studies, except for Glee Club; singing sustained her. Flunking out at the end of her freshman year, she returned home in disgrace, unable to tell her parents what had happened. She felt very alone. Again she turned to the library, and got a boost when she stumbled on gay fiction, novels such as *The Well of Loneliness, Dusty Answer, Nightwood, Claudine at School,* and *Extraordinary Women.* The stories mostly had unhappy endings, but at least the homosexual characters seemed to her like flesh-and-blood human beings with real lives and times of happiness. They made her feel better about herself.

She acquired her own copy of *The Well of Loneliness,* and when her father found it hidden in her room and told her to burn it, she hid it better. She signed up for a course in Abnormal Psychology, which led to more than book learning; she had a short love affair with another young woman in her class.

She took off for Philadelphia at age eighteen, without explanation. She settled in a rooming house, did frugal cooking on a hot plate, got a job clerking in a music store, and found a choral group to sing in. She took up hiking and biking and canoeing. She was making her own life. Even her father admired her spunk and wrote a formal note "relieving you of the onus of your disobedience" in running away from home. Despite his moralistic views, she seems to have been his favorite child. (He died in 1961 before becoming aware of Barbara's involvement in the gay rights movement.)

Although now free from parental control and the influence of Catholicism, Barbara still was lonely. She needed to find her people. By persistent hunting she got to some gay bars, first in Philadelphia and then in New York, but they felt alien to her. In the lesbian bars, most patrons looked butch or femme, and Barbara herself tried the butch role. But the role-playing so common in the 1950s wasn't congenial to her. Nor could she find in the bars others who shared her tastes in music and books and outdoor activities.

All those years she haunted libraries and secondhand bookshops to read more about homosexuality. She discovered Donald Webster Cory's *The Homosexual in America,* the first American book to proclaim the radical idea that gay people (although psychologically flawed as he saw it) are a legitimate minority group and should demand their civil rights. As a bonus, Cory had included a long list of fiction works with homosexual characters. Barbara was intrigued and arranged to meet Cory in New York. He told her about an early gay organization, ONE, Inc., in Los Angeles. With vacation time coming, Barbara flew out to the West Coast, went right to ONE's office with a rucksack on her back, and was hospitably received.

When told about the Mattachine Society, Barbara flew up to San Francisco to visit there, again got a welcome, and heard about a year-old lesbian organization, the Daughters of Bilitis. DOB members were about to hold a meeting to launch their magazine, *The Ladder;* Barbara got herself invited. In the congenial atmosphere of someone's living room, she met Del Martin and Phyllis Lyon and a diverse group of gay women who were serious about helping others. At last she'd found other lesbians she felt she had something in common with.

That was 1956. By 1958, Del and Phyl tapped Barbara to organize DOB's first chapter on the East Coast, in New York City. The Mattachine Society of New York gave encouragement and meeting space in its tiny office. Mattachine notified the handful of women on its mailing list, DOB in San Francisco notified its few *Ladder* subscribers on the East Coast, and with no more than ten women in attendance, DOB's New York Chapter got started and Barbara became president. She served for three years, taking the bus from Philadelphia twice a month to keep the chapter rolling with Gab-n-Java discussions, potluck suppers, business meetings, and lectures (often in conjunction with Mattachine). Turnouts were small—twenty was a crowd!—but Barbara wasn't discouraged. She composed, stenciled, and mimeographed a chapter newsletter and sent it out in sealed envelopes to ensure security.

In 1961, at a picnic in Rhode Island to explore starting a New England chapter of DOB, Barbara and I met each other. I was living in Boston then.

After a brief courtship, we settled into her efficiency apartment in Philadelphia. We've been together in the gay cause ever since.

"I've always been a joiner," she says. "If the gay rights movement hadn't come along, I might today be active in wilderness conservation—but the gay movement is a lot more fun!" In the late 1940s when our tiny groups began meeting behind locked doors, homosexuals were viewed as sick, weird, perverted, and immoral. Just banding together in those years helped gay people to overcome their feelings of inferiority. Having found her people, the community she belonged to, Barbara realized she could act with others to remedy the group's problems. The early 1960s were right for gay people to start pressing for our rights in an organized fashion. And in 1963 Barbara met Frank Kameny, an astronomer and physicist who had been fired from his federal job for being gay, had appealed his case to the U.S. Supreme Court which declined to hear it, and had then started the Mattachine Society of Washington as an activist group whose key mission was to reverse the antigay policies of the federal government.

Barbara was fired up by Frank.

> He had such a clear and coherent position about our cause! He said that homosexuality is fully the equal of heterosexuality and fully on par with it. He said that gay is good and right and healthy and moral, and those who claim otherwise are wrong. He said that homosexuality is not a sickness and that we must stand up and say so and not wait for so-called experts to do the right research and eventually persuade the public we aren't sick. Indeed he declared that *we* are the experts on homosexuality!

These were not the prevailing views in our movement at the time. But Frank's bold vision made sense to Barbara: "Until I met Frank, I had only a muddled sense of what we could do as activists. Frank crystallized my thinking."

In 1963 DOB again tapped Barbara, this time to take over editing its magazine, *The Ladder.* The appointment was to be temporary until a new permanent editor was found. Barbara agreed to help out for a few months; instead she was editor for three and a half years. "I discovered the power of the press, the power to put in what you want in order to influence readers," she says. She continued the magazine's popular fare of fiction, poetry, news items, readers' letters, book reviews, biographies of famous women known or thought to be lesbians, and essays. But she also expanded reporting on gay groups' early conferences, especially ECHO (East Coast Homophile Organizations). Barbara featured debates in *The Ladder* on controversies of the day. For example, in 1964 she published a lively exchange between

Frank Kameny and DOB's research director about gay groups' support of research into homosexuality. Then when organized gay picketing began in 1965, she printed pro and con views. A favorite back-and-forth of hers is the 1964 report "Act or Teach?" covering a close debate on whether we advance our cause better by pressing for favorable laws or by trying to change attitudes first. Barbara stretched the magazine's reach beyond its small list of a few hundred mail subscribers. No distributor would agree to handle sales, so Barbara and I personally delivered copies every month to a handful of progressive bookstores in New York and Philadelphia.

The most dramatic change in *The Ladder* was its covers. Barbara added the subtitle *A Lesbian Review,* and we moved to glossy photo covers. At first, we solicited photos of art works by professional artists and photos from the entertainment world. Then we persuaded lesbians to be pictured back to camera or in shadowy profile. Finally we had full-face photos of lesbians, a breakthrough!

Barbara felt strongly that tearing the shroud of invisibility was crucial to all our efforts to change social conditions for gay people. She used her own name from the start, while many activists still used pseudonyms to protect their jobs and their families. "At every point where I had to decide: shall I go on this radio show, and if so, shall I use my real name? Shall I talk to this newspaper reporter, and give my name and a picture if wanted? Shall I walk in the picket line, or work behind the scenes getting the signs ready? I felt I had less to risk than most gay people."

And walk the picket lines she did, in demonstrations in 1965 at the White House and the Pentagon in Washington, and at Independence Hall in Philadelphia every July 4th from 1965 to 1969. The picket lines were small. Barbara says, "It was scary to demonstrate for our rights and equality. Picketing was not a popular tactic in the 1960s. Certainly our cause wasn't popular. Even most gay people thought our efforts were foolish and outlandish." She adds,

> Only a tiny handful of us could or would take the risk of being so publicly on view. What if my boss sees me on the 6 o'clock news and fires me? What if my picture appears in my parents' hometown paper and causes shock waves? What if a bystander throws insults at us—or worse, bricks or stones? And what is the government going to DO with all those photographs and tape recordings they're making of us?

Still it was a heady time for the picketers. Barbara notes, "We all felt, as one of us put it, 'Today it was as if a weight dropped off my soul!' "

Barbara was fired as editor of *The Ladder* in the summer of 1966. She had had a number of frictions with DOB's governing board. She tried to drop "For Adults Only" from the cover, but it wasn't allowed. She wasn't allowed to change the magazine's name to *A Lesbian Review* so she added that as a subtitle. But the reason the board cited for firing her was her tardiness in shipping the monthly issues' mock-ups and covers to DOB headquarters in San Francisco. Mea culpa, says Barbara; she agrees her lateness was a hardship on the members there who physically produced the magazine.

There was plenty of other activism in the late 1960s. Barbara helped Frank Kameny challenge the Defense Department's moves to revoke security clearances held by gay people working in private industry. She teamed up with Jack Nichols for her first public lecture engagement beyond late-night radio shows, and then went on to make hundreds of appearances as a speaker and workshop leader. She encouraged her friend Craig Rodwell in 1967 when he opened the Oscar Wilde Memorial Bookshop, the nation's first bookstore devoted to better books on gay themes. She worked in the national umbrella association North American Conference of Homophile Organizations which was launched in 1966 and which peaked in 1968 with adoption of "A Homosexual Bill of Rights," and the adoption of the slogan "Gay Is Good" coined earlier by Frank Kameny.

Suddenly in late June of 1969 came the Stonewall rebellion. For the first time, gay people fought back physically against police harassment of a gay bar. Barbara and I cheered them from a vacation spot as we read about the riots, in *The New York Times*—a major breakthrough in media coverage of gay events. The Stonewall uprising itself was a turning point for the gay community, a leap in audacity and visibility. Out of three days of rioting in Greenwich Village emerged the loose-knit Gay Liberation Front, comprised mostly of Johnny- and Janie-come-latelys who proclaimed that all oppressed people must hang together to tear down "the system." Out of curiosity, Barbara attended two or three meetings in New York but was not sympathetic. Gay people who went to those chaotic GLF meetings were recruited to picket for the Black Panthers, women prisoners, and other nongay causes. Barbara, Frank Kameny, and others who had worked for years against great obstacles to change conditions for gay people were denounced as "dinosaurs" and "the enemy" and "lackeys of the establishment" by those wanting not reform but revolution.

Fortunately the veteran activists weathered GLF's storm of criticism and upheavals. GLF eventually fizzled out, replaced by Gay Activists Alliance, which was single-issue and reformist, yet militant and adept at daring confrontation tactics. The dignified pickets of the 1960s were replaced by the boisterous, free-wheeling Gay Pride marches that began in 1970. Barbara joined in, moving with the times, and was asked to be a main speaker at the 1973 march in New York.

Barbara and Lilli Vincenz were the first lesbians to go on a nationally syndicated TV show, the *Phil Donahue Show,* then out of Dayton, Ohio, in May 1970. Barbara remembers the live audience as "hostile housewives." She and Lilli appeared together again in the fall of 1971, with other lesbians, on PBS's nationwide *David Susskind Show.* At the supermarket a week later, a middle-aged couple recognized Barbara from the show and the wife told her, "You made me realize that you gay people love each other just the way Arnold and I do."

In the fall of 1970, Barbara acted as one of the newscasters on *Homosexual News and Reviews,* the pioneer gay radio show on station WBAI-FM in New York. One day a press release in her box excited her: gay librarians had organized within the American Library Association. Barbara turned up at the fledgling group's meetings in New York. Her enthusiasm and activist talent were welcomed; the group was a natural home for her even as a nonlibrarian. She spent the next sixteen years campaigning in the American Library Association to change attitudes about gay people as library patrons and employees, and to promote good gay materials.

She traveled at her own expense to ALA conferences around the country. At her first conference, in Dallas in 1971, the Task Force on Gay Liberation (later, the Gay Task Force) put on an ambitious program including the first Gay Book Award; a talk on discrimination by a gay librarian who had lost his job when he came out as gay; and a talk about changes needed in the way materials on homosexuality were classified. But few librarians outside the Gay Task Force showed up. So the gay group's founder and first coordinator, Israel Fishman, set up a publicity stunt in the exhibit hall, called "Hug a Homosexual," offering free same-sex kisses and hugs.

It was the first-ever gay kissing booth. Barbara and two other women were on the "Women Only" side of the booth and the GTF's leader with another man on the "Men Only" side. But there were no takers, only lots of oglers. Unflapped, Barbara and the others gaily showed the crowd How It's Done. For two hours they kissed and hugged each other, called out encouragement, handed out copies of the GTF's gay reading list, then kissed and hugged each other some more. "At last they noticed us!" says Barbara gleefully. "Also, our kissing booth made the point that there shouldn't be a double standard for love, that we gay people are entitled to be just as open as heterosexuals—no more, but no less—in showing our affection."

The Gay Task Force was now on a roll. Barbara became its second coordinator in 1971 and served until 1986. She joined the ALA so she could handle the GTF's bureaucratic needs, and she eagerly recruited other nonlibrarians to work in the group. Programs such as "The Children's Hour: Must Gay Be Grim for Jane and Jim?" about negative gay stories in novels for teenagers, and "It's Safer to Be Gay on Another Planet," about gay themes in science fiction, drew big crowds. One failure was the group's 1986 program, a fine presentation on "AIDS Awareness: The Library's Role." It drew only thirty-five persons, all core members of GTF. Most librarians and laypeople didn't yet want to confront the subject of AIDS.

Gay reading lists were a pet project of Barbara's. When GTF started, gay-supportive materials were so few that Barbara's first list of thirty-eight books, pamphlets, and articles fit onto a single page. But the 1970s signaled an explosion of gay materials, especially by gay and lesbian authors. Barbara's last edition of *A Gay Bibliography* in 1980 had almost 600 items including periodicals and audio-visuals. She also produced special lists of gay materials for use in schools, for professional counselors, for religious study, for parents of gays, and for start-up collections in small libraries. In 1986, Barbara's last act as GTF coordinator was to announce that the Gay Book Award had become an official award of the American Library Association.

Barbara had a key role in gains in another major arena in the 1970s: the American Psychiatric Association. "The sickness label was an albatross around our necks in the first decades of our movement. It's hard to explain to anyone who didn't live through that time how much gay people were under the thumb of psychiatry." That began to change in the 1960s. Barbara recalls,

> The pivot point was, we realized we'd have to wait forever for the researchers with accepted credentials to do studies that showed we are normal and healthy and then get the public to accept such unpopular findings. So we stopped deferring to the professionals and began to speak for ourselves.

At the American Psychiatric Association's 1970 meeting, a session on aversion therapy to change "undesirable" behavior was broken up by a group of gays and feminists who demanded, "Stop talking about us and start talking with us." Anxious to avoid future disruptions, APA set up a panel at its 1971 conference titled "Life Styles of Non-Patient Homosexuals." Barbara says, "We jokingly called it 'Life Styles of Impatient Homosexuals.' This was the first time the psychiatric establishment formally acknowledged that there were gay people who aren't in therapy and have no need for it."

Barbara and Frank were asked to join two psychiatrists at APA's 1972 convention for another breakthrough panel on "Psychiatry: Friend or Foe to Homosexuals? A Dialogue." Barbara felt strongly it wasn't right to just have two gay people and two psychiatrists pitted against each other, that the panel really needed someone who was both a psychiatrist and gay. But in 1972 it proved impossible to find a gay psychiatrist who would come forward.

Finally Barbara found one who said, "I'll do it—provided I can wear a wig and a full-face mask and use a voice-distorting microphone." Dr. H. Anonymous was born, despite the vehement protest of Frank Kameny who felt that a disguised gay person went against all we were fighting for.

Barbara smuggled Dr. H. Anonymous in his mask and wig through back corridors into the packed lecture hall. "He really rocked the audience," she says, "a masked gay psychiatrist telling his colleagues why he couldn't be honest in his own profession, how his career would be ruined." Barbara backed him up by reading poignant excerpts from letters she had received from other gay psychiatrists who had turned down her invitation to appear.

While this high-visibility panel was taking place, behind the scenes a few persistent gay activists were pressing APA to remove homosexuality from its list of mental disorders, as part of APA's overall revision of the profession's diagnostic manual. Contrary to some accounts, Barbara was not directly involved and can't be credited as a prime mover of that change. In late 1973, homosexuality was officially struck from APA's roster of psychiatric illnesses. Barbara relishes her local newspaper's headline: "Twenty Million Homosexuals Gain 'Instant Cure.'"

To spur changes in psychiatrists' views about homosexuality, Barbara set up and ran gay exhibits at APA conventions in 1972, 1976, and 1978. Her last display, "Gay Love: Good Medicine," emphasized gays as healthy and happy, and this time she was thrilled to find five gay psychiatrists willing to be shown in the exhibit with their pictures and credentials. The tide had turned. She also encouraged the emerging official group of gay and lesbian psychiatrists in the APA. "I think of myself as their fairy godmother."

Barbara loves fairy-godmothering; it gratifies her to stir up gay gumption. She also inspired nurses to form the Gay Nurses Alliance in 1973 and advised start-up gay groups in the American Public Health Association and the American Association of Law Librarians.

But she's not shy about being a public face for the cause. Since Stonewall she has been a Grand Marshal at Gay Pride celebrations in several cities (including New York, with Congressman Barney Frank as co-Grand Marshal). She continues her public speaking, including her illustrated lecture "Gay and Smiling: Tales from Fifty Years of Activism," and enjoys doing a bit of theater too. In 1986, gays staged a "Burger Roast" at Independence Hall to protest the decision by the Supreme Court under Warren Burger to uphold Georgia's sodomy law. Barbara, draped in a white sheet, played the allegorical figure of Justice in a tableau, but instead of the traditional scales, she held a Bible, and instead of a blindfold, she had binoculars "to peer into the nation's bedrooms." For a gay cabaret in 1998, Barbara donned other costumes to read a piece by Gertrude Stein and to sing a duet with the cabaret's lead drag performer.

Singing is actually Barbara's favorite activity. She began choral singing in junior high school in the mid-1940s. Today she sings second tenor with the Philadelphia Chamber Chorus which she joined in 1952. Her favorite music is Renaissance and Baroque, but she also enjoys the gay choruses and marching bands. A key event for her was a concert during the 1987 March on Washington when more than 500 gay men and women from all over the country sang and played at Constitution Hall, the very auditorium from which the great American singer Marian Anderson was excluded in 1939 because she was black. In summer 2000, Barbara spent an entire week hearing over 5,000 singers at the GALA international festival of gay and lesbian choruses. "All that gay energy, that fine singing, the great camp humor—it was thrilling!" In Barbara's view, gay music groups are not only fun for their members and fans, they're an important part of the drive for gay rights. "Amateur choruses and bands are a great tradition in this country," she points out, "and it'll be harder and harder to deny us a place in the parade."

She has done major political advocacy as well. She served on the charter board of directors of the National Gay Task Force, founded in 1973, later renamed the National Gay and Lesbian Task Force. She was on the first board of the Gay Rights National Lobby, launched in 1979; GRNL was the forerunner to the Human Rights Campaign. Boosting checkbook activism also appeals to her; she served on the initial board of the Delaware Valley Legacy Fund, which promotes philanthropy to benefit the gay community in the Philadelphia region.

Beyond group efforts to advance our goals, Barbara also strongly endorses individual action. "Each one of us can do something to make a difference. For example, in 1997 I got AARP, the American Association of Retired Persons, to treat Kay and me as spouses for membership and health insurance. I had to push for it. But every personal breakthrough opens the way for others to benefit."

For many years after we met in 1961 Barbara and I lived in small apartments, cramped by stacks of materials from our movement activities. We lived frugally; Barbara scraped by on low-paid clerical jobs so she could put her main energy into activism. Finally in 1980 we bought a house, a small row home in Philadelphia's University City, and for eighteen years enjoyed a succession of friends, gay activists, writers, historians, and documentary filmmakers who came to call. Barbara says: "We originally bought the house from a gay man friend, then finally we sold it to a gay couple. That house has gay spirits!"

And Barbara's spirit? What's she really like? "Just don't make me out to be a movement grind," she says. Her mother called her character "golden," and I agree. Plus she has the disposition of an angel—until she's crossed. She's mad about music and music comedians such as Anna Russell and Victor Borge. She loves reading mystery novels and *The New Yorker* and stories of whimsy such as *Ferdinand* and *Wind in the Willows*. She loves old movies and gay film festivals, rare books and prints, museums, theater, cartoons, ice cream, aerobic walks, sunsets, wilderness, parades, political satire. She loves to laugh, eat heartily, sip a little wine, and be merry with friends. She loves the gay cause and promoting it. She loves life, she loves her people, and thank heavens she loves me.

In spring 2001, a new branch of Philadelphia's public library opened near Independence Hall. It features the Barbara Gittings Gay/Lesbian Collection, a popular assortment of 2,500 books, periodicals, and audiovisual items. Financed mainly by gay community members, it was named to honor Barbara's longtime activism in the library field. Barbara is touched by the tribute. "This prominent special collection means that our work is bearing fruit," she says. "How exciting to see results! For me it's like a bit of heaven brought to earth."

As for her personal accumulation of over forty years of gay movement correspondence and materials, Barbara plans to organize it for donation to a gay archive to enhance gay history. Looking ahead, she says,

> I'd like to see us go out of business as a social change movement. Then we can be ourselves without special effort. Meantime, it's a wonderful experience, working with thousands of gay women and men to get the bigots off our backs and to show that gay love is good for us and for the rest of the world too!

BIBLIOGRAPHY

Books and Articles

"Gay Liberation: From Task Force to Round Table." Interview with Barbara Gittings in *American Libraries: The Magazine of the American Library Association,* December 1999, pp. 74-76.

Gittings, Barbara. "Gays in Library Land: The Gay and Lesbian Task Force of the American Library Association: The First Sixteen Years." Chapter 6 in *Daring to Find Our Names: The Search for Lesbigay Library History,* ed. James V. Carmichael Jr. Westport, CT: Greenwood Press, 1998. Also Chapter 7: "A Personal Task Force Scrapbook: 'Incunabula,' 1971-1972 and After." Photographs by Kay Tobin Lahusen, captions by Barbara Gittings.

Katz, Jonathan. *Gay American History: Lesbians and Gay Men in the U.S.A.* New York: Thomas Y. Crowell Co., 1976; Revised Edition, New York: Meridian, 1992. Interview with Barbara Gittings, pp. 420-433 both editions.

The Ladder. October 1956-September 1972. Reprinted by Arno Press, 1975.

Marcus, Eric. *Making History: The Struggle for Gay and Lesbian Equal Rights 1945-1990: An Oral History.* New York: Harper Collins, 1992. "The Rabble Rousers–Barbara Gittings and Kay Lahusen," pp. 104-126; "The Old Timers—Barbara Gittings and Kay Lahusen," pp. 213-227.

Perry, Reverend Troy D., and Thomas L. P. Swicegood. *Profiles in Gay and Lesbian Courage.* New York: St. Martin's Press, 1991, "New Thoughts on Unthinkable Subjects," pp. 153-178.

Stein, Marc. *City of Sisterly and Brotherly Loves: Lesbian and Gay Philadelphia 1945-1972.* Chicago: University of Chicago Press, 2000.

Tobin, Kay, and Randy Wicker. *The Gay Crusaders.* New York: Paperback Library, 1972; Arno Press, 1975. "Barbara Gittings," pp. 205-224.

Films

Before Stonewall: The Making of a Gay and Lesbian Community, film by John Scagliotti, Greta Schiller, and Robert Rosenberg, 1986, and *After Stonewall: From the Riots to the Millennium,* film by John Scagliotti, Janet Baus, and Dan Hunt, 1999. Information at (800) 229-8575.

Gay Pioneers, film by Glenn Holsten, 2001, produced for PBS by WHYY- Channel 12, 150 N. 6th St., Philadelphia, PA, 19106.

Out of the Past, film by Jeff Dupre, 1998. Distributed by Unapix, (818) 981-8592.

Barbara Grier (1933-   ):
Climbing the Ladder

Victoria A. Brownworth

She's taller, more zaftig, and has never worn anything by Chanel, yet Barbara Grier and legendary chanteuse Edith Piaf share something intrinsic. Piaf's signature song, "Je ne regrette riens," is also Grier's. "I absolutely have no regrets. I've had a wonderful time," exults Grier about her life. The American lesbian icon who edited the pathbreaking lesbian magazine, *The Ladder,* collected one of the world's largest compendia of lesbian literature, and co-founded the world's largest lesbian publisher, Naiad Press, while also finding true love along the way, has enjoyed her life immensely and reaped the benefits of her achievements.

Barbara Grier—whose noms de plume under which she penned her lavender prose for lesbian publications over the years include Gene Damon, Vern Niven, and Lennox Strang—is closing in on the seventh decade of a remarkable and iconoclastic life. Born at Doctors Hospital in Cincinnati, Ohio, on November 4, 1933, under the sign of Scorpio (which those who follow astrology would say explains her passionate and driven nature) and into an eccentric, theatrical family to an actress mother, feminist before her time, and a womanizing father who divested himself of a career as a small-town doctor to travel as a medical detail man, Grier's eclectic familial history includes James Jesse Strang, leader of a Mormon sect that split from Brigham Young and Joseph Smith in the mid-nineteenth century.

The eldest of three girls, Grier had two half-brothers, twelve and ten years her senior, William and Brewster (named for William Brewster, first governor of Massachusetts). Her sister, Diane, five years and eight months Grier's junior, is also a lesbian. Diane and her partner, Geyne Kent, have been together thirty-nine years. Grier's sister, Penelope, younger by a decade, is married with a grown child.

Now that her mother is no longer living, Grier remains closest to Diane, of whom she gleefully asserts,

> Diane is like I am except she's nice. I'm the "evil twin." Diane is a calm, peaceful, pleasant version of me. We have the same voice, interests, sense of humor. Diane and Geyne live in rural Willard, Missouri, so don't travel like I do, haven't seen as much. But Diane and I are incredibly similar.

When Grier speaks of being the "evil twin," it is only partly in jest. Her strong, no-nonsense manner has led some to term her a drama queen, characterized as much by the intensity of her personality as for her myriad achievements. To those who suggest she might woo more flies with honey than with her often abrasive, take-no-prisoners Midwestern approach, Grier merely shrugs. "I get things done," she states succinctly—a point few could argue in the face of her manifold accomplishments.

Just as Grier's passionate behavior and single-minded focus may derive in part from her astrological sign, her tendency toward flamboyance may be genetic; Grier comes from theatrical lineage, though accedes that her own major claim to theatrical fame is that she's fifth cousin to late British actor David Niven. All the theatricality did not go for naught. "When I trotted home at twelve and announced I was queer, my mother wasn't fazed because she had been exposed to gay men and lesbians in the theatre," Grier explains.

Precocious in most things, Grier discovered her lesbian identity early and came out quite young. Her family was living in Detroit, and as she tells the tale, she "went down on the streetcar to the library. I had looked in enough of my father's medical books that I knew the word homosexual. I went to the library to look up what I could on the word. I was twelve but I could have passed for much older. So the librarian didn't raise her eyebrows too high when I asked for books on homosexuals since she didn't know my actual age," Grier explains.

> Because Mother and I were always open with each other, I told her immediately. Mother said since I was a woman, I wasn't a homosexual, I was a lesbian. She also said that since I was twelve I was a little young to make this decision and we should wait six months to tell the newspapers.

It's a response few queers in the twenty-first century can imagine receiving, let alone in 1945 when out queers were the exception and parents were likely to disown a gay son or lesbian daughter.

"Years after that," Grier continued,

> she told me she was reading Radclyffe Hall's *The Well of Loneliness* when she was pregnant with me. Later I wondered why I hadn't asked her how she came to be a reading a book in 1933 that had been a big scandal only a few years earlier in 1929 [when it was involved in an indecency trial]. It had only just been published here, so that seems odd now in retrospect. I wish I had asked her.

That Grier's mother seemed so undaunted by the revelation speaks to the unprecedented level of acceptance Grier enjoyed growing up. "Mother gave me wider world validation," Grier states. "It's a pretty easy jump to see why I began collecting lesbian fiction a few years later—Mother opened me up to many, many things."

Grier asserts, "I grew up in a very loving family and I think that's why my mother's approach to my sister's and my being lesbian was just 'Okay, now what's for dinner?' My mother was really the strong person in the family. My parents divorced when I was fourteen, having separated when I was ten."

Grier credits the closeness of her immediate family for the acceptance she received as a young lesbian, but there were other intriguing elements to her upbringing that may have influenced her as well. Her great-grandfather, James Jesse Strang, also known as King Strang, head of the Mormon sect the Strangites, had five wives. One of Strang's wives dressed in men's clothing and traveled with him as a man during his evangelical tours. This wife was pregnant with Grier's grandfather while she was passing as a man, a fact Grier finds fascinating.

These familial revelations were Grier's entree into the complicated world we have come to call queer. Grier met her first transgendered person when she was eleven, a woman who lived in a cabin near Grier's then-home in Colorado. Grier would hike into an area in the Colorado Mountains near the town of Cascade. The woman lived in the mesa above Cascade where Grier says she would have been totally isolated for parts of the year. "She was probably in her later fifties," Grier muses.

> She was rough and crude, could easily have passed as a man and probably had at some point in her life. I was fascinated with her. I basically stalked her. She didn't make me leave. She let me pick flowers out of her yard. She wasn't friendly or welcoming, but she let me come near

her. Later I wrote a story about her for *The Ladder* and gave her a fantasy life to fit her appearance.

When Grier came out a year or so after meeting the passing woman in the cabin, she had another intriguing experience that also points to the complexities of being queer in the 1940s.

> My first serious girlfriend was two years ahead of me in school. She had a boyfriend and my mother discovered that he was a girl. The boyfriend was twenty-one, the girlfriend was sixteen, I was nearly fourteen. The boyfriend spent the whole day at my house [during the Christmas holidays] because my mother was so welcoming. We ate, decorated the tree. At some point the "boy" was sitting on the edge of the sofa, legs spread. Mother told me later, "You need to know this is almost certainly not a man." She told me there was no hint of beard stubble, even though he'd been at our house for twelve or so hours, and from seeing "him" sitting with "his" legs spread, my mother thought there were no male genitalia either. There is a kind of insularity that comes from big city living. People believe there can't be anything like that in other places, but there were all these different things and I was experiencing them from day one.

During her childhood and adolescence Grier's family moved from town to town throughout the Midwest and West. Divorced and struggling to eke out a living, Grier's mother kept herself and her daughters in proximity to Grier's father so child support did not become too elusive. The family traveled from Detroit to Colorado to Oklahoma City to Dodge City, Kansas, and then finally to Kansas City, Kansas. By her high school years the family had settled in the Kansas City area, where Grier remained for thirty years, until 1980. It was in Kansas City that she met her first long-term lover, Helen L. Bennett, a librarian.

Although she hasn't lived there in over two decades, Grier remains rhapsodic over the charming town at the confluence of the Kansas and Missouri rivers that fed her lesbian soul and introduced her to the two most important women in her life. "Kansas City has more boulevards than Paris, more fountains than Rome," Grier notes for those who think of queer life and queer culture as beginning and ending in huge coastal metropolises. "It's a beautiful city with the undeserved reputation of being a cow town." Kansas City proved no cow town for Grier, rather it became the locus of her literary career and romantic life.

Grier met Bennett when she was nineteen and Bennett was thirty-five. Bennett, whom Grier describes as "five foot two and one hundred pounds wringing wet," was partnered with Grier for twenty years, until Grier was wooed away by Donna McBride, her partner since 1972 and Grier's unabashed grand passion. After graduating from high school in Kansas City, Kansas, Grier traveled to Denver with Bennett while Bennett got her library science degree. While in Denver Grier worked for the *Denver Post* newspaper. Bennett's father was a Christian minister and her brother, who was gay, was an evangelist. While Bennett and Grier were living in Denver, Bennett's brother was killed in a train wreck and Bennett felt obligated to return to her family in Kansas City. Back home, Grier worked for Sears Roebuck and then for the Kansas City, Kansas, library. In 1960 she and Bennett moved to Kansas City, Missouri, where Bennett became curator of the Snyder Collection of Americana at the University of Kansas City (now University of Missouri at Kansas City). Grier notes with fondness that she used to say of the petite Bennett, "Helen was not as tall as her title." Bennett finished her career there.

The years spent with Bennett were tumultuous for Grier as well as for the budding lesbian feminist movement of which she became a key figure. Always a bibliophile, during her years with Bennett the librarian and archivist Grier herself began to work in libraries and develop her own bibliographic talents, cataloguing books with queer content. She poured over magazines and library journals searching out books that might have lesbian or gay themes imbedded in them. Having learned about the art and skill of bibliography from maverick researcher Jeannette Foster, author of the pathbreaking bibliography *Sex Variant Women in Literature,* Grier went on to compile her own extensive bibliographies, including several volumes of *The Lesbian in Literature* (1967, 1975, 1981). It was during this search for queer-themed literature that Grier stumbled upon the lesbian publication *The Ladder.* Grier says, "From the first issue I saw, the March 1956 issue, I said this is what I am going to spend my life doing. I thought it was wonderful. I wrote to them and offered my body, my soul, my heart, my money."

What would become Grier's literary legacy began then, with her letter to then-editor Phyllis Lyon. The first U.S. magazine for lesbians, *The Ladder* was published monthly by the lesbian organization Daughters of Bilitis (DOB) from 1956 through 1968, then bimonthly through 1970. Controversy over the feminist political content and management of the publication under Grier developed in 1968, and Grier and then-national DOB president Rita Laporte wrested control of the now highly visible and politically important publication from DOB leadership in 1970.

The Ladder was published independently by Grier from 1970 until it ceased publication in 1972. The magazine contained reviews, original fiction and poetry, news stories, political commentary, features, and letters. Grier worked on *The Ladder* in one capacity or another throughout its evolution, in part writing under the pseudonym Gene Damon. Grier's research on queer-themed books and her budding collection of lesbian literature found their way into *The Ladder* via a column she wrote called "Lesbiana," which reviewed queer-themed literature. She was also editor from 1968 through 1970, then editor and publisher until the final issue in the fall of 1972.

In its early days *The Ladder* was an obvious labor of love, mimeographed and distributed by volunteers such as Grier, Lyon, Del Martin, Laporte, and others. No mere bar rag, *The Ladder* was highly informative, particularly on issues of politics and culture. The quality of the writing was superb and included such lesbian literary luminaries as Rita Mae Brown, Marion Zimmer Bradley, and Jane Rule. The publication also sparked controversy throughout its lifetime, generating debate over a range of issues, including coming out: original editor Lyon had published under the pseudonym Ann Ferguson for several issues, then declared her true identity. Other controversies included discourse on the role of feminism in lesbian life. *The Ladder* showed prescience in other areas, with articles on queer marriage and military service predating current controversies by decades.

Because *The Ladder* had become a large publication—forty-eight pages for most of its lifetime, equivalent to most local weekly queer newspapers today—the costs and time required to produce it were prohibitive. As Grier notes, *The Ladder* always lost money, which is why it finally ceased publication. "*The Ladder* plateaued out," explains Grier.

> Our subscriptions cost $7.50 in 1972, which was considered incredibly high. We couldn't keep publishing—we couldn't get enough income. The only advertising we could have gotten would have sent our readers screaming into the night, especially given that we got lambasted for having women kissing in our stories. You can imagine the kind of advertisers a lesbian publication could have attracted in those days. It couldn't happen. And so October 1972 was the last issue.

Produced wholly by women devoted to the cause of connecting lesbians to each other through the written word, *The Ladder* had the same effect on most women as that first issue had on Grier. She remembers,

> The movement was entirely run by people who had no money to give. It's hard for this generation to understand, when we have these huge marches and events and lobbying organizations with hundreds of thousands of dollars changing hands. But I remember days like the day the box of pens came, the day the box of brown envelopes came. These were big moments in the life of a publication like *The Ladder*.

Grier adds, "I'm sure people were ripping off their bosses—cadging things here and there. Helen Sanders [second editor of the publication] worked at Macy's and went to the basement at work and used the mimeograph machine to print out copies." Grier's own tenure as editor proved a turning point for both her and *The Ladder.*

> I wanted to make it more feminist, less gay-oriented. I got Jane Rule, Margaret Lawrence, Martha Shelley, Rita Mae Brown to write for me. We got *The Ladder* more feminist, broadening the base, making it physically larger, getting good writers. Some people stayed over and became part of the early years of Naiad. The last two years of *The Ladder* we had amazingly good stuff in it. When I look back now it's kind of amusing because I went from doing that to doing Naiad, which isn't what most people consider highbrow. *The Ladder* was a very literate magazine. We even made Mary Renault angry enough at us to write us a letter and I really loved being able to put Mary Renault in *The Ladder.* Renault didn't like the fact that I wrote in *The Ladder* about her writing which in the forties had been very explicitly lesbian. And of course she wrote some very famous gay male novels. But that's the kind of publication we were.

The importance of *The Ladder* may be lost today, claims Grier, because times have changed so much. "People now can't imagine what it was like then, because there are at least a dozen TV programs now where gay is everywhere and there are books and magazines and newspapers and radio. But there were no gay images. That's why *The Ladder* was so important."

The demise of *The Ladder* coincided with a sea of change in Grier's own life. For years Grier had been "reading every piece of literature and belle letters that appeared in the U.S. and reading the reviews of everything that might be remotely gay and lesbian." She was infamous at the Kansas City, Missouri, Public Library for being "that woman who read those books" and had quite a reputation in the library for calling up and barking orders to hold this or that publication for her perusal. Donna McBride worked at the library for a woman Grier knew who was also a lesbian. "So unbeknownst to me she was trailing me," admits Grier. In March 1971 Grier called the library and told McBride, "You're new. Get a slip and write these numbers down of books I want to reserve." Grier got a shock when McBride asked if she could work for Grier at *The Ladder,* to which she was a subscriber. Grier went to live with McBride in 1972 when McBride was thirty-two and Grier thirty-eight. Bennett was fifty-four when Grier left her for the much-younger McBride.

"I didn't leave Helen because Donna was younger," Grier explains about the tumultuous period in her life. "If there was anything negative about Donna it was that she was younger because I was always involved with women who were older." As for the split with Bennett, "Helen did not take it well, as you might expect," Grier asserts. "Helen was raised to be socially correct. She was an entirely private individual and you were either on the inside of that wall or on the outside. She has very few friends and will not walk across the street to make a new one. Helen was never involved with another person after we broke up. Someone would have had to run her to ground to get involved with her, she's that private." Although Grier admits she and Bennett are no longer close, they still talk from time to time.

As for the partnership with McBride, life-long femme Grier admits, "Donna pursued me and nailed me down. Donna does not go around bushes; she goes through them. She wanted me, she got me, we've been together ever since." She adds, "If you asked what the most important thing I've ever done in my life was, I'd say it was meeting Donna and having a life with her."

Professionally the most important thing Grier has ever done was found Naiad Press, the publishing house noted African-American writer Donna Allegra calls "the place we go to find books that validate us as lesbians who love being lesbians, where the girl is never just going through a phase and doesn't end up with a man at the end." Although founded by several women on January 1, 1973, as a publisher of books by, for, and about lesbians, Grier was Naiad's driving force from the outset. Grier and McBride were joined in the venture by attorney Anyda Marchant, who wrote lesbian novels under the pseudonym Sarah Aldridge, and Marchant's partner Muriel Crawford.

According to Grier, Marchant "wanted to get her books published, so that's how it started. Now we've been all over the planet, published in eleven languages including Portugese, French, Flemish, Spanish, and German." In 1973 Grier and McBride lived in Bates City, Missouri, a town forty miles outside Kansas City. In 1980 the two moved to Tallahassee, Florida, where McBride had taken a library position. Naiad has been centered there ever since. Naiad has published nearly 500 original titles since 1973, making it the world's largest lesbian publisher. Grier's acumen as a bibliographer served her well when seeking out lesbian authors. Not only was Grier responsible for reprinting works by noted lesbian writers such as Margaret Anderson and Natalie Barney's poet lover, Renee Vivien, but she also published Ferro-Grumley award-winning novelist Sarah Schulman's first book as well as launched the career of noted mystery novelist Katherine V. Forrest.

During her years with Bennett, Grier had begun an enduring friendship with Canadian writer Jane Rule. The two had much in common—including lovers named Helen who were both nearly seventeen years each woman's senior. Rule and Grier remained close after Grier and Bennett split up, and Rule became one of Grier's most prized authors at Naiad. Her 1979 book, *Outlander,* was a critical success and Naiad's first big seller. This was followed by the comedic novel *Faultline* by Sheila Ortiz Taylor which sold 30,000 copies in the first two years—then an absolute marvel. While touring with Taylor, Grier met Forrest whose first novel, *Curious Wine* (1982), held the title of the world's best-selling lesbian novel for over a decade, selling nearly 200,000 copies. Forrest began a long association with Naiad, which included numerous novels as well as an editorship.

The book that put Naiad on the cultural map, however, was the 1985 anthology *Lesbian Nuns: Breaking the Silence,* edited by two former nuns, Nancy Manahan and Rosemary Curb. The book flew off the shelves and propelled the editors into the national spotlight. It also landed Grier at the center of a raging controversy. *Penthouse Forum* approached Grier about serializing the book and Grier, ever the astute businesswoman, agreed. The very same lesbians who would have been horrified to see sex-specific advertising on the pages of *The Ladder* were distraught at Grier's decision and believed she had courted the sex magazine simply to make money.

"*Penthouse Forum* approached us," Grier asserts. "We didn't even know they existed." But controversy swept the lesbian community and found voice in various lesbian publications. Although somewhat dismissive of the volatility that surrounded the serialization in *Penthouse Forum,* Grier believes the shift from so-called "downward mobility" in the lesbian community to moneymaking played a significant role in the controversy. "I actually believe retrospectively that people were angry with Rosemary and Nancy because being successful was a no-no in those days," she concludes. "It just wasn't cool to make money or even think about it. I think there was a lot of resentment about these women and Naiad making this kind of choice."

And that choice made Naiad a household name in households that weren't lesbian. "The stuff that happened around *Lesbian Nuns* wasn't like anything we'd ever experienced," Grier recalls.

> We'd come home and UPI and AP reporters would be racing up my driveway in the country. I wish I could convey how strange this was because of how incredibly rural the area was. And perfect strangers would stop us on the street and talk to us. We went from being barely known to being totally out to everyone. It was just amazing. The book was so successful there was even an excerpt in the Flemish TV guide!

The success of breakout books like *Lesbian Nuns* and *Curious Wine* afforded Grier the opportunity to expand the press with new titles and reprints of long out-of-print books and classics of lesbian pulp fiction, such as Patricia Highsmith's *The Price of Salt*. Grier finds "an ironic and funny coda" to Naiad's history of best-sellers. Jane Rule's novel *Desert of the Heart* became an instant best-seller for the press when Donna Deitch's film *Desert Hearts* premiered. In 1999, because of the attention, both critical and regarding the imbedded queer content, to the film *The Talented Mr. Ripley,* based on the Patricia Highsmith novel, *The Price of Salt* also became an instant best-seller. But Grier remembers when she first saw the Highsmith novel—published under the pseudonym Claire Morgan.

> In June 1952 I saw *The Price of Salt* in downtown Kansas City in the Jones Department Store. This was before the days of Borders and Barnes and Noble, of course, and department stores generally had big book departments. I remember it so clearly. Contrary to revisionist history the book wasn't a pulp novel but a hardcover. There it was on a table in Jones' with a picture of a salt shaker on a tablecloth on the cover. Highsmith had tried to get her publisher of *Strangers on a Train* to publish it. The Hitchcock film had been hugely successful so they found her a publisher, but she was forced to use a pseudonym. Of course anyone who worked in a library could find out who she was and I did. It was the only book she published under a pseudonym. Highsmith was a lesbian but feared republishing the book would lose her fans—she was from that era of intensely internalized homophobia. But it's an interesting story—for Naiad and for lesbians interested in where their books come from.

Despite these successes, Grier says it was nine years before anyone was paid to work for Naiad Press. "It was pure coincidence that I quit my job right before our first big seller happened," she concedes. "I was Naiad's first full-time employee and Donna became the second full-time employee in 1982." In the intervening years until 1999, when Naiad divested much of its list to the newly formed Bella Books so that Grier and McBride could "stop working eighty-hour weeks," the press employed eight full-time staff members.

When Grier hasn't been proving her mettle as a hardworking Midwesterner at Naiad, she has been honing her skills as a collector of lesbian literature. When asked what her single most defining contribution has been in life she says unequivocally, "I think the most important thing I have done is define lesbian literature."

Grier compiled the largest collection of lesbian literature in the world, now housed—having traveled from Tallahassee to San Francisco in an eighteen-wheeler—in the James C. Hormel Collection of the San Francisco Library in a section with a plaque bearing the names of Grier and McBride. "I am a historian by inclination even if I have no legitimate claim," explains Grier.

> I had the largest collection of lesbian books in the world. Almost fifteen thousand books and several hundred feet of papers went to library. We were looking for someplace to put this stuff. [Publisher] Sherry Thomas arranged the archive. Donna and I had been everywhere to find someone to take the collection. Sherry got the NEA and Xerox to CD-ROM and deacidify the whole thing, so even when the originals disappear, it will be around. Eighty percent of these books hadn't even been catalogued. It's instant immortality—it's a lot better than having children.

Grier did keep

> a couple hundred books for while I was still alive. I kept a few things—several hundred pounds of letters from Jane Rule—left untouched until we've both trotted on. I gave away a lot of things. It bothers me a little because now I am losing my memory a bit and so I don't have my references right there anymore. But I feel so gratified that all that collecting and work has a place now, forever.

Although Grier has no plans to wind down her life, a certain nostalgia tinges recollection of her past endeavors. "We were all wild-eyed maniacs then," she concludes.

> You had to be so earnest, so committed, think that you were going to save the world. I remember actually thinking things like, I am going to lead my people out of the wilderness. Everything was very, very different. There were different things wrong then than there are now. After a certain age you realize you aren't going to change the course of human history forever, things will change in ways you can't even anticipate and things will always need changing—nothing remains static.

Nevertheless, Grier concludes, hers has been an eventful and surprising life. "I didn't know it would be successful, but it was. And I have had such a wonderful time."

BIBLIOGRAPHY

Grier, Barbara. *The Lesbian in Literature.* Tallahassee, FL: Naiad Press, 1981.

Grier, Barbara and Reid, Coletta (Eds.). *The Lavender Herring: Lesbian Essays from* The Ladder. Oakland, CA: Diana Press, 1976.

Grier, Barbara and Reid, Coletta (Eds.). *Lives: Biographies of Women from* The Ladder. Oakland, CA: Diana Press, 1976.

Barbara also edited or co-edited a series of books reprinting erotic love stories by Naiad Press authors. Among them are: *Dancing in the Dark* (1992); *The First Time Ever* (1993); *The Touch of Your Hand* (1998); and *The Very Thought of You* (1999).

Stephen Donaldson (Robert A. Martin) (1946-1996)

Wayne R. Dynes

The outing of Robert A. Martin, who later chose to be known as Stephen Donaldson, came extraordinarily early, at the age of twenty, when he founded the first gay student organization in the history of the world. Later he became prominent as a theorist of bisexuality, an advocate of prison reform, and a determined opponent of the rape of males.

That was not all. For over the course of the half century of life allotted him, Donaldson played many roles: military brat, congressional intern, college student, gay and bisexual activist, journalist and cultural commentator, encyclopedia contributor and editor, poet, male prostitute, porn starlet, sailor, designer of war games, Buddhist priest and then convert to Hinduism, punk rock adept, user and advocate of drugs, rape victim, federal prisoner, crusader against violence, and lover of young men. His pivotal accomplishment, the founding of the Student Homophile League at New York's Columbia University, came while he was still an undergraduate.

Personally, he was a slight but appealing figure, retaining until the end the youthful quality he so much prized. Combining personability with eccentricity, in time he became an effective television spokesperson for the cause of prison reform. A punk brawl had inflicted a broken nose, lending an air of toughness he sometimes accentuated. Educated in the Ivy League, he could not disguise the fact that he was an intellectual through and through, although of a dissident, sometimes wayward sort. Long an extravert, he became somewhat reclusive in his last years, communicating often by e-mail. When necessary, he could recharge the skills of human contact acquired in his years as a journalist. This gift shone again in his final campaign against male rape, when he traveled for media appearances and conferences to Philadelphia, Cincinnati, Chicago, and other cities.

Some highlights of Stephen Donaldson's story emerge from his successive changes of the way in which he chose to be referred. Born Robert Anthony Martin, he never attempted to conceal his birth name after he adopted others. Of course pseudonyms are an old tradition, prudential in origin, among gay activists and writers, but Martin's reasons were more complex.

Stephen Donaldson was a designation he began to use in college and maintained throughout his public career. He created the surname after that of Donald B., a member of his high school baseball team in New Jersey who was his first love. The name incorporates the idea of sonship. Later he preferred to be called simply "Donny" so that he identified himself more closely with the beloved youth.

Two names refer to his religious interests. Sanghamitra Samanera refers to his training in Theraveda Buddhist orders, while Swami Lingananda reflects his ultimate religious commitment, which was to Hinduism (more specifically a branch of the Shaiva faith, professed in Bangalore, India, in February of 1988).

His searing account of his 1973 gang rape in a Washington, DC jail appeared under the name of Donald Tucker. His interest in contemporary youth music transpires in his moniker of Donny the Punk; under this name he wrote columns in *Maximum Rock 'n' Roll* and other alternative press papers.

All this variety shows a remarkable capacity for reinvention of self, of which he was rightly proud. Working usually on several fronts at once, his activities were time consuming and poorly remunerated, if at all—exposing him to the ongoing wear and tear poverty imposes. At one low point in New York City he remained homeless for eight months.

Greeting him as he went each morning to breakfast in his kitchen was a motto: "Life is too important to waste on a full-time job." Sometimes though, he disappointed his supporters by abruptly dropping one commitment to fulfill another. For this reason his editing of the *Concise Encyclopedia of Homosexuality* never reached completion.

The one constant in Donny's life was his allegiance to the values and lifestyle choices of the American counterculture, itself ultimately rooted in nineteenth-century Bohemia. Exposure to the counterculture was almost inevitable for a young man growing up in comfortable circumstances in the 1960s. Working-class youths, whom Donny professed to admire, were less susceptible to the siren call. As was the case for many who followed the Pied Piper of the counterculture, he overestimated the staying power of that prominent but ultimately unstable social phenomenon. He also did not realize how keeping to the counterculture lifestyle, easy enough for an attractive young man just out of college, would become increasingly hard to manage as the years passed. A stance of perpetual insurgency at length becomes wearying. He had early donned a mask that suited him for a long time but that he ultimately could not take off. He hoped, of course, to retard the aging process. Indeed, he did not reach old age, dying just before his fiftieth birthday.

As has been noted, he was born Robert Anthony Martin, the first name that of his father. He came into the world in a naval hospital in Norfolk, Virginia, July 27, 1946. His father was a naval pilot (later a college professor); his mother had artistic gifts. Later, after his parents divorced, his mother was diagnosed with the mental disorder known as porphyria. A touch of madness colored Donny's makeup.

Following military orders, the family moved every two years, promoting adaptability in the boy. At the age of ten he was a streaker, his first indication of interest in nudity. In later life he would surprise visitors to his apartment, including middle-class social workers assigned to help him, by appearing unclothed.

The eldest of four brothers, he is a counter instance of the fashionable social science thesis that maintains firstborns are likely to be conservative, allying themselves with the parents, while those born later are the rebels. In fact, Donny, the firstborn, was the rebel. Of his three brothers, two are in law enforcement and one is a Lutheran minister. The military side is another seemingly improbable feature, although its imprint remained in his lifelong identification with sailors and seafaring. Most efforts to detect the causes in later character and accomplishments in early childhood are probably destined to fail, first because there are some things from that stage the observer cannot know, and second, and of fundamental importance, because people adopt to changing circumstances. In Donny's case the climate of the 1960s in America was vital.

A precocious loner, he began reading science fiction in his early teens, crediting this avocation with "expanding my creative imagination and stretching my intelligence." In later life he became an avid follower of the original television series *Star Trek*.

His homosexual life was practical before it became affectional. As a Boy Scout, during a camping trip in 1957, he was lured by a slightly older boy into sucking his penis. As a result he acquired instant fame as a "blow boy." Eventually, these activities became known, and he was drummed out of the Scouts at age twelve. This disgrace triggered a family crisis, resolved by sending the boy to live in Germany, where he could be watched over by his stepmother's relatives. (His father had married a German woman, who proved an affectionate and concerned replacement for his biological mother.) For three years Donny attended classical gymnasium (elite high school) in Berlin, acquiring fluent German. He continued his oral servicing of schoolboys and a few adults but remained ignorant of the concept of the "homosexual." Donny observed the creation of the Berlin Wall in 1961. The city's location on a fault line of the Cold War fostered his interest in international politics.

In April 1962, at the age of fifteen, Donny sailed back to the United States to live with his grandparents in West Long Branch, New Jersey. In high school he was news editor of the school paper, an actor, and a student government officer. He also became active in politics as a libertarian conservative, supporting Barry Goldwater for president. His sport was baseball; he managed the school team for three years. A few dates with girls yielded no "action" and instead he had sex with a number of boys but without emotional involvement. Then, as he remarked, "in April 1965, the stars fell on me." He developed an enormous crush on Donald B., the shortstop on the baseball team. Donny stopped studying and dropped out of all activities but baseball. The crush was unrequited, but Donny decided to "read up" on homosexuality, coming out only to a few close friends.

As high school valedictorian in June 1965, he gave a speech against apathy. As the Bob Dylan song had it, the times they were a-changin'. On a school outing to New York City, he visited the headquarters of the Mattachine Society, then the leading gay organization.

Sent to live in Florida with his biological mother for the summer, Donny ran away to New York City, where he was in effect adopted by astronomer Frank Kameny, then a leading gay avant-guardist. In the fall he became a freshman at Columbia and came out—class of 1969. There he had to get a single room in Livingston Hall because his Carmen Hall roomies felt uncomfortable living with a "known homo." Political science and international affairs were what he studied; the aim, which he achieved, was to become a journalist. In 1966 he spent an impressionable summer at Cherry Grove, Fire Island, again under the tutelage of Kameny.

Growing wise to the ways of the city, he found that he could fund his education by working as a hustler, first at the infamous intersection of Fifty-third Street and Third Avenue, then as a call boy through a house. He claimed to have serviced several famous clients, including Rock Hudson and Roy Cohn (Senator Joseph McCarthy's counsel). He met a young woman, J. D. Jones, who became his lifelong friend and mentor. At that time a member of a psychedelic church, she turned Donny onto LSD. He in turn inducted others into the use of drugs, resolutely refusing to acknowledge that not every one of his acolytes benefited from the practice.

Donny first hatched the idea of the Student Homophile League (SHL) as a Columbia University undergraduate in October of 1966. His first idea for a gay group was as a chapter of Mattachine, but the Mattachine Society refused, reflecting a fear of anything remotely linked with pedophilia. Then came the idea of a completely autonomous group, the SHL, with the support of chaplain John Dyson Cannon. Not surprisingly, the powers that be at Columbia were none too keen. They demanded a list of members. As they well knew, this would be awkward because the list could be turned over to the

FBI. Donny passed the test by securing well-known "big men on campus" types (straight) as pro forma members.

After much foot dragging, Columbia finally acceded and SHL was accepted as an official group. Word got around and *The New York Times* ran a story with the headline: "Columbia Charters Homosexual Group." The publicity unleashed an avalanche of outraged letters on Columbia University authorities. On April 11, 1967, *Spectator,* the campus daily, published a two-page essay signed by Robert A. Martin, as he was then known, on the travails of being an out gay student at that time.

The Student Homophile League was a first in history (European countries, where the gay movement began at the end of the nineteenth century, generally did not have campuses, and therefore had few student groups of any kind). The SHL participated in the controversy over the Reserve Officers Training Corps (ROTC), then a hot issue, helping to force the military group off campus. Under Donny's leadership the members "integrated" dances and started some of their own.

The founding of SHL preceded the well-known 1968 blowup at Columbia that signaled a wave of campus disturbance across the nation. On two occasions buildings were occupied, Columbia's President Grayson Kirk's office was "liberated," and, after much dithering that revealed deep division in the university community, the police moved in to arrest the occupier. Donny was arrested twice and politically he moved from liberal to radical. This radicalism, and the counterculture heritage of oppositionality (which some would term simple orneriness), were two albatrosses he could not shake off.

Much of what he did could not have been accomplished without the complicity, as it were, of the climate of the times. In some ways the era was freer than today. I speak from personal experience, as my own teaching stint at Columbia lasted from 1968 to 1974. At this distance it is hard to recapture the fervor of those years, and the swiftness and apparent finality of cultural change. Rivers of psychedelic drugs, new styles of dress and deportment, and relentless attention to the counterculture in the media—the whole atmosphere encouraged experiment. The melody of rock suffused everything. Music was all important: it was the Woodstock generation.

Other SHL chapters sprang up at Cornell University and New York University (where Rita Mae Brown, later to gain fame and fortune as a novelist, headed the chapter). Donny threw himself into work for the North American Conference of Homophile Organizations (NACHO), the only real national grassroots organization. In 1969-1970 he held an office in the group.

In 1970, having graduated, he decided to fulfill an old yearning by enlisting in the Navy in the ranks. He served mainly in the Mediterranean. When his gay sexual activities become known, he was given a general discharge on

June 2, 1972. To avoid surrendering them, he smuggled his uniforms out and later, in 1977, became one of the first to get his less-than-desirable discharge upgraded to honorable, which is essential for veterans' benefits.

Late in the 1970s he began to experience burnout, owing in part to the hassling he received about his bisexuality, which was a complicated matter. On one hand, his deepest friendship was with a woman, J. D. Jones. On the other hand, his bisexuality had something of a forced, theoretical quality: despite his small collection of heterosexual pornography (assembled mainly for straight boys to look at), it did not seem a gut phenomenon. One of his oldest friends commented that the military tradition he grew out of required heterosexuality and that he therefore sought to retain some aspect of it. Although he had sex with women from time to time, it is clear that his deepest erotic feelings came from his experiences with young men, usually in their late teens to early twenties.

He sometimes confessed that his displayed attraction to women made it easier to get to first base with the straight-identified boys he was attracted to, as this was something they ostensibly shared. In some ways his profession of bisexuality recalls the transitional exploration of identity that some people go through in late adolescence. He knew, however, that his heterosexual side did not run deep, and his claim to it is tainted with inauthenticity, one of the ways in which he belied his surface commitment to honesty in all things.

On graduating from Columbia University he took a full-time job with the Associated Press. An exposé of the telephone company offended his bosses there, and he was fired. Later he wrote for various counterculture and music journals, generally without pay. At the end of the 1980s Donny worked on the *Encyclopedia of Homosexuality* and the thirteen-volume set, *Studies in Homosexuality,* both under my editorship.

In August 1973, while employed as a journalist in Washington, DC, he was arrested at a Quaker protest at the White House. Left unguarded in jail over the weekend, he suffered two traumatic gang rapes. Refusing to hide his misfortune, he courageously held a press conference after being released. This set of experiences led to his subsequent commitment to enhancing public awareness of male rape, a commitment made more vivid by a four-year prison stay, 1980-1984. His imprisonment on a federal charge resulted from a semideranged incident at a Veterans' Hospital in the Bronx. Having been denied medicine for a sexually transmitted disease (STD), Donny returned with a gun and fired it. Instead of prudently assuming a state of contrition at his trial, he self-righteously excoriated U.S. policies and culture. The judge threw the book at him.

Continuing to brood over what had happened to him, he wrote graphically about his experiences. Although some felt that he permitted himself to be dominated by the consequences of traumatic interventions not of his own making, he ultimately found the strength to make a sustained contribution to a cause that had long been taboo: the rape of males.

Still, the personal cost was high. From his ordeal in prison Donny developed a taste for abjection, the still mysterious condition whereby one comes to relish one's own humiliation. This might also be labeled masochism, but it was more than that. To the dismay of some of his associates, his refrigerator housed bottles of urine collected from favorite youths for later imbibing. This was only one of the counterproductive things that he did that complicated—and perhaps ultimately shortened—his life. He was reluctant to modify conduct that conflicted with his larger goals.

Donaldson's interest in South Asian religion scarcely ever flagged. He sometimes appeared in the flowing yellow robes of a Shaivite holy man and once, during a distressful episode, he was arrested in New Jersey in full regalia and sent to a mental hospital for observation. His youthful disciples were supposed to become "chelas" (Hindu-style disciples), but they usually had no understanding of the concept. During his stay in India in the 1980s, he was sometimes excluded from Hindu holy sites because he was Caucasian. He also found the spicy food difficult to tolerate.

His interest in the youth music scene, along with his sexual interests, brought much anguish, as the mainly straight youths he was attracted to were at best puzzled, at worst enraged by his interests. On several occasions he was beaten up, after being falsely accused of child molestation. His efforts to gain acceptance as one of the boys in the punk scene, for which he gained a local media award as "best punk," had its pathetic side.

In the mid-1980s he joined Tom Cahill in the leadership of the organization Stop Prisoner Rape, Inc., eventually becoming president in 1994. In a *New York Times* op-ed piece of December 29, 1993, titled "The Rape Crisis Behind Bars," Donaldson helped bring the issue to national attention. Here his activist energies found a significant outlet and the organization continues, offering public education and counseling for victims.

The problem of the rape of males raises questions regarding sexual identity that are yet to be answered, for in many instances neither the perpetrator nor the victim consider themselves to be homosexual. Similarly, a substantial number of the same-sex acts that are being performed every day involve individuals who do not consider themselves gay. One might argue that this self-concept was a delusional holdover from earlier times when to be identified as homosexual was a deep source of shame and social stigma. More disturbing, however, the rejection of the gay identity may fit with the postmodernist rejection of categories altogether. Most would agree with Donaldson that prison rape must be stopped, but it raises a series of difficult questions for which there is no answer.

Donaldson's last recorded speech, however, was to a New York City group opposing the death penalty. In his remarks he trenchantly observed that anyone entering activism for a social cause must expect that the work itself is its own reward. Expectations of fame or monetary gain must be "checked at the door." This caveat notwithstanding, Donny is in fact well remembered—by students, the punk rock community, bisexual theorists, and—above all—the movement for prison reform.

Stephen Donaldson died of AIDS complications, just a week short of his fiftieth birthday, on July 19, 1996.

His stormy career causes one to wonder whether an early attraction to causes exposes a vein of madness? Certainly mental disturbance was in his background even though his brothers are eminently conventional. It is perhaps more likely that Donaldson's creative madness, if so it is to be termed, was triggered by the times. He came of age just as the twin rebellions of the antiwar movement and the counterculture were cresting. When all is said and done, however, only a person of exceptional dedication and imagination could have founded Columbia's Student Homophile League, a first, and one that has happily produced many thorns in the sides of stiff college administrators and tight-assed alums everywhere. Today the "Queer Lounge" of the gay, lesbian, and bisexual community of Columbia-Barnard bears a plaque to his memory dedicated on November 15, 1996.

BIBLIOGRAPHY

Donaldson, Stephen. "The Bisexual Movement: Beginning in the 1970s," in Naomi Tucker (Ed.), *Bisexual Politics: Theories, Queries and Visions,* Binghamton, NY: Harrington Park Press, 1995.

Donaldson, Stephen. "Rape of Males," in Wayne R. Dynes (Ed.), *Encyclopedia of Homosexuality,* Volume 2 (pp. 1094-1098). New York: Garland, 1990.

Martin, Robert A. "The Student Homophile League: Founder's Retrospect," *Gay Books Bulletin,* 1983, 9:30-33.

Tucker, Donald. "The Account of the White House Seven," in Anthony M. Scacco Jr. (Ed.), *Male Rape: A Casebook of Sexual Aggressions,* (pp. 30-57). New York: AMS Press, 1982.

Tucker, Donald. "A Punk's Song: View from the Inside," in Anthony M. Scacco Jr. (Ed.), *Male Rape: A Casebook of Sexual Aggressions* (pp. 58-79). New York: AMS Press, 1987.

Randolfe Wicker (1938-   )

Jack Nichols

On July 11, 1984, I penned the following poem describing Randolfe Wicker and mailed it to him in celebration of our friendship, which had begun in 1963:

> *Just Like a Woman*, a song of the Sixties,
> floats its tresses in Eighties airwaves,
> and I feel the haunting sweetness of a bold,
> adventuresome time.
>
> Time of Underground Uplift, Mighty blasts of The Word.
> Time of Futurism, Time of Confidence.
> Time of Revolution, through flowers, herbs, and
> through Free Speech, Incorporated, founded by R.W.,
> gay, atheist, john.

> I recall a vision. It's R.W.,
> "An arrogant card-carrying swish,"
> riding the subway.
> I follow him through corridors.
> His, a swift gait,
> His, a loud mouth.
>
> An American voter, he, persevering,
> whining, enjoying a good cackle,
> holding tight to skepticism and his purse,
> generous to the undeserving,
> Odd revolutionary,
> praising Calvin Coolidge.
>
> I see, spread from coast to coast, a myriad
> of buttons,
> speaking the unspeakable,
> In keeping with R.W.,
> giving body to anarchism's era.

Illuminating the 1960s, the historian John Loughery (1998, p. 267) noted that "more than anyone else interested in rights for homosexuals," Randolfe Wicker "intuited that the new decade called for a new outlook."

Randy's new outlook, hinted at in my poem, was a hearty mixture of economic conservatism and social radicalism, a paradoxical wedding of characteristics that has provided the quixotic Wicker a persona ever at odds with convention but that has kept, at the same time, an ever-respectful eye on what he calls "The Almighty Dollar." Underground Uplift Unlimited, his mid-1960s' creation, was a counterculture store on New York's hippie superhighway, directly across from The Electric Circus, the city's foremost psychedelic dance hall.

I'd first met Randy Wicker in 1963, in Frank Kameny's home. He'd already begun producing his line of startling slogan buttons and as I entered the room Kameny was arguing with him in a friendly way over his proposed color for a button that would read, "Equality for Homosexuals." Randy remained dead set on his provocative choice of lavender while Kameny insisted the buttons should be black and white.

We were all newly charged pioneers—inspecting each other carefully, tweaking each other hopefully. Kameny, Wicker, and I were encouraged, it was clear, by our meetings with any new activist peers who demonstrated intelligence and ability. Around this same time Randy's friendship with pioneering couple Barbara Gittings and Kay Tobin Lahusen blossomed. He'd thereafter become the only male ever photographed as a house ad in *The Ladder* reading America's first lesbian review.

To me and to a few other crusading admirers, Randy had achieved a kind of minifame. He was a gay media star, one who boldly used his legal name! As a daring and "brash" gay crusader, says John D'Emilio's (1983) history, Randy had rattled New York's gay movement establishment as early as 1958, and in 1962 he did so even more loquaciously when he became the first openly gay male to initiate, on New York City radio, the broadcast voices of eight everyday gay males—including himself—speaking truths about their own lives.

During the summer of 1958, as a university student, he'd volunteered his services to The New York Mattachine Society, Inc. At age twenty, he passed himself off as twenty-one so as not to flout Mattachine admissions rules. Loughery's (1998) history reports how Randy ran up against some of the more timid elements in New York's homophile movement environs: "On his own frolicsome initiative, he had signs printed and displayed throughout Greenwich Village to publicize a talk on 'The Homosexual and the Law'" (p. 250).

Neither the lawyer who would deliver this lecture nor the Mattachine's board members, long accustomed to closeted word-of-mouth approaches, appreciated Wicker's "helpfulness," although nearly 300 persons showed up to hear their message. Many years later the then Mattachine president, Arthur Maule, affectionately recalled: "We didn't know what to make of Randy Wicker. . . . He was, let's say, a disturbing acquisition for the movement" (Loughery, 1998, p. 250).

Loughery's *Other Side of Silence* (1998) describes Wicker as "impressively energetic and frighteningly vocal" (p. 250), someone who—in 1958— struck a few Mattachine members as just what their organization needed, but to most of the others he was a troublemaker. Putting down permanent roots in Manhattan, Randy later pulled away from what he felt was the too-conservative New York Mattachine Society and founded what he jokingly called the "powerful Homosexual League of New York," a headline-grabbing phenomenon that, oddly, had only one member, namely himself.

Later, however, after he became an increasingly successful businessman, he made generous and regular contributions to sustain the late 1960s' leadership of the New York Mattachine Society, Inc. Randy argued persuasively, humorously, and passionately for his practical American visions, seeming to radiate the values of America's heartland, insisting on human rights and equal rights while promoting—wearing a suit and tie—equality for same-sex love and affection.

When he first spoke on Manhattan's WBAI-FM, a newspaper pundit denounced him as "an arrogant card-carrying swish," charging that by airing the views of openly gay males, radio station WBAI had scraped the very bottom of the proverbial barrel. The pundit's description of Randy was seized upon by his closest friends who tweaked him by pretending to give this description weight. But turn about is fair play, for such tweaking is, surely, Randy Wicker's own much-used talent.

Frank Kameny and Randy Wicker, Peter Ogren, Lige Clarke, Roz Regelson, Barbara Gittings, and Kay Tobin Lahusen, and I became close friends in those early-1960s' years, those prepicketing heydays. But when we later added picketing to our agendas late in 1964, we became bound together even more closely. Picketing remained anathema to movement conservatives who, when our lines emerged in public arenas, lumped us together as rowdy radicals.

Our small but militant grouping was also united by our unsparing opposition to the psychiatric establishment and to its "sickness theory" of homosexuality. Conservatives opposed militants such as Randy for daring to challenge the mental health establishment, whining: "Wait until more research has been done before we decide to take a stand." In public debates Randy Wicker ignored this advice, being adept at making the statures of shrinks shrink noticeably.

His militant East Coast elders hailed Randy's tough-as-nails, pirouetting debating style. He was an interesting person in talk show interviews too, being unexpectedly humorous and uncommonly direct. D'Emilio's *Sexual Politics, Sexual Communities* (1983, p. 159) describes him drumming up media coverage of homosexuality as no one had ever done before. "Wicker used his sudden visibility to induce further media coverage," recalls the historian.

After the WBAI broadcast, being public relations director for his own Homosexual League, Randy was greeted with a welcome blitz of publicity in *Newsweek, The New York Times,* the *New York Post,* the *Realist, Escapade,* and *Harper's* magazine. D'Emilio (1983) writes:

> Wicker's achievements had a snowballing effect. Each one of the articles expanded his ability to present himself as a spokesperson for the movement and provided him with added leverage in gaining a hearing for the homophile cause. (p. 159)

Soon afterward, he became the counterculture's national slogan-button king. I was later hired as his company's sales manager. Randy worried at first about hiring me, recalling a Yiddish warning that "business and friendship don't mix," but, with me, he confessed, he'd decided to make an exception.

A lead story in the business section of *The Washington Post* had earlier celebrated the volume of Randy's slogan-button sales. What people feared to say in everyday conversation, Randy knew, could be transformed into pithy satirical comments. Such buttons allowed their wearers the luxury of feeling both hip and humorous. There were buttons that decried censorship, made antiwar jibes, and celebrated the joy of sexual freedom. One said: "F*CK Censorship!" Another suggested "More Deviation, Less Population." There was a popular psychedelic seller too: "Let's Get Naked and Smoke."

Provided by him with a handsome Volkswagen van, I spread his colorful 1960s' slogan buttons—of which he'd been the nation's premier initiator and supplier—from Virginia to Rhode Island. It was 1967—the period labeled by the media as "The Summer of Love." Beatles' songs blared out of the front door at Underground Uplift Unlimited, especially those from the celebrated album *Sergeant Pepper's Lonely Hearts Club Band.*

Wicker's two biggest button sellers that were firsts in his collection also championed two causes Randy pioneered. The first button, "Legalize Pot," involved poet Allen Ginsberg with whom Randy Wicker had been a founding member of LEMAR, the League for the Legalization of Marijuana. The poet often dropped into Underground Uplift Unlimited after enjoying a cool beverage at Gem's Spa only a few doors away in the heart of hippiedom. Although he'd earlier been ticketed on the streets of New York for the "crime" of selling *The Marijuana Newsletter,* Randy still, in 1967, was optimistic that pot would be legalized in most states before the legalization of that other pleasure he championed, the love that dare not speak its name. Later, he backtracked, however, saying he no longer favored marijuana legalization but only its decriminalization.

Randy Wicker quickly became the foremost publisher of radical social ideas that were fueling the revolutionary causes of the 1960s. Although certain books performed the same task, it was his "hip" button business that became by far the most successful vehicle for making counterculture attitudes known to the public. In September 1964, history was made when the first march protesting antigay military policies, was cosponsored by heterosexuals, bisexuals, gays, and lesbians. This small group, marching at a draft board, the Whitehall Induction Center in Manhattan, included Jeff Poland and his Sexual Freedom League and Randy Wicker, Craig Rodwell, Nancy Garden, and Renee Cafiero, gay and lesbian activists.

How did Randolfe Wicker arrive, in the early 1960s, at a mind state wherein he felt comfortable identifying himself in public as a gay activist? His struggle to become himself had not always been an easy one; even when he'd distributed movement literature in New York's gay bars he got flack from apathetic conservatives who ridiculed the liberation struggle for which he stood.

He'd heard worried exclamations from his close relatives as well. His father, whom he'd admired, was particularly unhappy about Randy's activism. Randy's given name was Charles Gervin Hayden Jr. Charles Senior, an assistant comptroller at a company where he'd worked for three decades, had labored all his life to support Randy's mother and to assure that his son became the first member in the family to be college educated. But Charles Senior read Charles Junior's diary, one he'd kept during his first year of college, and discovered that he was gay. "Fortunately," recalls Randy today, "he went to a decent psychiatrist who told him that I would probably be gay all my life." When he confronted his son with his newfound knowledge, Charles Senior said that he just wanted his son to be the best-adjusted homosexual he could be because the concerned father wouldn't always be there to take care of him. Charles Senior had opted, however, not to share the diary discovery with Randy's mother "because" as he put it, "she could never accept it."

"In any case," recalls Randy, "in the summer of 1958, when we went out for lunch one day, I showed him materials put out by the Mattachine Society, the 'public educational research organization seeking to educate the public about homosexuality.' I thought he took what I showed him pretty well."

"I don't think you're ever going to get very far with this," Charles Senior opined. "But just do me one favor, will you?"

"Of course," offered Randy.

"Just don't involve my good name," cautioned the older man.

"How could I refuse such a 'reasonable' small request from a father who, while not close emotionally, was someone who put the needs of his wife and his child ahead of his own?" wondered Randy. He would adopt a pseudonym, he decided.

Randy was still young and antisocial enough in those days, he says today, that he found the surname he chose, Wicker, to be "charming," partially because it so resembled the word "wicked." Then he saw a movie starring Zachary Scott. "I just remember that he was dressed in a tuxedo, got off a yacht on a pier, and was named Randolph. Ah, there was a first name with real class," Randy recalls. So, as early as 1959, Charles Gervin Hayden Jr. proudly assumed the name Randolfe Wicker. He was careful to make sure the spelling would be a unique one. "After all, if my name was ever in lights, who could forget a 'Randolfe' spelled unlike any other in the entire world."

His self-chosen name had become, to Randy, his "real name," expressing how he truly regarded himself. "I named myself," he boasts. A journalist, surprised to find that he was only twenty-one years old, confided to him: "Your name, 'Randolfe Wicker,' does make it seem like you are soon due to inherit a barony." When Randy's business career became lucrative, he changed his name legally to Randolfe Hayden Wicker, his middle name a low-key tribute to his hardworking father who had died at the age of forty-nine.

By day Randy was, as his postcollege employment resumé shows, a business machine salesman, a trainee in an advertising agency, and a mass-circulation magazine editor. But by night he transformed himself, in the manner of Gotham's Clark Kent, into the crusading Randolfe Wicker. For a time, in fact, he became known affectionately among his East Coast movement friends as "The Gay Crusader" following the publication of an article which had profiled him under that title. "Where is your cape?" they joked.

In 1969, a week after the Stonewall uprising, Randy was asked to speak at a major counterculture gathering being held at Manhattan's Electric Circus. I encouraged him to wear his rare American flag shirt, one which had been blacked out on television screens when Abbie Hoffman had borrowed it to wear on a talk show. The trousers Randy wore were striped bell-bottoms. As he mounted the podium I tweaked him: "Is it a bird? Is it a plane? No! It's Superfag!"

Moving for a time in 1969 to Brooklyn, Randy turned over his spacious Manhattan apartment to Lige Clarke and to me—one located in the very heart of the East Village and kitty-corner from the famous rock theater, the Fillmore East (later to become a gay locale, The Saint). Randy's tribute to his admired mentor, Boston's pioneering activist Prescott Townsend, appeared in 1969's premiere issue of *GAY.* In the second issue of America's first gay weekly, Randy wrote a feature article about the joys of being self-employed, earning him a suspect reputation among Marxist sympathizers in those times. He retaliated against his literary critics by deliberately labeling himself a moderate Republican, even though he'd plainly relished those mushrooming sales in 1968 for his anti–Richard Nixon campaign button advising voters to "Lick Dick."

In the early 1960s Randy had penned a regular column, "The Wicker Basket," appearing in New York Mattachine's monthly magazine. In *GAY,* to which he contributed between 1969 and 1973, the tradition and title of that up-to-date news-nuggeted column were continued. Randy videotaped zaps in this period that were conducted by the spirited post-Stonewall group, the Gay Activists Alliance. In late 1968 Randy had helped secure for me my first job as an editor at Countrywide, a Fifth Avenue leader in the magazine business, a firm where his own quirky talents had earlier been utilized. Countrywide produced at least fifty mass-circulation magazines that focused on television and movie star secrets, true confessions, the occult, true crime stories, and crossword puzzles. Randy, as an editor, had been the Countrywide's best at publishing what is now called cutting-edge material, skating without fear into outrageous, anarchistic realms.

In particular I recall his writing an article about counterfeit coinage titled "Those Terrible Phone Cheats." It was an exposé that provided readers—under the guise of moral outrage—with knowledge of a perfectly sized metal washer, one usable in all machines that required dimes. A pound of such washers could be purchased for only two dollars, he explained, at any hardware store.

In the early 1970s, as the slogan button business slowed, Randy moved away from Underground Uplift's avant-garde perch on St. Mark's Place and, in Greenwich Village, he opened an antique lighting shop. His longtime lover, the late David Combs, had, because of his own interest in antiques, encouraged him. The new business, Uplift, Inc., was destined to support Randy for the next quarter-century.

Around him gathered a bevy of friends and activists, many of whom, like Sylvia Rivera, the feisty founder of Street Transvestites Action Revolutionaries, worked daily behind his store's counter. Sylvia's beloved transvestite friend, the late Marsha P. Johnson, lived for twelve years in Randy's Hoboken apartment, running errands and keeping house. Randy himself remained the patriarchal head of a close-knit family of youthful friends whose salaries he paid and for whom he often provided lodging. He particularly liked playing the role of a father.

Thus, in early 1997 when Dolly, a Scottish sheep, was born, he telephoned me when the news broke and exclaimed, "I want to be cloned." That same evening I deliberately recorded his impromptu defense of human cloning, printing it the following morning in *Gay Today*. "Heterosexuality's monopoly on reproduction is now obsolete," he exulted. The following morning Randy registered the world's first pro–human cloning activist group, Clone Rights United Front. Once again he was interviewed on television and radio talk shows, defending cloning from its worried detractors. "Human cloning is going to happen whether people like the idea or not," he explained, "and I'm just trying to lay the groundwork so that babies conceived through cloning will be properly welcomed in the future." After initiating the first pro–human cloning demonstration on Sheridan Square he found himself within the year addressing a special cloning subcommittee called into existence by the U.S. Congress.

Randy once again found himself becoming—for a still conservative gay and lesbian movement—what Mattachine's Arthur Maule had thought of him forty-two years beforehand: "a disturbing acquisition." While child rearing, adoption, and artificial insemination had become acceptable topics in activist circles, cloning had not. The Gay Crusader simply shrugs, convinced he'll one day be properly regarded as far ahead of his times because of his pioneering cloning activism. I tweak him, as usual. "Oh yes, Poppy," I laugh. "You'll be remembered by the cloned babies of the future as the Big Daddy of all clones."

BIBLIOGRAPHY

Alwood, Edward. *Straight News: Gays, Lesbians and the News Media*. New York: Columbia University Press, 1996.

Andrews, Lori. "The Clone Rangers." In *The Clone Age*. New York: Henry Holt, 1999 (pp. 245-247).

Caputo, Steven. *Alternate Channels: The Uncensored Story of Gay and Lesbian Images on Radio and Television*. New York: Ballantine, 2000.

D'Emilio, John. *Sexual Politics, Sexual Communities*. Chicago: University of Chicago Press, 1983.

Duberman, Martin. *Stonewall*. New York: Dutton, 1993.

Loughery, John. *The Other Side of Silence: Men's Lives and Gay Identities— A Twentieth Century History*. New York: Henry Holt, 1998.

McGarry, Molly, and Fred Wasserman. *Becoming Visible*. New York: 1998.

Teal, Donn. *The Gay Militants.* New York: Simon and Schuster, 1971; paperback by St. Martin's Press, 1995.

Thompson, Mark (Ed.), *Long Road to Freedom: The Advocate History of the Gay and Lesbian Movement.* New York: St. Martin's Press, 1994.

Tobin, Kay, and Randy Wicker. *The Gay Crusaders.* New York: Paperback Library, 1972. See Chapter 10.

Arthur Cyrus Warner (1918-   )

John Lauritsen

Photo by John Lauritsen

More than with other leaders of the homophile movement, there is a disparity between the public fame of Arthur Cyrus Warner and the magnitude of his accomplishments. An important intellectual force in the movement for half a century, he has evaded the glare of publicity so successfully that his name is unknown to the great mass of gay people and indeed to many of the newer "gay leaders."

With an AB degree (magna cum laude) from Princeton, an LLB degree from Harvard Law School, and a PhD degree from Harvard University (American and British history), Arthur Warner was well equipped for the roles he would play: mentor, theoretician, and strategist. His most important contributions have been in the legal sphere, where he and his colleagues intervened in state after state to overthrow sodomy, solicitation, and public lewdness laws.

Warner holds strong opinions and is not hesitant in expressing them. However, he does not mind hearing ideas that are different from his own. On the contrary, he is sometimes delighted; after the speaker has finished, he will pounce, like a cat on a negligent mouse. His speaking style on these occasions is inimitable. Enunciating with vigor, tempo adagio, he analyzes the offending argument. Factual errors are exposed, faulty arguments are carried to conclusions of manifest absurdity, and underlying philosophical premises are dissected. The experience is not easily forgotten, and some younger academics have emerged from it shaken and resentful. The present writer has received this treatment on more than one occasion and can say that—even if I still considered Warner to be wrong—I was grateful for the criticism, which at least constituted a safeguard against intellectual sloppiness.

Arthur Cyrus Warner was born in Newark, New Jersey, on February 14, 1918. His father's family had been in Newark for several generations and were in the wholesale grocery business. His mother was born in Paynesville, a small town in Minnesota; her family moved to St. Paul when she was about three.

It was not easy for Warner to come to grips with homosexuality, and his first experiences were informed by shame and horror. To understand this, it is necessary to describe his upbringing in terms of sex.

His mother came from a background which, although educated, reflected the Victorian ethos in matters of sex. As a child, Warner was not told myths about where babies came from, and he was allowed to see biology books showing the birth of animals, and so on, up to the point of fornication. However, when he was put to bed, his hands always had to be on top of the blanket, even on the coldest nights. Because the windows were always open for health reasons, his shoulders also would be cold.

Nevertheless, as with virtually all boys, he discovered the pleasures of masturbation, and at the age of seven or eight he did this several times a day, although without ejaculation. On one such occasion he was apprehended by his governess, who felt dutifully obliged to tell his parents.

Early the next morning the case was presented to his parents, who had just returned from a trip. His mother, "who wore the pants," took charge. She was in a frenzy and told him that if he ever did this again he would be taken to the state prison at Rahway, "where the bad boys go." He was also told that if he continued to do this, he would certainly become crazy. He was shaken by these warnings and for a year remained "good and pure."

However, his prepubescent sexuality reasserted itself. He was again caught, and this time he was told to pack his little bag, because he was going to the "home for bad boys." His parents put him in the back seat of the car, and they drove the twelve miles to Rahway State Prison, at which point he was almost hysterical. When the prison was reached, he was ordered out of the car, with his little bag. For about twenty minutes he stood outside the car and screamed for forgiveness, and finally was given "one more chance" and readmitted to the car. Arthur was then nine years old, and he began to realize the real problems of life.

This experience sufficed for about another year and a half of celibacy, after which he succumbed again. By now, however, he had learned the most important lesson: don't get caught. Because he performed the forbidden act so frequently, he believed that he had little time left before going completely insane—and since his future was hopeless and he was destined for the insane asylum anyway, he might as well enjoy himself during the short period of sanity remaining.

In prep school Warner was drawn to older boys with good bodies and became aware of the nature of his desires; yet he felt he was the only one in the
world with such feelings.

He was rudely disabused of this notion in the summer of 1934, when he
was a teenager due to enter Princeton in the fall. He and his parents were sitting in the living room, as his father read from the *Newark Evening News*
about the liquidation of Ernst Röhm. The head of the Schutz-Abteilung
[SA] of the Nazi Party during its rise to power, Röhm, together with dozens
of loyal SA officers, was murdered during the "Night of Long Knives" of
June 30-July 1, 1934. Hitler used Röhm's homosexuality as a pretext, claiming the murders were necessary to protect German youth from corruption.
Young Warner was wide-eyed at the news, and realized that there were other
people with propensities similar to his own—and that he was cursed, because only low, dirty people, such as Nazis, would have such proclivities.
This exacerbated his self-loathing, and he realized he would have to sup-
press his sexual desires even more.

His first sexual experience occurred during his sophomore year at
Princeton, when he was seventeen years old. On a cold, dark night in Tren-
ton, New Jersey, while waiting for a trolley to take him back to Princeton, he
was followed and then approached by a black man, who asked for a light.
Although terrified, he allowed himself to be taken to what appeared to be an
abandoned school yard, and there, through mutual masturbation, he experienced his first orgasm with a partner. The moment he came he was "overwhelmed with the most deep-seated sense of shame and disgust at myself
that I've ever had, before or since," and he rebuttoned his trousers and ran
the quarter mile back to the bus station. Inside the bus, he looked out the
window and saw that the man had followed him. He realized that his life
would end in total disaster, that he would be ruined and expelled from
Princeton in disgrace.

Later that year or the next year, a classmate of his at Princeton was
burned to death in his dormitory room, presumably from a fire caused by a
cigarette. A story ran the rounds in his class that the student was homosexual, and this was said with great loathing, as though he had deserved to die.
Believing that this was the attitude of his peers, Warner lived through his
four years at Princeton convinced that no one in his class would ever be so
degenerate as to have sex with another male.

After graduation from Princeton, and prior to entering Harvard Law
School, Arthur Warner worked for a year in New York City, as a messenger
for an advertising firm. There, in the summer of 1938, occurred an incident
that removed a layer of his sexual apprehension. As he was sitting in the
middle of a mostly empty auditorium in a Forty-Second Street movie house,
a man took the seat next to him, placed his leg next to his, and then placed

his hand on his knee. Arthur turned his head and was flabbergasted by what he saw: the person was a gentleman, wearing a suit and tie! So homosexuals were not all degenerates and low people. Suddenly he understood a number of things, including the reason so many men were congregating in the lavatory.

He now began going to the Forty-Second Street movies often and before long was going back to people's apartments. Within a month, and he still remembers the date, September 21, 1938, or rather two days after that, he noticed a burning in his urethra. When it got worse the next day, he told his mother, who sent him to the family doctor in Newark, who diagnosed gonorrhea. He was referred to a venereal disease specialist, Dr. Menck, who accepted Arthur's story that he had gotten it from a girl, told him that if he had simply washed his genitals and urinated afterwards, the chances were 95 percent he would never have contracted this. Dr. Menck said he was very careless for not having done this.

Those were the days before penicillin, and treatment for gonorrhea involved a six-week treatment, three times a day. A sulfanilamide compound was painfully injected into the urethra and then the penis was bandaged up for several hours. After eight weeks, the treatment appeared to be unsuccessful and Arthur had lost his job, as he couldn't do the walking that was required of a mail messenger. Finally, after nearly four months of treatment, he was cured. But the psychological trauma would last for the rest of his life. In reaction to Dr. Menck's rebuke, he developed a washing syndrome—pollution phobias and compulsive purification rituals—which greatly impaired his enjoyment in life and his ability to get things done.

At this point, in light of such painful experiences, Arthur Cyrus Warner would seem an unlikely candidate to become a homophile leader. But self-acceptance came gradually, and the Fates had a few tricks up their sleeves.

The following year he entered Harvard Law School. His studies there were interrupted by World War II, and he served a stint in the Navy (1942-1945), attaining the rank of lieutenant. Harvard Law School was completed after he returned from the service, and he received his LLB degree in 1946. Then for two years he worked for the American Association for the United Nations, as a field representative in Minnesota and North Dakota. In 1948 he returned to the East and was admitted to Harvard Graduate School, with the intention of working toward a doctorate.

Historians sometimes try to imagine what initially motivates individuals to dedicate their lives to social change. It doesn't always work that way. In 1951 a trick, a one-night stand, told him, out of the blue, that there was a gay group that met in a loft, not for purposes of sex but for discussion. For Warner this seemed oxymoronic, like talking about dry water. Nevertheless, his curiosity was aroused. He wanted to see what kind of people they were, and so he went to his first meeting of a group known only as The League.

Founded in 1948, The League appears to be the first American homophile group (although it was predated by Henry Gerber's short-lived Society for Human Rights in Chicago, and by the still earlier homosexual rights organizations in Europe and the United Kingdom during the nineteenth and early twentieth centuries). At his first meeting Warner could hardly believe what he saw: the men in attendance were wearing suits and ties. They looked thoroughly presentable, like bankers or lawyers.

Warner was hooked, and attended as many meetings of The League as he could, although he was then a graduate student at Harvard. As he remembers it, The League met in a rented space, a large loft, and there were generally about fifty to sixty persons at each meeting. The meetings were dominated by fear; entrance was scrupulously denied to anyone unable to prove he was at least twenty-one. A typical subject of conversation: "What is likely to be our fate if the authorities, either through the information given by the landlord or through some other means, discover what we are talking about?" Although they merely discussed the possibility of ameliorating the laws, not even abolishing them, they still shared an overall fear that they would end up in jail.

In January 1952 Warner was home for the Christmas recess and attended the first organizational meeting of what subsequently became the Mattachine Society of New York. The meeting was organized by Thomas Morford, a professor of psychology, who came as a representative of the Mattachine Society of California, which had been formed in 1950. It took place in a Times Square hotel shortly after New Year's. Most of those present were members or former members of The League, which passed out of existence shortly after the formation of Mattachine.

Although the new Mattachine retained the same phobias and comprised many of the same faces, there were some crucial differences. It was no longer furtive. Whereas meetings of The League had been held clandestinely, the Mattachine meetings were held in rented halls, open to the public and announced publicly, much like meetings of any other group.

After completing his doctoral course work at Harvard, Warner returned to the New York area, and from 1954 on he was continuously active in Mattachine. For all but two of its sixteen years of existence he was chairman of the legal department.

During the 1950s and 1960s he held various positions: research assistant, London School of Economics (1954-1956); assistant professor of history, Rider College, Lawrenceville, New Jersey (1956-1960); lecturer at Fairleigh Dickinson University, Rutherford, New Jersey (1960-1962); and associate professor, University of Texas (1962-1968).

In 1971 he founded the National Committee for Sexual Civil Liberties (NCSCL)—later renamed the American Association for Personal Privacy (AAPP)—of which he was and continues to be the director. This association is a high-level think tank, comprising lawyers, historians, theologians, and other professionals. Its paramount concern is legal reform.

One cannot record all of Arthur Warner's accomplishments in the legal arena, as his influence has often been indirect, as counselor and inspirer to other lawyers. His salient achievements include the following:

From 1976 to 1978 he worked with the Judiciary Committee of the New Jersey State Assembly and was largely responsible for having the sexual solicitation provision excised from the New Jersey Penal Code.

In collaboration with Thomas F. Coleman, Esquire (then cochairman of the AAPP), he won the case of *Pryor v. Municipal Court* (1979), in which the California Supreme Court judicially rewrote the sexual solicitation provision of the state's penal code (which had been the prime vehicle for arrests of gay men in California). Coleman wrote the brief for the defendant, and Warner wrote the one for the AAPP as amicus curiae.

He persuaded Professor Welsh White of the University of Pittsburgh Law School to accept the *Bonadio* case (1980), which resulted in the Pennsylvania Supreme Court invalidating both the sodomy statute and its companion homosexual solicitation provision.

He wrote the brief which induced the Criminal Law Revision Commission of Nebraska to delete the homosexual solicitation provision from that state's criminal code.

He initiated and directed the legal strategy in the *Albi* and *Gibson* cases in Colorado, which resulted in the invalidation of that state's homosexual solicitation statute by the Colorado Supreme Court (1974).

During the time when sodomy was still a felony in Ohio, he was called to testify before a special commission established by the Ohio Supreme Court to decide whether an acknowledged and practicing homosexual should be admitted to the state's bar. The commission's decision to admit was the first of its kind and set a precedent for other states. He later testified before the Judiciary Committees of both houses of the Ohio legislature during a hearing which in 1972 led to the decriminalization of private homosexual conduct between consenting persons above the age of sexual consent.

He acted as consultant to William H. Gardner, Esquire, of Buffalo, a fellow member of the AAPP and attorney in the *Onofre* case (1980), in which the highest New York court struck down that state's sodomy statute. Later he collaborated in writing the brief in the *Uplinger* case (1983), in which the same New York court invalidated the New York homosexual solicitation law.

He drafted the sexual solicitation provision of the proposed, but never enacted, Federal Criminal Code recommended by the National Commission on Reform of Federal Criminal Laws.

Along with Warner's activism for the homophile cause came a lessening of his sexual inhibitions. Some of his escapades, and his predilection for virile black males, are the stuff of legend, although this is not the place to recount them. Suffice it to say that he has described sexually himself as a "Dr. Jekyll and Mr. Hyde," and that he possesses two Eagle automobiles, made by AMC, whose relevant features are that the seats recline fully and the windows have blinds on them.

Arthur Warner has his own way of doing things. As he explained his approach in an interview for the present chapter, he prefers, as much as possible, to work with the establishment behind the scenes. He believes patriotism and good citizenship are principles that people working for social reform should embrace.

Since the members of Warner's group, the AAPP, tend to be prominent lawyers and academics, he was asked whether he would accept the terms *expert* and *elitist* as descriptive of his approach. His response: "Both! I'll accept both of them. If I want a doctor, I'll go to the elitist or the expert any time. You can go to the mediocres, the ones that are no different from anybody else. Three cheers for elitism!"

Finally, Warner's approach involves the element of time. He is in for the long haul and loathes undue haste. When speaking before a group a number of years ago, he contended that the homophile movement had accomplished more in a shorter time than any other reform movement. At that point, "a young gay whippersnapper got up and said: 'The hell with that, I want mine now!'" That particular philosophy is anathema to Warner, who stated in his interview: "At eighty-two years old, I still have not gotten mine, and I don't expect to get it all in my lifetime. We have a lot to learn—by this I mean gay people—from the patience that blacks and other disadvantaged people have demonstrated."

Arthur Warner's modus operandi is well illustrated by his interaction with editors of the *Oxford English Dictionary* (OED). He began in 1988 by writing to the head editor on the word *munitive*. He received a response from an assistant editor, Mrs. E. Bonner, with whom he became a correspondent. Having developed a rapport, he then broached the topic of the common slang words *blow* and its compound *blow job*. Although the OED supplements included such words as *fuck,* they did not give the oral intercourse/fellatio meanings of *blow*. Warner's suggestions were accepted, and he received a letter from Mrs. Bonner, in which she wrote: "You will be pleased to know that *blow* should appear in the second edition of the O.E.D. due to be published in 1989." She enclosed galley reproductions of the entries, not only for *blow* but also for *Princeton-First-Year* ("applied to a form of male homosexual activity in which partners achieve orgasm by intercrural friction").

Warner is critical of many aspects of the post-Stonewall movement—appalled by what he sees as the new movement's rashness and impatience, its irrationalism, its lack of patriotism and civility, its propensity to ally with left-wing causes, its "cult of victimhood."

When the Gay Academic Union (GAU) was founded in the early 1970s, Warner had high hopes for it but was soon disillusioned. Although GAU produced four successful conferences, it accomplished little in the way of serious scholarship. Warner describes many GAU members as academic dropouts who were more interested in getting their heads together than in achieving anything. The group had a powerful undercurrent of irrationalism and a hostility to free speech and free inquiry.

In reaction to these shortcomings, a minority within the GAU, calling itself the New York Scholarship Committee, "carried the true banner of intellectual scholarship." Meeting once a month in the New York City apartment of Wayne Dynes, professor of art history, the Scholarship Committee heard presentations in various areas of gay scholarship, followed by discussion. Warner drove up every month from Princeton to attend these meetings in which he was an enthusiastic participant.

When asked what he considered the greatest accomplishments of the homophile movement, Warner began by paying tribute to W. Dorr Legg, "an intellectual, who first of all recognized the absolute necessity of the linkage between education and homosexual law reform." In the legal arena, Don Slater and Dorr Legg won the only case before the Supreme Court that granted First Amendment rights to gay publications, so they were no longer banned from the mails as obscene.

In turn, New York Mattachine won—through three cases before the highest courts in New Jersey and New York—the right for gay people to go into a public establishment, such as a bar, without the bar's being threatened with closure by the Alcoholic Beverage Commission for violating the law which criminalized facilities that offered opportunities for homosexuals to congregate.

Warner also acknowledged the achievement of Troy Perry, who established the Metropolitan Community Church, the first gay organization within the Abrahamic tradition and the first gay organization to really begin mixing heterosexuals and homosexuals. Warner regretted that those not religiously inclined, himself included, sometimes did injustice to the pioneer efforts of religious gays who chose to work within the church.

In much bigger terms, Warner sees the gay movement as a central element in breaking the implicit prohibition against the pursuit of bodily pleasure. In effect, the homophile movement is undertaking unfinished business of the Enlightenment, which had unconsciously continued to accept the Judeo-Christian ethic that the human body was evil and shameful. This theme is developed in a recent unpublished monograph by Warner, *The Secularization of Knowledge.*

When asked what the movement should do next, Warner replied: "The movement ought to be looking toward working itself out of existence." He believes we should look forward to a time when "gays can meld into the population and become unrecognizable, as soon as their legitimate grievances have been redressed."

He maintains that we should pursue our goals in connection with other people, to end the "ghetto mentality," the "suffocating atmosphere of an all-gay group." He concludes an earlier paper, "Is There a Homosexual Culture?", with the following words:

> The way to political freedom is to recognize that the homosexual ghetto and its attendant deviant subculture are and should be temporary phenomena, direct products of anti-homosexual bigotry, and that they will disappear as soon as the bigotry itself disappears. Gay people will then be able to join the mainstream of American life with dignity and self-respect.

Although Warner's opinions are intensely held, they are not impervious to change. When the present writer first came to know him in the early 1970s, he was a Presbyterian, as were his parents. In recent years Warner has become a secular humanist who sees the gay cause as being, on one level, a struggle against superstition.

For almost all of the past half century, Arthur Warner has lived in Princeton, New Jersey, in the house built by his parents. Nothing in it has changed since they died about thirty years ago—except perhaps books and ideas.

REFERENCES

Various materials supplied by Arthur Warner.
Interviews conducted with Arthur Warner at his home in Princeton, New Jersey, August 15-17, 2000.

Richard Inman (1926?-   )

Jesse G. Monteagudo

On April 19, 1966, WTVJ Channel 4, Miami's leading television station, broadcast "The Homosexual," one of its *FYI* series of documentaries. Aimed "against the homosexual child molester and toward the parent who never thought it could happen to his or her son," "The Homosexual" was dominated by the likes of Detective Sergeant John Sorenson of the Dade County Sheriff's Department of Morals, and Lieutenant Duane Barker, former civilian advisor to the Florida Legislative Investigative Committee. The only person who dared to present a less-than-negative view of homosexuality was Richard Inman, described by *FYI* host Ralph Renick as "president of the Mattachine Society of Florida, whose goal is to legalize homosexuality between consenting adults." At a time when most gays hid behind an assumed name, a potted palm, or in a shadow, Inman used his own name and allowed his full face to be shown on television. Although Inman's television appearance left much to be desired, the fact that he was there at all made the showing of "The Homosexual" an important event in the gay history of Florida.

Who was Richard Inman? Unfortunately for posterity, Inman dropped out of sight around 1969, just when the Stonewall uprising revolutionized the lesbian and gay movement. Inman's departure from the scene kept the next generation of activists from learning from his achievements and from his mistakes. Florida's activists were forced to reinvent the wheel, often with tragic consequences. Not until the 1990s was Inman "discovered" by gay historians, who finally gave him the recognition that he deserved. James T. Sears, whose book *Lonely Hunters: An Oral History of Lesbian and Gay Southern Life, 1948-1968* (1997) contributes so much to our knowledge of Inman, called him a soldier of fortune turned taxi driver who challenged the homophobia and ignorance of heterosexuals as well as apathy and timidity among homosexuals. Other historians such as John Loughery (1998) called him a voice in the wilderness in Miami while Eugene Patron claimed he was a virtual one-man band for gay rights. Foster Gunnison Jr., who worked with Inman, regarded him as an unsung hero of the movement, while Jack Nichols (1999), who knew Inman as well as anyone still alive, dubbed him "the South's Pioneer." "Inman was the first Southerner to challenge anti-gay laws in the courts, to write in mass circulation publications about gay men and lesbians and to appear on local television and radio programs," adds Nichols (1999). As the Sunshine State's first out-of-the-closet activist, Inman dared to be openly and actively gay at a time and place when that was a dangerous thing to be. By challenging both an antigay political establishment and a closeted gay community, Inman earned the title of Florida's Gay of the Century.

Florida in the 1960s was, according to James T. Sears, the Mississippi of the homosexual. The state government, controlled by "pork chop" politicians, responded to the threat of homosexuality with a ferocity not unlike its earlier reaction to communism and the civil rights movement. The Florida Legislative Investigation Committee, chaired by State Senator Charley Johns (hence the "Johns Committee") targeted gays in state universities and other public institutions. A series of state and local laws outlawed gay sex, barred homosexuals from certain professions, and criminalized drag. Ordinances that prohibited gays from working or congregating in a bar were used to justify repeated police raids. Violence against "bachelors" was tacitly tolerated, if not actively encouraged, by the authorities. The media was uniformly hostile. Against such organized prejudice and terror, Florida's gays and lesbians retreated into their closets, hoping against hope that they'd be ignored. Jack Nichols was only slightly exaggerating when he told Jim Sears that in 1966, Florida was the worst place in the Union for gay people.

Only Richard Inman dared to challenge the status quo. Born in Tampa around 1926, Inman arrived in Miami in the 1940s. Although Inman's pre-activist past is murky, we know he married twice, had two long-term gay relationships, and was an active part of Miami's "furtive fraternity." We also know that he was arrested at least twice for "simply being in a gay bar"—not an unusual experience at a time when gay bars were illegal. During the 1950s Inman, either alone or with a partner, owned a mortgage company and "dozens of Miami properties," including several bars. However, in 1964 Inman filed for bankruptcy and was already working as a driver for Miami's Diamond Cab.

Frustrated in business, Inman turned to politics: "I had never before been a member of a homophile organization," he wrote.

Such organizations were entirely to be found only in the major cities of the North and in California. . . . I knew nothing about the history, aims, or goals of the homophile civil rights movement. . . . In the past, homosexuals had meekly accepted their arrests, paid their fines to the court, and then run for cover. Never before had anyone stood up to the Legislative Investigation Committee, the State Attorney, or the police departments when confronted by their harassment tactics. (Sears, 1997, p. 216)

It was a tough job, but someone had to do it.

Undaunted by the odds, Inman founded in 1963 the Atheneum Society, which, according to Sears (1997, pp. 213-214), was the first state-chartered, explicitly homosexual organization in the South. Its objective, wrote Sears, was to combat gross injustices affecting homosexual citizens which are perpetuated by certain heterosexuals who masquerade behind the guise of justice and decency. Although bartender Lea Surette and attorney Marty Lemlich were listed as vice president and secretary, the Atheneum Society was basically a one-man project. Even so, Inman's group benefited from the discreet but generous assistance of George Arents, an elderly millionaire who owned the U.S. franchise for Ferrari. "George is very closety," Inman later told Jack Nichols, "but he does provide me with pocket cash when there's printing to be done, or when I want to get a mailing out."

With his Atheneum Society in tow, Inman soon became, in Sears' words, "the lightning rod for Florida's nonexistent homophile movement." He tried to impress the Florida establishment by claiming to represent 200,000 homosexuals. When that didn't work, he threatened to stage a gay parade, "with hair-ribbons flying and 'bells-a-ringing' if the authorities continued to harass gay people" (Sears, 1997, pp. 217-218). Before long Inman was "privately engaged in correspondence and conversations with political leaders and kingmakers." The Society's newsletter, *Viewpoint,* although it never had the 4,000 subscribers in nineteen states that Inman claimed, was, according to Jack Nichols, certainly read by influential Florida politicians, members of the media, and law enforcement officers. Inman relied on these contacts, real or imagined, as allies in his long-running feud with two of Florida's most powerful politicians: State Senator Charley Johns and Dade County State Attorney Richard Gerstein.

It wasn't long before Inman caught the attention of Franklin Kameny, whose Mattachine Society of Washington helped revolutionize the homophile movement after 1961. In January 1965 Kameny asked Jack Nichols, his friend and cofounder of Mattachine Washington, to establish contact with the elusive Mr. Inman. Thus began what Nichols later called "some of the most remarkable letters of the Movement during that era." After six months of correspondence Nichols decided that it was time the two activists got together. In June Nichols and his lover, Lige Clarke, flew to Miami, where they arranged to meet Inman at Coconut Grove's tony Candlelight Club, already a favorite hangout for the rich and closeted. After a sumptuous dinner the trio decided to visit George Arents and his lover at Carousel, Arents's stately Coral Gables mansion.

Jack and Lige were impressed by their new friend. In his memoir of Inman, written for *GayToday,* Nichols described Inman as being

> In his forties, . . . tall and slim. He pontificated in earnest tones. He was dead serious about gay rights, and since he was the only person brave enough to stand up against Florida's bigoted establishment, we assured him—though we lived afar—that we wanted to help. We were conducting, after all, a challenge to state-sponsored cruelty. Because he was willing to take on both the politicians and police, we looked hopefully to him. It was apparent that because of our enthusiasm, he looked hopefully to us too.

Nichols and Clarke convinced Inman, "after a piña colada or two," to change the name of his organization from the Atheneum Society to the Mattachine Society of Florida: "By urging Inman to change the name of his fledgling organization so that it reflected, along with other Mattachine groups, a party line that emphasized gay equality, we argued that he could become part of a national trend, one that eased the isolation he was experiencing as he struggled alone." Inman (of course) became president of his newly renamed organization; Nichols became vice president and Clarke— since he did editing for the Army's Joint Chiefs of Staff—was appointed editor of the newsletter. For his part, Arents promised to subsidize Florida Mattachine: "You just ask when you need something" (Nichols, 1999).

Although Nichols and Clarke soon returned to Washington, they kept in touch with their new ally, primarily through a series of almost daily letters between Nichols and Inman, which are the primary source for all historical writing about Inman. Meanwhile, "Robert C. Hayden" (Lige Clarke) edited the Florida segment of the "Homosexual Citizen," published in conjunction with the Mattachine Society of Washington. Doubtlessly influenced by Lige and Jack, Richard soon adopted, in John D'Emilio's words, "a Kameny-like tone in his dealings with public officials" (1983, p. 233).

Although Mattachine Florida never had more than a handful of members, Inman and his friends managed to make it appear bigger than it really was. Lige contributed to this hoax by carrying, at a Mattachine-sponsored picketing of the State Department in Washington, a sign that read "This Demonstration Is Sponsored by The Mattachine Society of Florida, Inc." Meanwhile, according to Jack, Inman was bluffing Florida politicians with a threat to picket that would never materialize, promising a line around the Capitol Building in Tallahassee. The problem was that Florida's Mattachine had only subscribers, supporters, and contributors, and, like Inman's replaced Atheneum group, it had no active membership other than Inman himself.

There was a good reason for Inman's rash behavior. After the Johns Committee published its notorious "purple pamphlet" titled *The Homosexual Citizen* (1964) new antigay bills were introduced in the Florida Legislature. They included the Sexual Behavior Act, which would criminalize same-sex kissing and dancing, and the Criminal Sexual Psychopath Act which, according to Nichols, would have allowed the state to put those accused of "the abominable and detestable crime against nature" into mental hospitals and the state could confiscate their personal possessions to pay for their hospitalization. Inman was working overtime to stop passage of these repressive laws, in spite of his poor health—he had a heart condition—and the fear of losing his job with Diamond Cab. All this did not stop Inman from starting still another group, the Florida League for Good Government, to oppose the proposed legislation and to push for adoption of a Model Penal Code that would incidentally legalize homosexual acts in Florida.

It was at this time, according to Nichols' memoir, that Lige arranged to take a photo of our phony Florida sponsorship sign showing Washingtonians posing as Floridians clustered around it with the State Department building as its background. Inman distributed this photo among Florida's politicians to give credence to his picketing bluff. When the legislature quickly dropped the bill, he exulted that our bluff had worked. Whatever the reason behind the Florida Legislature's decision, Inman was quick to take credit for it.

Sears credited this unusual victory on "Richard's understanding of the intricacies of Florida politics, coupled with his diverse network of contacts." Inman did this in spite of Florida's closeted gays, some of who "sent critical, anonymous letters about him to various lawmakers" (Sears, 1997, p. 233). Inman's surprising success made him an important part of America's still-small homophile movement. One of the activists with whom Inman began to correspond at this time was Bob Basker, president of the Chicago-based Mattachine Midwest. Basker, whose involvement in leftist politics went back to the 1940s, shocked the conservative Inman by advocating the right of "commies" to serve in leadership positions. In spite of that, the two men maintained a firm friendship, which continued after both Basker and Inman moved to California in the 1970s.

In the fall of 1965 Florida Mattachine joined the East Coast Homophile Organizations (ECHO). Although Inman refused to attend the ECHO Conference held in New York City, he allowed Nichols to represent his organization. Finally in February 1966, Inman took Nichols' advice and agreed to attend the organizing meeting of the North American Conference of Homophile Organizations (NACHO), held in Kansas City. While in Kansas City, Inman and Nichols met Foster Gunnison Jr., "a kindly intellectual" (Nichols, 1999) from Hartford, Connecticut, who had recently become active with the Mattachine Society of New York. The overworked Nichols "begged" Inman to accept Gunnison as his new vice president, although Nichols remained in touch with the Floridian. As a result of this meeting, Inman and Gunnison began their own massive correspondence.

Inman was a master of "political dialectics," which he described in a 1965 letter to Mark Forrester

> as the way a politician will say one thing in his platform then do the opposite once elected and then get away with it without anyone calling his cards. It could be described as disagreeing with someone, but agreeing with them to their face so strongly that they don't hear you put words into their mouth and then before they know it, they are doing what you wanted them to do in the first place.

A born Machiavellian, Inman believed that the end justified the means and admitted he was not above playing the dirtiest kind of politics. "When pinned down, you either lash out at those who disagree, or you attempt to totally subjugate those who do agree," Inman wrote in a letter to Frank Kameny.

Jim Sears (1997, pp. 255-256) called Inman the "Gordon Liddy of pre-Stonewall gay politics." "His nonconventional tactics, web of contacts, and philosophy of 'political dialectics' differentiated him from other homophile leaders. In his legislative struggle he adeptly used the media both openly and surreptitiously." Nor was Inman afraid to work with people who would ordinarily oppose his cause:

> Richard used his closely guarded connections with those in the "rackets"..., federal agencies, and anti-Castro fronts who provided protection. He also relied on wealthy but closeted homosexuals like George Arents ..., on friendly capitol reporters who kept his lobbying efforts outside prying public eyes, on a cadre of gay politicos as well as state politicians who delivered key votes, and on longtime political insiders such as the chief clerk of the Florida House and former secretary of the Johns Committee, Mrs. Lamar Bledsoe (to whom he even sent a vase of red roses). (Sears, 1997, pp. 255-256)

Although Inman was more progressive than some California homophile leaders (who favored education over activism), in post-Stonewall terms he was very conservative. A firm anticommunist, Inman opposed the ideas and tactics of the New Left (which Basker embraced) and criticized the demonstrations and protests of the Vietnam era in a letter he wrote to Warren D. Adkins in 1965: "Civil disobedience like sit-ins," he wrote, "DEFINITELY NO! We start that and then we'll be classed right along with the Vietnam and Berkeley crowds. Why in hell do some of us think we must ape others? Can't we be original? Don't we have an original and unique problem?" The homophile movement, Inman insisted, should not be "contaminated" with any other agenda. Like other "conservative" activists before and since, Inman argued that

> diversions such as marriage, adoption and an unnecessary preoccupation with the subject of pornography all tend to create enormous resistance in the minds of the public and lawmakers against the homophile movement. These major and minor items should be listed and separated and the entire emphasis of the movement put upon [law reform, nondiscrimination and freedom of assembly]. Shove the others to the back, at least for now, until we get the items in the first group accomplished. (letter to Warren D. Adkins, July 1, 1965)

Although, according to Martin Duberman, Gunnison liked and admired Inman, he recognized that the Floridian was a "lone wolf" "halfway between a drifter and a taxi driver" (1994, p. 103). If Inman often seemed to contradict himself, as when (according to Duberman) he "helped in 1965 to organize, in conjunction with the South Florida Psychiatric Society, a program of free counseling for teenagers who 'want to get out of the gay life,'" he was probably just exercising his "political dialectics."

With that in mind, we could interpret Inman's equivocal performance in WTVJ's *FYI* documentary as another one of the master's Machiavellian gambits. Inman began his interview well enough when he remarked that "present laws are ineffectual and almost unenforceable" and should be replaced by laws that "make homosexual behavior between consenting adults, in private, not illegal." On the other hand, Inman shocked many gays when he said that homosexuality "is not a desirable way of life"; argued that reforming the law would "curb homosexuality"; and urged law enforcement agencies to "direct your efforts to prevent juveniles from becoming homosexual." When the interviewer asked about Inman's own sexual orientation, Inman lied: "I *was* a homosexual. But I gave it up about some years ago, over four years ago. It's not my cup of tea."

To many who watched the show, then and now, Inman's appearance in "The Homosexual" was a disaster. John Loughery, who reviewed "The Homosexual" while doing research for *The Other Side of Silence,* wrote that Inman's "performance" suggested gay men and lesbians would be better served by silence. Uncomfortable on camera and looking as if he had suddenly realized that acknowledging his sexuality was tantamount to admitting a crime for which he might be arrested, Inman squirmed before his interviewer's questions, ending with the claim that he had given up homosexuality four years earlier—"it's not my cup of tea"—although he believed that homosexuals deserved fair treatment. He giggled at the suggestion of gay marriage or gay adoption.

Others agreed with Loughery's sad assessment, which could be summarized by a quote from a Fort Lauderdale gay man who was in his twenties when the program took place: "You weren't exactly inspired to run out and join his organization." "Actually, he scared me more than the cop [Sorenson] they had telling the eighth-graders that any one of them could become a deviant if they weren't careful" (Loughery, 1998, p. 280). Although Nichols and Sears are willing to give Inman the benefit of the doubt, I cannot help but agree with Loughery and his unnamed subject. In his most important public appearance, Inman made a poor role model.

In his career as an activist, Inman received scant support from South Florida's frightened gay community. Then as now, gay men in positions of power, afraid of a backlash, worked to sabotage the activist agenda. "Everyone is hiding and . . . afraid that somehow they will be connected and exposed. Everyone now says 'count me out.' Last night, two bars asked me politely 'don't come around here anymore,' " Inman complained in 1965 in a March 12 letter to the *Citizen News.* Inman also received harassing phone calls from anonymous parties and tickets from the Miami Police Department. The police department also tried (unsuccessfully) to get Inman's employer to fire him. Increasingly frustrated, Inman sued the city of Miami in February 1966, arguing that the city's antigay legislation "arbitrarily denies to certain and various persons their rights to the equal opportunities upon which this great country was founded." Sears called this lawsuit the "first civil rights legal action brought in the South by an admitted homosexual" (Sears, 1997, p. 248). Although Inman lost his case, he laid the groundwork for trials that eventually overturned Miami's antigay laws.

Inman's leadership deteriorated. He quarreled with Miami's popular mayor, Robert King High; with the press; and with other gay men. In March 1967 Inman abolished Florida Mattachine. Inspired by San Francisco activist Guy Strait, whom he had met at a NACHO conference, Inman opened the Atheneum Bookshop, a Miami emporium that sold gay erotica. In October of that year the Miami vice squad raided Inman's shop, charging him with possession of pornography. Although Inman was acquitted on a technicality, it was his last stand as an activist. By August 1969, the *Miami Herald* could claim that the Miami gay subculture showed few signs of the minority group syndrome.

> Since the demise of the Mattachine Society of Florida . . . Miami has had neither homosexual organizations nor militants. A politically docile, socially invisible subculture, it attracts little attention, and less support. (Sears, 1997, p. 253)

It remained for a new generation of activists to revive a movement that Inman had led single-handedly through its 1960s' rise and fall.

What happened to Richard Inman? According to Jack Nichols, Inman visited him in New York in 1970 at his offices at *GAY,* a weekly newspaper that he and Lige Clarke edited from 1970 to 1973. "After that he disappeared. He'd had a heart condition which could have claimed him early" (Nichols, 1999). According to Professor Sears, Inman moved to California around the time of his last meeting with Nichols, not long before Bob Basker and other activists resurrected Florida's gay rights movement. Inman eventually settled in Long Beach, California, where he led a quiet life oblivious to the winds of change around him. One of the few people Inman kept in touch with was Bob Basker, who last spoke with Inman around 1987. Unfortunately, Basker has since lost contact with his old comrade in arms. When Basker tried to telephone Inman recently, Inman's numbers were disconnected.

Whether dead or alive, Inman the man has vanished into oblivion, not waiting for new generations to recognize his achievements. It remained for Nichols to summarize, in his chapter in Sears' *Lonely Hunters* and in his own memoir, Inman's contribution to America's GLBT community:

> Richard Inman, like a bright comet, soared through skies, lighting up America's early gay and lesbian liberation cause. Unique in our movement's history, he was committed to what he called "constitutional rights" and his brave willingness to step forward in a benighted area where savage antigay persecution had become standard government fare was, to me, a foremost inspiration in those heady times. I made Richard Inman my confidant and comrade-in-arms because I knew he was working virtually alone, sometimes despairing. I embrace the memory of him still. He serves our history as a shining example of what a single, committed, energetic individual can do—even though suffering setbacks himself—in the ongoing struggle to right the lot of the wrongly-persecuted. (Nichols, in Sears' *Lonely Hunters,* p. 255)

BIBLIOGRAPHY

This biography is based on an article "Richard Inman: Florida's Gay of the Century," which originally appeared in Miami's *The Weekly News,* Badpuppy's *Gay-Today,* and other publications in July 1999). A videotape of the program "The Homosexual," which appeared on WTVJ, April 19, 1966, is in the author's collection. The Stonewall Library and Archives in Fort Lauderdale also has a copy. It also has a copy of his letters and correspondence as well as a copy of the "purple pamphlet" issued by the Florida legislature, *Homosexuality and Citizenship in Florida.*

Basker, M. "The American Minority," *Tropic Magazine (Miami Herald Supplement),* August 24, 1969.

D'Emilio, John. *Sexual Politics, Sexual Communities: The Making of a Homosexual Minority in the United States, 1940-1970.* Chicago: University of Chicago, 1983.

Duberman, Martin. *Stonewall.* New York: Plume, 1994.

Loughery, John. *The Other Side of Silence: Men's Lives and Gay Identities: A Twentieth Century History.* New York: Henry Holt and Company, 1998.

Nichols, Jack. "Richard Inman: The South's Pioneer," *GayToday* (online magazine), Badpuppy Enterprises, May 17, 1999. <www.gaytoday.badpuppy.com/garchive/people/051799pe.htm>.

Sears, James T. *Lonely Hunters: An Oral History of Lesbian and Gay Southern Life, 1848-1968.* Boulder, CO: Westview Press, 1997. Chapter 7 by Jack Nichols is the fullest account yet written about Richard Inman.

PART IV: OTHER VOICES AND THEIR INFLUENCE

The challenge to standard stereotypes that Kinsey had made encouraged others from a number of disciplines to also investigate—even a handful of academics who had previously avoided the subject. Perhaps the most controversial individual included in this section is Walter H. Breen, who wrote under the name of J. Z. Eglinton. Wayne Dynes, who did the initial planning for this book, originally solicited Breen's biography because he felt Breen's belief that intergenerational sex (what Breen called Greek Love or ephebophilia) should be distinguished from androphile homosexuality (sex between adults) was important. The issue of pederasty or ephebophilia has been a hot issue in any discussion of male homosexuality, and it was with considerable trepidation that Breen's biography was included in this book. Although a believer in pederasty (he was arrested and convicted on child molestation charges) his research on the topics are a valuable source to the whole question of same-sex relationships in a historical perspective. It should be added that intergenerational sex is in part dependent on definitions of age of consent, and many countries have either long held or recently established the age of consent for males as fourteen or sixteen, the same as it is in those countries for females.

Among those he influenced to investigate homosexuality was Warren Johansson, a polymath, who tracked down some of the most obscure references to same-sex relationships in the past. Johansson knew more obscure historical facts about same-sex relationships than anyone else; many sought him when they had questions. Johansson corresponded with Kinsey, for example, providing him with information about Sigmund Freud's acceptance of homosexuality as a fact of life rather than as an illness.

Another controversial writer was Donald Webster Cory—Edward Sagarin by birth. His 1951 book on *The Homosexual in America* appears often in these pages as a source of information for many who were attempting to find out about their own sexuality. But Cory was, as his biography indicates, uncomfortable, to say the least, about his own same-sex inclinations. In fact, under his academic name, Sagarin, he often appears to be homophobic. It is this ambivalence that he has toward his own sex drives which make him an interesting subject.

Perhaps one of the most influential academics in bringing about change in attitudes toward homosexuality was Evelyn Gentry Hooker, whose studies indicated that homosexual men could not be identified as different on the standard projective tests then in use from the heterosexuals. Her conclusions remind one of the old children's story about the emperor who had no clothes, and it took a comparatively simple experiment to demonstrate this. George Weinberg, who coined the word *homophobia,* was one of a tiny handful of psychotherapists in the 1960s willing to take a stand against the psychiatric profession's classification of homosexuality as a pathology. Also included in this series of biographies is my own, insisted upon by the editor in chief of the series in which this book appears. Bullough was both a scholar and an activist, leading the charge to change the policies of the American Civil Liberties Union on gays and lesbians, and in the process becoming a public spokesperson for removing homosexuality from the lists of pathologies and perversions, at time when many gays and lesbians were still reluctant to go public.

Although many authors, playwrights, artists, poets, and others have been gay or lesbian, including many contemporary writers such as Gore Vidal, few took the public road that Allen Ginsberg traveled in debating, asserting, and demanding gay rights. For this reason he is included in this collection, and his biography begins this section.

Also helping to challenge public opinion on homosexuality was a number of other people whose contribution, although only peripheral to the issue of homosexuality, helped the public define what homosexuality was all about. Belonging in this group of people is Christine Jorgensen, whose surgical change from female to male forced psychiatrists and physicians to reexamine their own ideas about what was involved in sexual identity. Less well known to the general public but equally influential was Virginia Prince who believed that transvestism and homosexuality were two different phenomena and should not necessarily be linked together. She started a worldwide movement that includes a wide variety of behaviors usually now grouped together under the category of transgenderism.

As everyone knows there are also gay queens, and while their importance in the Stonewall riots finally has been recognized, they were early on the scene of being public about their sex preferences. Particularly important in this respect was José Sarria. The Empress of San Francisco who helped the citizens of San Francisco laugh with her and made the city much more tolerant of the acceptance of gays and lesbians. Her royal court became a standard ceremony in many of the cities of the United States. In a similar vein, not to be overlooked are the bar owners, not all of whom were exploitive of their gay clientele. Charlotte Coleman was particularly important in San Francisco and her activities again help explain how that city became so openly tolerant of its gay and lesbian citizens.

Probably the most important factor in enabling the gay movement to grow and expand from its initial base in Los Angeles was money. ONE, Inc. had a hand-to-mouth existence until Reed Erickson and the Erickson Education Foundation came to its rescue. Erickson, a female-to-male transsexual, became the angel for many gay causes, giving in the end several million dollars to the cause. The symbol of what he accomplished is the archival holdings of lesbian and gay topics in Los Angeles in the ONE/ILGA archives on the campus of the University of Southern California, and the Bonnie and Vern Bullough collection at California State University, Northridge.

A major breakthrough in the religious opposition to homosexuality was the establishment of the Metropolitan Community Church in Los Angeles. Troy Perry calls himself a Christian in spite of Christianity. His success led other religious groups to go further than they had before in coming to terms with homosexuality and lesbianism.

As the movement gained success, the nature of the leaders changed. Many retired but a few continued. One who continued on was Morris Kight in Los Angeles. Kight, who was long an activist in fighting for the civil rights of others and a closeted gay for much of his early life even though he worked for gay causes, emerged as an important out-of-the-closet leader in the 1960s, symbolizing the change in the gay movement even before Stonewall. In the aftermath of Stonewall, he played a more important role, just as many of the activists who had joined the battle earlier were being pushed out of leadership roles or began to be regarded as old fashioned and out of step, although many of them hung on through the changes. They were important, and it is their stories that this book tells.

Allen Ginsberg (1926-1997):
On His Own Terms

Gwen Brewer

Copyright Cape Goliard Press.
Photo by Tom Maschler.

Although many of the important twentieth-century writers were gay, most of them remained rather closeted about it. This was not the case of poet Allen Ginsberg, whose very fame in part rested on his willingness not only to proclaim his own homosexuality but to write seriously and poetically about it and to campaign for gay and lesbian rights. This, he insisted, was part of his being, and he gloried in it, proclaiming it everywhere, lending his support to gays when it was not popular to do so. As gay power grew, he remained controversial, even defending the National American Man-Boy Love Association (NAMBLA). He enjoyed being a spokesman for those who were different, and he did make a difference.

Allen Ginsberg was born in Paterson, New Jersey, to Russian Jewish parents. His mother, Naomi Levy, immigrated to the United States when she was ten with her Marxist family, who opposed Czarist Russia. A bright, outspoken woman, she loved poetry and loved to sing as she played the mandolin. She evidently enjoyed being a mother and had strong ties to her two sons, Allen and Eugene. She was a strong communist all her life; her sons heard many political arguments and even attended doctrinaire communist camps during alternate summers. Unfortunately Allen's mother developed paranoid schizophrenia and spent increasingly frequent periods in asylums while the boys were growing up. During periods when she was home, Allen often had to miss school to care for her. She separated permanently from Allen's father in 1943, and she died at Greystone Sanatorium in 1956. Allen's feelings about his paranoid mother haunted him all his life. He dealt with them in two poems: the long "Kaddish," written shortly after "Howl," and "Black Shroud," written twenty-five years later.

His father, Louis Ginsberg, was a poet who earned his living as a schoolteacher. He was an agnostic Jew who observed traditional Jewish holidays, and he was an active socialist. He married Naomi Levy in 1919 and cared for her and supported her through many illnesses. In 1949 he married Edith, a bright, lively woman who formed a warm, understanding relationship with Allen. Although they disagreed in politics and poetry, in both of which Louis was more conventional than iconoclastic Allen, father and son were close. They wrote each other frequently, with Louis objecting to what he considered crude and vulgar passages in Allen's poems, but praising and being proud of his son's fiery, imagistic poetry. Louis died in 1976.

Ginsberg's personal aesthetics matured slowly. Growing up in a home in which both father and mother were passionate about poetry, Ginsberg was surrounded by words and was a prolific reader. His decision to become a poet, however, did not crystallize until he was in college. At Columbia University, influenced by Lionel Trilling and Mark Van Doren as well as his father, he played with traditional aesthetics. As Ginsberg matured, he was more influenced in what and how he wrote by Walt Whitman, Ezra Pound, and William Carlos Williams, all of whom opened up the literary canon. Williams, also from Paterson, critiqued Ginsberg's early poems, and later, at Ginsberg's request, wrote an introduction to "Howl," the poem that shocked the world and made Ginsberg famous. Ginsberg came to think that artists should put "the raw material of your own actual experience in your work, whether it fits accepted aesthetics or not" (Ginsberg, 1993, p. 15). Photographers such as Alfred Stieglitz did that, as did William Carlos Williams in his poetry, which was built through visual images. Ginsberg liked Ezra Pound's description of one kind of poetry in *How to Read:* phanopeia, "the casting of images upon the visual imagination." Phanopoeic artists such as the photographers Alfred Stieglitz, Charles Sheeler, and Robert Frank, and poets such as William Carlos Williams and Hart Crane appealed to Ginsberg. These artists "shared a common aesthetic of precise observation, and understood the importance of close attention to detail" (Ginsberg, 1993, p. 15). Shared human experiences, feelings, and ideas were always extremely important to Allen Ginsberg.

In 1948 he had an experience that strongly affected his aesthetic consciousness for the next fifteen years. He had been reading deeply in the works of visionary William Blake. Ginsberg had a visionary experience of eternity, which he thought took him beyond himself into deeper creativity. Aesthetic exploration became his great aspiration. Largely to that end, he tried to recapture that experience by experimenting with mind-altering drugs: marijuana, mescaline, heroin, LSD, psilocybin, ayahuasca. To Ginsberg, drugs were not for partying; they were for expanding the mind, for opening up the consciousness. But a terrifying vision of death caused by his prolonged drug use eventually caused an oppressive anxiety within him that was so horrendous it made him vomit. Yet, he still wanted to recapture that Blakeian vision that would take him beyond his human limitations.

His release from drugs came through his study and eventual espousal of Zen Buddhism. In 1953 he spent many hours poring over Buddhist texts in the New York Public Library. Chanting mantras became another way to expand consciousness. Later, he and Jack Kerouac had a serious correspondence about Buddhism. In 1962 he and Peter Orlovsky traveled extensively in India, participating in many Hindu rituals and ceremonies. For example, in Calcutta, he participated in celebrations praising the Hindu goddess Kali and smoked ganja while spending nights in burning ghats. In India, his negative feelings about drugs were reinforced when he received word of the suicide of his friend Elise Cowen due to a breakdown from use of amphetamines. Depressed, he asked many holy men in India what he could do to attain his vision. He was told that he should accept his humanness, fulfilling his needs within his human self. Taking this advice, he liberated himself from drugs, and in 1972 took Buddhist vows. During the 1970s, he meditated a great deal, sometimes even eight hours a day. He chanted mantras during poetry readings and used a Tibetan bell and a harmonium as props. Over the years he met many Zen masters. The most influential was Tibetan Buddhist Chögyam Trungpa, whom he met in 1970.

Ginsberg reported that he became conscious of sexual fantasies at age eight and by fourteen had sexual crushes on many of his male classmates. Conscious that he was different, he did not tell anyone about his same-sex preference until he became close friends with Bill Burroughs and Jack Kerouac, with both of whom he eventually had a sexual relationship. Although he had long-term intimate friendships with these men, neither he nor his two partners regarded the relationships as sexually fulfilling. Kerouac preferred women, and Burroughs never really came to terms with his bisexuality.

His first complete sexual experience was with his Beat friend Neal Cassady, a socially fluent, self-assured, confident, smooth, virile, handsome, married bisexual hustler. Cassady was open to anything. Ginsberg reported his relationship with Cassady as intense and exciting. It was also a sadomasochistic one in which Cassady was the dominant. As described in detail in his poetry, dominance/submission roles excited Ginsberg. The relationship was fairly shortlived, but later briefly renewed in Denver where Cassady carried on simultaneous affairs with his former wife, LuAnne Henderson, with his wife to be, Carolyn Robinson, and with his old friend Ginsberg. Cassady ultimately rejected Ginsberg.

Ginsberg had many brief sexual encounters with other men and even had some experience with women, notably Sheila Williams Boucher, with

whom he briefly lived in San Francisco. During this time he also participated in a series of ménage-à-trois as well as group orgies. Then he met Peter Orlovsky, with whom he had his first completely reciprocal lovemaking
experience. The relationship, which they considered to be a marriage sealed
by vows (Ginsberg listed Orlovsky as his wife in *Who's Who*), began in the
mid-1950s and continued, with some periods of separation, for thirty years.
It was an open relationship, in part because Orlovsky was bisexual, and
Ginsberg did not object to Orlovsky's periodic affairs with women. Ginsberg divulged in a *Playboy* interview, however, that their sexual relationship
had ended by 1968 (Schumacher, 1992). Orlovsky was moody and dependent; Ginsberg was the dominant person, and his heavy-handed advice and
criticism caused considerable resentment in Orlovsky, who not only became
increasingly alcoholic but had several bouts with mental illness. Ginsberg
recognized that his experience with Orlovsky repeated his experience with
his "mother and the chaos she created" (Miles, 1989, p. 527).

The core of Beat group included Allen Ginsberg, Jack Kerouac, and Bill
Burroughs. These three had an intimate camaraderie in the 1940s. They
trusted each other and had the same attitude toward "hyper-militarization,
. . . the Atomic Era and the Age of Advertising, . . . Orwellian double-think."
Ginsberg says of them in retrospect, "Well, I had a sacramental sense of
these friends. . . . I was in love with them both in one way or another—with
Kerouac physically and with Burroughs sort of spiritually. I admired Burroughs as a seventeen-year-old boy would admire a man of about thirty
years—it was almost a kind of hero worship. They were teachers to me, and
I have a very strong devotional sense toward them both." They were all interested in writing, and by 1953 they had all written their first major works
and were "sort of cemented together for life" (Ginsberg in *Snapshot,* 1993,
p. 9).

Other people became part of the Beat group—Neal Cassady, Gregory
Corso, Lawrence Ferlinghetti, Peter Orlovsky. The Beatnik movement fed
the countercultural revolution of the 1960s. Rejecting traditional values and
codes of the "Establishment," especially materialism, it heralded individual
freedom and creativity and the value of intimate friendship with its candor
and honesty. Ginsberg's poetry reflects his beliefs. Ginsberg was an erudite
man, but he rejected intellectual analysis and opted for the spontaneous verbal outpouring of his being. Such spontaneous outpouring was reinforced
by the Buddhist belief in living in the moment. His poems reflect immediacy. No slow, careful composing for him; instead a capturing of what his
mind was thinking in the passing moment. The words on the page were not
superficial. Their immediacy came only after hours of meditation. William
Deresiewicz (2001) accurately describes Ginsberg's poetry: "Long lines of
thought unspool in image after startling image, gradually weaving them-

selves into argumentative structures of stunning density, originality and depth" (p. 6). His poetry reflects his intimate thoughts—condemnation of political actions of the United States; feelings about his mother and other relatives and friends; responses to daily happenings; explicit references to penises, anuses, juicy intercourse. In a section of his poem "I Went to the Movie of Life," for example, written from 4:30 to 6:25 a.m. on April 30, 1987, Ginsberg asks whom he should love, describes in sequence two men, and then realizes that there is no one to bring him scrambled eggs in bed when he wakes up, naked, from a dream.

> Who should I love? Here one with leather hat, blond hair
> strong body middle age, face frowned in awful thought,
> beer in hand by the bathroom wall? . . .
> No one I could find to give me
> bed tonite and wake me grinning naked with eggs scrambled
> at noon assembly when I opened my eyelids out of dream

(Ginsberg, 1994, p. 21)

Ginsberg became seriously interested in photography in 1984. He was coached largely by Robert Frank, author of *The Americans,* which had a strong impact on twentieth-century art photographers (Kohler in Ginsberg, 1993, p. 7). Under the influence of Frank, Ginsberg looked discriminately at the snapshots he had taken in the 1950s and 1960s. The art photographer Berenice Abbott also helped develop his photographic sensibility. Bob Dylan took an interest in Ginsberg's snapshots, asking that Ginsberg send him a large number to critique (Ginsberg sent 140) (Ginsberg, 1993, p. 14). These people helped Ginsberg look with a new eye at the many old snapshots that he took, "not to show others, but as keepsakes of my own total sacramental, personal interest in intimate friends." This capturing of important moments with intimate friends pervades his poetry also. He describes the pictures taken in Tangier in 1957 and 1961 as capturing "occasional and intermittent epiphanies" (Ginsberg, 1993, p. 10). Many of the pictures that had caught these fraternal moments turned out to be have artistic merit, and Ginsberg published them in 1993 in *Snapshot Poetics: A Photographic Memoir of the Beat Era.* Ginsberg realized that good photography had much in common with his own poetry: in both, the individual artist captured specific, real images of his chosen focus. After 1984, Ginsberg thought and taught about the parallels between photography and poetry (Kohler in Ginsberg, 1993, p. 7). He continued taking pictures and had many shows—in New York and throughout the world.

In spite of Ginsberg's conscious desire to gain media attention, in person he was kind and generous. He was interested in other people and looked for what held people together, what they had in common, not how they were different. One of his biographers, Michael Schumacher, reported that after eight years of doing research on Ginsberg, interviewing him many times and interviewing friends, family, and even nonfriendly acquaintances, he "came away in admiration of Ginsberg's candor, generosity, and overall spirit of humanity" (Schumacher, 1992, p. ix). Ginsberg needed love, approval, attention—and, sensitive to other people's needs, he gave these to family and friends.

To support himself he worked at a variety of unskilled jobs, and mooched off and shared with friends who were often as broke as he was. After "Howl" made him famous, his fees as a guest lecturer helped support him. For most of his life, he existed near the poverty level, but this did not seem to hinder him. He helped found the Jack Kerouac School of Disembodied Poetics at Boulder, Colorado, taught there for a time, and continued to give readings and lectures there. Ginsberg ultimately achieved financial security when he was appointed to a permanent position at Brooklyn College.

As his fame grew (and his fees rose), his tours extended. He traveled all over the world lecturing and reading his poetry. In his travels, however, he was never just a tourist. He read extensively about the places he visited to understand the history, the people, the culture, and the beliefs. He particularly enjoyed China, where many of the Chinese intellectuals seemed envious of his ability to be so candid. Ginsberg wrote in his journal that in China there seemed to be different levels of discourse: a public one and another, private level of consciousness with entirely secret views. What men really think, he said, "they tell only their wives, not even their children" (Schumacher, 1992, p. 683).

Ginsberg had a knack for working with people well known in other fields. With composer John Cage's music, he matched his photographs. He and Philip Glass paired poetry and music, and he did the same with rock musicians. With Russian poet Yevgeny Yevtushenko he wrote a political manifesto about Nicaragua. He collaborated or dialogued with W. H. Auden, the Beatles, Paul Bowles, Jean Genet, LeRoi Jones, Timothy Leary, and Andy Warhol. He had active exchanges with other poets—Robert Bly, Robert Creeley, Gary Snyder, and Philip Whalen. Not all was sweetness and light, however, and he had powerful enemies. Norman Podhoretz, for example, repeatedly attacked him for glorifying "madness, drugs, and homosexuality," charging that he ridiculed anything that society believed to be "healthy, normal or decent." He claimed that Ginsberg and Kerouac (and other Beats) played a major part in ruining a great many young people who were influenced by their "distaste for normal life and common decency" (Miles, 1989, p. 530).

Ginsberg was always fighting for the underdog and against the accepted protocol of the mainstream. Everyone knew where he stood, whether it was condemnation of Israel's actions on the West Bank, the unjustness of the Vietnam War, the injustice of America's role in overthrowing President Allende of Chile, or his vociferous opposition to any kind of censorship. Because he was just as outspoken abroad as at home, he was thrown out of both Cuba and Czechoslovakia for voicing his opinions about what was taking place in those countries.

Overall, he had a tremendous impact on his times while living in the world on his own terms. As far as homosexuality is concerned, he has to be counted as a moving force in encouraging other gays and lesbians to come out of the closet, if sometimes only to indicate that not all gays and lesbians were like him. He was a leader of the Beat generation; and although the movement has been criticized, as it has been by Norman Podhoretz and others, for challenging the status quo and by feminists for its sometimes misogynist views, the camaraderie and openness, the warmth and flamboyance of Ginsberg and his many male friends helped give strength to those who did not want to be forced to publicly conform to what they did not believe in, but who wanted to be themselves as they really were. He helped gays and lesbians realize they could be open about themselves.

BIBLIOGRAPHY

Cassady, Carolyn. *Off the Road: My Years with Cassady, Kerouac, and Ginsberg.* New York: William Morrow, 1990.

Deresiewicz, William. "First Thought, Best Thought." [A review of Allen Ginsberg, *Spontaneous Mind, Selected Interviews, 1958-1996,* David Carter (Ed.)]. In *New York Times Book Review,* April 8, 2001, Late Edition, Final, Section 7, p. 6.

Ginsberg, Allen. *Collected Poems, 1947-1980.* New York: Harper and Row, 1985.

Ginsberg, Allen. *Cosmopolitan Greetings: Poems 1986-1992.* New York: Harper Collins, 1994.

Ginsberg, Allen. *Howl and Other Poems.* San Francisco: City Lights, 1956.

Ginsberg, Allen. *Snapshot Poetics: A Photographic Memoir of the Beat Era.* Intro by Michael Kohler. San Francisco: Chronicle Books, 1993.

Ginsberg, Allen. *Wales—A Visitation. July 29th, 1967.* London: Cape Goliard Press, 1968.

Ginsberg, Allen. *White Shroud: Poems 1980-1985.* New York: Harper and Row, 1986.

Ginsberg, Edith. Personal interview. January, 1991.

Haggerty, George E. (Ed.). *Gay Histories and Cultures.* New York: Garland, 2000.

Hampton, William. "Allen Ginsberg, 70, Master Poet of Beat Generation," Obituary. *The New York Times,* April 6, 1997, Final, Section 1, p. 1.
Miles, Barry. *Ginsberg: A Biography.* New York: Simon and Schuster, 1989.
Schumacher, Michael. *Dharma Lion: A Critical Biography of Allen Ginsberg.* New York: St. Martin's Press, 1992.

Walter H. Breen (J. Z. Eglinton)
(1928-1993)

Donald Mader

Copyright 1991 by COIN WORLD.

Recent scholarship has emphasized homosexualities rather than simply the term *homosexual*. It is startling to note that, although coming from a very specific point of view, one of the pioneering studies by an American, *Greek Love,* anticipated this by at least thirty years. Walter Henry Breen (also known under his pseudonym J. Z. Eglinton) was the most important theorist of man-boy love to appear since the German figures (Benedict Friedlaender, Hans Blüher, the *Der Eigene* circle, Gustav Wyneken, and John Henry Mackay) in the first third of the twentieth century. Although retrograde (at least as compared with Mackay) in explicitly looking back to a Greek model, Breen independently affirmed, as they had, the distinction between what he termed "Greek love" (pederasty, or intergenerational homosexual relationships) and "androphile homosexuality" (eroticism between adult males). Although he himself argued that androphile homosexuality had usurped the "true" tradition of homosexuality which belonged to Greek love, viewed in a critical perspective this renewed insight opened the way in the United States for an understanding of homosexual behavior as a protean rather than a unitary phenomenon. In addition, he applied critical and historical research skills he had honed in his other areas of expertise to the exploration of the whole span of nearly 3,000 years of the recorded history of homosexuality. In an era—the 1950s and 1960s—when most writers favorable to homosexual behavior were either celebratory (Garde/Leoni) or wrote from a descriptive, sociological perspective (Stearn, Cory/Sagarin), Breen made a notable academic contribution to uncovering the history of homosexuality, and in the short-lived scholarly journal he conducted, encouraged others to do so too.

It has been over twenty years since I last saw Walter Breen. Although I vividly remember his general appearance—gray mane of hair and Whitmanesque beard flowing down over a gaudily flowered shirt unbuttoned to reveal a vast, hairy breast—I have difficulty fixing his height. Sober reflection indicates he was probably no taller than I, about six foot, but I am inclined to picture him as half a head taller. He literally left a larger-than-life impression.

This impression was the result of a remarkable force of personality that made Breen the center of attention in any gathering—be it a coin fair, a science fiction convention, or a movement meeting—of his prodigious intellectual energy, and, it must be admitted, of a carefully cultivated flair for the outrageous. For instance, although one of America's leading numismatic authorities, his best known pronouncement on the subject was, "I don't collect coins myself. That's only for rich people."

On the other hand, he had a good deal in the way of talents to cultivate, and a totally fallow field to work. Literally without precedents, he had been a foundling child, discovered in San Antonio, Texas, in 1928 (he used September 5 as his birth date). Developing a forceful personality and a drive for intellectual distinction may have been a coping strategy for claiming attention in the institutional and foster settings in which he grew up. Certainly his interest in reincarnation and his exploration of his "past lives" in Atlantis, Greece, Arthurian and Elizabethan England, and other eras might be seen as an effort to compensate for his lack of roots in this life; in effect, he created an identity for himself on *both* sides of his birth. He also found the etiology for his sexuality in his past lives; if it was classically Greek, that was because he had once sat literally at Socrates' feet.

He obtained his BA from Johns Hopkins in 1952, completing the four-year curriculum in just ten months, and qualifying for membership in Phi Beta Kappa. He also later completed the premedical course at Columbia and went on to complete a master's degree at University of California, Berkeley, in 1966, producing a thesis on "The Changing Social Status of the Musician." He was an accomplished pianist and an acknowledged expert on medieval and baroque music.

Even before his graduation, however, he was moving into the field where he would gain his greatest distinction. His earliest scholarly articles on the history of American coinage appeared in the *Numismatist* in 1951. His first book on numismatics, *Proof Coins Struck by the United States Mint, 1817-1901,* appeared in 1953. Following a number of similar specialized studies, beginning in the 1970s he came into his own in publishing with *Walter*

Breen's Encyclopedia of United States and Colonial Proof Coins, 1722-1977 (1977), *The Encyclopedia of United States Gold and Silver Commemorative Coins, 1892-1954* (with A. Swiatak, 1981) and *The Complete Encyclopedia of United States and Colonial Coins* (1988). For his studies in the field of numismatics he twice received the American Numismatic Association's Heath Literary Award, in 1953 and 1991, and the Rittenhouse Society awarded him the title of "Numismatic Scholar of the Twentieth Century" in 1992, citing his "generous contribution to knowledge through [his] enormous number of books, catalogues and magazine and newspaper articles and columns, . . . [and] amazing breadth and depth of extensive research on all phases of American numismatics" ("Rittenhouse," 1992, p. 81).

It is one of his specialized books, *Dies and Coinage,* published in 1962 by Robert Bashlow, which provides a link to our topic here. Breen and Bashlow shared more interests than numismatics: both had an erotic interest in younger males. A wealthy coin and bullion dealer who had already created one press for numismatic publications, Bashlow was persuaded to fund another press for issuing material on "sexual questions." Called the Oliver Layton Press, its first book was *Greek Love* (1964), by Breen, who for it adopted the pseudonym created for him by Bashlow, by which he was to be known in homosexual circles, J. Z. Eglinton. Their next project was a scholarly magazine on the topic, the *International Journal of Greek Love,* edited by Breen under his pseudonym. The first issue appeared in January 1965 and included, among other things, an article on Ralph Nicholas Chubb by Timothy d'Arch Smith (writing as "Oliver Drummond"), a discussion of the identity of the "Mr. W. H." of Shakespeare's sonnets by Breen himself, Warren Johansson's translation of Nacke's essay on Albanian boy-love, and "Feminine Equivalents of Greek Love in Modern Fiction" by Marion Zimmer Bradley. The second issue appeared nearly two years later, in November 1966, with articles on an anonymous pederastic manuscript, by Toby Hammond (d'Arch Smith again), pederasty in Turkey by Jonathan Drake (J. Parker Rossman), and the later career of John Francis Bloxam, the author of *The Priest and the Acolyte,* by Breen. In the meantime, Oliver Layton had published the classic *Asbestos Diary,* the first book by Casimir Dukahz (pseudonym of Brian Drexel, d. 1988). There were two other items from the press: a second edition of Tuli Kupferberg's *Book of the Body* (1966)—Kupferberg had been involved with Allen Ginsberg, Julian Beck, Frank Kameny, Paul Krassner, and others in the New York City League for Sexual Freedom, which was the only advertiser in the first issue of *IJGL*)— and the first edition of Michael Davidson's *Some Boys* (1969). Other projects announced—such as an English translation of Antonio Rocco's *Alcibiade Fanciullo a Scola* (a project which has defeated at least three publishers who have announced it, so that, scandalously, this important historical work became available in English only in 2001 by a different translator and publisher)—never came out. Editorial disagreements regarding how political *IJGL* should be led to a break between Breen and Bashlow in the early 1970s; an attempt to continue the journal with a new publisher under the title, *Kalos: On Greek Love,* but still under Breen's editorship yielded only one issue in the summer of 1976 before a second issue, the plates for which were later destroyed, was blocked by further editorial wrangling. Bashlow died in a hotel fire in Spain in 1980.

The dedication of *Greek Love* "to my beloved wife," and the presence in *IJGL* of Marion Zimmer Bradley, the science fiction author who had been incorporating homosexual themes in her stories since the mid-1950s and had also contributed to the *Mattachine Review* and the lesbian periodical *The Ladder,* is a link to another area of Breen's life and scholarship. Breen and Bradley had been married in February 1964. They had two children—a boy and a girl—from their marriage. In 1976 Breen, a frequent presence at science fiction conventions, published the first thorough study of Bradley's Darkover stories, *The Gemini Problem: A Study in Darkover,* and he also discusses her work, with that of many others, in his essay on science fiction and gender in the second issue of Sidney Smith's small press magazine *Dragonfly* (March 1976). (In that article he was also, as far as I know, the first to draw attention in print to homoerotic subtexts in the relation between Captain Kirk and Spock in *Star Trek.*) In *The Ladder,* in 1957, Bradley had defended lesbians entering heterosexual marriages, and Breen advocated the Greek model of married men who also loved adolescent boys. They separated after about twenty years of marriage, and were divorced in May 1990. Bradley died September 25, 1999.

Although based in Berkeley, California, Breen was frequently in New York for business in the 1970s and 1980s. He regularly stayed with Patrick MacGregor (b. 1947), bicycle repairman, poet, and proprietor of Blind Duck Press in the East Village, but if his stay extended to more than a few days I could count on him giving his host a break by calling and asking to visit my home in Brooklyn for an "after-dinner chat." He'd arrive around 7:00 p.m., and somewhere around 9:30 p.m. he would take out his Y Ching and throw his changes. This would inevitably produce something to the effect that it was "dangerous to cross the great water," which he would interpret as a warning that it was inadvisable to take the subway back under the East River, and ask to stay the night. He would then go to the spare bedroom to return with his stash and rolling papers. If it was at all a warm night, without a stitch of clothes on he would subsequently settle in on the couch and hold forth for another six hours or so on his research on Greek love (he was constantly revising the book for a proposed second edition); or other things such as explorations of his former lives; or the occasion when he had to defend his family and friends by making "sigils of power" with his fingers and hurling "flaming pentacles" at Lovecraftian monsters which had attacked them while they were ensconced in a hot tub in Marin County; or the time he had been overcome by a mystic trance on a visit to Glastonbury and was granted a vision of purple flames towering above the ruins and visited by the Wise Old Man. (Another acquaintance, a New York University writing instructor who in the 1960s had penned a classic of pederastic pornography under the pseudonym Colin Murchison, had also heard this tale, and always insisted the Wise Old Man was probably Breen's confused recollection of a custodian trying to extract him from the flower bed into which he had toppled backward after ingesting too much of some mind-altering substance.) You never knew quite what to expect from Walter; but one can imagine the effect such vivid accounts must have had on thirteen-year-olds.

On another of his visits, with malice aforethought, I arranged for another Atlantean, Rick Nielsen, photographer and owner of a gay cardshop-annex-gallery on lower Seventh Avenue in the Village, to come around so they could compare their past lives. They could agree on nothing: one insisted Atlanteans wore yellow robes; the other insisted on white, and so forth. By 4:00 a.m., when they decided they must have lived on the lost continent in different eras, I had long since ceased to find the confrontation amusing. These were also the years when Breen was close with the artist and micropress publisher Sidney Smith (b. 1950), who has left a portrait of him as the enthroned Pan in his book of drawings, *Manchild*.

It is not, however, his personal eccentricities, but his book *Greek Love* for which Breen deserves notice. The 500-page volume is divided into two almost equal parts: the first is a theoretical discussion and justification for man-boy homosexual relationships; the second is a survey of the cultural history of such relationships. It is very difficult to properly evaluate the book today, either for its theoretical argument or its historical scholarship.

It is almost impossible today to imagine oneself back in 1964. In light of the mass of historical research available on the subject today, it may seem absurd to think of attempting a cultural history of homosexuality in only 225 pages. But in 1964, aside from a burgeoning psychiatric literature which, while it disagreed on the causes of homosexuality and the prospects for its cure, was in total agreement that homosexuality was a mental illness which, untreated, doomed those afflicted with it to unhappiness and even suicide, one had a scattering of novels (many of which ended with suicide), and only a small handful of other texts such as Stearn's *Sixth Man,* Donald Webster Cory's *The Homosexual in America,* and, if one could find them, magazines such as *ONE* or the *Mattachine Review,* or, from France, *Arcadie.* The historical study most often cited as pioneering, *Jonathan to Gide,* by Noel I. Garde (Edgar H. Leoni), did not appear until that same year, 1964—and in comparison with Garde's almost exclusive use of secondary sources, Breen's fifteen years of research in primary sources has produced a far more thoroughly grounded and reliable work. There are remarkably few errors, and although there are certainly many points where Breen's work has been superseded by further studies, the breadth and quality of his research is astounding. As a scholarly history of homosexuality and its manifestations in culture, Part II of *Greek Love* is simply the first thing of its kind ever undertaken in the United States, the first research anywhere in decades to pick up the work of the scholars in Hirschfeld's *Jahrbuch,* and several decades ahead of its time, standing out all the more for the absence of anything similar around it.

But is it a "scholarly history of *homosexuality*"? If we have difficulty imagining how little positive or even objective information was available about homosexuality in 1964, we will have even greater trouble today imagining a "homosexuality" that does not conform to the present hegemonic gay model of relations between individuals exclusively oriented to their own sex and that does not transgress either gender definitions or age or power distinctions—a model that denies any place within "homosexuality" to relationships where the age and power of the partners differ, and indeed denies them the status of "relationship" between "partners" altogether, relabeling them "sexual abuse," with "perpetrators" and "victims." (It also—although it does not affect us directly here—tosses overboard effeminate homosexuals and transvestites and has no use for anyone who is not an exclusive homosexual, except to demand that they "come out of their closet.") We have in fact invented for ourselves a new "problem in Greek ethics": not that the founders of Western civilization practiced homosexuality, but that they were "child abusers."

It is ironic that the gay community has become most vocal in its denunciation of "child abusers" at precisely the time that ever-accumulating research is making it increasingly clear that such age-differentiated relationships between individuals who were not exclusively homosexual have always been a major strand—if not *the* major strand—in the phenomenon we call homosexuality. Even those gays who grudgingly admit this fact, however, regard it as a sign of the "maturity" that their movement has gained over the past twenty years and now repudiate this current as part of their history. Yet it is equally possible to regard contemporary self-definitions of the gay community not as "maturity" but as a recent and perhaps short-lived response to cultural trends which are at best less than a century old. It may well be that as research progresses and the prevalence of age-differentiated relationships in male-male erotic relations (at least when viewed historically and cross-culturally) is forced upon us, we will come to view a work such as *Greek Love* as ahead of its time in another way, through its insistence on examining relations of this sort as a dominant, if recently repressed, component of what we understand as homosexuality.

I have formulated that carefully because, to be totally frank, that is not what Breen is claiming for his Greek love, which he defines as the relation between an adult man and a younger boy (generally between ages twelve and seventeen) in which neither is exclusively homosexual—for only a man with heterosexual experience could guide the boy to a heterosexual outcome, which is the goal of Greek love. The man supplies a role model and the love (unconditional positive regard), which enables the boy's personality to develop healthily, performs a pedagogical function by teaching specific skills and generally initiating the boy into the adult world and its complexities and responsibilities (including preparing him for eventual heterosexual relations), and within this framework shares sexual or erotic experiences with the boy, who will then apply this experience in heterosexual practice. In return the man accepts the boy's love and admiration, and attains sexual satisfaction from their shared experience. In a position that harks back to the attitude taken by Friedlaender, Brand, and the *Der Eigene* circle toward Hirschfeld and "third sex" theories of homosexuality (arrived at independently, incidentally, as Breen does not seem to have known at the time of their critique of Hirschfeld), Breen in fact argues that Greek love has nothing to do with androphile homosexuality in any of its manifestations from Achilles and Patroclus through Genet (nor, for that matter, with Ulrichs' and Hirschfeld's "inverts"); for Breen, Greek love is the *true* tradition of male-male relations, to whose history these others have wrongly laid claim. This deposition of Greek love from its rightful place is largely, he argues, the result of antisexual mores, changes in the role and status of the adolescent in our culture over the past couple of centuries, and explicit campaigning on the part of the usurpers. He also, however, clearly distinguishes Greek love from pedophilia, or attraction to boys under the age of puberty; although he cites studies which indicate that in the absence of force or coercion, or later damaging interventions producing guilt, such activities are generally not harmful, he strongly denies that they can have any of the positive effects he associates with Greek love.

Not unexpectedly, then, the heart of Breen's argument is found in the chapter of the book entitled "Greek Love As a Solution to a Social Problem," and the two chapters of "case histories," "Uncomplicated Greek Love Affairs" and "Difficult Greek Love Affairs," in which the personal and social benefits he claims for Greek love are demonstrated, either by the success of an affair in making the boy a productive adult, or in showing the potential for that outcome destroyed by hostile social reactions. Also not unexpectedly, given the era in which he was writing, the "social problem" resolves itself into those 1950s bugaboos, juvenile delinquency and alienation. Friedenberg's *Vanishing Adolescent* is much cited, and the spirit of Paul Goodman, particularly in *Growing Up Absurd,* hovers over the whole (the footnotes reveal that Goodman and Breen evidently carried on a correspondence on this topic). If one is clued in to look, and knows the connection between the two authors, echoes of Breen's argument (in more academic garb and minus the sexual dimension) can be found a decade and a half later in *After Punishment, What?* (1980), by Yale's J. Parker Rossman.

One of the book's most curious features is a concluding written exchange on Breen's claims between Breen and Dr. Albert Ellis. Ellis was evidently approached because of his views—somewhat more liberal than his professional colleagues'—on homosexuality, as espoused in his *Sex Without Guilt.* Although Ellis praises the thoroughness of the research and clarity of his argument, he flatly rejects Breen's thesis: he doubts that love or even positive regard is the solution to the problems of alienated youth, and if it was, therapists and not passionate male lovers would be the proper individuals to administer it. Neither was the gay community as it developed after 1969 impressed, although some figures such as Jim Kepner, who have stood somewhat outside the mainstream of post-Stonewall gay organization, have acknowledged Eglinton's influence on their understanding of homosexuality.

Nor, finally, were later boy-love activists impressed. Daniel Tsang labels Greek love "the over-romanticized, idealized and often sexist and ageist relationship between a male adult 'mentor' and his young 'student' "; since gay liberation, he says, we have seen the light and rejected such "archaic" ideals with their goal of "a man guiding a young boy on his road to marriage, nuclear family, good citizenship and other aspects of straightdom" (Tsang, 1981, pp. 8-9). Tom Reeves took a similar potshot at men who "help boys grow up to be normal drones and good citizens" (Reeves, 1980, p. 3). They had hit the mark squarely: unquestionably *Greek Love* is vulnerable in attempting to apply an argument from utility to sexuality, seeking to justify the acceptance of a category of sexual relationships on the grounds of its purported social benefit, rather than demanding its equal right simply because it exists—and worse yet, like other artifacts of the 1950s, it was making the production of conforming individuals the criteria for that utility. Had they stopped there they would have been better off, but these critics seem oblivious to the fact that, although changing the goal, they apparently replicate the structure they also claim to detest, merely replacing "mentors" with members of a sort of revolutionary vanguard leading boys *away* from the evils of "straightdom." Others in the new movement, seeking also to avoid the charge of seduction, chose to emphasize the role of man-boy love in socializing "gay boys," ignoring the reality that most boys who become involved in such relationships ultimately become practicing heterosexuals.

Once again, the "mentor" structure was affirmed, this time explicitly, while rejecting the social goals Breen proposed for Greek love.

In view of Breen's rejection of Bashlow's desire to make *IJGL* more "political" and this hostility from the founders of NAMBLA, it is perhaps surprising to find Breen involved with the North American Man-Boy Love Association at all after its founding. However, J. Z. Eglinton was one of the keynote speakers at the organization's second conference in New York, at the Church of the Beloved Disciple, in the spring of 1979. Notes of his speech are found in *NAMBLA News* 2 (June 1979); it is striking that he no longer argues for acceptance of Greek love on the ground of its purported benefits to society, instead merely insisting that boys often benefit from experiencing loving intergenerational relationships. The major problem, he still maintains, is that these relationships are illegal; society should understand them, tolerate them, give them room to develop and flourish, and judge each relationship by its result. In *NAMBLA Journal* 3 (successor to the *News,* March 1980) he favorably reviews *Puppies,* by John Valentine (Chester Anderson, 1932-1991, of Haight Ashbury's "news before it happens"), the journal of a boy lover who, although wearing Levis rather than a toga, comes close to embodying Breen's ideal of Greek love. Except for occasional letters to NAMBLA publications, J. Z. Eglinton then fades from view as an advocate of Greek love.

In 1990 Breen was arrested on child molestation charges; the exact circumstances are hazy, as his legal strategy was to keep the arrest quiet and try to negotiate a settlement without publicity. He eventually (and perhaps suspiciously) was offered and accepted a plea bargain of three years' probation in return for pleading guilty to a felony charge involving a boy of fourteen or under. Shortly thereafter, in September 1991, at a public coin valuation day in Beverly Hills, he was arrested again—this time on eight felony molestation counts involving the thirteen-year-old son of acquaintances. There have been suggestions that these accusations were already in police hands when the bargain was offered, meaning that law enforcement officials knew this anticipated arrest would constitute a violation of his probation leading to automatic imprisonment and a long mandatory sentence when convicted on the new charges. In March 1992, after having surgery, he was diagnosed with terminal liver cancer. The trial on the new charges was delayed several times because of his health, but he eventually was sentenced to ten years' imprisonment. Walter Breen died on April 28, 1993, in the hospital ward of the state prison at Chino, California.

Although one numismatic journal carried an obituary, no gay publication reported his death—nor did NAMBLA's *Bulletin.* After many "past lives," to take him at his word, in eras when his Greek love could be expressed and appreciated, he had the misfortune this time to be born into our time, when such activity is calumniated and persecuted. He left behind his book, a monument of scholarship in its time. As idiosyncratic, romanticized, idealized—and dated—as its apologia for Greek love may be, it is a testament to an irradicable strain in human experience, one of the many facets of homosexual love: the love of a man for a youth and of a youth for a man.

BIBLIOGRAPHY

Breen, Walter, writing as J. Z. Eglinton. *Greek Love*. New York: Oliver Layton Press, 1964; second printing, 1965; British edition, London: Neville Spearman, 1971; German edition, *Griechische Liebe,* trans. Albert Y. Millrath. Hamburgh: Gala Verlag, 1967.

Breen, Walter, writing as J. Z. Eglinton. "Introducing a New Journal," *International Journal of Greek Love* 1:1 (January 1965), 3-4.

Breen, Walter, writing as J. Z. Eglinton. "Shakespeare's Boyfriend and Sonnet XX," *International Journal of Greek Love,* 1:1 (January 1965), 24-30.

Breen, Walter, writing as J. Z. Eglinton. "The Later Career of John Francis Bloxam," *International Journal of Greek Love* 1:2 (November 1966), 40-42.

Breen, Walter, writing as J. Z. Eglinton. "Responses to Letters to the Editor from Noel I. Garde," *International Journal of Greek Love* 1:2 (November 1966), 50-52.

Breen, Walter, writing as J. Z. Eglinton. "Review of John Valentine's *Puppies,*" *NAMBLA Journal* 2:3 (March 1980), 15.

Breen, Walter, writing as J. Z. Eglinton. "An Open Letter from J. Z. Eglinton," *NAMBLA Bulletin* 2:3 (April 1981), 4-5.

"Prolific Researcher Walter Breen Dies," *Coin World,* May 17, 1993, 3.

Reeves, Tom. "Letter." *NAMBLA Journal,* 3 (March 1980), 3.

"Rittenhouse Society Honors Breen," *Coin World,* August 10, 1992, 81.

Smith, Sidney. *Manchild*. Brooklyn, 1978.

"Summary of a Speech Given by J. Z. Eglinton," *NAMBLA News* 2 (Spring-Summer 1979), 4-5.

Tsang, Daniel. *The Age of Taboo*. Boston: Alyson/Gay Men's Press, 1981.

Warren Johansson (1934-1994)

William A. Percy III

Warren Johansson was, quite simply, the most extraordinary person I have ever known. Although a good number of our other pioneers in the homophile movement combined keen intellect and passionate commitment with various forms of eccentricity, none, in my opinion, matched Warren's mélange of brilliance, erudition, generosity, and mystery. As all who knew him well can attest, he was a gay cabalist par excellence, a labyrinth of profundities and secrets. I spent much time with him for almost a decade, during the last half of which he lived in my house, yet for years I did not even know his real name. To this day, eight years after his death, he remains a fascinating enigma.

Born Peter Joseph Wallfield in Philadelphia, February 21, 1934, Warren early on exhibited a genius for linguistics. In time he mastered every modern European language except Basque (unrelated to any other known language) and the Finn-Ugrian (Siberia-derived) tongues. He read Greek and Hebrew in their multifarious forms, and although I am a professor of medieval history, a field noted for its Latinists, I've never met anyone who equaled Warren's facility with ancient, church, and modern scholarly Latin. These skills gave him access to the wellspring of true historical scholarship: original texts and their mutations. He could read them all. More than anyone, perhaps, he really *did* read them all, including, while he was still an undergraduate, the entire twenty-three–volume set of the *Jahrbuch Für Sexuelle Zwischenstufen (Yearbook for sexual intergrades)*, the world's first periodical to publish articles on homosexuality by experts in numerous fields, edited by the legendary Magnus Hirschfeld in Berlin between 1899 and 1923. Warren was, perhaps, the leading American authority not only on Hirschfeld but also on all Germanic and Slavic writers on homosexuality. His reach extended far beyond that, however. He mastered, for example, the papyrological antecedents of important biblical passages. From all of this flowed a vast knowledge of history, philology, and etymology, which he applied to uncovering nuances of homosexual experience since ancient times. Indeed, Warren documented historical evidence from many obscure foreign language sources that would have remained unknown to us but for his tireless efforts. His passion to look things up and track details down assisted countless academics and journalists throughout the world on myriad projects concerning the gay and lesbian past.

But Warren didn't confine himself to scholarship. He belonged to many activist groups, often as a founding member, including the NYC Gay Liberation Front of 1969, GLAAD/NY, the NYC Coalition for Lesbian and Gay Rights, ACT UP, Queer Nation, and Gay and Lesbian Americans. His first contribution to the queer cause came in 1955, when he mixed scholarship with activism in sending an obscure but crucial statement by Sigmund Freud to the Wolfenden Committee, the parliamentary body that initiated the decriminalization of sodomy in Great Britain and subsequently throughout most of that nation's former empire. The statement, made in an interview with the editor of the Vienna newspaper *Die Zeit* and printed in the issue of October 27, 1905, was Freud's earliest published advocacy for tolerance for homosexuals. It had been overlooked until Warren called it to the Wolfenden Committee's attention. Prompted by the prosecution of a professor who had had sex with two young men whom he had hired to pose for photographs, the statement read, in part:

> [L]ike many experts, I uphold the view that the homosexual does not belong before the bar of a court of justice. I am even of the firm conviction that the homosexual cannot be regarded as sick, because the individual of an abnormal sexual orientation is for just that reason far from being sick. Should we not then have to classify many great thinkers and scholars of all ages, whose sound minds it is precisely that we admire, as sick men? (reprinted in the *Encyclopedia of Homosexuality,* 1990, p. 434)

Warren later provided expert testimony to the legislative bodies and policymakers of several countries that were considering the reform of laws that affected gay people.

Warren's "guru" was Walter Breen, a world-renowned numismatist who, with Warren's extensive assistance, authored the "bible of the pederasts," *Greek Love* (1964), under the pseudonym J. Z. Eglinton. In fact, Warren virtually co-authored the book, which today still remains the starting point for the study of the cultural history of pederasty and pedophilia and a vital source of information; many scholars have mined the footnotes and followed their pioneering clues. A groundbreaking survey of boy love in the Western world from ancient Greece to modern times, *Greek Love* naturally contained a number of errors that increasingly were recognized as knowledge in the field burgeoned. Eglinton and Warren intended to put out an expanded second edition to correct the errors but could not agree on a vital point: Eglinton insisted on advocating no age limit for sex with boys, while Warren backed a cutoff of fourteen.

Warren contributed important articles to a journal, published by the Scholarship Committee of New York's Gay Academic Union, which appeared under three different names: *Gai Saber* (1977-1978), *Gay Books Bulletin,* and *Cabirion* (1979-1985). "The Etymology of the Word *Faggot*" (*Gay Books Bulletin,* 6, 1981), definitively showed that "faggot . . . is purely and simply an Americanism of the 20th century" (p. 16)—not, contrary to a popular gay myth, derived from a practice of using homosexuals as kindling to burn witches at the stake in medieval times. With characteristic authority and clarity, Warren wrote:

> On a conscious level it [the notion that "faggot" as a pejorative term for gays entered the language because homosexuals were thought to have been used as fuel for witch-burning] serves as a device with which to attack the medieval church, by extension Christianity in toto, and finally all authority. On another level, it may linger as a "myth of origins," a kind of collective masochistic ritual that willingly identifies the homosexual as victim. (p. 16)

In another article, "Whosoever Shall Say to His Brother, *Racha* (Matthew: 5:22)" (*Cabirion,* 10, 1984), Warren trained his formidable philological acumen on a biblical passage to undermine another myth, widely believed by both straights and gays, that Jesus "never mentioned homosexuality." In a subsequent version of the article, he concluded:

> What the text in Matthew demonstrates is that he [Jesus] forbade acts of violence, physical and verbal, against those to whom homosexuality was imputed, in line with the general emphasis on self-restraint and meekness in his teaching. The entire passage is not just a legalistic pastiche of Jewish casuistry, but also a polished gem of double entendre and irony. (*Encyclopedia of Homosexuality,* 1990, p. 1093)

Warren also provided indispensable editorial contributions to three quite significant books assembled under the direction of Wayne R. Dynes: *Homolexis: A Historical and Cultural Lexicon of Homosexuality* (1985),

which contained Warren's "The Sodomy Delusion: A Typological Recon-
struction"; *Homosexuality: A Research Guide* (1987); and the prizewinning
two-volume *Encyclopedia of Homosexuality* (1990). With me he co-
authored *Outing: Shattering the Conspiracy of Silence* (1994), and he offered utterly essential assistance with my *Pederasty and Pedagogy in Ancient Greece* (1996), as well as with numerous book reviews, articles, and
anthology chapters, including "Homosexuality" in *Handbook of Medieval
Sexuality* (1996) and "Homosexuals in Nazi Germany" in *Simon Weisenthal
Center Annual VII* (1990).

   The Encyclopedia of Homosexuality was an important vehicle for trans-
mitting Warren's findings to a larger public. Unfortunately, a leftist-feminist
cabal attacked the volume for failing to propagate their "revolutionary"
views. Among other complaints, this group disapproved of the pseudonym
Evelyn Gettone, employed (along with Ward Houser) by both Warren and
Wayne Dynes. For more than a century pseudonyms had been in common
use among gay scholars and activists. Generally, male names had been used
by women and female ones by men.

   In 1995 the cabal used the controversy to accomplish its aim of suppressing the *Encyclopedia*. With professed outrage over the name Evelyn Gettone having been used by men, and wielding threats of boycotts, they persuaded Garland Publishing to withdraw the *Encyclopedia* despite the fact
that no significant inaccuracies had been detected. Now unavailable for purchase, the work, with many signal contributions by Warren Johansson, can
still be consulted in many libraries.

   Despite his learnedness and dedication, Warren never sought the limelight. In fact, he often published pseudonymously, and most of the rest of his
work saw print as collaborations with other writers who usually received top
billing on the title page, often the only billing. This reflected two major
components of Warren's personality, to which I've already alluded: a spectacular capacity for generosity, and a general secretiveness deployed to such
a degree that it could be fairly termed a fetish.

   The aforementioned Wayne Dynes met Warren in the early 1970s, a time
when gay studies had not yet become an established academic discipline,
and the very notion of queer studies would have been considered science
fiction. I, and many others, hold that there have been three phases in the recent studies of homosexuality and lesbianism. The first phase, labeled the
homophile phase, might be called an apologetic one: homosexuals are here
to stay but are nice people; the second or gay studies phase held that gay is
good and society should accept this as a fact of life; the third or queer studies
phase is an unapologetic, assertive, in-your-face attitude using the tactics of
street theater. No formal system then existed to codify knowledge of homosexuality's significance; to be a student of the subject perforce made one an

autodidact. But Dynes observes that those lucky enough both to know Warren and learn from him got the rough equivalent of a graduate school education in the history of same-sex eros. He was, in short, a mentor for gay intellectuals. Besides Dynes, those who benefited from his tutelage included Gene Rice, John Lauritsen, David Thorstad, Jonathan Katz, James Steakley, Steve Alt, a host of others, and, as must by now be clear, me.

It's worth noting in passing that although Warren worked on a dissertation on the gay Russian poet Alexander Pushkin, under the direction of the distinguished Columbia professor Ihor Sevcenko, for whom Warren also served as an assistant, he never received a PhD. His advanced degrees were limited to an MA in Slavic languages and a certificate in Sovietology from Columbia's Harriman Institute. But then, Warren wasn't inclined to pursue a conventional academic career, possibly because it would have entailed too much scrutiny of his personal life.

More broadly, regarding his generosity, Warren was unstinting in sharing his knowledge and research skills with almost anyone. Friend or stranger had but to ask him a question—on a huge range of topics—and he either would deliver a comprehensive discourse on the spot or head for the appropriate library. C. A. Tripp, author of the acclaimed best-seller *The Homosexual Matrix,* recalls that Warren helped him resolve a dispute with Paul Gebhard, a senior associate of Alfred Kinsey, after Gebhard had objected to a passage in Tripp's book that addressed certain Jewish traditions of family members kissing the penises of newly circumcised boys. "You picked that up from Kinsey, didn't you?" Gebhard had asked Tripp.

"Well, yes, I certainly did," Tripp replied. "What's the matter?"

Gebhard declared, "I checked it with the local rabbi, who walks by my house every day, and he said he'd never even heard of this penis-kissing business. I think Kinsey made it up."

The very idea incensed Tripp, who himself had been closely associated with Kinsey. He said, "Kinsey did not *make things up.*" To settle the matter he turned to Warren, who said with his customary pixieish alacrity, "I'll be back to you in two days" (Tripp, 1999).

Warren proceeded to find references that fully corroborated the passage in Tripp's book. Tripp was delighted. "So I then sat down, *armed by Warren,* and wrote a sharp letter to Gebhard. He wrote back saying, 'Well, you've certainly won *that* argument.'" Tripp also notes that as eccentric as Warren was, he always wrote with superbly balanced perspective: "His personal oddness never crept in" (Tripp, 1999).

A lot of people won arguments with Warren's help, for nothing pleased him more than to ferret out the most recondite underpinnings of an intellectual controversy, particularly if he could expose falsities in conventional or superficial thinking. As seen previously in the discussions of "faggot" and "racha," he loved to demystify; to challenge myth was a kind of crusade. It is, then, no small irony that he chose to mystify quite thoroughly all who knew him when it came to the topic most central to his own life: Warren himself.

To impart a sense of just how slippery a character Warren was with regard to his identity and background, one must begin with his appearance, style of living, and habits. His narrow shoulders and ample tummy made him pear-shaped, a fact somewhat disguised by his unvarying custom of wearing a jacket and a tie in settings both public and private. His bushy beard gave him a rabbinical aura; Wayne Dynes remembers that when Warren was marching in one of New York City's Gay Pride parades, a spectator approached him and exclaimed, "Ah, Rabbi, what an honor to have you here!" The salutation pleased Warren, for he enjoyed projecting a sense of cultivated authority. Dynes thought he resembled Karl Marx; Warren, fastidious in such matters, preferred to be likened to Friedrich Engels. Warren's self-image, which sprang from complex depths, wasn't merely a question of vanity. He saw himself as conforming to the ideal of the Talmudic scholar, a role with ramifications: in exchange for dispensing wisdom to his community, he expected food and lodging free of charge. This Warren took to amazing lengths, which indeed his circumstances obliged him to do, for as far as anyone could tell, he never held even one paying job after he gave up his graduate school assistantship at Columbia.

In consequence Warren literally was homeless for extended periods of time. He often stayed overnight in various New York City libraries, particularly those affiliated with Columbia. For hygiene and, probably, sex (although on this point as with so much else about his life, no one really knows), he frequently relied on gay bathhouses. Food he scrounged from hors d'oeuvres tables at art gallery openings or academic receptions and from the largesse of friends such as Wayne Dynes, Gene Rice, and me. A gourmand as well as a gourmet, Warren was something of a scandal when taken out to restaurants: he often would order two full courses or sometimes as many as four or five entrées. Dynes used to remark that he was like a camel, able to eat so much at a single sitting that he could go for days on very little. I have never seen anyone eat such quantities and enjoy it so much. When he lived with me in Boston during the last five years of his life, countless roasts traveled from my stove to the dining table and down his gullet—goose, lamb, beef, ham, with all the accoutrements; he didn't disdain lobster, shrimp, and crab. In line with his self-image as a Talmudic sage, one to whom certain deferences must be accorded in recognition of his contributions, he never helped with cooking, washed dishes, or even took his plates back to the kitchen. That bothered me not a bit, for I never had any doubt that Warren's contributions were priceless and unique. During those last years he grew immensely fat, approaching 300 pounds until cancer struck him, after which he slowly wasted away to almost nothing.

Earlier, in New York City, where Warren lived most of his life, Wayne Dynes, Gene Rice, Steve Alt, and others saw to his welfare, but with the exception of Alt, with whom he stayed for about three years, they didn't house him on a regular basis, hence his reliance on libraries and bathhouses. One might wonder how, under such circumstances, Warren maintained his uniform of jacket and tie. The answer is that he wore the same set of clothes until they nearly decayed, then replaced them. The only known repository for his personal effects was a rental locker at Columbia, hardly a place to keep a wardrobe. The locker, incidentally, became the subject of lore: Warren intimated that he kept fabulous treasures in it, without ever quite specifying what they were. Whatever the contents were, a custodian threw them out after one of Warren's benefactors forgot to pay the locker fee.

In short, Warren did not always present the tidiest of appearances. Dynes remembers that Warren's ties tended to become "symphonies of squalor," casualties, among other things, of his gourmandizing ways. They accumulated months of dietary history that a forensic expert no doubt could have reconstructed—an idea Warren would have found deeply alarming.

For reasons never satisfactorily explained, Warren had a horror of anyone reconstructing *anything* about his past. He refused to be photographed, for example, and would go to great lengths to avoid it. I have but two pictures of him, one the photo in his passport (which he never used to go abroad), the other a small detail blown up from somebody's snapshot of a Gay Pride parade. We know that he wrote under three pseudonyms in his articles for the *Encyclopedia of Homosexuality* alone, but do not know, and never will, how many other literary aliases he used elsewhere. About his family and upbringing he maintained the strictest silence, except to claim that his father was a gentile emigré from one of the Baltic states, that his mother was Jewish, and that some twenty-odd relatives had attended either the University of Pennsylvania or Columbia. I assumed that many of these relatives were rabbis, but Warren wouldn't confirm or deny that. In fact, he not only refused to talk about his family, but he also, as far as we know, had absolutely no contact with even one member since shortly after his mother's death during his graduate school years.

Some of the few details I've gleaned about his family came from his high school classmate and academic rival, Howard Reilly. Howard was my classmate at Princeton, a Rhodes scholar, and a Harvard Law School graduate. He went on to practice law at an exclusive Denver firm until a gay sex scandal quite completely wrecked his career; rumors had it that he was reduced to waiting on tables in Mafia-connected restaurants. When I contacted him, against Warren's repeated and emotional forbiddings, he was working a modest legal-aid job in upstate New York, and losing a war with AIDS.

Howard told me that Warren's mother had been a schoolteacher, his father a druggist "who worked seven days a week and saved his money," and that both parents had strongly supported Warren's scholarly endeavors in high school. The father's job situation struck me as descriptive of the many Jews whom prejudice and quotas had kept out of medical school, and I wondered if Warren had fibbed about his father being a gentile.

Just recently I learned that Warren had indeed misrepresented his father's religion. A man called my house out of the blue and asked for Joseph Wallfield. The caller identified himself as Roger Nyle Parisious. He said that he'd met Warren at Columbia in 1958 and had stayed in touch with him off and on, but never had learned that his old chum from graduate school days had changed his name. However, he knew facts about Warren's past that Warren painstakingly concealed from his gay-movement friends, among them the brutal 1957 murder of his father in Philadelphia.

Jacob Wallfield, Warren's father, died at age seventy-five of a shotgun blast to the abdomen during an attempted robbery of his pharmacy. The fact that the shooter and his two accomplices were fifteen-year-old blacks, coupled with Jacob's status as a beloved pillar of his community, made the story big news in the then racially charged atmosphere of the city. Parisious recalls that when he first met Warren about a year after the murder, Warren insisted on showing friends a sheaf of clippings from newspaper articles on the tragedy. He would proffer the clippings with reverent intensity, "smiling at them in a chilling, even terrible fashion"; his father's passing and the manner of it clearly tormented him. That isn't so very remarkable, of course. What *is* remarkable is that, years later when Warren entered his prime as a gay intellectual, he never once mentioned his father's death to any of his activist friends. Why did he erase an event that he had freely disclosed to friends in the late 1950s? Why did he conceal the fact that his father was indeed Jewish?

Whatever the reasons, he remained obsessed with the history of the Jews, whose intellectual capacities he naturally admired, but whose homophobia and superstition he despised. Indeed, he spent most of his life attacking the Judaic homophobic tradition. It's possible, I suppose, that he felt a degree of self-loathing both about being Jewish and about being gay.

Warren proceeded to abandon his Pushkin dissertation, and at this time also became close to J. Z. Eglinton. Warren once told me that Eglinton "saved" him and hinted that his guru helped him stave off a nervous breakdown. Another factor transformed his life as well: he inherited $5,000 from his father, the equivalent of about $50,000 today. Warren went on a spending spree, indulging in bespoke suits and expensive meals at the very best restaurants. When his mother died a couple of years later, in 1959 or 1960, she much to his surprise left him a large sum, the equivalent of perhaps half a million today, and Warren's extravagances correspondingly expanded. The inheritance must have been the source of another of Warren's mysteries: his "trust fund," to which he made cryptic allusions from time to time even into the early 1990s.

None of us ever saw any proof of such a fund. When he died the only bank account we found, in New York City, contained just $1,500, which I had paid him. (As he left no will, and had no known relatives, it went to the state.) But when Charley Shively first met him at a "New Left Gathering of Tribes" in Atlanta (August 1971), Warren had arrived in a Mercedes, wearing a black suit with tie, which he never loosened in the hot Georgia sun. As the gay tribal contingent changed into women's dresses and called for the straight men to come out of the closet, Warren remained to one side. He nonetheless made friends with Lee Stone, a young, half-nude, dancing street boy revolutionary hustler, and they slipped away to a nearby motel.

Years after Warren's death, Ihor Sevcenko, his Pushkin dissertation advisor at Columbia, lunched with me at the faculty club at Harvard (where he then taught) to discuss the mystery of Warren's name change; we didn't settle it, needless to say. Ihor mentioned that "Joseph," as he couldn't help calling Warren, often spoke of taking his nephew out to dinner at the finest New York City restaurants. I was amused by what I thought to be Ihor's naïveté, for I assumed that this "nephew" was one of the ephebe types that Warren courted—but was even more amused by the eminent professor's remark, delivered with great indignation, "And you know, he never once invited *me* out!" However, I recently learned that Warren did indeed have a nephew, a football star at the University of Pennsylvania, on whom he may well have doted.

By his middle New York City years, he had no apparent income. That fact, coupled with his other oddities and his penchant for attending every gay event to gather all available literature, generated a persistent rumor among New York City activists: "This Johansson weirdo has to be an undercover police agent."

I always found that idea preposterous. Dynes observes that, politically speaking, Warren veered from the far left to the far right and abhorred the comfortable middle. He was something of a mugwump, however, reluctant to take a stand on volatile issues, and he rarely spoke up at meetings unless he was specifically addressed. Furthermore, because he never mentioned his sex life, Warren made it easy for acquaintances to construe him as a deeply conflicted closet type. To many, in those justifiably paranoid times, this presented the profile of an informant.

As to Warren's sex life, almost no one with whom I've discussed the matter seems to have met any of his tricks. He always professed to be an ephebophile, attracted to late adolescents, but with a guru such as Eglinton—author of the "bible of the pederasts," cowritten with Warren—well, who knows? John Lauritsen recounts to this day with astonishment how he and Warren once were invited by Eglinton to meet for dinner at a good New York restaurant. When they arrived, Eglinton already was seated, outfitted from head to toe, for reasons he didn't explain, in a Santa Claus costume. He proceeded to dine, drink, and converse as if there were nothing out of the ordinary about his apparel.

Later, a couple of years before Warren's death, Eglinton was sentenced in California for activities with two brothers of nine and eleven—not, I think, his first brush with the law, but his first imprisonment. I said to Warren, "A little money goes a long way in prison. Why don't I send him some?"

To my surprise, Warren became terribly agitated, more upset than I'd ever seen him. He exclaimed, "We could get in trouble!"

I replied, "But I've never done anything felonious." (Except sodomy, of course.) Warren was so perturbed, however, that I broke off the conversation. When I again brought up the subject several days later, he was equally adamant, and I dropped it. His fearfulness made me wonder if his name change, refusal to be photographed, estrangement from his family, and secrecy about his erotic encounters might stem from legal trouble, possibly for underage sex. At some point or another, had Warren himself played "Santa"?

The question wouldn't be significant or even interesting if Warren's life weren't very much both of those things, but it is, which to my mind justifies subjecting all of his secrets to speculation. Not a day passes that I do not think of him, for I loved him and still miss him more than anyone I have ever lost. Daily, too, I curse the illness that took him from us when he had so much yet to contribute, and which, as if manifesting the bleakness that underlay Warren's mordant sense of humor, provides an uneasy coda for a world-class linguist who loved to eat and hated to talk about himself: Warren Johansson, a lifetime nonsmoker, died of cancer of the tongue in 1994. I wish he were still feasting at a laden table. I wish he were still reclining in his chair, belching with contentment, confident that others would bear his plates back to the kitchen.

BIBLIOGRAPHY

Bullough, V. L. and Brundage, J. *Handbook of Medieval Sexuality*. New York: Garland, 1996.

Dynes, W. R. (Ed.). *Encyclopedia of Homosexuality*. 2 volumes. New York: Garland, 1990.

Dynes, W. R. *Homolexis: A History and Cultural Lexicon of Homosexuality*. New York: Scholarship Committee, Gay Academic Union, 1985.

Dynes, W. R. *Homosexuality: A Research Guide*. New York: Garland, 1987.

Johansson, W. "The Etymology of the Word Faggot," *Gay Books Bulletin,* 6 (1951), 16-18, 33.

Johansson, W. "Whosoever Shall Say to His Brother, *Racha* (Matthew 5:22)," *Cabirion and Gay Books Bulletin,* 10 (1984), 2-4.

Percy, W. A. *Pederasty and Pedagogy in Archaic Greece*. Urbana: University of Illinois Press, 1996.

Percy, W. A. and Johansson, W. *Outing: Shattering the Conspiracy of Silence*. New York: The Haworth Press, 1994.

Tripp, C. A. Personal interview by the author, 1999.

Donald Webster Cory (1913-1986)

Stephen O. Murray

> In a world in which one is rewarded for concealment and submission, it would be difficult to expect the reverse.
>
> Cory and LeRoy (1963, p. 213)

Donald Webster Cory was the pseudonym under which Edward Sagarin wrote about the plight of homosexuals during the 1950s and early 1960s. His 1951 book, *The Homosexual in America,* was important in its day for describing from the inside something of the experience of stigmatization and discrimination homosexuals experienced. Cory participated in the incipient homophile movement and—in work that hid his involvement and bitter feelings of rejection—wrote about the Mattachine Society of New York.

Photo by Sal Terracina

Edward Sagarin was the youngest of eight children of a Russian Jewish immigrant couple. He was born in Schenectady, in upstate New York, on September 18, 1913, with scoliosis (a "humpback"). His mother died in the Spanish influenza epidemic of 1918. Edward did not get along well with his stepmother, and broke with his father. He also spent more than a year in France before starting at the City College of New York.

Under the auspices of the National Student League, he was an observer (until asked to leave by the lead defense counsel) at the 1933 "Scottsboro boys" trial, a

I am grateful to Wenshen Pong for an extended loan of Sagarin's doctoral dissertation; to Barry Adam, Don Eckeman, Vern Bullough, John Gagnon, David Greenberg, Frank Kameny, Brian Miller, Peter Nardi, Ken Plummer, and Dennis Wrong for prompt and helpful responses to my flurry of questions. This chapter's readability has been enhanced by comments on an earlier draft by Wayne Dynes, John Alan Lee, and Peter Nardi.

notorious case of young African Americans accused of raping white women that was cause celèbre at the time in left-wing circles.

Under the pseudonym Donald Webster Cory (a variant on the title of André Gide's apologia *Corydon,* which in turn is the name of the shepherd in Virgil's second eclogue in love with the handsome boy Alexis) Sagarin reported that since his early adolescence, he had been aware of the "homosexual problem." His first awakening came with the "bewildering attraction" he felt for a young man a few years his senior. He had never before realized that there were men who were attracted to other men and "no one had attempted to seduce . . . or . . . tempt" him. He knew only that he had a drive "of a vague and troublesome character" for another person of the same sex whom he wanted to be near and to embrace. Still, he remained completely ignorant of any facts of homosexuality until a teacher in high school took him aside and, after engaging him in conversation, explained that there were people called "inverts."

He wanted to know more and spent his years of later adolescence and early manhood delving into every volume of literature that he thought might give him enough information to understand why he could not be like others. He was, he reports, deeply ashamed of being abnormal and was aware of the heavy price he would pay if anyone were to discover his secret. Similar to many other homosexuals at that time, he struggled against his homosexuality, sought to discipline himself and to overcome it, punished himself for failures to resist sinful temptations, yet the struggles did nothing to diminish the needs within him (Cory, 1951, p. 11). What did diminish was the length of his relationships with other males:

> A friendship of a rewarding character developed when I was sixteen, lasted for two years, but ended, as others were to end later. Then the passions endured only a few months, and then a few weeks, and I was scornful of those who would use the word love to describe such relationships. Homosexual love, I told myself, is a myth. . . . At the age of twenty-five, after determining that I was capable of consummating a marriage, I was wedded to a girl whom I had known since childhood. (Cory, 1951, p. 12)

Esther Gertrude Lipschitz, a fellow student leftist, married Sagarin in 1936. She became a housewife but continued to be politically active. He later reported that she was "the only woman I had ever had erotic feelings towards" (quoted by Duberman, 1997, p. 8; see also Cory, 1951, p. 203). It is unclear whether her "deep understanding" of Sagarin originally included knowledge of his homosexual history and frequently acted-upon desires. I infer that Esther did not know from one of Sagarin's passages: "I resolved that marriage would be the end of my sins, that I would sever my ties with the homosexual circles and with my dear friends therein, and built what appeared to be the only life that might be fruitful for me" (Cory, 1951, p. 12), and from the representation of the usual pattern Cory (1951, p. 204-205) posited. The coupling was literally fruitful: they had a son, Fred. Nonetheless, Sagarin "was not long in learning that marriage did not reduce the urge for gratification with men. . . I needed my former companionships, but I would not allow myself to admit, even in the silence of the thought process, that I wanted them" (1951, p. 12).

He must have thought about it, however, because he began a long psychoanalysis. As it proceeded, he realized that it "was going to help me overcome my feelings of shame, guilt, remorse, rather than overcome the impulses which brought forward these feelings" (1951, p. 12). In a chapter from *The Homosexual in America* (1951) that was also printed in the journal *Sexology,* he challenged not only the likelihood of "curing" homosexuality but the consideration of it as a disease. Far from hostile to therapy, even psychoanalysis, Cory insisted that the purpose of therapy was not to make a person a heterosexual, but to transform him into a well-integrated and happy invert. That such a goal was impeded by social conditions beyond the control of the therapist or the patient merely meant that it was a problem that extended to all society and thus could not be entirely solved on the analyst's couch. In this respect, it was not unlike the psychological problems that arise from racial discrimination. "Self-acceptance is the basis of the adjustment of the homosexual" (Cory, 1951, p. 178). Advocating conscious sublimation of homosexual urges rather than repression or suppression, he described a continued acting on urges such as his by primarily homosexual men who married women.

The book has a strikingly ambivalent three-page introduction by Albert Ellis, PhD (then chief psychologist for the New Jersey Diagnostic Center and recent author of *The Folklore of Sex*), that "take[s] issue with Mr. Cory's pessimism concerning the possibility of adjusting homosexuals to more heterosexual modes of living" and with the inborn and compulsive natures of homosexuality (Cory, 1951, p. 8). Ellis denied to Martin Duberman (1997, p. 11) that he was close to Sagarin or had ever been his therapist, although Sagarin's views about the pathology of exclusive homosexuality moved closer to Ellis's after publication of *The Homosexual in America.* Ellis claimed that "after their 'few, informal sessions' together, Cory was able to get more pleasure from sex with his wife." Duberman (1997, p. 11) also records Ellis's disbelief in the extended analysis Cory claimed in *The Homosexual in America,* noting that "when I met Cory he was an exceptionally promiscuous gay man."

Having had to drop out of college for lack of money during the 1930s, Sagarin put his fluency in French to use, handling French correspondence for a cosmetics company. He moved into sales and management, acquiring considerable knowledge about the manufacture of perfumes. As an adjunct instructor at Columbia University, he taught a course on the chemistry of perfume, published a book on *The Science and Art of Perfumery* in 1945, followed in 1947 by *Natural Perfume Materials,* a three-volume copiously illustrated collection on the materials and their combinations in *Cosmetics, Science and Technology,* published in 1957 (second edition, 1972-1974) and still in print.

Sagarin (1951, p. 245) considered the epoch-making publication of the Kinsey report on the human male in 1948 and included what he saw as two significant breakthroughs: showing that homosexuality was not rare, and bringing the subject out into open discussion. Sagarin decided that its objectivist survey of sexual outlets needed to be supplemented by "the expression of the opinion [about homosexuality] as seen from within that group," believing "that the majority of homosexuals will be able to identify themselves with the thoughts and experiences related in many sections of" *The Homosexual in America* (Cory, 1951, p. 10).

Although then lacking any professional training in social science research, Sagarin had the assistance of John Horton, who was financially independent and had earned a BA in anthropology at Columbia. Horton suggested that the basis of their friendship "maybe [was] because I had a black lover. Cory had had a number of affairs with black men. He used to boast about the frequency with which he was able to pick men up along the benches at Central Park West in the Seventies" (quoted by Duberman, 1997, p. 9).

In an era in which there were considerable social mobilizations to end discrimination against blacks and Jews, the analogue of a minority group persecuted by the majority would likely have occurred to someone contemplating the situation of American homosexuals even without a preference for black sexual partners. Harry Hay, for example, had independently described homosexuals as a minority group.

What is notably lacking (all the more so in contrast to Hay), especially for someone with a background of political action in support of black civil rights, was any conception of resisting persecution—either the laws or police procedures legitimated by often vague laws. Although *The Homosexual in America* was written during an era in which white liberal support was mobilized for ending exclusion of Jews and Negroes, there were Jewish and black organizations directly involved in challenging laws, social mores, and widespread negative attitudes about them. Cory described a subculture (with an argot, cruising locales, bars, and patterns of concealment) and pled for less social contempt. Fighting back was far beyond what he conceived.

The book minimizes police depredation and direct application of laws against sodomy and related statutes. In a chapter "World of Law-Abiding Felons," Cory wrote, "There are few homosexuals who are ever arrested or convicted of crimes, and relatively few who are successfully subjected to blackmail" (1951, p. 57). The book completely fails to anticipate the then-coming changes in laws and the protests against police entrapment, raids, etc. Although indignant, he described the situation as impossible to challenge:

> The homosexual is, unfortunately, in a position before the law where he cannot effectively fight back. The civil liberties groups show little interest, and their lawyers are loath to engage in such cases. Laws whose unconstitutionality is considered by many to be patent remain unchallenged, because no one dares come forward with courage to issue such a challenge and take the consequences thereof.
>
> The homosexual cannot stand up in court and say: "Your laws are behind the times. I cannot be ashamed of what I have done, but only of those who have pried into my private life and arrested me." Even if he were successful in his day in court, he would be exposing himself to the blows that must fall on those who would drop the mask. (Cory, 1951, p. 62)

Almost immediately, a Mattachine Society founder, Dale Jennings, provided a counterexample by challenging his own arrest; even though he admitted his homosexuality, the jury in June 1952 voted eleven to one not to convict him, after which the district attorney dropped the charge.

Although wrong in his belief that no one could fight back, Sagarin experienced one of the feared consequences of advocacy: he lost his job after his employer found he had authored such a book. He, however, quickly found another position in the cosmetics industry.

The Homosexual in America went through seven hardcover printings by 1957, was translated into French and Spanish, and was issued as a mass-market paperback in 1963. It prompted thousands of letters to the author, mostly grateful ones, and revealed to many readers, including Norman Mailer that "homosexuals are people, too." Good businessman that he had become, Sagarin (as Cory) used the correspondence as a mailing list for a gay-themed book-of-the-month club in 1952. From the first issue of *ONE Magazine* in January 1953, through the next three years, Cory was listed as a contributing editor. He wrote several articles pleading for understanding for internal differences among gays, particularly advocating compassion for effeminate males.

The second Cory book was an anthology of short stories dealing with homosexuality from insider and outsider perspective called *21 Variations on a Theme* (Cory, 1953). Many of the stories focus on repressed or suppressed passions, but several provide glimpses of men or women in relationships and supportive networks. Cory himself had become an activist of sorts, joining the Veterans' Benevolent Association, a New York City group that "sponsored parties, picnics, and discussion, and gave advice to members; it made little effort to conceal its homosexual orientation, except to use an innocent-sounding name" (Sagarin, 1969, p. 84). "It functioned primarily, but not exclusively as a social club for members. It did not publish, it did not proselytize. . . . Former officers state that there were between 75 and 100 regular members but that some of the social functions were attended by 400 or 500" (Sagarin, 1966, p. 65).

By 1955 the league had dissolved. Five former league members and two others (one female) formed a Mattachine Society chapter. It produced a newsletter and had regular public lectures (Sagarin, 1966, p. 82); Cory delivered one in 1957. He became more involved, although he did not become a member until May of 1962.

Mattachine founder Harry Hay completely distrusted Cory. Cory was not well liked even by Curtis Dewees, who "probably got to know him better than anyone else in Mattachine and recalled that "he wasn't much fun to be around," being "thin-skinned, easily offended, aggressive" (quoted by Duberman, 1997, p. 12). Frank Kameny recalls that Cory "exhibited no reticence or negativism whatever about his quite unequivocal and enthusiastic same-sex tendencies, when we went out 'on the town' with some friends, here in Washington" in 1962 (September 4, 2000, e-mail).

Sagarin, at age forty-five, had entered an adult undergraduate program at Brooklyn College in 1958. He and his son Fred both graduated in 1961. He then wrote a master's thesis that was published in 1962 but was rejected by the Brooklyn College sociology department. Ironically, for the respectability-craving new academic, the author photo on the book, *The Anatomy of Dirty Words* (Sagarin, 1962) made his real name known to other Mattachine members, although everyone already knew from *The Homosexual in America* that he was married.

In the early 1960s he visited a young, attractive, and more militant Mattachine member, Barry Sheer (John LeRoy), two or three times a week for sex. Sheer told Duberman (1997, p. 12) that Cory "would give me a little money and have me help him with some of his research and I would let him have sex with me," although unattracted to the older, deformed man with a high-pitched, loud voice. The book that they co-authored, *The Homosexual and His Society* (1963) did not have the same influence as his early work although it is not without interest. The chapter on hustlers does not altogether disguise Cory's considerable familiarity in hiring them. One chapter challenges the conventional wisdom about homosexuals being security risks, closing with a lengthy quotation (without attribution) from Frank Kameny's brief to the Supreme Court (Cory and LeRoy, 1963, p. 147). Another chapter rationalizes the senior author's separation of (homosexual) sex and (marital) love. The book definitely notes that homosexuals had begun to organize and to fight back (pp. 146, 242-250).

Considering that Sagarin was a sociology graduate student when he wrote the book, it is also notable that the early sociological work on homosexuality (which notably lacked Sagarin's own subservience to psychoanalytic assumptions such as those of Albert Ellis) was not cited. Similarly, although there was a chapter on "the better-adjusted" homosexual, it did not mention Evelyn Hooker's research. The only mention of Rorschach testing is in a six-page exposition of a ludicrous study by Albert Ellis that found zero percent of effeminate homosexuals to be highly creative, in contrast to 26 percent of heterosexuals (although Cory and LeRoy did note that patients in therapy are not a typical sample of any population).

Sheer/LeRoy himself abandoned Cory's view that homosexuality was a disturbance that should be treated with compassion and embraced the "Gay Is Good" view proclaimed by Frank Kameny to a 1964 Matttachine Society of New York (MSNY) meeting and adopted by many of its younger, more militant members, as well as by the chapter's president, Julian Hodges.

Sagarin enrolled in the sociology doctoral program at New York University (NYU) in 1961, leaving the cosmetic and perfume business behind. He was a lecturer at Brooklyn College the 1962-1963 academic year, at the Pratt Institute the next year, and at City College the year after that. He became an assistant professor there upon completion of his PhD, and received tenure in 1970.

After the first year of taking classes at NYU, Sagarin became more active in Mattachine New York and made the organization the subject of his doctoral dissertation. He had the cooperation of Mattachine officials to query members (an appendix to his dissertation includes his questionnaire and a cover letter from Mattachine New York's president Hodges, dated January 1965, assuring respondents that "we expect our Society, and the homophile movement as a whole, to benefit from this research."

It is not clear that his doctoral committee knew how participant an observer he was. Robert Bierstedt, the department chairman, who was a member of Sagarin's doctoral committee, told Martin Duberman (1997, p. 14) that not only did he not know that Sagarin was Cory at the time but did not learn that until a decade after Sagarin's death. Dennis Wrong, however, wrote me that "I certainly knew that Sagarin was Donald Webster Cory when I went to NYU in 1963. Bierstedt told me so, whatever Duberman may say he said to him some years later. And I'm pretty sure Larry Ross knew too. . . . I spoke to Ed Sagarin on several occasions about his dissertation though I was not on his committee and remember being amused when with a straight face he cited Cory as an authority with, or so I imagined, a certain twinkle in his eye based on his suspicion that I knew of Cory's identity" (August 30, 2000, e-mail). Another of the sociologists not on his committee whom Sagarin acknowledged in his dissertation, John Gagnon, told me that he knew that Sagarin had been Cory, knew that Cory was writing about a political struggle he had lost, and that this colored his views (September 1, 2000, e-mail).

Wrong added that "while I can't positively verify it, as I can in the case of Bob, I'm sure Erwin [Smigel], knowing him well, and his pal Larry Ross, likewise, who were both on Ed's committee, knew he was Cory" and "I doubt very much that knowledge of this fact would have influenced his dissertation committee in the slightest. . . . I remember speaking to him [Duberman] over the phone and denying that we didn't know in the NYU department that Sagarin was Cory. If we had known [at the time of his admission to doctoral studies] we would doubtless have welcomed him even more as a lively if controversial writer who would make an interesting student and write an interesting if possibly controversial dissertation (legalizing homosexuality was very controversial then)" (August 31, 2000, e-mail). Perhaps anachronistically Wrong was claiming that there was nothing to hide, that someone who was a homophile activist would have been welcome in the department.

But more was involved than Sagarin being and citing Cory. Cory was a member of the Mattachine board of directors and was heavily involved in factional politics within the organization, and even ran for president. It is far from the case that his name was simply put up without his knowledge. Although Sagarin's dissertation portrays the backers of Hodges as a clique, "early in 1965 some of them [the old guard] constituted themselves as 'the committee' and began holding strategy sessions . . . and aggressively sought proxies from inactive members of the society for their slate" (D'Emilio, 1981, pp. 166-167). Upon his two-to-one defeat by the younger advocates of a direct action civil rights strategy who did not agree that homosexuality is an inherently pathological, Cory left the organization immediately and permanently.

Frank Kameny suggested that "President of MSNY [was] a position to which I suspect that Cory felt himself entitled almost as a matter of royal succession" and confirmed that Cory "became deeply embittered at his rejection by MSNY and others in the Gay Movement, and his consignment to the sidelines exactly as I had predicted in my much-quoted letter to him . . . [and] expressed bitterness, of course, in his PhD thesis . . ." (September 4, 2000, e-mail). In the letter, prior to the MSNY election, Kameny had warned Cory "you have become no longer the vigorous Father of the Homophile Movement, to be revered, respected and listened to, but the senile Grandfather of the Homophile Movement, to be humored and tolerated at best; to be ignored and disregarded usually; and to be ridiculed at worst" (quoted by D'Emilio, 1981, p. 167).

There is certainly valuable historical information in Sagarin's dissertation. Yet readers informed about his failed bid for leadership of Mattachine New York, the venom of the campaign, his position on its board of directors, the existence of a faction led by himself, and its mass exodus following his electoral defeat would approach statements such as the following with greater skepticism if they realized the nature of Sagarin's participant observation and instances needing to be separated. "What seems noteworthy in MSNY is the existence of a formal structure that is evaded, despite a Board and against its will, in favor of one man and his personal coterie" (Sagarin, 1966, p. 294). The one man being singled out was the very one who signed the cover letter urging cooperation with Sagarin's research.

> Within Mattachine, the "go fast" group consists largely of those who have little to lose, in the way of position, public anonymity, and business; they are also likely to be more youthful, politically more liberal and radical; have lesser ties in New York with Families; are generally aggressive in their social attitudes; and sympathetic to other militant movements, which they seek to imitate. The "go slow" are more moderate, more frequently professional, more aware of the hard road ahead in striving to make progress in a difficult social atmosphere. (Sagarin, 1966, pp. 207-208)
>
> [It] is likely to sink deeper into untenable ideological distortions. . . . The Mattachine Society has little regard for truth. . . . It is part of a movement that participates in blackmail. (p. 405)

There may well be rational kernels and defensible analyses in these and similar statements about factions within MSNY—and, perhaps, even those about "counterfeit love" and "compulsivity," etc.—but the very deliberate concealment of his stake and history in MSNY evaded questions that surely would have been raised about how much of his purportedly "objective analysis" was "sour grapes." Given Sagarin's position that advocacy undercuts objectivity, enhancing his own credibility has to have been one of the conscious motivations for concealing the nature and extent of his MSNY participation in his dissertation, and, subsequently (in oral presentations and written work, including a chapter based on his dissertation in his 1969 book *Odd Man In*), from the profession of sociology.

Donald Beckerman, who also entered the NYU doctoral sociology program in 1961, told me that Sagarin continued to be very promiscuous up until his heart attack in a rent-by-the-hour hotel where he had taken a black hustler (this event is further elaborated in Duberman, 1999, pp. 91-92). Beckerman has the impression that Sagarin stopped tricking then, whether from fear of death or fear of the disgrace of dying under such compromising circumstances. Sagarin eventually died in 1986 of another heart attack.

One could say that Donald Webster Cory died in May of 1965 when his bid for the presidency of Mattachine New York went down to resounding defeat. Under the name of Edward Sagarin he soon retaliated in an "objective" analysis that hid his ego involvement and personal bitterness at being passed by conceptually and politically, as well as sexually. In a chapter titled "Dirty Old Men Need Love, Too," Humphreys (1972, p. 116) wrote, possibly thinking of Cory and the younger Mattachines rejecting him in these multiple ways: "If an ideological conflict is at the heart of the struggle between potential helmsmen of the movement, there is a personal dynamic that often intensifies acrimony between the reformers and liberationists. Simply put, the severity of the aging crisis for homosexuals is apt to produce resentment, even bitterness on the part of older leaders" (see also Sagarin, 1966, pp. 321-334).

Cory undoubtedly contributed to consciousness of a kind among homosexuals during the 1950s and early 1960s and inspired some compassion from others for the difficulties homosexuals faced. In that *The Homosexual in America* did not imagine organization and resistance, and that Cory did not join any homophile organization until 1962 (when he was an NYU doctoral student seeking a dissertation topic), the title "father of the homophile movement" seems undeserved. He not only failed to reach the Promised Land of self-acceptance and sociocultural acceptance but refused to look for it, rejected any such goal, and consistently derided those who viewed their homosexuality as nonpathological. Especially in his publications as Edward Sagarin, he held up Alcoholics Anonymous as the proper model of what an "organizations of deviants" should be, i.e., "one that preserved the anonymity of participants and focused on suppressing forbidden urges and ending the 'deviant' behavior" (Sagarin, 1969, pp. 97-99, 105-106).

Increasingly Sagarin criticized sociologists and others for "hiding behind" the safety of their wives and children while advocating that lesbians and gay men come out of the closet, yet he himself refused to identify himself as Cory. He died in 1986, alienated and embittered from most of the homosexual community that no longer subscribed to his ideas or would-be leadership, and had no interest in following his proffered advice.

REFERENCES

Cory, Donald Webster. 1951. *The Homosexual in America*. New York: Greenberg (quotations are from the 1963 Paperback Library edition).

Cory, Donald Webster (Ed.). 1953. *21 Variations on a Theme*. New York: Greenberg.

Cory, Donald Webster, and John P. LeRoy. 1963. *The Homosexual and His Society: A View from Within*. New York: Citadel Press.

D'Emilio, John. 1981. *Sexual Politics, Sexual Communities*. Chicago: University of Chicago Press.

Duberman, Martin. 1997. "The 'father' of the homophile movement." *Harvard Gay and Lesbian Review* 4(4):7- 14. Revised version, pp. 69-94 in *Left Out: The Politics of Exclusion*. New York: Basic Books, 1999.

Ellis, Albert. 1951. *The Folklore of Sex*. New York: Boni.

Humphreys, Laud. 1972. *Out of the Closets: The Sociology of Homosexual Liberation*. Englewood Cliffs, NJ: Prentice-Hall.

Sagarin, Edward. 1962. *The Anatomy of Dirty Words*. New York: L. Stuart.

Sagarin, Edward. 1966. *Structure and Ideology in an Association of Deviants*. Doctoral dissertation, New York University. Facsimile published in 1975 by the Arno Press, New York.

Sagarin, Edward. 1969. *Odd Man In: Societies of Deviants in America*. Chicago: Quadrangle Books.

Evelyn Gentry Hooker (1907-1996)

Sharon Valente

Evelyn Hooker, nee Gentry, was an instrumental figure in bringing about changes in attitudes about homosexuality in the scientific community and envisioning a future where homosexuality would not be diagnosed as a "severe and pervasive emotional disorder."

She was born in her grandmother's house, which sat next to Buffalo Bill Cody's house, on September 2, 1907, in North Platte, Nebraska, the sixth of nine children. Her mother, who had completed schooling only through the third grade, had traveled to Nebraska in a covered wagon and inspired Evelyn to "get an education—they can't take that away from you." Her parents eked out an existence as farmers and Evelyn's only exposure to books occurred during her attendance of a series of one-room schoolhouses. She loved to tell of a "sun bonneted child named Evelyn Gentry, being perched on the front seat of a covered wagon, a genuine prairie schooner, moving with her parents and eight siblings from North Platte to their new home in Sterling" (Shneidman, 1998). Sterling, Colorado, boasted of its position as the county seat and had a large high school. As a senior, Evelyn enrolled in the honors program with a course in psychology. She planned to attend a Colorado teachers' college, but the faculty recommended she attend the University of Colorado instead.

In 1924, she became a freshman at the University with a tuition scholarship but no money for board and room; she paid for this by housecleaning. Her entry into psychology was initially opportunistic. After learning that seniors in the psychology department could become paid teaching assistants in quiz sections, she concluded that this kind of teaching seemed far superior to earning her way by housekeeping, and so she became a psychology major. In a course on comparative psychology with Karl Muenzinger, she was inspired by and intrigued with the notion of the scientific investigation of behavior. The University, upon her graduation in 1928, offered her an instructorship and she began her studies on her master's degree with Muenzinger. Her master's thesis in 1930 examined vicarious trial-and-error learning in rats. At the American Psychological Association meeting, the president, Edward Tolman, used graphs from Hooker's thesis to illustrate his discussion of vicarious learning in rats.

In this era, discrimination against women commonly prevailed in higher education. Although she preferred to attend Yale for her doctoral work, the psychology department chair there refused to accept a woman. Muenzinger suggested that instead she study with Knight Dunlap at Johns Hopkins even though Dunlap did not generally approve of women doctorates (Shneidman, 1998).

Her faculty at Hopkins discouraged further study of learning in rats; instead, she concentrated on humans. She earned her PhD in psychology in 1932 at Johns Hopkins in experimental psychology with a dissertation on discrimination training. She was elected to the honor societies of Phi Beta Kappa, Sigma Xi, and Phi Gamma Mu. Her first academic appointment was at the Maryland College for Women where she taught from 1932 to 1934, when she was diagnosed as having tuberculosis. With support of her friends, she came to a sanitarium in California for two years of reading and recuperation. Faculty positions for women were hard to find in the Depression era, but she did teach part-time at Whittier College for a year after leaving the sanitarium.

She then received a fellowship to study psychotherapy in Berlin. Although her fellowship was interesting, the events in Germany and other parts of Europe were even more captivating. She lived with a Jewish family and viewed Germany through their eyes. After seeing the rise of Nazism and traveling to Russia with a tourist group after the purge of 1938, she was impressed with the impact of totalitarian regimes and dedicated herself to make her life count in helping to correct social injustice (APA, 1992).

After returning to Whittier College for a year, she applied for a faculty appointment in psychology at UCLA. Her request was denied because they already had three women faculty and the faculty were unwilling to consider another woman. She found a more receptive hearing in the UCLA Extension Division which appointed her as a research associate in psychology. She taught in UCLA Extension from 1939-1970 and never was on a tenure track and was not necessarily a full-time teacher. This fact probably allowed her considerably more freedom in her own research than otherwise would have been the case and allowed her to delve into topics that academic psychology departments would not touch. Teaching was a source of reward and pleasure, and she was well respected as an excellent teacher. She also taught herself to be a qualified clinical psychologist and she became a diplomat in clinical psychology (Shneidman, 1998).

Her studies on homosexuality were the earliest within the psychological community to break with standard stereotypes of homosexual men—who were then considered maladjusted or mentally ill, were forcibly ejected from government jobs, and were arrested in police raids. The prevailing psychiatric opinion about the adjustment of homosexual men was illustrated by a quotation from the Group for the Advancement of Psychiatry: "When such homosexual behavior persists in an adult, it is then a symptom of a severe emotional disorder" (GAP, 1955, p. 7). At this time, few clinicians ever had the opportunity to examine homosexual subjects who did not come from psychiatric agencies or prisons. The one major exception to this was George Henry's 1941 study, but he was too much part of the psychiatric mainstream to see the similarities between homosexuals and heterosexuals that Hooker did. Those patients diagnosed as homosexual by psychiatrists were usually sent for drastic treatments, including electroshock therapy, to reverse their perversity.

Hooker's exposure to homosexuality was serendipitous. While teaching a class in the UCLA Extension in 1943-1944, Hooker had a gay male in one of the classes with whom she later became friends. The student, known as Sam From, introduced Evelyn and her then husband, Donn Caldwell, to a number of his homosexual friends. According to Shneidman, From told Hooker that she had a moral responsibility to study his "condition." She asked what his condition was and upon hearing it was homosexuality, she noted that she knew nothing about it. From responded, then "you'll have to learn" (Shneidman, 1998). As he introduced her to the topic, she came to the conclusion that the men she met were as well adjusted as any of the heterosexual men she knew.

Her marriage to Donn Caldwell was short lived; he died from a heart attack with her at his side six months after their marriage (Shneidman, 1998). She remarried in London, England, in 1951 to Edward Hooker, a distinguished professor of English at UCLA. Encouraged by some of her colleagues and friends in the gay community as well as her new husband, she began her investigation of homosexuality despite the stigma associated with such studies. Much to the surprise of many of her colleagues, she even obtained government funding from the National Institute of Mental Health (NIMH). In 1953, she applied to NIMH for a six-month grant to study adjustment of nonclinical male homosexuals and a comparable group of heterosexuals. Intrigued by such a remarkable proposal, the chief of the grants division, John Eberhart, came to Los Angeles to meet Hooker. This grant application was extraordinary, particularly because this was the height of the McCarthy era, when there were severe legal penalties for homosexuality. Eberhart was interested in such a study because scientific data about normal homosexuals from nonclinical and nonprison environments was nonexistent. He told her that they could give her the grant but that "you may not receive it and you may never know why and we won't know why." She later learned that her project was referred to as the "Fairy Project" by some of the federal grant officials. NIMH continually renewed her funding until 1961 when she obtained a Research Career Award.

While prior research by psychologists and psychiatrists had used clinical samples of psychiatric patients or military or prison inmates, the studies by Alfred Kinsey had already challenged most such conclusions, and both she and NIMH felt that mental health professionals needed to know more about the topic. Hooker selected a sample free of psychopathology and examined thirty homosexual men and thirty heterosexual men matched for age (from twenty-five to fifty), education, and IQ. She carefully selected homosexual subjects who would have been classified as a five or six on the Kinsey scale, and heterosexuals who would fall in the zero to one category and who were not receiving psychotherapy. Since finding such homosexual subjects was not easy because of the closeted nature of so many of her potential subjects, she sought assistance from the Mattachine Society, whose members volunteered as subjects and enlisted their friends also to do so. Hooker precisely details the data on selecting the homosexuals but notes that the "heterosexual subjects came because they were told that this was an opportunity to contribute to our understanding of the way in which the average individual in the community functions, since we had little data on normal men" (Hooker, 1992, p. 144).

She administered a series of standard projective tests including the Rorschach, which then was believed to be the best measure of personality and was instrumental in diagnosing homosexuality, the Thematic Apperception Test (TAT), and the Make a Picture test (MAP) to the sample. After removing all the identifying information except age from the test results and profiles, she arranged them in random order. Then three expert outside clinicians reviewed the tests and described the personality of the subject and then attempted to distinguish the homosexuals from the heterosexuals. The judges, who were unaware of the subjects' sexual orientation, were unable to distinguish the homosexuals from the heterosexuals on the basis of the projective tests. The two experts reviewing the Rorschach agreed only on the sexual orientation of sixteen of the sixty cases, and then they were mostly wrong. After completing the judging, the expert clinicians commented that the profiles did not resemble those of the homosexual men they saw in clinical practice.

One of Hooker's conclusions was that clinicians should be very skeptical about the so-called homosexual content signs in the Rorschach. Hooker called Dorr Legg, one of the gay men in the study, and reported that although he did not know it, the evaluators had determined that he was a heterosexual. Findings of the study where none of the experts (even after one repeated his analysis) could do better than chance were presented at the annual meeting of the American Psychological Association in Chicago in 1956 and published in the *Journal of Projective Techniques* the following year. Although this was not a widely read journal, these findings helped set the stage for removing homosexuality as a disorder in the diagnostic manuals of psychiatry and psychology. Her conclusions included:

> Homosexuality as a clinical entity does not exist. Its forms are as varied as those of heterosexuality. Homosexuality may be a deviation in sexual pattern, which is within the normal range psychologically. The role of particular forms of sexual desire and expression in personality structure and development may be less important than has frequently been assumed. (Hooker, 1992, p. 154)

Her critics alleged that she had a biased sample because her sample of homosexuals came from gay rights and advocacy groups and these groups were better adjusted than the average.

As a sign of the times, when Hooker began her study she received a letter from the chancellor at UCLA identifying her as a faculty member and researcher in the event of a police raid or arrest. Even before the publication of her projective technique study, she had published an article suggesting that homosexuals think of themselves as members of a minority group with a separate culture. In the process she became one of the first published ethnographers on the topic in English. Impressed by her findings, the NIMH initial grant expanded into a Research Career Award which she held until she retired in 1970. Subsequently, she opened a clinic practice serving mostly gay men and lesbians.

Probably her most important contribution was as chair of the Task Force on Homosexuality established by NIMH in 1967, which provided a stamp of validation and research support for other major empirical studies (APA, 1992) . The report recommended, among other things, that homosexuality be decriminalized through the repeal of sodomy laws. She worked, albeit indirectly, with Judd Marmor to have homosexuality removed from the list of clinical diagnoses of the American Psychiatric Association in 1973 and from the American Psychological Association terminology in 1975. In short, she was instrumental in changing the definitions (Shneidman, 1998).

The task force argued that homosexuality presented a major problem for American society because of the amount of injustice and suffering it entailed not only for homosexuals but also for those concerned about them. Unfortunately, by the time the report was ready the Nixon administration was in power in Washington and publication was delayed. This led to its publication instead by the *One Institute Quarterly*. The task force also encouraged better public education on homosexuality.

She went on to become a devoted if somewhat reticent spokesperson for gays and lesbians. During her later years, she was much honored by the gay community, and one of her subjects, Wayne Placek, left a bequest for her to administer designed to encourage research into homosexuality.

She had a rich life and many episodes of high drama. According to Shneidman, she, like some of her subjects, was once arrested and booked in the Los Angeles County jail (Shneidman, 1998). At another time, she passed as a male to enter the bathhouses to interview homosexual subjects.

The Division of Clinical Psychology of the American Psychological Association (APA, 1992) honored her with the Award for Distinguished Contributions. She also received the APA Award for Distinguished Contributions to the Public Interest. The Association of Gay Physicians recognized her for contributions also. In 1992, Dave Haughland and Richard Schmiechen made the documentary film *Changing Our Minds: The Story of Evelyn Hooker*. It was nominated for an Academy Award (Shneidman, 1998). She told the *Los Angeles Times* that the documentary "Gives a kind of finality to one's life, doesn't it? I don't exactly say my last goodbye to the world on film, but it does sum me up like nothing else" (Oliver, 1996). The Los Angeles Gay and Lesbian Community gave her its highest honor in 1989.

Many homosexual men have reflected that she changed their lives by removing stigma and allowing societal and self acceptance. Shneidman (1998) comments that her life, first in an academic setting as an experimental psychologist and then in community action, raises important questions about the role of psychology in the making of social policy.

Although she wrote comparatively little in refereed journals and published fewer than twenty articles, and most of the publications are in collections edited by others, it was more what she did than how much she wrote. For more than three decades she was a tireless advocate for an accurate scientific view of homosexuality. The University of Chicago honored her for establishing homosexuality as a field of study by establishing the Evelyn Hooker Center for the Mental Health of Gays and Lesbians.

She died at her home in Santa Monica, California, at the age of eighty-nine.

BIBLIOGRAPHY

American Psychiatric Association. *Diagnostic and Statistical Manual: Mental Disorders DSM-IV*. Washington, DC: American Psychiatric Association, 1952.

American Psychiatric Association. *Diagnostic and Statistical Manual of Mental Disorders* (DSM-IV). Washington, DC: American Psychiatric Association, 1994.

American Psychiatric Association. "Evelyn Hooker: Biographical Sketch." *American Psychologist 47* (1992), 499-501.

Boxer, Andrew A., and Joseph M. Carrier. "Evelyn Hooker: A Life Remembered." *Journal of Homosexuality 36* (1998), 1-17.

Group for the Advancement of Psychiatry. (GAP) Report on homosexuality. Committee on Cooperation with Government (Federal) Agencies. *Report* No. 30, January 1955, p. 7.

Henry, George W. *Sex Variant: A Study of Homosexual Patterns*. New York: Hoeber, 1941.

Hooker, Evelyn. "The Adjustment of the Male Overt Homosexual," *Journal of Projective Techniques 21* (1957), 18-31.

Hooker, Evelyn. "The Adjustment of the Male Overt Homosexual." In W.R. Dynes, S. Donaldson (Eds.), *Homosexuality and Psychology, Psychiatry, and Counseling, Studies in Homosexuality,* Volume 11 (pp. 142-145). New York: Garland Publishing, 1992.

Hooker, Evelyn. "The Case of El: A Biography," *Journal of Projective Techniques 25* (1961), 252-267.

Hooker, Evelyn. "An Empirical Study of Some Relations Between Sexual Patterns and Gender Identity in Male Homosexuals." In J. Money (Ed.), *Sex Research: New Development* (pp. 24-52). New York: Holt, Rinehart and Winston, 1965.

Hooker, Evelyn. "Male homosexuality." In N.L. Farberow (Ed.), *Taboo Topics* (pp. 45-55). New York: Atherton, 1963.

Hooker, Evelyn. "Male Homosexuals in Their Worlds." In J. Marmor (Ed.), *Sexual Inversion: The Multiple Roots of Homosexuality* (pp. 83-107). New York: Basic Books, 1965.

Hooker, Evelyn. "Parental Relations and Male Homosexuality in Patient and Nonpatient Samples," *Journal of Consulting and Clinical Psychology* 33:2 (1969), 140-142.

Hooker, Evelyn. "A Preliminary Analysis of Group Behavior of Homosexuals," *Journal of Psychology 42* (1956), 217-225.

Hooker, Evelyn. "Reflections of a 40 Year Exploration: A Scientific View on Homosexuality," *American Psychologist* 48:4 (1993), 450-453.

Oliver, M. "Evelyn Hooker: Her Study Fueled Gay Liberation." *Los Angeles Times,* November 22, 1996, p. 32.

Shneidman, E.S. "Evelyn Hooker (1907-1996)," *American Psychologist* 53:4 (1998), 480-481.

George Weinberg (1935-   )

Jack Nichols

George Weinberg, PhD, coined the term *homophobia*. In the mid-1960s, at a time when most other members of his profession were classifying homosexuality as a malfunction, Weinberg, who self-identified as a heterosexual, was passionately and publicly proclaiming them mistaken. In the process of defining homophobia, he proffered a radical concept: healthy homosexuality. Only one of a handful of psychotherapists who were willing to take such a stand, Weinberg gave unrelenting assistance to the East Coast's pioneering gay and lesbian activists. A lover of poetry, especially Shakespeare, he used his forceful literary and speaking talents on behalf of gay and lesbian liberation.

In September 1965, addressing the second annual ECHO conference (East Coast Homophile Organizations), Weinberg critiqued his professional peers, bemoaning among other cruel therapies electroshock treatments. In 1969, without bothering to identify himself as a heterosexual male, he began writing regularly for *GAY,* America's first gay weekly. In 1972 St. Martin's Press published Weinberg's groundbreaking work, *Society and the Healthy Homosexual.* This book, which for the first time explained his conception of homophobia, began with a direct statement that sent shock waves through the memberships of both the American Psychological Association and the American Psychiatric Association: "I would never consider a patient healthy," he wrote, "unless he had overcome his prejudice against homosexuality" (1972, p. 1).

George Weinberg was born in 1935 in New York City and was raised entirely by his mother, Lillian, who had only a seventh-grade education. She taught herself shorthand and typing, however, and secured employment as an assistant to a well-known lawyer, Harold Riegelman, regarded by her son as his godfather. Riegelman rose to prominence in the Empire City's Republican circles with the assistance of Lillian, who wrote speeches for him dur-

ing a period when he ran unsuccessfully for mayor. Weinberg met his actual
father only briefly and for the first time when he was eighteen.

It was Lillian, however, whose advice to her son set a standard by which
he would thereafter appraise all people he knew: "The way to judge someone," she said, "is by how he or she treats the least important person in his
life." Weinberg's childhood, in spite of Lillian's loving care, became a tur-
bulent period. He was diagnosed as "emotionally disturbed" by the New
York City public school system. Lillian scrimped and saved in order to place
him in the Riverside School, a private facility where he enjoyed the attention
of first-rate educators (Nichols, 2000).

There, his prodigious success in mathematics gave him a sense of sanity
that was bolstered by his enjoyment of classical literature and history. Not
being wealthy by his classmates' standards, however, the young student
found himself excluded from their social gatherings in the countryside. He
spent his afternoons on New York City streets, making friendships on his
own, choosing companions based not on their social stations but on their
characters. Although initially he felt like an outsider, his solace was summed
up for him as he self-identified with Marcellus in a verse by Alexander
Pope:

> More true joy Marcellus, exiled, feels
> Than Caesar with a senate at his heels

As an exiled youth, George Weinberg looked on the brighter side. He enjoyed that he didn't have to wear jackets and ties. Most of his friends in high
school, he was later to discover, were gay, although neither he nor they
themselves had yet realized it. In his 1996 foreword to my book, *The Gay
Agenda,* Weinberg recalled his fond remembrances of those gay high school
chums, reflecting the kind of warmth and enthusiasm he'd learned to bring
to his same-sex friendships. "I valued these friends," he explained, "for their
encompassing, loving vision of literature, their gentleness of spirit, their
subtlety."

"Eventually," he said, "a few disclosed to me what they had considered
the dark truth of their not being 'like others,' like me. It was difficult for
them to reveal their notion that they did not draw their passions from a common spring."

Weinberg, in one of his typical flights of masterly prose, sounded a clar-
ion call to embrace what society had denied. "Society," he said, had been
failing to "recognize that passion is its only excuse for being and that all
love is conspiratorial and deviant and magical. The 'mainstream' could not
accept that isolation is universal, as is every individual's desire to bridge it

with love and truth. In this sense we are all the same" (Clarke and Nichols, 1986, p. 13).

By the time his high school friends had confided in him, however, George Weinberg had already become a psychotherapist with a doctorate in clinical psychology from Columbia University. He'd also earned a master's degree in English literature from New York University. At Columbia he'd noted with alarm how psychologists were being taught to instill conservative values. Their aim, he decided, was to make people conform "to the most homogenous, controlling standard" (Nichols, 2000).

More specifically, educators had taught him to treat gay men and lesbians as though they were inherently sick, and he recalled how many of his colleagues "were so phobic about gays that it even seemed reasonable to torture homosexuals if this would 'cure' them." Such attitudes found the young doctor "tormented" by his profession's showy blindness to injustice. He began, he indicated to me, by trying gently to change their perspectives. He introduced them to gay male friends. Although his psychoanalytic colleagues liked gay men and lesbians as long as they thought them to be heterosexuals, the very news that Weinberg had, by design, introduced them without first outing his gay friends elicited their extreme disgust, and, recalled Weinberg, his experiment had "had no effect on their views. They simply reversed their fondness for those individuals they had liked. They insisted on their repugnance and on despising homosexuals, calling them mentally disturbed, and shunning them" (Nichols, 2000).

Summing up their behavior in clinical terms, Weinberg made his diagnosis: "Clearly this was a phobic attitude." In 1967, he began calling them homophobes, labeling their behavior homophobic. Once the youthful outsider, he sympathized now with society's outcasts: "It was hard to enjoy being one of the chosen people, 'the heteros,' when so many people whom I admired were not invited to the party" (Nichols, 2000).

One of the people he most admired—his lifelong mentor, in fact, about whom he would later write two books—was William Shakespeare. George Weinberg had not been the first scholar who had concluded after conducting prodigious studies that Shakespeare was gay. This conclusion furthered the young psychotherapist's determination to do his part to eliminate antigay prejudices. He said "I felt terrible for Shakespeare, my hero, when, in a sonnet, the poet begged an unnamed lover not to mourn for him too openly after he died":

> Lest the wide world should look into your moan
> And mock you with me after I am gone.

"Clearly," Weinberg argued, "Shakespeare was speaking to a gay lover. No one would have mocked a woman for mourning a man. I was outraged that even the greatest of all writers had lived in fear because of his unpopular preference. Love is love, after all" (Nichols, 2000).

George Weinberg became infuriated by the difficulties he witnessed as experienced by his gay male friends. He was quite certain about his own heterosexual inclination but also empathetic enough to see that his friends felt equally decisive about their own preferences. "Most of them confessed that they lived so alone," he recalled, "so hopelessly, feeling so unwanted" (Nichols, 2000).

That they had not even trusted him enough to confide in him gnawed away at him, expanding at the same time his awareness of how repressive were his peers' insecure claims about sexual propriety. He noted that on the question of same-sex love and affection they were moving in sheeplike formations and wandering outside any known field of scientific credibility.

Before opening a private practice, Weinberg pursued a doctorate in mathematics at the Courant Institute at New York University. Eventually, however, he decided that he'd be happier in a profession that did not isolate him in the way that mathematics seemed to promise. While attending City College, he suspected that some of his English teachers might be gay, those who had awakened his consciousness to a wealth of literature. After coming out to him, his gay male friends found themselves drawn closer to George than before. It soon become clear to them that he wasn't judgmental—nor would he have been judgmental toward lesbians, had he known any personally in those poststudent days. He worried about his male friends' safety, however, especially about "the beatings and blackmailings," which were taken for granted by most upright citizens as an expected price for being openly gay.

Weinberg's friend, Nelson W., told him how a sailor had pulled a knife on him in a hotel room and how the young man had successfully escaped through the window onto a ledge, teetering many stories above the pavement before reaching safety. Other commonplace instances of antigay prejudice were never thereafter lost on Weinberg. He was infuriated when he saw how "even the families of homosexual men disowned them, disenfranchised them" (Nichols, 2000).

On September 26, 1965, at New York's Barbizon Hotel, Weinberg delivered a scathing critique of the ideologically inspired misbehavior of his own profession. He had bravely come forward to address activists at the second East Coast gay and lesbian conference, which had taken place prior to the movement's first national conference the following year. In his clear, unmistakable style, Weinberg's speech, titled "The Dangers of Psychoanalysis," regaled that early assemblage with reflections on the blind spots that had afflicted members of his profession. "With the aid of pseudoscientific literature, superadded to our early cultural bias to loathe the homosexual, too many of us are able to take his time and money while treating him as deranged, without any evidence that he is" (*The Homosexual Citizen,* 1966, p. 5).

Only during the spring and summer of 1965 had two major gay movement organizations first passed policy statements directly challenging the ideologies of the psychiatric and psychological professions when, nearly simultaneously, Weinberg said:

> As a beginning therapist working under a supervisor, my immediate instructions were clear: to regard the homosexual's behavior as a symptom of lurking disease and not to consider him cured until his pathological taste was changed. To say the least, it is hard for anyone who is concerned about people to ask someone to give up what counts most to him, for no apparent reason except to escape public condemnation—a price which every homosexual implicitly understands better than his therapist could ever explain it to him. The request is especially hard to make when, as with the homosexual, there is nothing even vaguely commensurate to promise him in return. (*The Homosexual Citizen,* 1966, p. 5)

The prejudices Weinberg saw manifesting in his colleagues and reflected in social register etiquette found him remembering the early 1950s and scornfully hurling cultural critiques that would become useful to his 1965 gay activist audience:

> When I was a graduate student in clinical psychology, in the early fifties, sex was hardly discussed at all. I don't remember being assigned a single reading from Kinsey's work, though he was already famous and ours was a research-oriented department. The attitude toward all sexual behavior was as embarrassed as in the average American home. Toward the homosexual it was the current "enlightened" one: "Don't laugh at him but pity him because he is sick." This attitude, by the way, has begun (in 1965) to replace American-Gothic contempt, for the simple reason that it brings its own reward, the feeling of being considerate and sage, in contrast with some imaginary bigoted group, hostile to the homosexual. (*The Homosexual Citizen,* 1966, p. 4)

In 1969 I met Weinberg shortly after Lige Clarke and I began editing *GAY.* Our friendship grew steadily because of the mutual love we shared for literature and for useful values we had discovered in certain poems. We harbored similar hopes, an expansion of human happiness among them. On

lazy summer afternoons we would introduce each other to our favorite passages in the works of both Shakespeare and Walt Whitman, often swimming
in a spectacular hillside pool at the home of Weinberg's colleague and
friend, Dr. Clarence Tripp. Tripp was busily writing his scholarly tome, *The
Homosexual Matrix.*

Weinberg's regular essays in *GAY* became increasingly and stridently
critical of antigay psychiatric and psychological theories. He began, in these
essays, to describe the causes of homophobia. But he also wrote to encourage the ranks of the newly formed militant New York Gay Activists Alliance. In 1972, his groundbreaking statement on homophobia, *Society and
the Healthy Homosexual,* was published. Author Merle Miller noted at the
time that not only could Weinberg write expertly but that he had something
to say to gays and straights alike. Feminist author Germaine Greer wholeheartedly praised Weinberg's pioneering views. Thane Hampton, among
GAY's most sophisticated writers, gave his immediate reaction to Weinberg's revolutionary manifesto: "I would like to share a subjective but nonetheless valid historic pronouncement with you. Dr. George Weinberg's *Society and the Healthy Homosexual* is by far the best book ever written about
homosexuality."

Hampton noted how we gays are enormously fortunate that George
Weinberg is also here to stay. He is probably the greatest ally we have ever
had, and we owe him our loyalty and support. . . . Some of us may even owe
him our lives." Philosopher Arthur Evans, author of the monumental *Critique of Patriarchal Reason* (1997) and a 1969 founding member of New
York's Gay Activists Alliance, recalls Weinberg's influence at the time:

> It was clear to those of us who were GAA activists that George was a
> compassionate and far-sighted soul, that he had uncommon common
> sense. I remember how he encouraged and mentored our militant or-
> ganization at a time when most people in the professions thought we
> were crazy. He knew that it was the system that was out of kilter. He
> wasn't afraid to tell his colleagues so, but in a way that even his most
> intransigent critics could hear. You don't often find that combination
> of verve and balance in the same person. (Evans, 2000)

Over lunch one day, Weinberg introduced Lige Clarke and me to his book
publisher. A year later, as a result of that meeting, Clarke and I became the
authors of the first nonfiction memoir by a male couple. In our acknowl-
edgements to those who'd encouraged us to write and who'd broadened our
horizons, George Weinberg's name was listed first for having suggested the
book itself. Our title was *I Have More Fun with You Than Anybody* and we
described "those welcome summer afternoons" spent swimming in com-

pany with George Weinberg and his lady friend. In a nutshell, we described his indefatigable desire to end preventable sufferings. We told how each member of our little group had relaxed in our own ways around the swimming pool, but observed how it was George whose time was doggedly devoted to the welfare of tiny struggling creatures: "George, kindly soul that he is, picks drowning insects out of the pool."

There were a number of occasions when George Weinberg and I appeared together in New York media, each of us so comfortable with the gay topic and with each other as friends that our more serious themes of homosexual rights often became occasions for happy-go-lucky exchanges, punctured by Weinberg's good-natured laughter. Shortly following the publication of *Society and the Healthy Homosexual,* Weinberg decided to throw a grand party in his large Central Park apartment. It was to honor four of his gay and lesbian friends who'd seen their own co-authored books published. Lige Clarke and I were one of the duos while Kay Tobin Lahusen and Randolfe Wicker, co-authors of *The Gay Crusaders,* were the other.

The interviewees in *The Gay Crusaders*—those who had most helped to shape nationwide activist strategies—were mostly all present too, including Frank Kameny, Marty Robinson, Arthur Evans, Barbara Gittings, Craig Rodwell, Jim Owles, Lige Clarke, and me. George had, by this time, developed vibrant friendships with several lesbian movement pioneers, including Lilli Vincenz, Barbara Gittings, and Kay Tobin Lahusen. On this special occasion, he allowed his guests of honor to invite a hundred comrades each. The party became a *Who's Who* of the gay liberation movement on America's East Coast. Attendees also included famous New York City artist-provocateurs. Andy Warhol's superstars, Jackie Curtis and Candy Darling, arrived fashionably late in the company of Vicki Richman, a brilliant transvestite columnist for *GAY.*

The latter part of the 1970s found the good doctor maintaining a steady but deliberately small therapy practice; he also devoted himself to his real love, writing. Earlier he proved to himself that it was possible for him to get published in the largest of the mainstream publications, including *Reader's Digest* and *TV Guide.* Now he began offering, in a series of books, unique insights into consciousness, designed to be of help to the many and not just to a limited few. He had begun this line of work much earlier when he wrote his second book, *The Activist Approach,* bringing the influence of American psychologist William James to bear on his approach to therapy. Weinberg's first book had been, literally, a textbook about psychology and statistics, one in which his mathematical insights had come into play.

Now, however, he aimed at a popular market, and in 1978 his *Self Creation,* a colloquial self-control manual, was selected by both the Psychology Today Book Club and the Book-of-the-Month Club, clearly demonstrating his appeal to a self-help–conscious mass audience. It was translated and published in fourteen languages.

George Weinberg was particularly busy during the 1980s and 1990s unveiling in a series of books his visions of human potentialities. One of his major works, *The Pliant Animal: Understanding the Greatest Human Asset,* emphasized what he knew about the strengths inherent in our species' elasticity. He wrote:

> Far from being a creature who cannot change, the human being has incredible pliancy . . . to study sameness with the intention of classifying people as like or unlike one another is to set one's sights on seeing how we do not change. Yet this is essentially what psychology has done. (Weinberg, 1981, p. 233)

Next published was a 1984 overview of his profession, *The Heart of Psychotherapy: A Journey into the Mind and Office of a Therapist at Work.* Scorning traditional ways therapists often approached their patients, his criticisms exposed practices he thought of as little more than hocus-pocus. He deplored signs of greed among psychologists wherever he saw them. I was once witness to his unhappiness at finding that a small hourly fee he'd charged to tutor a student-therapist was being exceeded by the high fees that same student was already charging his new patients.

Among some of the more significant approaches to a pleasured life that George Weinberg and I agreed upon, I think, pertained to beauty. In his introduction to a second book Lige and I wrote, he zeroed in on advice we'd given about approaching new relationships. "I like them especially," he said of us, "when they are rebutting the criteria of physical beauty according to which all but one in ten-thousand is ugly." Within this context Weinberg offered his own challenging but characteristic perspective that "the art of life consists largely in the ability to see beauty, to remain open to beauty, for nature never tires of showing it to us in new forms" (Clarke and Nichols, 1974, p. xiii).

In 1990, with the publication of *The Taboo Scarf,* George Weinberg offered his readers dramatic tales from his experience as a therapist, altering patient histories to make them unrecognizable, but describing their progress in unforgettable terms. A *New York Times* (November 18, 1990) reviewer found in this book "complex investigations of a master sleuth searching for the demon within, the repressed evil, the killer of the psyche."

Brian L. Weiss, MD, chair of the Department of Psychiatry at Mount Sinai Medical Center in Miami, characterized *The Taboo Scarf* as a "rare treasure" in which readers "become the therapist and the patient," learning about themselves in the process (Weiss, 1990).

In the same vein as *The Taboo Scarf,* Weinberg wrote *Nearer to the Heart's Desire,* more tales from therapy, his title borrowed from a haunting verse in *The Rubaiyat* of Omar Khayyam. This particular verse seems somehow best to capture George Weinberg's deep passion to act:

> Ah, love, could you and I with Fate conspire
> To grasp this sorry scheme of things entire,
> Would not we shatter it to bits?
> And then remold it nearer to the heart's desire?

BIBLIOGRAPHY

Books by George Weinberg

The Action Approach. New York: St. Martin's Press, 1969.
The Heart of Psychotherapy: A Journey into the Mind and Office of a Therapist at Work. New York: St. Martin's Press, 1984, reprinted, 1996.
Invisible Masters: Compulsions and the Fear that Drives Them. New York: Grove/Atlantic Press, 1993.
Nearer to the Heart's Desire. New York: Grover/Atlantic Press, 1992.
Numberland. New York: St. Martin's Press, 1987.
The Pliant Animal: Understanding the Greatest Human Asset. New York: St. Martin's Press, 1981.
Self Creation. New York: St. Martin's Press, 1978.
Shakespeare on Love. New York: St. Martin's Press, 1991.
Society and the Healthy Homosexual. New York: St. Martin's Press, 1972.
Statistics: An Intuitive Approach. Belmont, CA: Brooks/Cole, fourth printing, 1981.
The Taboo Scarf. New York: St. Martin's Press, 1990.

By George Weinberg and Dianne Rowe

The Projection Principle. New York: St. Martin's Press, 1988.
Will Power! Using Shakespeare's Insights to Transform Your Life. New York: St. Martin's Press, 1996.

Columns

GAY, Four Swords, Inc., New York, see George Weinberg's columns, 1970-1973. St. Martin's Press, New York, 1969.

Other

Clarke, L. and Nichols, J. *The Gay Agenda*. Buffalo: Prometheus Books, 1996.
Clarke, L. and Nichols, J. *Roommates Can't Always Be Lovers*. New York: St. Martin's Press, 1974.
Evans, Arthur. E-mail communication to Jack Nichols, March 5, 2000.
Nichols, J. Interview with G. Weinberg. February 25, 2000.
The Homosexual Citizen, "ECHO 1965" by Warren D. Adkins and Michael Fox, published by the Mattachine Society of Washington and the Mattachine Society of Florida, Inc., January 1966.
Weiss, B.L. Personal letter to G. Weinberg, March 10, 1990.

Vern L. Bullough (1928-):
Making the Pen Mightier Than the Sword

John P. De Cecco

As editor in chief of the Harrington Park series on gay and lesbian studies, I want to explain why Vern L. Bullough was selected as editor of this collection, and why I feel his biography should also be included, despite some opposition from him. Bullough has been a longtime supporter of the gay liberation movement and helped launch and sustain the field of gay and lesbian historical studies. It is an extraordinary example of how scholarship can be used without being compromised to further political freedom and equality.

In my visit in the summer of 2000 to his home in Southern California, besides the de rigueur swimming pool, the patio, and the garden off the living room, the first things anyone would notice are the books. Vern's home, which he shares with Gwen, his new wife and also a retired professor, is virtually encased in books, neatly shelved and lining the walls of the living room, the dining room, the entrance way, halls, and his study. These are not all the books he has owned in an academic life stretching over six decades. Many he has given away to universities and other collections, particularly the library associated with the Center for Sex Research at California State University, Northridge. The section of his library that contains books on homosexuality, particularly those that are historical in substance, shows that he is remarkably current with the burgeoning literature in the field of gay and lesbian studies.

Books, his own and others, have been Vern's loves of a lifetime. Writing comes easily to him. He has enjoyed it since he was a teenager. His style is clear, smooth, and unadorned, increasingly rare attributes in modern academia. He believes the writer/historian should tell a story as it emerges from documents before engaging in postmodern flights of interpretation. He

361

writes for three or four hours every morning. This is followed by his daily swimming dishabille, the tiniest and only hint of impropriety that I detected in my weekend visit. I should add that the garden where the pool is located shields him from his neighbors.

Vern's interest in homosexuality was sparked by the mother of his late wife and lifelong collaborator, Bonnie Bullough, with whom he worked over a period spanning five decades. Bonnie's mother had abandoned her, her stepfather, and their two children (Bonnie's half brother and half sister) early in the 1940s to enter a long-term relationship with another woman, Berry Berryman, which lasted over thirty years. Within a couple of years, however, she reestablished relationships with her children.

Vern and Bonnie, who began going together in their midteens, often visited the two women and much of their early conversation dealt with homosexuality, particularly lesbianism. Vern says he was the goggle-eyed teenager finding out about life from them. They gave Bonnie and him books to read and introduced them to other lesbians and gays at parties. Both became intensely interested in the subject. Berry, who had done an early study of lesbians, however, did not let them read her study because she said it was unfinished. Shortly after Berry's death, Bonnie's mother sent them the still-uncompleted manuscript, which Vern and Bonnie then published in a scholarly journal, identifying Berry as the original compiler and their relationship to her.

As an undergraduate at the University of Utah and later as a graduate student in history at the University of Chicago, Bullough read any books on homosexuality he could find in the library that his mother-in-law did not have. Knowing that his professors would frown upon his interest in studying sexuality—horrible dictum homosexuality—he never revealed to them the subject matter of the books he assiduously searched for and read. This clandestine ferreting of the few volumes he could find on homosexuality, usually in the section that housed books on sexual perversion, is not an unfamiliar experience of many gay and lesbian scholars in the period before libraries and bookstores opened their shelves to gay and lesbian studies in the late 1970s. At the University of Chicago, Vern earned a doctorate in late medieval/early modern history, with an emphasis on the history of science and medicine, subject matter not entirely unrelated but still a closeted distance from sexuality.

While still living in the Midwest, Vern published a review in the *Humanist* of a study of the Wolfenden Report, which had been issued in 1957 by a committee of the British Parliament charged with the responsibility to study "homosexual offenses and prostitution." One of its major recommendations was the decriminalization of homosexual acts occurring in private between consenting adults ages twenty-one and older. A publisher, impressed with

Vern's review, asked him to write a book on one of the two topics. After considerable soul-searching and with Bonnie's encouragement, he decided to do a study on prostitution, although he feared it might well end his academic career. He admits that he, at that time, avoided writing on homosexuality because of the possibility of being stigmatized as a homosexual—yet there was little fear of being labeled a prostitute. Only later when his academic status was secure did he feel confident enough and less worried about what others might think to write publicly about homosexuality.

Active in the American Civil Liberties Union as a graduate student in Chicago, when he moved to Ohio to teach at Youngstown University he became a member of the state board of the Ohio Civil Liberties Union and unsuccessfully urged that the affiliate adopt a policy to decriminalize homosexuality. He had a long talk with the then-national director who said such a policy would be enacted only over his dead body. Fortunately, that director later left his position.

After Vern moved to Los Angeles in 1959, and feeling more confident in his ability to withstand any labeling, he became more directly involved with the gay and lesbian community. He quickly became a member of the board of the ACLU of Southern California and began planning with then-executive director Eason Monroe to change ACLU policy on gays and lesbians. The Southern California affiliate was the oldest affiliate of the ACLU, having been established early in the 1920s, and had considerable independence from the national union. The Southern California ACLU was noted for its attempt to expand the scope of the issues with which the ACLU dealt, and Vern and Eason Monroe agreed that homosexuality and sexual identity in general was an issue that involved civil liberties. Still, it took a two-year campaign, with several draft statements, to get the board to acknowledge this civil liberty, which they did unanimously. Closely involved in the campaign were Dorr Legg and Don Slater, as well as representatives of DOB. As part of the campaign to get the ACLU involved in the issue and the subsequent adoption of the statement, Vern spoke widely to chapters of the ACLU, as well as service organizations, and participated in public debates on the decriminalization of homosexuality in public forums, on radio, and on television. The Washington, DC, affiliate, at the urging of Frank Kameny, soon followed the Southern California ACLU, as eventually the national itself did. Most of the legal staff members, however, came to be centered in Los Angeles where they remain today. As Vern later found out, a couple of the board members were then closeted homosexuals who were supporting him in all his efforts.

Vern also became involved in ONE, Inc., and in the Homosexual Information Center. He became vice president of the Institute for the Study of Human Resources, the tax-free foundation set up for ONE, Inc., by Reed

Erickson, who chaired it. Because Erickson almost never attended meetings, Bullough usually acted as chairperson. He was involved in most of the activities associated with both ONE and the Homosexual Information Center until he left Southern California at the end of 1979 for Buffalo, New York. One of the more vivid memories is his and Bonnie's participation in the auto caravan, organized by Don Slater and others, which paraded through the streets of Hollywood and West Hollywood in the mid-1960s demanding that gays be drafted to serve in Vietnam, a war that Vern strongly opposed.

He wrote articles and book reviews for *ONE Magazine,* published in *The Ladder,* the magazine of the Daughter of Bilitis, the lesbian organization founded by Del Martin and Phyllis Lyon, and also wrote for *Tangents,* the magazine Don Slater established after the break from ONE.

With a little prompting from me and with wry smiles Vern recalled some of the movement pioneers he knew, particularly their motley array of political allegiances and their inevitable factionalism, which in his marginal status as a straight man he was mostly able to avoid. He described Harry Hay as a mystic who tried to build "cells" within the Mattachine Society after the fashion of the Communist Party. He knew screenwriter Dale Jennings, one of the founders of the society, a person he believes was never comfortable in the gay movement. He recalled with admiration, however, Jennings' coming out during his trial on a charge of soliciting in West Hollywood, one that ended in acquittal. He described Jim Kepner as always gathering materials for what has become one of the core collections in the gay and lesbian library at the University of Southern California. Kepner, who was never outspoken, kept peace with all factions, writing for *Tangents,* the offshoot of *ONE Magazine,* and pursuing his interest in science fiction. Then there was Don Slater, the anarchist, who would not pay his traffic tickets. Dorr Legg was the conservative, the prototypical Log Cabin Republican and the indefatigable founder of ONE who kept the organization, if not its publication, going at all costs. It was through Legg that Vern met Reed Erickson, who had established the Erickson Foundation and who provided him the financial support for his major study, *Sexual Variance in Society and History* (1976). Bonnie and Vern, but mostly Vern, spoke for decriminalization of homosexuality before gay and straight groups all over Southern California.

Vern also knew Evelyn Hooker, who, after her pathbreaking studies on gay men, had been appointed as head of a task force by the National Institute of Mental Health that was intended to frame policy and initiate research on homosexuality. Evelyn invited Vern to be the task force's historian (he had to decline because he was living in Egypt at the time). Vern and Bonnie were among early members and consultants of the newly organized (and still-thriving) Parents and Friends of Gays in Los Angeles (two of their five children, three of whom were adopted, are gay—a son and a daughter). With colleagues at Northridge, Vern founded the Center for Sex Research early in the 1970s, which in 1999-2000 underwent a state auditor's investigation after holding conferences on prostitution and pornography. The Center for Sex Research was recently officially granted a new charter. After Vern moved to Buffalo to serve as a dean and later as a distinguished professor of the State University of New York, he served as a consultant to William H. Gardner, the attorney who successfully filed the suit that struck down New York's antisodomy statute. Interestingly, for a person who felt he was going to be ostracized from academia for his sex research, particularly that on homosexuality, Vern later found that several members of the selection committee which chose him as dean were gay, and he was probably chosen *because* of his research, rather than despite it.

Vern has undoubtedly led the way for gay and lesbian studies. Before I became editor of the *Journal of Homosexuality* in 1977, he had published two articles in the very first issues in 1974. The first article, "Homosexuality and the Medical Model," appeared the year after the declassification of homosexuality as a mental illness by the American Psychiatric Association. The article described how this decision marked the reversal of a trend that began in the latter part of the eighteenth century and had gradually transformed a moral conception of sexuality into a medical one that pathologized all forms that were not procreative. His conception of the "medical model" and its relationship to homosexuality preceded the related publications of Michel Foucault (1976) and Jeffrey Weeks (1977), whose views have become so influential in the field of gay and lesbian studies. In this article Vern introduced to this new field the name of the pioneer par excellence of gay liberation, Karl Heinrich Ulrichs. This article was followed by another, "Heresy, Witchcraft, and Sexuality," which appeared in the second issue of the journal (also in 1974). It described the association of heresy and witchcraft with sodomy—how religious and political dissent was tarred with the brush of "deviant" sexuality. It is an association that dramatically reared its ugly head during the McCarthy hearings of the 1950s in which communism and disloyalty to the flag were associated with homosexuality.

The topic of homosexuality remained central to Vern's research and writing well into the 1970s. In 1976 Garland Press published *An Annotated Bibliography of Homosexuality,* which was mostly based on a bibliography that Vern had compiled but included major contributions by Dorr Legg and James Kepner. It appeared in two volumes and contained about 13,000 entries. In that same year he published a magnum opus, *Sexual Variance in Society and History,* a study of attitudes toward sexuality. Homosexuality received much more attention than any other sexual variation. After Magnus Hirschfeld's work, to which I refer next, *Sexual Variance* is probably the first cultural history of the subject; it preceded by several years the work on medieval homosexuality by John Boswell, *Christianity and Social Toler-ance,* published in 1980, and by other gay and lesbian historians.

As editor of the Prometheus Press, Vern has been energetic in supporting the English translations by Michael Lombardi-Nash of the nineteenth and early twentieth-century work on homosexuality by Karl Heinrich Ulrichs and Magnus Hirschfeld, both German pioneers of the gay and lesbian move-ment and of gay and lesbian studies: Ulrichs' *Riddle of Man-Manly Love* (1993) and Hirschfeld's *Transvestites: The Erotic Drive to Cross-Dress* (1991) as well as his *Homosexuality of Men and Women* (2000). In his intro-duction to the latter book, Vern points to the biological reductionism inher-ent in Hirschfeld's conception of homosexuality and that current notions have gone beyond his "monism" in both causation and typology. We now speak of *homosexualities.* Vern describes his present position on the issue of "causation" as "interactionist"—one that includes both biological and envi-ronmental factors. Since we can confidently assume that all human erotic states, preferences, behavior, and attitudes are an indistinguishable complex of body, mind, physical environment, and society, any singling out of the "causes" of homosexuality has an inescapable whiff of the old medical pa-thology that he so clearly described in 1974.

Vern has had several identities, all of which have come into play in his contributions to gay liberation and gay and lesbian studies. His primary pro-fessional identity is that of historian of human sexuality, an identity that he ranks higher than "sexologist." He takes pride in the fact that in the Ameri-can Historical Society he pioneered sexuality as a serious, acceptable area of research and teaching. His interest in the field extends well beyond ho-mosexuality although he was one of the founding members of the gay cau-cuses in both the historical and sociological associations. He has written or edited about fifty books, about half of them on sex or gender topics, from contraception (the subject of his latest writing) to prostitution and trans-genderism, from pornography to sadomasochism to a history of sex re-search. He jokes about the fact that as he publishes on each new sexual vari-ation, there are renewed speculations about his own "true" sexual and gender identity—e.g., is he a cross-dresser, transsexual, or simply a closet gay? Regretfully, I must report, he is not a transvestite, neither is he gay nor bisexual.

The issue of his gender identity arises as a kind of a guilt by association. He has had a long friendship with Virginia Prince, a transvestite man who publicly always appears cross-dressed. Prince was the pioneer leader and organizer of the transvestite movement. Vern, who might have been hesitant early in his career about being identified with stigmatized sexual groups, is clearly quite comfortable in his gender identity—comfortable enough to go back to college to get his nursing degree to gain greater clinical experience.

Nursing was Bonnie's primary professional affiliation, to which she later added a doctorate in sociology, and the two of them wrote extensively on nursing. His advocacy of women's rights has been a continuing commitment throughout his career in his research, writing, teaching, and political action. This includes women's right to engage in prostitution, to work in the pornography and stripping industry, and to employ various forms of contraception.

His political identity, of which he never makes an issue, is that of the classic liberal, in the mode of John Stuart Mill. He has cultivated fundamental respect for individual rights and individuality, particularly of those persons and groups whose lives fall outside of conventional sexual and gender norms. He does not impose his values on others; he avoids the tyranny of political ideology. He does not harbor grievances or injustices that lead to severed relationships. In the field of sexology, he is one of the few professional people who has not been swallowed up in controversy and ambition and manages to keep a civilized relationship with individuals in all factions. Although many of the pioneers of the gay movement whose biographies appear in this book, and others, ended up not speaking with each other, Vern has managed to remain connected with most of them.

Considering that he was born in the bosom of the Mormon Church, which he left in his teens, his work delights with a subterranean puckish, irreverent edge. Whereas Mormonism has been to this day a bastion of procreative sexuality, almost all of Vern's work and advocacy have dealt with the nonreproductive forms. He acknowledges that studying the "forbidden" forms of sexuality and gender, although still working well within the boundaries of scholarly respectability, provides an illicit frisson for his work. He can write and speak about forbidden forms of sexuality and gender with a very straight voice and steady voice.

His scholarly achievements and respectability, combined with his open-mindedness, have over the years provided a crucial link between gay and straight communities. Although several of the gay and lesbian homophile pioneers were well-educated and articulate people, their credibility and authority were clouded under stigma from the start. It would take two more decades before we as gay and lesbian students and advocates of gay liberation could find our own voices and draw support from our own communities. That independence, however, would not have been possible (and still is not) without the contributions of scholar-advocates such as Vern Bullough, who lent their reputations and shared our struggles long enough for us to gain the confidence to take them on for ourselves. As editor in chief of the Harrington Park series on gay and lesbian studies, which this volume now joins, I wish to express to Vern Bullough the deepest gratitude of our gay and lesbian scholarly community for all the work he has done these past forty years on our behalf.

BIBLIOGRAPHY

Selected Books

Bullough, Vern L. *Homosexuality: A History.* New York: Garland, 1978; New York: New American Library, 1979.

Bullough, Vern L. *Science in the Bedroom: A History of Sex Research.* New York: Basic Books, 1994.

Bullough, Vern L. *Sexual Variance in Society and History.* New York: Wiley, 1976; Chicago: University of Chicago, 1978.

Bullough, Vern L. *The Subordinate Sex: A History of Attitudes Toward Women.* Urbana: University of Illinois Press, 1973; Penguin Books, 1974.

Bullough, Vern L., and Bonnie Bullough, *Cross Dressing, Sex, and Gender.* Philadelphia: University of Pennsylvania Press, 1993.

Bullough, Vern L., and Bonnie Bullough, *Human Sexuality: An Encyclopedia.* New York: Garland, 1994.

Bullough, Vern L. and Bonnie Bullough, *Sexual Attitudes, Myths, and Realities.* Buffalo, NY: Prometheus Books, 1995.

Bullough, Vern L., Bonnie Bullough, Marilyn Fithian, William Hartman, and Randy Klein, *How I Got into Sex.* Buffalo, NY: Prometheus Books, 1997.

Bullough, Vern L., Howard Fradkin, and Dorr Legg, *Homosexuality: Twenty-Five Questions.* Los Angeles: Institute for the Study of Human Resources, 1972. (Pamphlet.)

Bullough, Vern L., Dorr Legg, James Kepner, and Barrett Elcano. *An Annotated Bibliography of Homosexuality.* New York: Garland, 1976.

Selected Articles

Bullough, Vern L. "Heresy, Witchcraft, and Sexuality," *Journal of Homosexuality,* 1 (1974), 183-201.

Bullough, Vern L. "Homosexuality and the Medical Model," *Journal of Homosexuality,* 1 (1974), 99-116.

Bullough, Vern L. "Lesbianism, Homosexuality, and the American Civil Liberties Union," *Journal of Homosexuality,* 13 (1986), 23-32.

Bullough, Vern L., and Bonnie Bullough. "Lesbianism in the 1920s and 30s," *Signs,* 2 (1977), 895-904.

Chesser, Eustace, "Live and Let Live: The Moral of the Wolfenden Report," *Humanist,* 19 (1959), 119.

Christine Jorgensen (1926-1989)

Vern L. Bullough

Courtesy of ONE, Inc.

At the beginning of the 1950s, psychiatric opinion dominated any discussion of homosexuality. It and almost anything else that was not heterosexual was pathological. To change ideas about sexual identity required a major change not only in psychiatric thinking but in public opinion. Instrumental in initiating this process was Christine Jorgensen, ne George Jorgensen, who became an international media sensation in 1952.

Jorgensen, an ex-GI, believed that nature had made a mistake in giving him a male body. Searching for solutions, he planned to go to Sweden where he had heard that some surgical intervention was possible, but he first stopped in Denmark to visit relatives. There he met Christian Hamburger, a Copenhagen surgeon, and he told Hamburger he simply could not go on living as a man. He had, before coming to Denmark, secretly acquired women's clothes, often wore them, had shaved his pubic hair to be shaped more like a female's, and in his work as a laboratory technician he had access to estrogen which he had for a time administered to himself. After further examination, Hamburger and his associates decided to treat him with additional female hormones, although in doses much larger than he had given himself, and his body gradually gained more feminine contours, while his behavior, gait, and voice (after some training) became more feminine. As his beard grew sparser, electrolysis was used to removed the remaining facial hair. He was then castrated under provisions of a Danish Sterilization and Castration Act, which permitted castration when the patient's sexuality made him likely to commit crimes or when it involved mental disturbance. In 1952, Jorgensen expressed an ardent wish to have the last visible remains of his detested male sex organs removed, so his penis was amputated one year after his orchiectomy had been performed. Technically, however, as a castrated man, the patient had not undergone a sex change, and no attempt was made at that time to construct a vagina or other female sex organs; but the hormones had given him a very feminine look, and the U.S. government changed his sex on his passport to female. Later, there were somewhat successful efforts to make a vagina for Jorgensen from her intestines. It was not until much later that the male-to-female transsexual surgery was perfected, which involved using the scrotum and the penis, from which the meatus had been removed, to make a fairly successful vagina and labia.

When the news of what was called a "sex change" reached the media, probably initiated by Jorgensen herself, Jorgensen became famous worldwide. Seizing the opportunity, she sold her story to journalists from the Hearst newspapers and went on the stage. Reading about Jorgensen caused an outpouring of requests to Hamburger by hundreds of others to change their sex—requests which he refused, although a few other operations were done.

Special clinics to deal with transsexualism and similar issues were set up by Johns Hopkins, Stanford, and other institutions, and a number of surgeons began to specialize in the operations in places such as Morocco and in Trinidad, Colorado. Many, but not necessarily the majority, were homosexual in orientation when they presented themselves for treatment. This in some ways was troubling because it seems that many believed that the stigma or sinfulness of homosexuality was so great that they felt they could overcome it only by changing their sex.

Jorgensen herself, however, had contacts with ONE, Inc., in Los Angeles, where she eventually settled down and participated in conferences sponsored by ONE. She considered herself a missionary for changing public attitudes about sex. Her appearance as a speaker always guaranteed an audience, most of whom ended up supporting her and even admiring her. Her case also undermined the psychiatric domination of sexuality and made the public more willing to listen to different views.

Psychologists, sociologists, anthropologists, and even historians had begun to conduct investigations into human sexuality from their own disciplinary interest, and Alfred Kinsey, whatever else he had done, had mounted a full-scale attack on the psychiatric domination. Transsexualism brought surgeons, endocrinologists, and others who were making decisions about sex changes without even consulting psychiatrists and resulted in some turf battles in the medical profession.

Although Christine Jorgensen later deliberately removed herself from the limelight, she never forgot where she had come from and helped out would-be transsexuals, gays, transvestites, lesbians, and others in whatever way she could. By going public as she did, she forced the public as well as the professionals to rethink standard stereotypes and encouraged many to come out of the closet.

BIBLIOGRAPHY

Vern L. Bullough and Bonnie Bullough, *Cross Dressing, Sex, and Gender.* Philadelphia: University of Pennsylvania Press, 1993.
Christine Jorgensen, *A Personal Biography.* New York: Eriksson, 1967.

Virginia Prince (1913-   )

Vern L. Bullough

Homosexuality was a catchall term for a variety of activities in the first half of the twentieth century, and demarcating differences and emphasizing that there was a variety of behaviors both homosexual and heterosexual was an important task in pre-Stonewall America. Virginia Prince was a major factor in this movement. He, or rather she, since it was by her feminine persona that she was known, was the founder of the transvestite movement in the United States and around the world. Her emphasis on the heterosexuality of what she believed to be the majority of cross-dressers challenged traditional ideas about sex and gender, emphasizing that many behaviors which had been subsumed under the category of homosexuality were separate and distinct behaviors from a person's sexual orientation. Because the public's tolerance for transgendered persons was closely allied to its acceptance of homosexuality, Prince's "crusade" for a medical and psychiatric reconsideration of cross-dressing was an important factor in a growing public acceptance of same-sex preferences as well as in gender behavior.

Born into an upper middle-class family in Los Angeles in 1913, she began cross-dressing in her teens and collected a wardrobe of women's clothes. By the age of eighteen she was sneaking out of her house cross-dressed, riding the streetcar, and engaging in adventures as a teenaged girl. She reported that on such occasions she often achieved orgasm without masturbating. Both the fear and excitement about being caught and the actual cross-dressing were important to the sexual high. She continued to cross-dress until she married, at which time she went through an event that is standard in transvestite literature: a purge of everything associated with her "feminine self" and an oath not to do it again. Marriage was followed by a move from Los Angeles to the San Francisco area where she earned a doctorate in biochemistry. She soon began cross-dressing again. While participating in grand rounds in the medical school affiliated with the university, she attended a session featuring a man who had recently changed his name to Barbara Wilson and was living as a woman. Other cross-dressers were presented and Charles, a male pseudonym Virginia adopted, contacted them. Charles also had a private session with Karl Bowman, a psychiatrist knowledgeable about cross-dressing and who, unlike other psychiatrists he had consulted, told him that there were thousands of others like him out there and to accept himself as he was and to enjoy it.

Charles, in the meantime, had become a father and after completing a research project in San Francisco returned to Los Angeles and told his physician father about his cross-dressing and even dressed for him. His father's advice was to visit an endocrinologist, implying that additional male hormones might help him. After that, he refused to talk with his son about cross-dressing and never reconciled himself to his son's behavior. Charles, who had adopted the name of Virginia for his feminine persona, had also told his wife about his activities while they still lived in northern California. She was upset but reluctantly agreed to let him do so as long as she did not see him. In Los Angeles, unable to cope with Virginia's cross-dressing, she began seeing a psychiatrist who convinced her that her husband was a homosexual and concluded that the only solution was for her to get a divorce. The divorce provided a media bonanza, and the story of Charles/Virginia was featured in lurid newspaper stories. One effect of the stories was that Virginia was contacted by other transvestites and they began meeting together and publishing a newsletter. Virginia soon emerged as a dominant figure in the group and began publishing a magazine, *Transvestia,* on her own. She soon had a variety of publications and out of these came organized groups. Her activities soon came to the attention of the U.S. Post Office and she was charged with mailing obscene material. The charges grew out of some personal correspondence from Virginia to an individual whom she thought was a woman sympathetic to cross-dressing and in which Virginia let her fantasies go wild. The person turned out to be a man who himself was under investigation by postal officials for illicit activities, of which Virginia was believed to be a part. Although admitting she wrote the letter, Virginia was successful in the court in separating this activity from her publishing activities. Pleading guilty to writing the letter, she was given a three-year sentence in a federal penitentiary, which was suspended providing she avoid any illegal conduct for a five-year probationary period. If she was arrested for any reason, she would automatically go to prison. Since cross-dressing in public was prohibited by the Los Angeles criminal code of the time, this meant she would be subject to arrest if she cross-dressed publicly. To get around this prohibition, her attorney persuaded the court to allow part of her probation to be served in educating the public about cross-dressing. The court agreed, and the result was a number of public appearances as a woman before service clubs and other groups where she talked about gender differences and in the end revealed that she was a man. She also took great pains to distinguish cross-dressing from homosexuality, although she emphasized that both were unfairly persecuted. In the mid-1960s, she began living full-time as a woman, traveling around the country and the world, establishing transvestite clubs and groups along the way.

As the movement spread and other groups appeared, different views of transvestism appeared as did other publishers. Many groups welcomed homosexual cross-dressers and would-be transsexuals; other factions associated transvestism with bondage and domination and various fetishes. Many transvestite groups made coalitions with the gay and lesbian groups in their community, and the homophobia so prevalent in Virginia's early writings was not accepted by large segments of what came to be called the "transgender community." Increasingly Virginia herself recognized her antihomosexual bias and ultimately even went on a cruise with a gay man who pretended to be her husband.

An important incidental result of Prince's early efforts and of the club movement that ensued was that it gave researchers opportunities to study populations of transvestites who were not necessarily clients of a psychiatrist or psychologist and who had not been drawn from a criminal population. This significantly broadened the focus of the research on both cross-dressing and homosexuality. Prince was one of the first to take advantage of this and did a pioneering study of 504 subjects. Many people who identified as homosexual were found in the study, and there were probably more than entered the literature since often researchers excluded them from their reported data, giving a skewered view of the topic.

Transvestites, similar to homosexuals, were burdened by the psychiatric definitions of homosexuality and transvestism. As the definitions of homosexuality changed and it was eventually removed from the *Diagnostic and Statistical Manual of Mental Disorders,* so were those of transvestism. Magnus Hirschfeld, in his pioneering work on both homosexuality and transvestism published early in the twentieth century, had attempted to distinguish similarities and differences between the two phenomena, but much of his research was ignored by the English-speaking world. One of Hirschfeld's basic points was that although there were differences between homosexuals and transvestites, he felt that the two had to be allies in trying to change misleading public perceptions. This was ultimately the contribution of Virginia Prince to the movement, bringing a different group into the struggle for individual rights.

BIBLIOGRAPHY

Virginia Prince's autobiography appeared in her magazine, *Transvestia,* 100 (1977).

Vern L. Bullough and Bonnie Bullough. *Cross Dressing, Sex and Gender.* Philadelphia: University of Pennsylvania Press, 1993.

José Sarria (1923-   )

Vern L. Bullough

José Sarria early on recognized that he was a homosexual, and brags he screwed his way into the U.S. Army after the Japanese attack on Pearl Harbor on December 7, 1941. Turned down by the Navy and Marines because he was slightly under five feet tall and weighed only ninety pounds, he vowed to get into the Army even if he did not meet the height minimum. He believed he had found a way to do so when he became acquainted with an Army major whom he had met at several gay gatherings he had attended in San Francisco. The major had been interested in Sarria, but José had only flirted with him until he found out that the officer was assigned to the recruiting station. Knowing what he had to do, Sarria contacted the major; the two had lunch together and then went to a nearby hotel on the condition that the major would approve him for enlistment. Sarria soon found himself in the Army, where he was sent to attend classes to be a cook and baker. Eventually he ended up as an aide to a high-ranking officer and from there became the operator of an officers' dining hall in occupied Germany. He also became an expert in dealing with the black market and throwing parties. Although there was a lot of gossip about his possible sexual orientation, he was accepted by most of his colleagues.

Born to an unmarried woman, Maria Dolores Maldonado, and fathered by Julio Sarria late in 1922 or early 1923, Sarria was brought up by Jesserina and Charles Millen, while his mother lived with another family as a full-time maid. In fact, she used her wages to buy a house and to move the Millen family into it. José's mother tolerated his early cross-dressing and encouraged his artistic development by having him take lessons in dancing, violin, and voice, and the young boy had dreams of becoming an opera star. His adult voice was a high tenor, and he could reach high C in his normal voice and so he never had to camouflage his voice to sing as a woman in his shows. Unlike many other female impersonators, he always sang in his own voice.

When he left the Army in 1945, he enrolled in college and on the side became a cocktail waiter at the Black Cat bar in San Francisco, a Bohemian bar in the North Beach area used as a hangout for people on the fringes of acceptability in society, from actors to anarchists, including a significant number of gays, prostitutes, writers, and others. It served food, drinks, and irreverent entertainment. Sarria was the only male cocktail waiter and he soon became hostess and began singing and doing female impersonation on the side. He quickly became a star and a centerpiece of the San Francisco nightclub scene. He also became deeply involved with Jimmy Moore whom he had met at the Black Cat.

Angry over a growing estrangement between him and Jimmy, Sarria went out for a night on the town on his own and found himself arrested in the men's room at the St. Francis hotel by a vice squad officer whom he knew. He felt then and still feels that it was a set-up since all José did was use the urinal. Although the trial was handled discreetly, the fine was heavy and he had to sell some property of his to pay for it. Believing that the arrest and conviction ruined any possibility for getting a teaching credential, he left college without getting a degree. Feeling he was labeled a homosexual and a queen, he decided that he would be "the best goddam queen that ever was!"

He was also a crusader. San Francisco, as did many other cities at that time, had a law prohibiting men from dressing in women's clothing with an intent to deceive. Although the police usually looked the other way on Halloween, as soon as midnight passed anyone cross-dressed on the street would be arrested, even though the bars and clubs did not close until 2 a.m. Sarria, with the cooperation and advice of attorney Melvin Belli, had tags made up for each cross-dresser to wear, stating that "I am a boy." He distributed them widely advising everyone that when the police attempted to arrest those leaving the bars after midnight, the person could clearly state that there was no intention to deceive and show the tag. This marked the beginning of the end of police Halloween raids.

Sarria became a well-known female impersonator in the San Francisco clubs. He was increasingly flamboyant; for example, once a week, he would ride in a sidecar of a motorcycle in drag and red high-heeled shoes to make a deposit at a local bank, and then go shopping for a dress or shoes. When he didn't want to be flamboyant he dressed in men's clothes. Still, he enjoyed the role of impersonator, not only on stage; occasionally, in real life, he would appear as a housewife. He performed in the first camp opera at the Black Cat in 1958, a parody of *Madame Butterfly*.

Sarria, known everywhere as a gay queen, quickly became an activist for gay rights, preceding the actions of the gay queens of Stonewall. In 1960, he organized the League for Civil Education to do public education programs on homosexuality, to provide support for men trapped in the police sweeps, and to hold public meetings at which men facing discrimination and ostracism because of their homosexuality could vent and get support. To gain publicity for his cause he ran for county supervisor in 1961 on a program of equal justice for all. Although he lost, he became a San Francisco fixture.

Although Sarria had been the organizer and the financial angel of the League for Civil Education as well as its treasurer, the public spokesman was Guy Strait, and the two, after some three years, split apart over publication of a newsletter. A new foundation was organized in 1963 under the title of Society for Individual Rights (SIR) and the league disappeared. Both men remained active in the new society, and to raise money the SIR began putting on shows called "Celebritycapades" with dinners featuring female impersonators including Sarria.

Unfortunately for the Black Cat bar, Sarria's reputation led to a change in the nature of the clientele, which increasingly came to be identified as a welcome place for gays and lesbians. This reputation caused the state liquor commission to revoke its license in 1963. Because it could not survive without a bar, the Black Cat closed its doors the next year. Sarria, however, continued to fight in his own indomitable way. The Tavern Guild, which had been organized by tavern owners and their wholesale liquor supplier allies to fight incidents such as what happened to the Black Cat, began sponsoring an annual event featuring female impersonators.

In 1964, at a Tavern Guild ball, José was proclaimed queen of the ball. A week later, when he was asked as a San Francisco celebrity to appear at the opening of the Ice Follies, he declared himself Empress José Norton the First. He deliberately planned to be tardy. When he finally appeared with a court of attendants and in his capacity as empress, he proclaimed the opening of the follies, which brought the house down.

Sarria had looked to San Francisco tradition to establish his court, using the example of Joshua Norton, a prominent merchant during the gold rush era. After disappearing from San Francisco for a number of years, he reappeared wearing a feathered top hat and a blue military-style tailcoat, proclaiming himself Joshua Norton the First, Emperor of North America and Protector of Mexico. The amused newspapers treated Norton with all the deference due an emperor, and all of San Francisco joined in the game, treating him as a ruler in all social matters. Restaurants served him free meals, the board of supervisors appropriated funds for his clothing, and children followed him when he appeared on the streets because of his habit of throwing candy to them. Following his death at the turn of the century, his story became part of the folklore of San Francisco, and it was on this legend that Sarria seized, proclaiming himself the widow of the emperor who had died long before he was born. All of San Francisco joined in the game just as they had in the earlier era.

Encouraged by his success at the Ice Follies, Sarria in 1965 founded the Court System both as an outlet for gays to make fun of themselves, and also as a political statement. Sarria felt he was free to stand up for gays and lesbians, in part because he had much less to lose than his closeted brothers and sisters. He was not going to be fired from his performance jobs for being gay, because being gay was an integral part of his stage persona and he was used to taking flak for his unabashed belief in the basic equality of gays. He believed that dressing in drag itself was a provocative and defiant act, which emphasized that it took courage to be different; from the first he included women in his movement, and Del Martin and Phyllis Lyon became the first duchesses.

His willingness to go public as a homosexual meant that he was a political figure, sought out by others who wanted to make contact with or get support from the gay community. He expanded his influence by nominating empresses in San Diego and Los Angeles and many other communities. Each year in San Francisco there was a new empress, along with a slate of offices including an emperor, dukes, duchesses, and assorted czars, czarinas, jesters, and keepers of this and that. Initially he had tried to appoint the court members, but soon gave this up, taking a motherly delight in each new court and empress. He, however, remained Empress One of San Francisco, overseeing her growing family and heirs, and the ceremonies, which grew increasingly elaborate. Sarria began an annual memorial service for "her" late departed husband, the Emperor Norton, in Woodlawn Cemetery in nearby Colma. Even the cemetery got into the act by putting a new marker over the grave, a marble obelisk declaring the plot to be the final resting place of Emperor Joshua Norton I, Emperor of North America and Protector of Mexico.

As the movement has spread across the United States and Canada, Sarria's influence has become more tangential, but the growth of the movement remains an indicator of the ability of the gay and lesbian community to make fun of itself. Although the Mattachine Society named itself after the court jester, Sarria's imperial court brought the whole royal family into the game, and in the process made gays and lesbians more part of the mainstream, even while laughing at themselves. Quite clearly, as the Stonewall riots later demonstrated, the gay and lesbian community owe a lot to the pioneering gay queens of whom Sarria is a prime example.

REFERENCE

Gorman, Michael. *The Empress Is a Man: Stories from the Life of José Sarria.* Binghamton, NY: Harrington Park Press, 1998.

Charlotte Coleman (1923-   )

Roberta Bobba

Charlotte Coleman was more or less forced to resign from the Internal Revenue Service because of her suspected lesbianism, and, deciding to become more open about her same-sex preferences, she opened the first lesbian-owned bar in San Francisco, The Front. This was the first of many gay bars and restaurants she established; when one closed she moved on to another, including the Golden Cask and the Mint. She was not a passive owner but an active one, and her bars and restaurants hosted many a fund-raising event in the gay community and served as a safe meeting place for others. She was among the founders of the San Francisco Tavern Guild, which, aided by the wholesale liquor dealers, served as an effective political force in opening up the bar scene in San Francisco. She was instrumental in the foundation of the first gay bank, was important in the development of the Gay Olympics, and was a strong supporter of the Daughters of Bilitis.

Born September 5, 1923, in Rhode Island, she grew up in the small town of Somerset, Massachusetts. Because of her growing awareness of her attraction to other women, she believed it best to leave home and enlisted as a member of the women's reserve SPAR in the U.S. Coast Guard. She received an honorable discharge after completing two years, and wearing the "Ruptured Duck"—the pin given to discharged veterans—on her uniform, she decided to see the United States, which she could do for three cents a mile, courtesy of the U.S. government. The government also gave returning veterans twenty dollars a week for fifty-two weeks to get back on their feet. After visiting most of the major cities in the country she ended up in San Francisco, where she decided she wanted to live. She got a job as a book-keeper, where she spent her days, while her evenings were spent socializing in gay bars where she met many friends with whom she still keeps in contact. In 1950 she passed a government examination that enabled her to work as an auditor for the Internal Revenue Service. Shortly after this the IRS cut back on hiring new employees and the New Employee Investigation staff, determined to keep busy in this slack period, made a decision to reinvestigate all employees who were about to be elevated to a new grade raise, of which Charlotte was one. She was soon summoned to the investigation office, where she found the IRS had collected a file four inches thick of information about her. The investigators had read her mail, tapped her telephone, followed her to parties, bars, and even on weekend trips that she had taken to Sacramento and Santa Cruz. Events in her life that she had been unable to explain became clear. For example, at a Santa Cruz weekend party, the hostess observed an unknown driver circling the block both day and night throughout the weekend. At a Walnut Creek party a heap of cigarette butts had been discovered under a window shortly after the party. IRS agents had recorded all vehicle license plate numbers and traced down the names and addresses of everyone who had driven to these and other parties.

During her interrogation, the investigators mentioned many names of people, some of whom she knew well, others with whom she had only a fleeting acquaintance. She later learned that several of her friends had been arrested but had not communicated this fact to anyone. Although the IRS was not able to prove definitively that Charlotte was a lesbian, they concluded that she was guilty of "association with persons of ill repute" and should be released. Even though the head of the IRS personnel department confidentially advised Charlotte that she probably would win her case with the IRS if she contested it, Charlotte felt that then everyone in the IRS building would know she was a lesbian, a situation that might have been difficult to confront in 1959. Shortly after she left, she was invited by the IRS to participate in an awards ceremony at which she was given the Superior Performance Award for her exemplary service to the IRS, one of three such awards given in California that year. Such was the life of a lesbian woman.

Using the small amount she had received from her retirement account, Charlotte invested in a small beer and wine bar in the produce area of San Francisco, which she named The Front. Because the area was deserted at night, it was unlikely that women would be seen entering the bar, and it quickly became popular—before it was demolished to make way for a massive redevelopment project. Before that happened, however, the Alcohol Beverage Control (ABC) agency had filed "morals charges" against the bar in an attempt to revoke the liquor license, mainly for the observed actions of homosexual men in the bar. Charlotte did not fight the charges because the building was going to be demolished, but when she opened her new bar and restaurant, the Golden Cask, on Haight Street, she had to use a friend's name (who became her bartender) for the liquor license. The night of the grand opening, four police cars and a paddy wagon with sirens blaring sped up to the front door, and several cops swarmed into the restaurant, arrested and handcuffed the bartender, and drove her off in the paddy wagon. When Charlotte pressed the police on why they were arresting her bartender, an irate policeman replied that she had a "two-month unpaid parking ticket." Obviously this was part of a police harassment campaign that continued for several months. Police no longer entered the bar but rather arrested patrons as they left the bar, charging them falsely with being drunk in a public area. Charlotte bailed out her patrons the next morning and had her attorney seek dismissals of all cases, a demand in part motivated by the fear that the ABC board would use records of the arrests to deny her a license. Interestingly, all charges were dismissed.

Her bars and restaurants served as venues for many money-raising events in the gay community. The Daughters of Bilitis, spearheaded by Phil Lyon and Del Martin, used The Front for a St. Patrick's Day brunch. The Golden Cask was important in fund-raising for the Council on Religion and the Homosexual. She and her staff helped raise funds for the gay and lesbian community through a series of auction sales, but also sponsored the Memorial Day tricycle race to raise money for guide dogs for the blind. Still there was widespread homophobia, which was blatantly manifested in the city's police department who made a regular practice of harassing members of the gay community, particularly focusing on the city's restaurants and bars which catered to them. After the organization of the San Francisco Tavern Guild, aided by wholesale liquor dealers who did not want the lucrative businesses closed, police harassment decreased. Charlotte and various partners then opened a series of bars and restaurants in the San Francisco area including Gilmore's, The Answer (in Redwood City), the Campground (in Berkeley), and others. She sold her last two establishments in 1996 after thirty-seven years in the business.

She was very active in launching the first all-gay savings and loan bank in San Francisco, Atlas Savings and Loan Association, which, after great initial success, went bankrupt in the savings and loan crisis of the late 1980s. Charlotte still believes that it could have been saved if it had not been for the homophobia of the government officials involved. She was instrumental in raising money to support Tom Waddell in organizing the competitive event that initially was called the Gay Olympic Games. Although the International Olympic Committee refused to allow the use of the name "Olympic," the games have continued to grow and survive.

Since Charlotte has retired, she has become interested in creating a gay senior retirement home in San Francisco and is still talking and planning for it as of this writing.

Reed Erickson (1917-1992): How One Transsexed Man Supported ONE

Holly Devor

Courtesy of the Holly Devor collection

In order to succeed, all social movements need a vision of where they are going, dedicated people to do the work of getting them there, and material resources with which to support their efforts. In the 1960s, there were very few people who could freely offer any of these for the nascent gay and lesbian movements. Reed Erickson was one man who came forward during this time to provide ongoing financial support for gays and lesbians and to show remarkable vision and leadership, as well as financial support, for the development of transsexual/transgender advocacy on all fronts.

Reed Erickson was an extremely wealthy transsexed man who lived a colorful and eccentric but very private life. In June 1964, Reed Erickson launched the Erickson Educational Foundation (EEF), a nonprofit philanthropic organization funded and controlled entirely by Erickson himself. A brochure describing the Erickson Educational Foundation stated that its goals were "to provide assistance and support in areas where human potential was limited by adverse physical, mental or social conditions, or where the scope of research was too new, controversial or imaginative to receive traditionally oriented support." Through the EEF Erickson contributed millions of dollars to the early development of the gay, lesbian, bisexual, transgendered, and queer movements between 1964 and 1984.

REED ERICKSON'S PRIVATE LIFE

Reed Erickson was born as Rita Alma Erickson in El Paso, Texas, on October 13, 1917. Erickson's U.S.-born mother, Ruth Herzstein Erickson, came from a large German-Jewish family but was a practicing Christian Scientist during Erickson's lifetime. Erickson's German-born father, Robert B. Erickson, who may also have had Jewish roots, was an inventive intellectual businessman who spoke seven languages fluently. Erickson had one sister, Sylvia Roberta, who died in 1990.

When Erickson was still quite young the family moved to the Olney area of Philadelphia, Pennsylvania. Erickson was a good student who attended Wagner Junior High and the Philadelphia High School for Girls, where s/he became involved with a circle of lesbian women and started using the nickname Eric when among them. Erickson attended Temple University, 1936 to 1940. In 1940 the Erickson family moved to Baton Rouge, Louisiana, where Erickson's father had transferred his lead smelting business. In Baton Rouge, Rita/Reed Erickson worked in the family smelting business and attended Louisiana State University. In 1946, Erickson became the first female graduate from LSU's school of mechanical engineering.

In the early 1940s Erickson became the lover of a woman who was to become an integral part of the lives of Erickson and of his subsequent family. Anne (her name has been changed to protect her privacy) was a working-class New York Jewish woman who came from a family of left-wing political radicals. She held strong opinions about social justice and political activism, which she shared freely with Erickson. People who were close to Erickson have attributed his later social conscience and support of political activism largely to the influence that Anne had on the development of his thinking.

After graduating from LSU, Erickson and Anne lived briefly in Philadelphia. There Erickson worked as an engineer until losing her/his job for refusing to fire a woman who was suspected of being a communist. In the early 1950s Erickson and Anne returned once again to Baton Rouge, where Erickson resumed working in the family business and started an independent company, Southern Seating, making stadium bleachers. Anne and Erickson brought with them a pet Siamese cat named Sappho who was soon joined by a leopard kitten named Henry. Over the next twenty years, the full-grown Henry was Erickson's constant companion, living in each of his homes and frequently traveling with him in a crate on commercial and private aircraft. Henry more than once became front-page news as a result of his frequent appearances in the otherwise quiet residential streets of Baton Rouge's more well-to-do neighborhoods.

After Robert Erickson's death in 1962, Erickson inherited a major interest in the family enterprises, Schuylkill Products Co., Inc., and Schuylkill Lead Corp., and ran them successfully until selling them to Arrow Electronics in 1969 for approximately $5 million. Erickson continued to be financially successful, eventually amassing a personal fortune estimated at over $40 million, most of which came from canny investments in oil-rich real estate. Over a period of years, Erickson's ongoing income was often hundreds of thousands of dollars per month.

In 1963, Erickson became a patient of Dr. Harry Benjamin and began the process of masculinizing and living as Reed Erickson. Erickson's official name change took place in 1963 with the sex change following in 1965, setting legal precedent in the state of Louisiana. In 1963 Reed Erickson also married for the first time to a woman who was an entertainer and was related to the U.S. diplomats W. Averell Harriman and Florence Jaffray Harriman.[1] Sometime in 1964 the relationship ended and they ultimately divorced in 1965.

In 1964 Erickson started seeing a New Zealand woman, Aileen Ashton, who was working as a dancer and an escort in New York City when they met. Erickson was so entranced with her when he met her that he asked her to marry him on their second or third date. They were married in December 1965 in a small private ceremony in the United States. They followed this in March 1966 with a large traditional wedding which was hosted by Erickson's new wife's family and which was held at St. Mary's Church in Christchurch, New Zealand. After the wedding, the newlyweds returned to the United States where they took up residence in Baton Rouge. Within four years their lives had changed again in two significant ways: They became the parents to both a daughter and a son, and Erickson began to experiment with recreational drugs. In 1973 the family, including Henry the leopard, moved to an opulent custom-built home in Mazatlan, Mexico, which Erickson dubbed the Love Joy Palace. While there, Erickson increasingly indulged his interest in hallucinogenic drugs and before the end of the next year Erickson and his second wife were divorced. In 1979, after a few years of trying to coexist in Mazatlan, Erickson's ex-wife moved to Ojai, California, taking the children with her. By 1981, Erickson had followed and also taken up residence in Ojai to be near his children.

Around the time of Erickson's divorce from his second wife, he met and began a relationship with a Mexican woman, Evangelina Trujillo Armendariz, whom he met at the tourist bureau in Mazatlan. Early in 1977 they flew from Mazatlan to Baton Rouge where they were married in a small ceremony at the home of a friend of Erickson's sister. During the course of the relationship, both in Mazatlan and later in Southern California, Erickson's overindulgence in the use of illegal drugs increasingly came between them.

By the end of 1983 Erickson had run afoul of the law for his drug problems and his third wife had filed for divorce.

Over the remaining years of his life, Erickson's personality and judgment became undeniably distorted by the effects of his drug problems. Sadly, by the time of his death in 1992 at the age of seventy-four, he had become addicted to illegal drugs. He died alone in Mazatlan as a fugitive from U.S. drug indictments.

REED ERICKSON'S PUBLIC LIFE AS A PHILANTHROPIST

In 1952, seven men, Martin Block, Dale Jennings, Don Slater, Merton Bird, W. Dorr Legg, Antonio Reyes, and Bailey Whitaker, banded together in Los Angeles to found ONE, Inc., one of the earliest and longest-running gay and lesbian organizations in the United States. The men who started ONE dedicated themselves to an ambitious course of action, which included publishing literature, conducting educational activities, supporting research concerning homosexuality, providing homosexual peer counseling, and making the acquisition of property in aid of these goals.

Throughout the 1950s and early 1960s ONE, Inc., achieved remarkable success in many of these areas. They established *ONE Magazine* and mounted a successful challenge against the U.S. government's claim that it was a priori obscene and could not be sent through the postal system. Later, ONE began publishing a scholarly journal, the *ONE Institute Quarterly*. ONE also set up a telephone hotline in a rented office that was quickly transformed into a kind of de facto gay community center. In addition, ONE sponsored lecture series, miniconferences, short and full-length college-level courses, and graduate seminars on topics related to various aspects of homosexuality. All of these activities were sustained with the most minimal of financial resources.

In 1964, shortly after Erickson founded the Erickson Educational Foundation, Erickson's path crossed that of ONE. In need of funds to support their activities and to finance a much-needed move to improved premises, ONE sent out a mailing requesting donations. Erickson was one of the few who replied with an offer of money. Erickson soon established a relationship with Dorr Legg, the man who was the driving force of ONE during much of its existence. Erickson continued to work and to battle with ONE and with Dorr Legg over the next twenty years.

Erickson's first move was to advise ONE to establish a nonprofit tax-exempt charitable arm, the Institute for the Study of Human Resources (ISHR) to make it more attractive for potential benefactors to donate freely to ONE. The establishment of ISHR shifted ONE's research, social service,

and educational work into the nonprofit ISHR and allowed ONE the freedom to work for the legalization of homosexuality and other law reforms.
Reed Erickson was named as president of ISHR and remained in the post
until 1977 when the Erickson Educational Foundation temporarily suspended operations. Erickson's then bride to be, Aileen Ashton, was also a
founding director, a position she held until 1975. Dorr Legg was noted as the
secretary of ISHR; he retained that post until his death in 1994.

The money immediately began to flow from Erickson's EEF to ISHR.
The first $2,000 went to the cost of incorporation of ISHR. Another $1,000
arrived in early October 1964 even before the by-laws were drawn up. In
December 1964, a check arrived at ISHR for $10,000 as a first installment
on a "Research Study Project in the Bibliography of Homosexuality." By
January 1965, ISHR was receiving $1,000 a month from Erickson's EEF.
Erickson's EEF continued to fund ISHR directly from 1964 to 1976 and
again from 1980 to 1983 during which time 70 to 80 percent of ISHR's
operating budget came from Erickson through the Erickson Educational
Foundation. In total, ISHR's official records showed them having received
over $200,000 in direct grants. These monies were channeled through ISHR
to the ONE Institute's educational programs, to the development of the
Blanche M. Baker Memorial Library, and to a variety of other educational
and research projects. In addition to the money channeled directly to
ISHR/ONE, Legg and other activists and researchers also received private
grants from Erickson's EEF in aid of their activities.

The establishment of ISHR allowed Erickson a vehicle through which to
make tax-exempt charitable donations to support the activities of ONE. Although there were other donors to ISHR and ONE, it would not be an exaggeration to say that *without* Erickson's support many of ONE's activities,
and perhaps even ONE itself, would not have been possible on the scale that
they obtained *with* the benefit of EEF money. The expansion of ONE Institute's nondegree courses, a great many of ONE's several hundred Sunday
afternoon lectures, and extension division courses given by ONE in other
cities were all facilitated by Erickson's generous donations to ONE through
ISHR.

For example, among the many projects supported by Erickson's EEF was
a public program staged on a topic of particular interest to Erickson. In June
1974, a widely publicized three-day "Forum on Variant Sex Behavior" took
place in Los Angeles, organized by Professors Vern and Bonnie Bullough,
under the auspices of ISHR. Speakers for the event included Vern Bullough,
vice president of ISHR; Zelda Suplee, director of the Erickson Educational
Foundation; Virginia Prince, editor of *Transvestia* and widely attributed as
being one of the founders of transgender activism; Laud Humphreys, author
of *Tearoom Trade: Impersonal Sex in Public Places;* Christopher Isher-

wood, widely acclaimed author; and Evelyn Hooker, author of the revolutionary 1957 research study, "The Adjustment of the Male Overt Homosexual." Christine Jorgensen was also there

The earliest of ISHR's research projects funded by Erickson and the one
that took the longest—over twenty years—to come to fruition was also one
of great significance. The members of ONE were well aware that there was
an abysmal dearth of information available on homosexuality—beyond that
which was most damning. In 1955, ONE announced plans to compile an annotated bibliography on the topic of homosexuality to at least partially remedy this situation. However, due to limited funds, very little was accomplished until Erickson appeared on the scene and agreed to fund the project.

Work was begun in late 1964; two volumes of *An Annotated Bibliography of Homosexuality* were eventually published in 1976 by Garland Press.
The completed work contained 12,794 entries and, as such, constituted an
unprecedented foundational contribution to the study of homosexuality. At
the same time as work was under way for *An Annotated Bibliography,*
Erickson also funded Vern Bullough for work on three other important
books on human gender and sexuality.

Another important project cosponsored by Erickson's EEF and by ISHR
was the one-month coast-to-coast speaking tour of the United States by Antony Grey, a key figure in the British organizations The Albany Trust and
The Homosexual Law Reform Society. The Report of the Wolfenden Committee, commissioned in 1954 in response to a series of scandalous U.K.
court cases concerning homosexuality, was released in 1957. It recommended the legalization of homosexual acts performed in private and between consenting adults. The Homosexual Law Reform Society was set up
in spring 1958 to apply social and political pressure in hopes of seeing action taken on the Wolfenden recommendations. The Albany Trust was its
nonpolitical tax-exempt charitable arm. Antony Grey, as the secretary of
both organizations from 1962 to 1970, headed up the fight for legalization
of homosexuality in Britain. When homosexual activities between consenting adults in private were legalized with the passing of the 1967 Sexual Offenses Act, Grey was widely acknowledged as a key player in spearheading
the campaigns that culminated in this victory. Due to Erickson's largess,
Grey was able to come to the United States to share what he had learned.

Perhaps ONE's most proud accomplishment was its 1981 accreditation
by the state of California as a graduate degree-granting institution after
twenty-five years of offering graduate-level education. In August 1981, history was once again made by ONE when authorization was granted for the
first time for degrees to be offered in homophile studies. The first-ever degrees in homophile studies were awarded early in 1982 at the thirtieth anniversary celebrations of the founding of ONE, attended by over 600 people

gathered in the Wilshire Room of the Los Angeles Hilton Hotel. Presentations at the banquet were made by, among others, Lisa Ben, Del Martin, and Phyllis Lyon. Lisa Ben was the pseudonym of the publisher of *Vice Versa,* "the earliest known American periodical especially for lesbians." Del Martin and Phyllis Lyon founded the Daughters of Bilitis in 1955, "the earliest lesbian emancipation organization in the United States . . . dedicated to understanding of, and by, the lesbian." The highlight of the evening was the convocation ceremonies wherein two honorary doctoral degrees were awarded: one to ONE's and ISHR's benefactor Reed Erickson and the other to Christopher Isherwood which, remarkably, was the first and only college degree that he had at that time yet received.

Soon after the creation of the ONE Institute Graduate School, Erickson suggested that a campus should be founded which would be suitable for housing the school, its libraries, ONE's business and "community center" offices, and the Erickson Educational Foundation's offices. For a sum of $1.9 million, Erickson purchased a 3.5-acre property in the Country Club Estates area of Los Angeles from Elizabeth Clare Prophet of The Church Universal and Triumphant. On the property, known as the Milbank Estate, were situated an elegant 1913-built twenty-seven-room mansion, another smaller but still grand home, tennis courts, and other smaller buildings, all of which were turned over to ONE for their use.

A crew of people from ONE moved its large library and archives as well as all of ONE's other possessions out of the building on Venice Boulevard where they had been located for twenty-two years, between 1961 and 1983. ONE proudly proclaimed: "A landmark event will be celebrated here May 1 when ONE Institute announces its occupancy of the historic Milbank Estate as its permanent campus for Homophile studies, the first such campus of its kind in the world." Eight months later, January 29, 1984, ONE Institute held an open house and convocation ceremony at the Milbank mansion during which ONE Institute awarded a master's degree to Deborah Ann Coates, and two doctoral degrees in homophile studies to Paul David Hardman and Michael Anthony Lombardi, the world's first in homophile studies.

ONE AND ERICKSON:
THE UNRAVELING OF A RELATION

Sadly, it seemed that no sooner had the ink dried on the contract for the purchase of the Milbank Estate for ONE than the first signs of trouble in the relationship between Erickson and ONE began to surface. The deed to the property was originally supposed to have been turned over to ONE in a gala publicity event on May 1, 1983. That transfer was postponed until June 1, and then apparently Erickson abandoned the idea altogether.

By May of 1984, Erickson was fully engaged in trying to remove ONE from the premises and began to file legal suits against ONE in California State Courts. The aggressive actions of Erickson himself and of those whom he hired worsened ONE's tenuous financial position. Both the move from a low-rent location to the expensive Milbank property and ONE's loss of funding from the EEF left ONE facing possible ruin. In order to protect their interests, ONE obtained a series of restraining orders and injunctions against Erickson and the EEF. The effort expended in defending their hold on the Milbank estate effectively paralyzed much of the public operations of ONE. By 1986, ONE Institute had ceased to be an authorized degree-granting institution under California state law. ONE did, however, manage to continue to publish the *ONE Newsletter,* to keep the library open for researchers, and to offer its lecture series.

The battle for Milbank raged over a period of ten years, from 1983 to 1993. Late in 1988, Erickson's daughter, then twenty years old, was appointed conservator of Erickson's affairs due to Erickson's ill health. She, in conjunction with her mother, continued to fight for possession and ownership of the Milbank estate. On April 4, 1990, a judgment was reached. The title to Milbank was ordered to ONE and ISHR. Subsequent appeals were launched on behalf of Erickson and the Erickson Educational Foundation, which continued until late 1992. Three days into 1992, Reed Erickson died in Mazatlan, Mexico. His daughter became the executor of his estate and ultimately agreed to a settlement in the dispute in October of that year. The property was divided between Erickson's heirs and ISHR. The 1992 assessed value of the property received by ONE in the settlement was over $1 million. By 1997, all of ISHR/ONE's part of the property had been sold and ONE's activities were largely transferred to locations under the auspices of the University of Southern California (USC).

ONE AFTER ERICKSON

As the relationship between Erickson and ONE began to deteriorate, so too did the ability of ONE to function at full capacity. Throughout the ten years of ongoing court battles for possession of the Milbank property, most of ONE's human and financial resources were engaged in that fight. At the same time, their primary source of income, the Erickson Educational Foundation's grants to ISHR, had ceased.

For the first few years, Dorr Legg, USC professor Walter Williams, and a few others continued to provide courses to a handful of graduate students.

However, by the late 1980s only Legg continued to teach at the ONE Institute graduate school, which he did until his death in 1994. No further degrees were granted to students of ONE Institute.

ONE's successful monthly lecture series was also maintained for more than forty years since the inauguration of ONE's Sunday afternoon lecture series. As of this writing, ONE Institute continues to cosponsor it with the Los Angeles Gay and Lesbian Center. Similarly, ONE's library was maintained throughout the years of difficulties. It has since moved to a building near the University of Southern California.

In 1995, ONE Institute reclaimed a place of prominence in gay and lesbian history. In January of that year, ONE and the International Gay and Lesbian Archives (IGLA) officially merged operations under the name of ONE Institute. ISHR, which continues to function as a separate entity, supported the merger with a donation of $35,000 and has continued to provide grants to ONE Institute in subsequent years. The newly reconstituted ONE Institute has dedicated itself to several projects: to ONE's ongoing lecture series and educational outreach, to ONE Institute Press, to the ONE Center for Advanced Studies, and to the maintenance of the combined ONE library and the IGLA archival collections.

Thus, ONE has come through the difficult years of strife and depletion of resources and has grown strong once again. ONE has regrouped, joining forces with others who share their vision, and has found a new benefactor in the University of Southern California. While ONE Institute has revived, Erickson has died, and the EEF has ceased to function. However, the proceeds from Erickson's philanthropy quietly continue to help fund ONE's gay and lesbian outreach, education, and research more than thirty-five years after Erickson first saw the need and offered his wealth and expertise to help make it happen.

NOTE

1. I use the term "married" advisedly. I have not yet been able to find an official record of this marriage although numerous people (including Harry Benjamin) noted that they were married. The sex on Erickson's birth certificate, however, was not changed to male until May 1965. Before the surgery I refer to Erickson as s/he.

BIBLIOGRAPHY

Erickson's work on behalf of transsexual and transgendered peoples was considerably more extensive than what he did for lesbians and gays, and many trans people have come into contact with or have been members of gay and lesbian communities.

BEFORE STONEWALL

I have mentioned in this article some of the work in support of trans people that Erickson sponsored through ONE. My research into the history of Erickson's work through the EEF on behalf of trans people is still in progress. Visit <http://web.uvic.ca/-erick_123> for highlights.

Bullough, Vern L., W. Dorr Legg, Barrett W. Elcano, and James Kepner. *An Annotated Bibliography of Homosexuality*. New York: Garland Publishing Company, 1976.

The Erickson Educational Foundation. No date. A brochure published by the foundation describing its activities, a copy of which is in the collection of the author.

Hooker, Evelyn. "The Adjustment of the Male Overt Homosexual," *Journal of Project Technique,* 21 (1957), 18-31.

Legg, W. Dorr. Press release issued April 20, 1983. IGLA archives.

ONE, Incorporated, "ONE 1952-1982—Thirty Year Celebration: Program of Events," ONE, 1982. Collection of the author.

Books by Vern Bullough That Grew Out of Research Sponsored by Erickson:

Homosexuality: A History. New York: New American Library, 1979.

Sexual Variance in Society and History. New York: Wiley, 1976.

With Bonnie Bullough, *The Subordinate Sex*. Urbana, IL: University of Illinois Press, 1974.

Troy Perry (1940-   )

Lee Arnold

Troy Perry is a Christian in spite of Christianity. Thrown out of two Protestant denominations for being gay, he ended up founding a Christian church—the largest of its kind—that primarily serves the needs of gay men and lesbians. It was a long road from the fire-and-brimstone churches of the southern United States to heading up the Universal Fellowship of Metropolitan Community Churches in Los Angeles.

Troy Perry was born in Florida on July 27, 1940, and grew up there and in Georgia and Texas. Familiar with both Pentecostal and Baptist traditions, by the age of fifteen he was licensed to preach by a local Baptist church. And preach he did: to churches, to fellow students at his high school, to anyone who would listen. Perry loved his church; he loved the preacher's daughter he would eventually marry; and he also loved other men.

Baptists and Pentecostals played a formative role in Perry's life. Yet these were two very different traditions. The Baptists (his mother's faith) were mainstream and fundamentalist who had a more traditional form of worship. The Pentecostals (his relatives' faith), on the other hand, were evangelical and believed in the actual manifestation of the gifts of the Holy Spirit, including speaking in tongues (also known as glossolalia). Their services were more animated as members, who were moved by the Spirit, would stand up and utter words unknown to man. Other members stood and provided divine interpretation of this utterance following this manifestation. The merging of these two religions made for a rich source of the best of both faiths but also caused dissension by those who believed one tradition dominated the other. This conflict spilled over not only to Perry's personal life but also into the Metropolitan Community Church, which he would found years later.

Perry had a horrific childhood. At age twelve, his father, a bootlegger, had been immolated in a car crash following a police chase. Perry's mother soon remarried to a no-account man with a severe drinking problem. The new husband not only went through the family's savings and assets but was physically abusive to young Troy, his mother, and his four brothers. After a particularly violent night, Troy called the sheriff and his stepfather went to jail for three days. A week after his release, a shiftless man—passed off as his stepfather's brother—came to stay with them. That man sexually abused young Troy and threatened him with violence if he told anyone. Troy ran away from home and lived with relatives throughout the South until his mother divorced. It was in this situation that he gravitated toward Pente-costalism, eventually becoming involved with the Cleveland, Tennessee-based Church of God.

He met the daughter of a Church of God pastor and eventually married her, even though he knew he had sexual feelings for other men. He tried to verbalize his reservations, but his future father-in-law simply told him that the love of a good woman would take care of anything. Even though he did fall in love with his wife, that love alone was not enough to stop those de-sires. Throughout his Pentecostal years Troy maintained liaisons with will-ing men from the churches he ministered. However, he chalked it all up to youthful exploration and did not consider himself gay. He was, after all, a Christian; and he had been taught one could not be both gay and Christian.

At age nineteen, shortly after his marriage, he took a calling at a Church of God church in Joliet, Illinois. All went well until a state overseer and dis-trict coordinator wanted to meet with him. They confronted him with the fact that someone in the denomination whom he had had sex with tipped off the officials that Troy was gay. The officials made Troy tell his wife and forced them to leave the church immediately. After a tense discussion, Troy and his wife Pearl decided to stay together and make the marriage work. He took a job in a local plastics factory and relocated to Torrance, California, when the company opened a branch there. It was there that Troy accepted the call of another Pentecostal church, the Church of God of Prophecy. This church had broken away from the Church of God in 1923 and had very little contact with its former brethren. No one would know that Perry had been excommunicated from the Church of God for being gay. By this time the Perrys had two small boys and were a model example of a young ministerial couple. Yet Troy still knew that he had homosexual desires; he could not continue to live a lie. While his wife and children were away visiting family, he went to the district overseer and told him that he was gay. When his wife and children returned, the bishop contacted Pearl; she knew what to expect.

Troy Perry was thrown out of his second Pentecostal denomination for being gay, and his wife and children left him. He then went to work for Sears until the Army drafted him at age twenty-five, despite his claims of homosexuality. Stationed in Germany, he met other gay servicemen and eventually toured Europe with one while on leave. In 1967 he returned to California and his job at Sears. He fell in love and had a torturous affair which ended with his lover walking out the door. Troy, despondent, locked himself in the bathroom and slit his wrists. Fortunately a roommate came home, heard the water running, and broke down the door. In his autobiography, Troy tells how in the hospital a nurse told him, "I don't know why you did this, but what you did tonight was crazy—why don't you look up?" Perry knew he had to get back on track with the Lord. How, he wondered, could he do this and still accept his gayness? Perry believes God answered his prayers by speaking to him and letting him know that He loved him just the way he was. He believes that God told him we are all children of God, and God does not have stepchildren.

In the summer of 1968, while on a date at a gay bar, the policed raided and arrested people; Troy's date was one of them. It took him several hours to get his friend out of jail, but by then the damage had been done. The police had harassed and humiliated the man so much that his spirit was broken. He confided to Troy that nobody cared about gay people. No amount of protesting by Perry could convince his friend that God did care. It was then that Troy believes God told him to establish a church that would care about gay men and lesbians. God wanted it done now.

The history of Troy Perry then becomes the history of the Metropolitan Community Church (MCC). On October 6, 1968, Troy Perry held a worship service for a dozen people in his home in Huntington Park, California; this was nine months prior to New York City's Stonewall riots. Within two years, MCC owned a piece of property in Los Angeles, the first piece of property ever owned by a gay organization in the United States. From an interview in *The Christian Century* in 1996:

> If you had told me twenty-eight years ago that the largest organization in the world touching the lives of gays and lesbians would be a church, I would not have believed you. So many members of the lesbian and gay community feel that they have had violence done to them by religious groups that it is very difficult to evangelize any members of our community. But we do evangelize. That evangelism is not limited to gay folk. (p. 896)

In 1992, the National Council of Churches (NCC) denied not only membership to the Metropolitan Community Church (MCC) but also observer status. Perry did not take this as a bad sign. At least in the whole process dialogue was established between the NCC member churches and the Metropolitan Community Church. (Ironically, MCC *was* granted observer status in the World Council of Churches and attended its assembly when it met in Australia.)

Yet changing the establishment has never been easy. One unholy alliance appears to be between fundamental Christianity and violence. Twenty-one MCC churches were arsoned and burned to the ground; several of its leaders have been threatened or assaulted; four MCC clergy have been murdered. From an interview with the *Orange County and Long Beach Blade* in 2000: "We will never, ever, be chased out of a city; we've never, ever, left a city where we've faced persecution." Troy also stated in his interview with *The Christian Century* (1996):

> I believe that we are the last minority left in America that you can hate in public and still get away with it. The radical right in America continues to raise millions of dollars to oppose us, claiming that our community is demanding special rights. My agenda is only one thing: to be treated like every citizen is supposed to be treated under our Constitution. I don't expect more, but I refuse to accept any less.

A staunch opponent of Anita Bryant's Save Our Children campaign in 1977, Perry even refused to drink the complimentary orange juice provided on a cross-county flight to protest the former beauty queen's feckless use of the specter of children's welfare in order to attack gay civil rights. (Anita Bryant was a former Miss Oklahoma—and runner-up for Miss America—as well as a spokesperson for Florida orange juice. She eventually lost her job as a citrus saleswoman after her foray into the antigay rights movement. Perry once referred to her as an overripe beauty queen. Bryant later admitted that her then-husband, Bob Green, manipulated much of her activism during this time.)

The battle with Bryant's Save Our Children was lost in Miami. There followed a domino of defeats for gay rights in Wichita, Kansas, St. Paul, Minnesota, and Eugene, Oregon. Perry watched these with dismay and vowed that it had to stop. The next target of the antigay agenda was California. In 1977 the amendment debate, proposed by State Senator John V. Briggs to ban gays and lesbians from being public school teachers in the state, was in full swing. Perry worked tirelessly to get politicians (including such diverse ones as Jimmy Carter, Jerry Brown, and Ronald Reagan) to endorse "No on Proposition 6." Briggs, however, had the support of the man behind the Dade County, Florida, campaign: Jerry Falwell and his fund-raising ability. Yet ultimately Briggs was shown for what he was—just another bigot with a hateful agenda and a bankroll. The antigay forces lost in every California county.

Troy Perry had the sad task of going to San Francisco and meeting with civic and community leaders after the murders of Mayor George Moscone and gay City Supervisor Harvey Milk in 1978. His presence helped keep the response to the murders peaceful.

With comedienne Robin Tyler, Perry helped organize the first gay march on Washington in 1979. MCC members didn't want only to show up in Washington; they wanted to do it with style (and with the press present). They rode from San Francisco to Washington on Amtrak, dubbed the Freedom Train, picking up people and publicity along the way. The first march was a success. It made its goal of focusing on gay rights and immigration reform. By 1987, there were two new reasons to return to Washington. The first was the United States Supreme Court sodomy decision against Michael Hartwick. The second was AIDS. The Reagan administration was seen as apathetic to the crisis. President Reagan had a hard time even saying the word AIDS. Perry helped organize the second march and made sure that MCC was well represented in the crowd. The MCC is the oldest ongoing AIDS ministry of any Christian denomination in the United States.

Perry and the MCC were part of the 1993 March on Washington, and Perry was one of the three people who called for, and a subsequent member of the board that resulted in, the Millennium March on Washington on April 20, 2000.

Troy Perry has long been a champion of human rights and a recognized leader in both the gay and religious communities. In 1973 he was appointed to the Los Angeles County Human Relations Commission, the first openly gay person to be appointed to such a position anywhere in the nation. In 1977 he was invited to the White House by President Jimmy Carter to discuss gay rights. In 1978 he received a humanitarian award from the American Civil Liberties Union Lesbian and Gay Rights Chapter. He was invited to the White House three times by President Clinton: in 1993 to participate in the White House Conference on AIDS, in 1997 to participate in the White House Conference on Hate Crimes, and in 1997 as an honoree at a breakfast honoring 100 national spiritual leaders. Perry received an honorary doctorate of ministry from Samaritan College in Los Angeles for founding the Metropolitan Community Churches, and an honorary doctorate in human services from Sierra University of Santa Monica, California, for his work in civil rights. He also received a humanitarian award from the Gay Press Association. Besides Perry, other MCC clergy in the news are the Reverend Mel White (former ghost writer for Jerry Falwell, Pat Robertson, and Billy Graham), and the Reverend Elder Nancy Wilson, pastor of the mother church, MCC Los Angeles.

Troy Perry's relationship with his family has had it highs and lows. His mother, deceased for over ten years, was the first heterosexual member of

the Metropolitan Community Church and one of her son's biggest supporters. Separated for over nineteen years, he has reunited with his youngest
son, Michael, and even married him and his daughter-in-law. He is still es-
tranged from his oldest son, Troy Perry Jr.

Troy Perry has had his share of love and loss. In 1983 his partner and
MCC employee, Greg Cutts, died from a reaction to medication while work-
ing on a church video project in Vancouver, Canada. On a happier note,
Perry later began a relationship with Phillip Ray DeBlieck. He and DeBlieck
have been lovers for over fifteen years and live in the Silverlake section of
Los Angeles.

One can find an MCC float or contingent in almost every gay pride parade. They are out there, unashamed to be both gay and Christian. Their
mission statement is threefold: We embody and proclaim Christian salva-
tion and liberation, Christian inclusivity and community, and Christian social action and justice. The MCC vision statement is even more ambitious:
to embody the presence of the Divine in the world, as revealed through Jesus
Christ; to challenge the conscience of the universal Christian Church; and to
celebrate the inherent worth and dignity of each person. Again from the
Christian Century (1996) interview:

> I am very hopeful about our future. I used to say years ago that we
> were working to put ourselves out of business. . . . I see now that
> we will not be shutting our doors, and that there is a need for our
> church. Today there are gays and lesbians in church groups outside of
> my own denomination, but there are tens of thousands [over 48,000
> members in eighteen countries; over 500 clergy serving 310 churches]
> who want to be part of the Universal Fellowship of Metropolitan
> Community Churches. We continue to expand and grow and carry the
> good news that Jesus died for our sins, not our sexuality. (p. 896)

BIBLIOGRAPHY

Amster, Joseph S. Reverend Troy Perry: The Cornerstone of the Gay Spiritual
    Movement, *Orange County and Long Beach Blade* (January 2000).
Perry, Troy D. *Don't Be Afraid Anymore: The Story of Reverend Troy Perry and the
    Metropolitan Community Churches.* New York: St. Martin's, 1990.
Perry, Troy D. Gays and the Gospel: An Interview with Troy Perry. *The Christian
    Century,* 113: 27 (1996), p. 896.
Perry, Troy D. *The Lord Is My Shepherd and He Knows I'm Gay: The Autobiogra-
    phy of the Reverend Troy D. Perry.* Reprinted, Austin, TX: Liberty Press, 1987.
Universal Fellowship of Metropolitan Community Churches. Who Is Rev. Troy
    D. Perry? Available online at <http://www.ufmcc.com>.

Morris Kight (1919-   ):
Community Activist

Felice Picano

Photo by Tom Bianchi

Any volume of important gay rights figures in our time would be incomplete if it
did not include Morris Kight. A simple listing of the organizations, groups, and events
he has begun, spearheaded, or revived makes
it immediately apparent how dynamic and
how effective Kight has been in seeing that
gay men and lesbians achieved political
and social rights and recognition. Kight
founded the Gay Liberation Front; he was
cofounder of the Gay Community Services
Center of Los Angeles; founder of the Christopher Street West; founder of the Stonewall Democratic Club of Los Angeles; cofounder of the Lesbian and Gay Caucus of
the California Democratic Party; cofounder
of Asian and Pacific Lesbian/Gays; Com-
missioner of the National AIDS vigil in Washington, DC, in 1983; leader of
the 1987 March on Washington; organizer of the 1988 March on Sacramento; cofounder of the Van Ness Recovery House for Alcoholism and Ad-
diction in Los Angeles; and founder of the nationally celebrated twenty-
fifth anniversary of the Stonewall Rebellion March in New York City in
June of 1994. Before and since, he has been involved with many nongay organizations.

These activities and successes, however, must be weighed against other
factors: Morris Kight remains one of the more controversial, scrutinized,
and at times criticized of our gay leaders. He calls himself a feminist, a paci-
fist, a generalist, a universalist, and, above all, a humanist. Unquestionably,
personal, philosophical, and political opposition to Kight coming from
many sides within the gay-lesbian-transgender community has arisen and
become a constant in his life.

Partly this has come about as a result of the inherent combativeness within any revolutionary movement. Partly it has been exacerbated by the extreme individualism, even orneriness, of many in the community toward any leader: More than one gay psychologist has noted that for most gays, growing up in an overwhelmingly homophobic society often leads to a tendency to internalize that hatred. By extension, it also leads to fierce self-analysis and a willingness, even an eagerness, to apply the same harsh critique to other gay men and women, especially those who ask for trust and power. As the old saying goes: He who rises high makes the best target.

On the other hand, Kight himself has—either unconsciously through his personal exuberance or by design—left himself open to attack. The most frequent points made against him have been the scattering of his force into areas outside the gay community and his support of sometimes unpopular ideas and causes. Yet the most egregious of his shortcomings noted have been Kight's instinct for grabbing attention and personal publicity whenever possible and, to some critics, his seemingly infinite capacity to receive—and even negotiate receiving—honors, even when they are most deserved. Kight himself perceives those accolades far less personally than do his critics. He sees himself an exemplar: whenever he receives another kudo, he feels he is standing in for many other gays who do not wish to be or who through circumstances cannot be as highly recognized.

To many in the community, Kight is an imperfect person in need of corralling: an unrelenting activist, at times running over or eliminating those in his path. To others, he is a bright and charming person, one of the most astonishingly effective leaders we've had. As his field of endeavor for half a century, Los Angeles in particular owes a debt to him.

Morris Kight was born November 19, 1919, at 11 p.m. into a poor farming family in Comanche County in central Texas. Because his parents didn't have the entire fee for Virginia Morris, the midwife brought from town to help birth him, they named him after her, using her last name as his first. Kight's father died in an accident when he was seven years old, and the boy was forced to grow up quickly as an around-the-house, then an around-the-farm worker.

He felt from a young age that he was "different" and said that he was "never invited into the games" of other children. He found solace in nature and in books. He also began collecting art in the form of fine art prints, and his many years of collecting eventually resulted in a substantial collection. His childhood reading was so extensive that later on, at Texas Christian University, he was passed through freshman literature class and promoted ahead.

But Morris wasn't "arty" and impractical. As a boy he planted seeds, and experimented in botany and also with local water control. He also taught himself, through trial and error, how to keep the engine of the family's Model A Ford running. Kight's older siblings departed the farm while he was still a preteen. Left with the support of himself and mother during the difficult mid-1930s, and years of poor weather and extensive drought in the region, he opened and operated a roadside diner when he was sixteen years old. This enterprise led to Kight's first encounter with hatred of difference and with institutionalized prejudice. He was witnessed serving food to a traveling African-American family who could not get fed anywhere else and was arrested for "mixing the races." Young Kight was tried in court and avoided serving time only when friends of his deceased father intervened. Asked if he had "learned his lesson," Kight said he had. The rebellious boy would thereafter throw himself into various forums of intense civil rights activism.

Another crucial life lesson Kight says he learned was from the girl in his tiny high school graduating class who was forced to leave school in her final year to have a baby. Her anger at the teacher who made the pregnant teen leave and at her poor treatment by the authorities led the boy to begin to think for himself about issues such as the lack of women's privileges—especially their lack of abortion rights.

Kight worked his way through college, first as a gardener and later in the dean's office. He also took the rigorous test for the Roosevelt administration's U.S. Career Services Training Academy through which those needed to operate the various New Deal agencies were enlisted. He won a spot over many thousands and graduated from the Academy in 1941, in the process forming an acquaintance with the First Lady, Eleanor Roosevelt. During World War II Kight served as a civilian administrator adjunct to the military in the Pacific Theater, where his task was to plan governments and policies for the islands reoccupied or recently conquered.

After the war he lived in various areas of the Southwest, on his own and with his mother, opening and running hotels and restaurants. He briefly worked for the Bureau of Indian Affairs, but the institutionalized inequality and substandard treatment of Native Americans he witnessed led him to quit. He soon joined local tribal leaders in organizing social services and public health services for New Mexico's indigenous people.

Despite the fact that by the time he was in college Kight was sexually active with other males, he resisted accepting the identity of a homosexual, an understandable action shared by millions of closeted American gays at the time. A few years later, in Albuquerque, Kight married a woman with whom he had two daughters. He remained married only five years but stayed in contact with his family thereafter.

By the time Kight moved to California in 1957, he was already a seasoned and dedicated activist, and was considered a radical. First the civil rights movement, then the movement against the war in Vietnam were his chief arenas. As part of the latter, in 1967 he formed and headed the Dow Action Committee, dedicated to stopping that chemical company from manufacturing the napalm that was being sprayed from U.S. warplanes, with lethal effects upon both the population and the environment of South Vietnam. He also worked for gay causes—not as an openly gay man but as part of his struggle for civil rights for all.

Out of the Stonewall riots in New York City and the subsequent days of political action that swirled about their confrontation with the authorities, was born the Gay Activists Alliance and eventually the entire gay rights movement. Precursors to the GAA and Stonewall had existed for decades: the small but daring openly homosexual Mattachine Society, formed in Los Angeles during the 1950s, picketed the U.S. Post Office and other government offices for discriminating against homosexuals, and it sponsored the first homosexual publication, a newsletter called *ONE*. The Daughters of Bilitis was a comparable organization for lesbians. Although few gays were actually organized within cities such as New York, San Francisco, Chicago, and Los Angeles, openly gay lives were being led by thousands of men and women, and their choice of neighborhoods, so-called "gay ghettos," were already solidly established.

It was only a few months after Stonewall, during a massive demonstration by mostly young, educated, and middle-class people against the Vietnam War in San Francisco's Polo Grounds that Kight realized that homosexual rights could also be made to attract large numbers of "clean, well-bred, ordinary men and women" who, in his words, "saw their dentist twice a year," and who, he recognized, constituted the mass and character of gay life. Kight recognized that—like the groups of students and professionals who marched against the war and who influenced public opinion sufficiently to end the conflict in Southeast Asia—their lesbian and gay counterparts should also be able to sway public favor to their cause. Kight, the closeted activist for gay causes, came out in the open.

Shortly afterward, Kight moved from Albuquerque to Los Angeles in part because it had the large middle-class gay population. However, because it also possessed an official environment hostile to homosexuals—predominantly due to an outspoken homophobic police chief—Kight judged the southern California city prepared for some incisive political action. Kight moved to the Westlake area of the city, which was close to downtown and popular with many gays who lived there. Once there he soon formed the Gay and Lesbian Resistance. Unlike the Gay Activists Alliance in New York City, the GLR dealt not only with the issue of gay and lesbian rights but also with social issues such as health care and poverty in general, which were problems of interest to a wide variety of politically active groups. By

1969, the GLR and its activities were subsumed under the banner of the Gay Liberation Front, or GLF.

At the time of his move to Los Angeles, Kight was fifty years old and already a longtime experienced activist on many social and political fronts. At that same age, many other men are thinking of how to solidify their career position, even considering retirement; for Kight it was the start of an entirely new life.

Kight's first target for the Gay Liberation Front was a West Hollywood restaurant named Barney's Beanery. That neighborhood had become increasingly populated by lesbians and gays; police activity against establishments serving homosexuals had correspondingly increased. The owner of Barney's Beanery put a sign on the door reading "Faggots Stay Out." In January of 1970, the GLF began holding actions—"shop-ins," "change-ins," and "sit-ins"—inside the restaurant, and they continued until the management agreed to take down the sign.

The success of that action led to 175 more protests and demonstrations by the GLF in the next two years. Kight became such a thorn in the side of Los Angeles Police Chief Ed Davis that official retaliation ensued, including three police raid/searches of Kight's home. Many gays were convinced that the worst was yet to come. Kight held to his constitutional guns; hearing that, in New York City, gay activists had made plans for a parade to celebrate the previous year's Stonewall bar riot, Kight quickly formed plans for a corresponding West Coast version. Chief Davis was unsuccessful in his attempts to stop the parade and, although Kight received multiple death threats, the parade went on nonetheless. Like its East Coast version, it was small and dowdy, but it was also brave and it raised many people's spirits and raised gay awareness: achieving—many people feel—exactly what the huge festivals of drugs, dancing, shirtless torsos, and commercialism that today call themselves gay parades cannot achieve.

In 1971, Kight joined Don Kilhefer and several other men to form the Gay Community Services Center in an old clapboard Victorian house. The first such focal point, it provided social, medical, and legal aid to gays, as well as giving them a place to gather, feel at home, and air their grievances. The structure has since been razed, but its descendant, Los Angeles's current Gay and Lesbian Center, consists of two enormous, well-funded, well-equipped, well-staffed, up-to-date Hollywood locations, with one campus given entirely over to the arts. Other American cities such as New York, Chicago, most recently San Francisco, and many foreign cities, from Vienna to Tel Aviv, have used the Kight-Kilhefer pilot as a model for their own lesbigay community centers.

As much work as all that was, soon enough Kight and colleagues had their hands full with other more pressing, specifically political matters. In

the late 1970s, singer-spokesperson Anita Bryant's war against lesbians and
gays in Florida under the cynical disguise of "saving the children" quickly
led to various imitations around the country, the most significant being John
Briggs, who managed to get gay discrimination clauses onto the state of
California's ballot. Seeing how serious the threat was, Kight and other gays
sprang into action, calling for aid from homosexuals, heterosexuals, friends,
celebrities, business groups, and individuals across the country.

The national effort that Kight and others helped develop to defeat the
Briggs Amendment displayed for the first time to opponents and adherents
alike the true financial and organizational power and reach of lesbians and
gays—in effect, proving that Kight's original thesis, when he'd relocated to
Los Angeles, had been correct. It also showed that consequential civil rights
associations, such as the distinguished American Civil Liberties Union,
would join the fight for gay rights.

In an interview he gave to *The Advocate* a few years later, Kight provided
a few reasons why a man such as himself, who had worked for the NAACP,
Southern Christian Leadership Council, and other national forums, would
concentrate all his efforts toward the issue of gay rights.

> No matter where I am in the world, when I meet another gay person I
> feel recognition. We're a new race of people, writing our own script.
> . . . We have a chance to be the first people in history to define itself.
> We can break the heterosexist mode and create something entirely dif-
> ferent. (Sarf, 1974)

Possibly because that potential is so general, Kight has branched out
from the specifically political, leaving several civic issues to younger
people. Meanwhile, his interest in art, his collecting of various souvenirs
from the many demonstrations and protests he was involved in, and his personal relationship with friends who died and whose own collections of
GLBT memorabilia were destroyed or disposed of, led him to open the
McCadden Place collection, containing work ranging from Southwest folk
art to documentary film and photos specific to the beginnings of gay activism. Every year, Kight hosts an exhibit of parts of this collection at Christopher Street West's Gay Pride Festival in West Hollywood.

He has also become reinvolved in the needs of others besides gays,
chiefly the homeless: Kight was president of the board of directors and
consultant on housing beginning in 1978. He aided in forming the County of
Los Angeles Commission on Human Relations in 1980 and has served on its
board as commissioner, secretary, and vice president. Officials of City Hall
who snubbed him for years, hoping he would just go away, have instead

gone themselves, replaced by people his activism has influenced, who now honor him and appoint him to municipal positions.

In recent years, as he has aged, Kight has become increasingly aware of the predicament faced by many of the elderly. That new interest has retied him to the gay community, where he sees ageism and the disregard of senior lesbians and gays as an acute current and future ongoing anxiety. He recently involved himself with a photographer putting together a book of portraits of seniors from our community. Will Morris Kight's work ever be done?

Over the past decades as an activist and politician, Morris Kight may very well have been humanly imperfect, but he has also been perfectly humanitarian, a model for future activists. And that's just how he'd like to be remembered.

BIBLIOGRAPHY

Paul Ciotti, "Morris Kight: Activist Statesman of L.A.'s Gay Community," *Los Angeles Times,* December 9, 1988.

Pete Conroy, "Get Centered," *Our Paper,* May 17, 1989.

Miki Jackson, "A Brief, Inadequate Biographical Sketch of Morris Kight," *Self-published,* November 19, 1996.

Jack Nichols, "Interview with Morris Kight." Available online <www.gaytoday. badpuppy.com/>. December 3, 1998.

Personal interviews with Morris Kight, June and August 2000.

Doug Sarf, "How Gay Community Service Came of Age in Los Angeles," *The Advocate,* February 13, 1974.

Nancy Wride, "The Liberator." *Los Angeles Times,* Southern California Living. June 8, 1999.

Index

Abbott, Berenice, 308
Abbott, Sidney, 165
Abraham Lincoln School, 58
Activist Approach, The (Weinberg), 357
activist strategies
civil disobedience, 217, 297
civil rights movement and, 209, 212-214, 225-226
controversy over, 245, 275, 297
militancy of, 122, 131, 213
military inclusion protests, 111, 174, 277, 364
multi-issue versus single-issue, 200, 225-226, 246
picketing, 112, 245, 275, 295
White House protests, 213, 227, 232, 233-234
zaps, 238, 279
Adam, Barry, 131
Addams, Jane, 197
Adkins, Warren D., 297
Adonis Bookstore, 158
Advocate, The, 112, 131
African Americans. *See also* race issues
civil rights movement, 7-8, 209, 212-214, 225-226
culture of, 195, 230
Glenn (Bonner), 189-190
in organizations, 128, 195
Scottsboro trial, 333-334
Walker, 191-192
White people's sexual desire for, 236, 288, 336, 342
After Punishment, What? (Rossman), 319
age, 16, 167-168, 176-177, 405. *See also* intergenerational relationships
AIDS, 248, 272, 397
Alcibiade Fanciullo a Scola (Rocco), 314-315

Aldridge, Sarah. *See* Marchant, Anyda
Alfred C. Kinsey: A Public/Private Life (Jones), 22
Alice B. Toklas Memorial Democratic Club, 165
Alien Registration Act of 1940, 57
allies. *See* heterosexual allies
Alt, Steve, 326, 328
American Association for Personal Privacy (AAPP), 287, 288
American Association of Law Librarians, 249
American Association of Retired Persons (AARP), 250
American Civil Liberties Union (ACLU)
activists in, 138, 148-150, 196, 200
chapters led to national support, 7, 212, 213, 363, 404
club closing contested by, 186
American Committee for the Protection of the Foreign Born, 58
American Historical Association, 131-132
American Historical Society, 366
American Law Institute, 7, 170
American Library Association (ALA), 53, 247-248
American Psychiatric Association (APA)
convention protest, 166, 214-215, 248
DSM revision, 167, 215, 249, 348, 365
pressure on, 166-167, 214-215, 248-249, 351
American Psychological Association, 345, 348, 351
American Public Health Association, 249
anal sex, 33, 224. *See also* sodomy laws

SPECIAL 25%-OFF DISCOUNT!

Order a copy of this book with this form or online at:
http://www.haworthpressinc.com/store/product.asp?sku=4646

BEFORE STONEWALL
Activists for Gay and Lesbian Rights in Historical Context

_____in hardbound at $37.46 (regularly $49.95) (ISBN: 1-56023-192-0)

_____in softbound at $20.96 (regularly $27.95) (ISBN: 1-56023-193-9)

Or order online and use Code HEC25 in the shopping cart.

COST OF BOOKS_____

OUTSIDE US/CANADA/
MEXICO: ADD 20%_____

POSTAGE & HANDLING_____
(US: $5.00 for first book & $2.00
for each additional book)
Outside US: $6.00 for first book
& $2.00 for each additional book)

SUBTOTAL_____

IN CANADA: ADD 7% GST_____

STATE TAX_____
(NY, OH & MN residents, please
add appropriate local sales tax)

FINAL TOTAL_____
(If paying in Canadian funds,
convert using the current
exchange rate, UNESCO
coupons welcome)

☐ **BILL ME LATER:** ($5 service charge will be added)
(Bill-me option is good on US/Canada/Mexico orders only;
not good to jobbers, wholesalers, or subscription agencies.)

☐ Check here if billing address is different from
shipping address and attach purchase order and
billing address information.

Signature_____

☐ **PAYMENT ENCLOSED: $**_____

☐ **PLEASE CHARGE TO MY CREDIT CARD.**

☐ Visa ☐ MasterCard ☐ AmEx ☐ Discover
☐ Diner's Club ☐ Eurocard ☐ JCB

Account # _____

Exp. Date_____

Signature_____

Prices in US dollars and subject to change without notice.

NAME_____

INSTITUTION_____

ADDRESS_____

CITY_____

STATE/ZIP_____

COUNTRY_____ COUNTY (NY residents only)_____

TEL_____ FAX_____

E-MAIL_____

May we use your e-mail address for confirmations and other types of information? ☐ Yes ☐ No
We appreciate receiving your e-mail address and fax number. Haworth would like to e-mail or fax special
discount offers to you, as a preferred customer. **We will never share, rent, or exchange your e-mail address
or fax number.** We regard such actions as an invasion of your privacy.

Order From Your Local Bookstore or Directly From
The Haworth Press, Inc.
10 Alice Street, Binghamton, New York 13904-1580 • USA
TELEPHONE: 1-800-HAWORTH (1-800-429-6784) / Outside US/Canada: (607) 722-5857
FAX: 1-800-895-0582 / Outside US/Canada: (607) 722-6362
E-mailto: getinfo@haworthpressinc.com
PLEASE PHOTOCOPY THIS FORM FOR YOUR PERSONAL USE.
http://www.HaworthPress.com   BOF02

VERMONT STATE COLLEGES

0 0003 0744526 2

VOTC Library
Hartness Library
Vermont Technical College
Randolph Center, VT 05061